THE PURSUIT OF
CERTAINTY

THE PURSUIT OF CERTAINTY

DAVID HUME   JEREMY BENTHAM

JOHN STUART MILL   BEATRICE WEBB

BY

SHIRLEY ROBIN LETWIN

CAMBRIDGE

AT THE UNIVERSITY PRESS

1965

PUBLISHED BY
THE SYNDICS OF THE CAMBRIDGE UNIVERSITY PRESS

Bentley House, 200 Euston Road, London, N.W.1
American Branch: 32 East 57th Street, New York, N.Y. 10022
West African Office: P.O. Box 33, Ibadan, Nigeria

PRINTED IN GREAT BRITAIN BY WILLMER BROTHERS LIMITED
CHESTER STREET, BIRKENHEAD
Library of Congress Catalogue
Card Number 65-12494

CONTENTS

Introduction   *page* 3

PART I

DAVID HUME:

PAGAN VIRTUES AND PROFANE POLITICS

1   A Man of Moderation   13

2   The Kirk   18

3   The Combat of Reason and Passion   29

4   A New Scene of Thought   41

5   Virtue in a Bundle of Perceptions   59

6   The Philosophical Enthusiasm Renounced   72

7   A Matter of Degree   78

8   The Science of Politics   85

9   The Proper Political Disposition   94

10 The End of Profane Politics   112

PART II

JEREMY BENTHAM: LIBERTY AND LOGIC

11 Blackstone's Challenger   127

12 Utilitarianism—A System of Tolerance   137

13 A Perfect System of Legislation   155

14 Gadgets for Happiness   176

15 A Modest Utopian   183

PART III

JOHN STUART MILL:
FROM PURITANISM TO SOCIOLOGY

16 James Mill   *page* 191

17 The Young Disciple   203

18 The Failure of Utilitarianism   212

19 Intimations of a New Creed   223

20 Many-Sidedness   235

21 The Creed of Progress   244

22 Radicals in Politics   253

23 Sociology   263

24 Sociology Applied   282

25 Liberty and the Ideal Individual   291

26 The Liberal Gentleman   312

PART IV

BEATRICE WEBB:
SCIENCE AND THE APOTHEOSIS OF POLITICS

27 A New Climate of Opinion   *page* 321

28 The Making of a Socialist   342

29 The Apotheosis of Politics   365

    Index   379

portant that their philosophies were inspired not by metaphysical convictions, but by moral preoccupations. What concerned them was how their ideas affected the world they lived in, rather than how completely they had captured or conformed to some abstract truth. Their ultimate objectives were not philosophical, but moral.

In temperament, too, the four have some important affinities. Although each summed up and reflected currents of thought and emotion common in his day, all had the reputation of being radical and all shocked their more conventional contemporaries. Each of them rebelled against what he had learned, or believed he had learned as a child. At the same time, all of them esteemed moderation and tolerance. There is among them no true revolutionary, no one who actually tried to blow up the house, no one who advocated or even welcomed the use of violence. While they all wished to influence practice, they hoped to do so through theory, and relied mainly on the power of the pen.

In these ways, all four are excellent representatives of what is distinctive in British political thinking. Nevertheless, the change that can be traced through their lives is a story of a departure from, a decline of, a uniquely British pattern.

The story not only begins with, but, in a way, rests on David Hume because he more than anyone else has given expression to the peculiar genius of British politics. The political outlook he voices lived and breathed most freely in the eighteenth century, in an elegant, witty, and careless civilization. Yet it was alive in Britain before the eighteenth century. And it has lived on to temper every other theory that has gained a hold there. It accounts for the curious, unexpected, incoherent mixture that any theory becomes when applied in Britain, and it has contributed at least as much as anything else to the unparalleled peaceful development of her political institutions.

Although Hume is best known today for having made a revolution in philosophy, his philosophy was designed to support a revolution in morals. He set out to destroy the traditional Christian view of man as divided between divine reason and brute passion, and directed his attack at the metaphysics that had since Plato's time supported it. He proposed to show how the human powers that had hitherto been traced to a faculty that man shared with God could be accounted for otherwise, that man's much vaunted reason was nothing that set him apart from the rest of nature, or required him to renounce his earthly connections. But as his attack on reason denied to man any possibility of discovering a rational warrant for his beliefs, Hume's philosophy in effect undermined itself. He thereby involved philosophy in dilemmas from which it has not yet managed to escape. For himself, Hume solved the problem he had created in the simplest fashion, by retiring from the field and turning essayist and historian, teaching the moral spirit he

3

admired by means of examples without the encumbrance of a doubtful epistemology.

But throughout, his view of the human condition remained unchanged. It was, as he saw it, neither good nor evil, neither unknowing nor omniscient; it could be pleasant, but never secure. His notion of goodness included all things that men love, honour, and enjoy, without elevating any one activity or kind of life above all others. If a man exercises courage, temperance, justice, and wisdom, he does, according to Hume, as much as can be expected of him. He is not required to transcend his nature, or to struggle against evil. There is no more harm in the passions than in the reason, and they naturally work together. Virtue flows from harmony and a disposition to heed natural sentiments.

The sternness in Hume was entirely reserved for one enemy, the puritan. The puritan believes man is a divided creature, that virtue consists in making brutish passion submit to divine reason; he feels certain he can penetrate the ultimate mystery of the universe and achieve a single unifying vision of life that will free him from uncertainty and confusion. He is righteous, austere, godly, an enemy to everything that makes human life a pleasure. Worst of all, he insists on remaking all men to fit the one image he admires. All the rogues and villains that Hume discovered were somehow tainted by puritanism. The men he admired were averse to anything like dogma or rigid definition; they preferred the near to the far, the seen to the unseen; they valued a steady judgement and a lively capacity for enjoyment; they accepted and were even amused by the variety and vicissitudes of human life. They were pagans who respected the power of their gods, but expected no mercy, not even justice, from them.

Hume thus denied the possibility of demonstrating the superiority of any single way of life, or of any set of rules. There was no ideal to be enforced on all, nor any City of God to be reached. And nothing very exalted was left for politics to do. Government has to look after certain things that individuals cannot do for themselves. Without these activities, civilization cannot survive, but they are no more than an indispensable condition of a good life. For the purposes of politics, society is merely a web of interests that has to be managed so as to let each man live as he likes without fearing either his neighbours or his rulers. To reach for perfection, to seek an ideal, is noble, but dangerous, and is therefore, according to Hume, an activity that individuals or voluntary groups may pursue, but governments certainly should not. Politics is just one of many social activities, by no means the highest, concerned with the ordinary business of life, with things as they are, not as they should be.

What was fixed in Hume's politics was not any set of policies, not even any general principles about the best form of government or constitution, but simply the conviction that the office of government is to protect men against arbitrary interference, or, in other words, to enforce the rule of law. Everything else had to be subordinated to this, for where there is no rule of law, force prevails and civilization is impossible. One is obliged to remember how dangerous it is to unsettle established rules, but beyond that politics offers neither any absolute truth nor any fixed goal. The politician never can choose between good and evil, but merely between greater and lesser evils. What he ought to choose cannot be known beforehand because what is right today might be wrong tomorrow. There is no escape from the uncertainties of politics either through technical knowledge or esoteric learning; one can rely on nothing more than political wisdom, that is, a good working knowledge of what men are like, and how to deal with them, a sense of proportion and delicacy.

Those who hold this view of politics would never criticize a government for failing to be daring, bold, or inspiring, but rather for being rash, crude, or dishonest. Nor are they likely to encourage glorious deeds or to want sweeping reforms; they are reluctant to go to war or to inflict suffering. They leave great changes to take place over a long time, and content themselves with making piecemeal and somewhat haphazard adjustments to circumstances. The world never appears to them as divided between saints and villains, because they expect even virtuous and reasonable men to differ.

Some of these sentiments continued to rule in Jeremy Bentham. He was as anxious as Hume to preserve diversity in opinion and action, to protect liberty and the rule of law. Nevertheless a new temperament was at work, a temperament that could not bear either uncertainty or the intrusion of personality. While Bentham's work was inspired partly by a sensitivity to injustices that had been allowed to accumulate, the way in which he proposed to deal with them reflected more than a desire for justice. He represented in England the spirit that possessed France in the late eighteenth century, the urge to remake the world according to a rational pattern. There is perhaps no better evidence of the nature of the British temper than the fact that in England this urge took the form of Benthamism.

For Bentham concerned himself even less than Hume did with men's souls; he did not undertake to make them secure of bliss in the hereafter, not even on earth. But within the limited province he allotted to politics, essentially the same as Hume assigned to it, he proposed to change the character of politics. It was no longer to be an art, or left to gentlemen amateurs. It was to become a technical activity. Not merely the particular reforms he outlined, or his insistence that English law needed reform gave Bentham such influence and reputation, but the suggestion implicit in everything he did that political wisdom could be reduced to a technique. This technique would enable men to dispense with experience; it could be put down complete and self-contained in a book, so that anyone could learn it and apply it

5

almost automatically. Unlike Hume, Bentham did not expect political needs to be constantly changing. He was certain of having discovered the key to perfection, to a system of law that would need but minor correction once in a hundred years.

Moreover, Bentham taught his successors to equate political order with one kind of order. Only in the realm of economic affairs was he content to accept another sort of order, and his interest in mechanisms enabled him to explain, as lucidly as anyone has, how from the self-interested activities of individuals social order could result without recourse to mystical natural harmonies or unseen hands. About law, however, he thought very differently. He denounced the Common Law not only because of its complications and inefficiencies, but because he opposed the whole notion of law as the product of growth, necessarily unpredictable, never complete or perfect. Instead, he advocated another concept of law, as the product of purely logical operations. The issue raised by Bentham was not whether the law was to be reformed, not even whether it ought to be codified, but in what manner it was to be reformed. Bentham did not want slow, limited innovations that would continue to be made always, but one grand sweep. Change was to come not in response to some specific defect, some particular injustice or inconsistency. It was to throw aside what had grown up over the centuries as simply chaos; it was to create a perfect, comprehensive, new design. For Bentham, legislation ought above all to be an activity of invention and logic, free of any need to consider what went before. It should make politics largely a matter of technical skill.

Thereby politics could also, Bentham hoped, be made impersonal. All his suggestions were designed to limit or eliminate the need to make judgements. Whereas the old Whig rulers believed they had something better than brains to rely on, Bentham's politician was to be pure brains. Yet this love of impersonality grew out of the same interest that moved Hume to emphasize personal qualities. Hume argued that motives and character must always be considered because no two men do the same thing for the same reasons; Bentham's sensitivity to the wide variation in human behaviour was expressed in a desire to rule out any question about a man's character or motives even from ethics, and certainly from politics. He would have confined ethical judgements to the impersonal question of how a man's actions affect others, without presuming to say anything about the man himself. In politics, his techniques were designed to make any personal judgement about a politician or the people he ruled irrelevant. He hoped in this way to free men altogether from subjection to anyone else's opinion.

Nevertheless Bentham's sensitivity to the feelings of real people came to haunt his dream of reducing politics to a technique. In the end, for all his preaching, he himself produced mainly a great number of ingenious devices, more nearly gadgets for reform than sweeping panaceas. He opened the door, however, to a world where politicians need not be men of prudence and taste, but merely qualified technicians.

A more profound change was introduced by John Stuart Mill, who endowed politics with a new meaning. Altered conditions made Bentham's theories seem less relevant, while modifications introduced by disciples gave them a more vulnerable character. At the same time, young intellectuals were being exposed to influences from abroad. All this led Mill to question the central tenet of the British political tradition, never jeopardized by Bentham, that the City of Man has no connection with the City of God. Within a century the protest against puritanism fashioned by Hume became the foundation for the revival of puritanism in a new form. Mill reminds us that puritanism is as permanent a strain in the British temper, at least since the seventeenth century, as is the tolerance opposed to it.

Although Mill's renunciation of his early beliefs is celebrated, he never rejected the puritanical discipline that James Mill had quite unconsciously taught him. It was a secular puritanism, unconnected with God, but just as the older forms did, it dismembered human nature and made repression, rather than harmony, its moral ideal. Like all latter-day puritans, Mill tried to give the emotions their due, but for all his efforts, he could think of them only as naturally hostile to reason, unless curbed by it. Although he cultivated an interest in art and poetry, he never could accept a full, spontaneous reaction to life. Instead he followed the old puritans in trying to draw a detailed picture of what a man ought to be, of how he should order his faculties and all his activities. To Mill, as to the early Christian puritans, man was a corrupt and fallen being, who had to struggle constantly against the sin within him.

But with this he combined an unprecedented optimism in man's ability to save himself through his reason. John Mill was not a man to tolerate doubt about anything, however profound, nor to be amused by confusion. Earnestness, moral certainty, righteousness were more natural to him. His interest in giving emotion its due did not move him to abandon his father's moral spirit, but to reject the prevailing British suspicion of comprehensive views of the universe. The upshot of his personal search for something spiritually more inspiring than Benthamism was an ambition to contain the whole world in a single theory, which constituted his real break with Benthamism. By comparison, Bentham's most grandiose schemes were child's play. Whereas Hume, like Hobbes and Locke, had used philosophy to underscore the limits of human powers and to advocate more modest aspirations, Mill saw in philosophy the guide to complete and final truth.

Yet he failed to rid himself altogether of the prejudices bred in him by his early training. As a philosopher, he remained within his native tradition.

But his flirtation with alien ways of thinking left its mark—his early interest in a comprehensive philosophy turned into an interest in a comprehensive politics and science, animated by a faith in progress. Only those who were cold-hearted or philistines, he came to think, considered politics merely a means to peace and security and liberty. Those who were aware of man's higher potentialities would make politics a means to human perfection. And a new role for science would make this feasible. From his father, Mill had learned the puritan notion that society is best governed by an élite, although they were to be elected by a wide suffrage. He came to identify this élite with those who had scientific knowledge and to believe that a new set of intellectual leaders would conduct men to salvation on earth. The new priesthood were to be sociologists, able to understand the true course of events, and on the basis of this information to tell people how they should live.

But a science of sociology had still to be developed, and while he devoted much thought to it, Mill did not get far beyond suggesting some modifications in classical economics. He persisted in founding his social analysis on individuals, just as Bentham had done, and from such an assumption the results he wanted were difficult to come by. Nor could he ever renounce his allegiance to the traditional liberties even while preaching his new spiritual politics. He marked the birth of the 'liberal intellectual', so familiar today, who with one part of him genuinely values liberty and recognizes the equal right of all adults to decide their lives for themselves, but with another wants the government, under the direction of the superior few, to impose what he considers the good life on all his fellows.

Precisely how politics could be based on science and made to serve spiritual ends was proposed in a consistent and clear-cut manner by Beatrice Webb. In her, the urge for improvement was altogether freed of inhibitions inherited from the eighteenth century. That she and Sidney Webb should both have become such important figures in the history of British political practice is in itself significant. For though Beatrice Webb was an impressive and moving figure, and in her way deeply reflective, she cannot be ranked with the greatest among either philosophers or statesmen. Yet she offered most eminently what her time demanded. Englishmen, even thoughtful ones, had come to care above all·for getting results at once. The pressure of social problems and a changed understanding of civilization made them indifferent to discussions of eternal dilemmas and impatient of anything that encouraged them to be undecided or troubled. They were ready to dispense with profundity and elegance, if only they could find some simple directions for improvement. This sort of need Beatrice Webb could satisfy.

Although she was not, like John Mill, strictly born into puritanism, it was easily available to her and early in life she adopted it as her own. In time she learned to equate the triumph of reason over passion with the rule of science over all of human life. For Mill, science still retained the character of a technique, though a very superior and broad technique. For Beatrice Webb, science assumed the quality of a religion. It represented not only man's victory over nature but a superior discipline that could truly purify human life. Diverse influences helped to shape this image of science—the impact of new discoveries in the physical sciences, Darwin's theory of evolution, Spencer's grand synthesis, idealist philosophy, and Evangelical morals. It did not correspond very well to what scientists actually did or believed, but it came closer than anything else to satisfying her emotional and intellectual wants.

Above all, it transformed her image of political activity. Science, Beatrice Webb believed, taught that politics should concern itself with the generations of the future more than with individuals living here and now, that in fact it ought not to deal with persons but with constituents of a social organism. The new politics could depend wholly on impersonal knowledge. For since science taught her, she believed, to think of society as an organic whole, the sociology that Mill had failed to develop seemed ready at hand. It followed that just as with the advancement of medicine, the physician replaced the barber, so politics had now to be taken out of the hands of ordinary men, however well educated or discerning, and turned over to the only ones who could be trusted with it, scientific experts. To the ordinary man was left a greater opportunity to join in public discussion and the joy of dedicating himself to Humanity, an infinite, possibly eternal being, though, happily for a scientific age, not a transcendental being.

Beatrice Webb continued to speak of a mysterious realm of values that neither science nor politics could reach, but doubts about ultimate truth never interfered with her dreams of human perfection through politics. She sanctioned only the usual parliamentary means, but in all other ways her view of political activity broke profoundly with the British tradition. Politics was at one stroke both destroyed and sanctified. It was destroyed in the old sense because political wisdom, all the skills once considered necessary in politics, even the old moral standards, became irrelevant. In its new sense, politics was no longer one of several human activities and at that not a very noble one; it encompassed all of human life. The City of Man was to be not a means of reaching the City of God, not even a reflection of it, but the Heavenly City itself.

Thus Hume's picture of man as a balanced whole whose object is merely to live decently and enjoyably was replaced by a view of man as essentially sinful, obliged to struggle against the evil within him, and most likely to succeed if he submits himself wholly to reason and puts his life at the service of future generations. In the new picture, man acquired new resources— accurate and very detailed knowledge about how to live, untainted by anyone's prejudices or interests. The earth was no longer peopled by free moral agents deciding their own actions, in a world as far as possible removed from the consistency of a machine because every moral problem was unique. There was no longer merely a great variety of goods, but a coherent, all-inclusive system of life, arranging the things men seek in a clear hierarchy. The old dilemmas of human life, it seemed, could be disposed of, the difference between man and God reduced to a bare minimum, and tragedy translated into inefficiency.

But these are only the bold outlines in the pattern. There is besides a wealth of surprising detail. Apparent affinities hide the widest divergence— Hume uses Newton's method to thwart the scientific spirit; the aversion to magic, that more than any other sentiment unites John Mill to Bentham, leads him to qualify liberty for the sake of progress; the established picture of Benthamite individualism is taken from a Darwinist who cares nothing for individuals. But the real affinities are often no less startling—Hume shares Montaigne's preference for Catholicism; John Mill denounces nature in the same terms as the Scots Presbyterian ministers castigated by Hume; the collectivist, T. H. Huxley, and the Comtist, Frederick Harrison, echo the *Westminster* reviewers on education, art, and science; the same antipathies shape the lives and work of Bentham, Spencer, and Beatrice Webb. The masters rarely teach what they intend—Hume becomes the patron saint of men utterly devoid of the scepticism and irony he had carefully cultivated; Bentham's gadgets for tolerance come to serve as a dogma of the righteous; Locke's psychology, designed to restrain human ambition, inspires James Mill to believe that men can be remade to order; John Mill's rejection of organic sociology prepares Englishmen to accept it. The same sentiment felt with equal passion and sincerity comes to bear very different connotations—we move from Hume's detached ironic tolerance to Bentham's 'gadgeteering' tolerance to John Mill's geometric tolerance. And the anomalies are endless—two model conservatives, who seem to repeat one another's words, are as far apart as heaven and earth; a radical critic of conservatism denies the necessity for change; a leading admirer of Germany preaches against the love of system, while an arch opponent of German metaphysics becomes the most influential purveyor of the German pursuit of system; England's empire is opposed by advocates of capitalism and cherished by those who wish to transform England's social system; the 'progressives' choose God, while their opponents choose man.

In short, we are forcibly reminded that names and doctrines collect a variety of associations and hide a limitless stock of temperaments, beliefs, and purposes. These are arranged and rearranged in unforeseeable patterns. And neither affinities nor divisions, in politics as elsewhere, are ever complete or simple.

PART I

DAVID HUME: PAGAN VIRTUES AND PROFANE POLITICS

CHAPTER I

A MAN OF MODERATION

PURITANISM does not often breed defenders of pagan virtues. Yet it was partly because he grew up in a culture preoccupied with hell that David Hume came to speak so profoundly for the tolerant civilization, devoted to living gracefully here and now, that flourished in the great Whig houses of eighteenth-century England.

He was born in Edinburgh, in 1711, the younger son of the Laird of Nine-wells, a modest and picturesque estate near the village of Chirnside. After a few years at the University of Edinburgh and a faint-hearted attempt to study law, he settled on being a man of letters. At twenty-three, he left home to seclude himself in France for three years; and in the cloisters of the Jesuits' college in La Flèche where Descartes had been a student, he wrote most of his revolutionary *Treatise on Human Nature*. The book was barely noticed when it appeared. But the hopeful author, 'being naturally of a sanguine and cheerful temper', soon consoled himself and retired to Nine-wells to prepare a volume of essays, which was published in 1742 and met with some small success. As his literary efforts did not, however, provide enough to supplement his slender patrimony, he was obliged to look for more immediate ways of increasing his income. For a year, he lived as a companion to the mad Marquis of Annandale. Then in 1747, he became secretary to General St Clair, and attended him on some clumsy and ill-fated expeditions, as well as in his embassies to Vienna and Turin. Hume performed his duties carefully, observed with detached interest the warlike operations in which he participated, and enjoyed the sights on the way. It was amusing to be presented at court in Vienna, especially since he could not manage a bow, but he disapproved of Maria Theresa's efforts to establish a 'Court of Chastity'. Everything was most enlightening: 'There are great advantages in travelling', he wrote in his journal to his brother, 'and nothing serves more to remove prejudices'. He had not, for instance, expected to find Germany so 'fine a Country, full of industrious honest People . . . it gives a Man of Humanity Pleasure to see that so considerable a Part of Mankind as the Germans are in so tolerable a Condition'. He predicted (with the insight that led him to foresee a little later the disturbed state of America that if Germany were united, 'it woud be the greatest Power that ever was in the World. . . .'[1]

By the time his appointment with General St Clair came to an end, he had

[1] *Letters of David Hume*, ed. by J. Y. T. Greig (Oxford, 1932), vol. I, p. 126.

become the David Hume familiar to us, no longer a rawboned, rustic Scotsman, disposed to be intense and a recluse, but a portly man of the world. He still spoke English with a broad Scottish accent, and French very badly, all in a thin, somewhat effeminate voice. His appearance was even more misleading, or so it seemed to one companion who has given us the most vivid picture of him:

His face was broad and fat, his mouth wide, and without any other expression than that of imbecility. His eyes vacant and spiritless, and the corpulence of his whole person, was far better fitted to communicate the idea of a turtle-eating alderman than of a refined philosopher. . . . His wearing an uniform added greatly to his natural awkwardness, for he wore it like a grocer of the trained bands.[1]

But the portraits by his friend Allan Ramsay show more than the blandness— a half amused, half melancholy man, with a dreamy quizzical expression, a man who enjoyed watching mankind and did not mind being thought more simple than he was. He appears to be an accepting man, resigned to whatever fortune granted him. And it is not surprising to find him writing as he did to Henry Home when, at the end of St Clair's campaign, it seemed that he would return home with no gain in resources:

I shall stay a little time in London, to see if anything new will present itself. If not, I shall return cheerfully to books, leisure, and solitude in the country. An elegant table has not spoilt my relish for sobriety; nor gaiety for study, and frequent disappointments have taught me, that nothing need be despaired of, as well as that nothing can be depended on.[2]

Things turned out better than he expected. Hume accumulated enough for an income of about fifty pounds a year, sufficient for his wants. Within the next few years, he became established as a literary man: another volume of essays, his *Political Discourses*, was at once successful. His *Enquiry on Human Understanding*, as well as his *Enquiry on Morals*, into which he had recast the *Treatise*, were very well received. He began to think of establishing himself somewhere permanently. As he agreed with Bayle that town was 'the true scene for a man of Letters', and had decided against London, he moved in 1751 to a flat in Edinburgh.

His life was orderly and social. In the mornings, after a walk round Salisbury Craigs, he worked; four or five times a week he dined out and returned home early to his studies. Other evenings he could be found at some tavern, like Cleriheugh's, where his friends often gathered with other men of letters, lawyers, and magistrates. At home he provided his friends with modest fare—roasted hen, minced collops, and punch, but the best in com-

---

[1] *Memoirs of the Political and Private Life of James Caulfield, Earl of Charlemont*, by Francis Hardy, p. 8, in *Life and Correspondence of David Hume*, by John Hill Burton (Edinburgh, 1846), vol. I, pp. 270 f.

[2] *Letters*, vol. I, pp. 99 f.

LIST OF PLATES

I David Hume, from a portrait by Allan Ramsay (reproduced by kind permission of the National Galleries of Scotland) *facing page* 112

II Jeremy Bentham, from a portrait by H. W. Pickersgill (reproduced by kind permission of the Trustees of the National Portrait Gallery) 129

III John Stuart Mill, from a portrait by G. F. Watts (reproduced by kind permission of the Trustees of the National Portrait Gallery) 304

IV Beatrice Webb, from a photograph by George Bernard Shaw 321

ACKNOWLEDGEMENTS

I would like to thank the William Volker Foundation, the Earhart Foundation, and the Rockefeller Foundation for grants during the early stages of my work. I owe a special debt of gratitude to the Radcliffe Institute for Independent Study and its director, Miss Constance Smith, for enabling me to complete the book under circumstances most unusually encouraging and agreeable.

I am grateful to the Passfield trustees for permission to read and quote from the unpublished diaries of Beatrice Webb, and to Mr C. G. Allen of the library at the London School of Economics for his kind assistance.

INTRODUCTION

Although nothing inspires dispute more easily than matters of politics, there is wonderful agreement about the questions at issue. Not only is the nature of political controversy in the distant past supposed to be clear. What has more recently agitated men seems equally certain. And hardly anyone denies that the distinctive political issue since the eighteenth century has been whether government should do more or less.

The agreement extends to accounts of how this came to be such an important question in England. Toward the beginning of the nineteenth century, the historians all tell us, new social conditions aggravated the problem of poverty. The lower classes began to insist on a measure of equality, and the upper classes came to recognize in that demand a claim on their consciences. Those who welcomed change and novel solutions, that is, those who were 'progressive', became collectivists or socialists. They were so successful in converting others to their opinions that the activity of government has vastly expanded. The opposition, which has declined to move ahead—so the story runs—is led by 'reactionaries', who desire less government and long for a return to times past. They are the individualists or defenders of capitalism or perhaps *laissez-faire*. The image of modern politics is accordingly that of a debate. It is presumed to have two sides, and anyone who declares a political opinion is classified as either forward or backward.

While this image corresponds to something real, it is not altogether satisfying. It seems to be lacking a dimension. For not everyone who speaks on politics at any given moment may be addressing himself to the same issues. A dispute on how much government ought to do for social welfare may be related to a disagreement on what welfare comprises. There may be no independent clockwork which is wound up to answer political questions. Not only a man's worldly interests, his compassion, or knowledge of objective circumstances may determine his political convictions. They may depend even more on his character, his tastes, his notion of the relation between man and God, his preference for a quite particular way of living.

If we look at modern politics from this point of view, the presumed debate between more government and less dissolves. Instead, political disagreement emerges as clusters of conversations. Party lines no longer seem to mark out groups of soul-mates, and the important divisions are not between progressives and reactionaries, or collectivists and individualists. The divisions are defined rather by basic differences in temperament—philosophers are opposed to artists, logicians to historians, puritans to pagans. The most striking change is no longer in the attitude toward the role of government, but in the conception of what sort of activity politics is.

I

How the conception of politics changed in England can be traced through the lives and work of four writers—David Hume, Jeremy Bentham, John Stuart Mill, Beatrice Webb. Each represents a distinctive way of looking at politics, which has become intertwined with others and obscured in political practice, and yet remains a vital part of the political tradition in England. Nevertheless, each writer contributed to a transformed outlook on the nature of politics. It was first suggested by Jeremy Bentham; its shape was defined by John Stuart Mill; and the finished product appears in the work of Beatrice Webb. But the significance of what happened becomes plain only by comparison with the earlier view of David Hume.

The four writers are taken here to speak for something more than their individual preferences, but not for any mysterious reason. As people who meet together very often, whether directly or indirectly, tend to communicate to one another their convictions and inclinations, there is likely to be a kinship in any given time and place between the reactions and ideas even of very different sorts of people. And what is common to the group may be stated unusually well by some member. In this manner, Hume may be said to express better than anyone else the dominant attitude to politics in the eighteenth century. But it does not follow that Hume's contemporaries all looked at politics exactly as he did, or for just the same reasons. Nor would any attempt to make an abstract of Hume's outlook and call it 'the eighteenth century view' produce anything short of a monstrosity. One must see the portrait of Hume as one among many portraits of a family. The resemblance cannot be analysed or isolated. It is stronger in some faces than in others. Like a shadow, its outlines are never sharply defined, but somehow it can be discovered in all the family faces. In this sense, and only in this sense, the patterns found in the four writers may be considered generic patterns for their time, and the changes from one pattern to another may be said to represent a broad change in moral and political ideals.

What makes the differences among the four writers especially impressive is that in a way they all owe allegiance to the same intellectual tradition. The name, utilitarian, most readily comes to mind. They have all been called utilitarians, and they themselves have claimed some such kinship with one another. Bentham said he had discovered the idea of utility in Hume; Mill, who first made utilitarianism a popular name, was tutored by Bentham himself, as well as by Bentham's chief disciple, James Mill; and the Webbs often liked to describe themselves and other Fabians as latter-day utilitarians. In fact, the name is misleading because it suggests that they all shared a common philosophy. But it does point to certain common sympathies. All these writers praised a common sense, matter-of-fact, concrete, experimental approach to human affairs. All tried to justify their arguments ultimately by referring to something that any man could see with his own eyes. It is even more im-

pany and conversation. His visitors included besides the leading Scots literary men and disbelievers, some liberal defenders of the faith, very often William Robertson, historian and minister, leader of the church Moderates. His old ties with Lord Kames and other friends of his youth were renewed; and he became very attached to Adam Smith, with whom he remained on the closest terms until he died.

His tone was always easy and good-humoured, never righteous. It suited his ideal of society, 'the happy times when Atticus and Cassius, the Epicureans, Cicero, the Academic, and Brutus, the Stoic, could all of them, live in unreserved friendship together, and were insensible to all those distinctions, except so far as they furnished agreeable matter to discourse and conversation'.[1] Afraid of no one, and not disposed to guard his tongue, the host was often far from reverent—ready with a tale about churches and bishops and crowds of immortal souls, or about the Mohammedan converted to Catholicism who concluded that God no longer existed because he had been eaten yesterday in Church. He could as easily gossip about the divorce of a duchess or the paternity of a lord, as discourse on the immorality of Restoration drama, or Shakespeare's lack of refinement. Ordinary affairs of business were well within his province—he quarrelled with his publishers, inquired into the credentials of a Latin tutor, used his influence to solicit favours for his friends, and followed the politics of the day with critical and sometimes caustic impartiality. He was disappointed when the pious and respectable thought him unfit to teach moral philosophy at Glasgow, but he generally dismissed them with a laugh. When there was a move to excommunicate him, he wrote to Allan Ramsay:

You may tell that reverent gentleman the Pope, that there are many here who rail at him, and yet would be much greater persecutors had they the power of doing. The last Assembly sat on me. They did not propose to burn me, because they cannot. But they intend to give me over to Satan, which they think they have the power of doing. My friends, however, prevailed, and my damnation is postponed for a twelvemonth. . . . Anderson, the godly, spiteful, pious, splenetic, charitable, unrelenting, meek, persecuting, Christian, inhuman, peace making, furious Anderson is at present very hot in pursuit of Lord Kames.[2]

He did succeed, soon after moving to Edinburgh, in becoming Librarian for the Faculty of Advocates, and used his access to the library to write a history of England. It was meant to be an impartial account, and it turned out to offend no one, Hume found, other than the Whigs and Tories, English, Scots, and Irish, churchmen and sectarians, free-thinkers and pious, patriots and courtiers. Nevertheless, it sold, and he became more than independent, indeed 'opulent'. Between volumes of the history, he also

[1] *Ibid.* p. 173.
[2] *Ibid.* p. 224.

published a *Natural History of Religion*, which was, to his satisfaction, violently attacked by the pious. In the summer of 1758, in order to put his Tudor volumes through the press, he went to London for his first visit in ten years. It had always attracted him, and now the freedom from bigotry, and the respect for himself as a literary man that he found there pleased him so much that he was disposed never to leave. He met everyone: at the table of David Garrick, he became acquainted with Burke, whose 'very pretty *Treatise on the Sublime*' interested him. The young Gibbon boldly sought him out. Through his old friend, Gilbert Elliot, Lord of the Admiralty and favourite of Pitt, he met George Grenville, Charles Townshend, and Temple; he played whist with the Duke of Argyll; and Shelburne invited him to join the distinguished circle he was gathering around him. Still, partly in disgust with the London mobs and the general nationalist hysteria inspired by Pitt, he decided to forsake 'that mobbish people'. The big world with its wit, its elegance, and gaiety attracted him, but he preferred, after all, his simple independent life in Edinburgh. When Boswell came to see him in 1762, he found Hume 'sitting at his ease reading Homer', in his 'pretty little house', actually the third story of a vast building, James's Court, where he had hung classical engravings around the sitting room.

But his plans to remain peacefully in Edinburgh were broken by an invitation in 1763 to assist the Earl of Hertford in his embassy to Paris. With a short interruption, Hume stayed on in Paris for five years, first as secretary to the embassy, then as *chargé d'affaires*, and finally, under General Conway, as undersecretary, serving ably in all these capacities. In Paris, his history and his essays had won him more fame than at home—Voltaire admired him, he became an intimate of Diderot and d'Alembert, Mme. du Deffand and the other leading hostesses vied for his presence in their salons, and his popularity amazed and wounded Horace Walpole. He became so fond of Mme. de Boufflers that he was tempted to become her permanent admirer, but remembered in time, assisted by her ambitions to marry the Prince de Conti, that he was but an awkward fat Scotsman, and fled back to Edinburgh.

From France Hume took home, along with a host of gratifying memories, a volatile French genius, Jean-Jacques Rousseau, who had been commended to his care by Mme. de Boufflers. Hume undertook to get for him a pension from the king of England, and to arrange for his living quarters, refusing to heed friends who assured him that Rousseau's suspicious nature was beyond rescue. But a man like Rousseau was not within Hume's comprehension; when the storm broke Hume was, most unlike himself, enraged, and the quarrel became an international scandal. But not even Rousseau's strange ingratitude could for long disturb his serenity. He was immune to rancour, just as he was a stranger to sin and tragedy. His only regret was, he wrote to Gilbert Elliot, that his old house in James's Court was too small to display my great Talent for Cookery, the Science to which I intend to addict the remaining Years of my Life; I have just now lying on the Table before me a Receipt for making *Soupe a la Reine* copy'd with my own hand. For Beef and Cabbage (a charming Dish), and old Mutton and old Claret, nobody excels me. I make also Sheep head Broth in a manner that Mr Keith [Ambassador to Vienna, St Petersburg, and Copenhagen] speaks of it for eight days after, and the Duc de Nivernois would bind himself Apprentice to my Lass to learn it.[1]

He lived long enough to congratulate Gibbon on reviving English letters and to rejoice that Smith's *Wealth of Nations* lived up to all expectations. During the long illness that preceded his death, his only worry was to arrange for the publication of the *Dialogues Concerning Natural Religion* which his friends, solicitous for his reputation, wished him to suppress. He continued to pay calls and receive visitors, and was amused, though never convinced, by the varied, hopeful prognostications of his physicians. There was much to laugh about in death as in life. Not long before he died, he read Lucian's *Dialogues of the Dead* and tried to think, he told Adam Smith, of what excuses he might make to Charon: could he stay for a new edition of his works?

But Charon would answer, 'When you have seen the effect of these, you will be for making other alterations. There will be no end of such excuses; so, honest friend, please step into the boat.' But I might still urge, 'Have a little patience, good Charon, I have been endeavouring to open the eyes of the public. If I live a few years longer, I may have the satisfaction of seeing the downfall of some of the prevailing systems of superstition.' But Charon would then lose all temper and decency. 'You loitering rogue, that will not happen these many hundred years. Do you fancy I will grant you a lease for so long a term?

After all, Hume pointed out to his friends, he had done all he had meant to do, and left his friends and relations in good circumstances—'I therefore have all reason to die contented'.[2]

When Boswell came to investigate the dying man's state of mind, Hume was reading a new book, Dr Campbell's *Philosophy of Rhetoric*, and much to Boswell's dismay, showed no sign of either repentance or agitation. Johnson, the devout Christian, could not bear even to discuss death; Hume expected annihilation very shortly, and was content. He wanted nothing beyond his span on earth and feared nothing thereafter. He had no quarrel with the natural lot of man. For he was, as he said in his funeral oration on himself, 'a man of mild Dispositons, of Command of Temper, of an open, social, and cheerful Humour, capable of Attachment, but little susceptible of Enmity, and of great Moderation in all Passions'.

[1] *Ibid.* vol. II, p. 208.
[2] Smith to Strahan, 9 Nov., 1776 in *Hume's Dialogues Concerning Natural Religion*, ed. by Norman Kemp Smith (London, 1947), p. 245.

CHAPTER II

THE KIRK

HUME'S moderation had, however, been acquired. It was fashioned by rebellion against the dogmatic and austere civilization that bred him. Beneath the bland surface of his life, there is another story that begins with Scotland in the early decades of the eighteenth century, where Calvinism still ruled with much of its early strength but little of the grandeur. It produced a tension that shaped Hume's genius, and determined his development from a son of the Kirk to an outrageous infidel philosopher and finally to a worldly essayist and historian. Although puritanism survived in England as well, and inspired Hume's heirs, there it took on subtler, sophisticated shapes. In Scotland puritanism had its last moment of simplicity, and the emotions it fed on and generated, obscured later by intellectual wrappings, could still be seen plainly.

The Reformation had not, as in England, reduced religion to a political and individual concern. Instead, it replaced Catholicism with another complete interpretation of all the facts of existence. The Calvinism that took over in Scotland (everywhere but the Highlands) removed from Christianity all pagan vestiges. It not only forbade outward emblems, ceremonies, and images, and emphasized the justice and infinite, awful majesty of God, rather than love or hope of salvation; it aspired to read the Divine Will, and in place of the contemptuous indifference that had characterized Scotland under Romanism, it brought an unqualified dogmatism. The Old Church was swept away rather than reformed and there was little left to temper the zeal of the Reformation.

The events of the following centuries confirmed the most extreme tendencies. Under Cromwell, all but rigid Covenanters were excluded from power, and Scotland was placed thoroughly under the heel of the Church. When the Episcopal clergy returned during the Restoration and in turn dismissed the Presbyterians, they effectively destroyed any hope for a moderate Presbyterianism. In exile, the older men acquired what Bishop Burnet called 'a tangled scrupulosity', a habit of enlarging minor differences into great issues, in short, a fanaticism that pursued victory at all costs. The younger men had little opportunity to become learned and knew only that the Lord's Word was worth more than all the pagan learning. They were 'rude in mind and manners, grimly religious and bigotted in spirit'.[1] As a result, the Presbyterians restored to power upon the landing of William of

---

[1] H. G. Graham, *Social Life in Scotland* (London, 1899), vol. II, pp. 10 f.

Orange were distinguished chiefly by their zeal in purging the Episcopal clergy. They were proud of their vulgarity and ignorance, opposed to philosophy, to the classics, to all learning, addicted to a puritanism that, having excluded the most powerful intellectual elements, was left with little more than its harshness.

A decline in their influence began as a result of the union with England in 1707. The union re-opened Scotland to the outside world and stimulated the growth of another spirit, along with industrial and commercial changes that were to transform it from a poor, barren country into one of the more enterprising and prosperous industrial nations of the world. In the Church, the group of Moderates who came to dominate it in the middle decades of the century began gathering strength. But during the youth and early manhood of David Hume, the prevailing spirit in Scotland was still that of the Covenanters. Their spiritual austerity found a natural environment in the material conditions of the country, which still bore the marks of years of turbulence. Trade was stagnant, houses deserted, agriculture poor. There was nothing left of those earlier days when Scotland was much closer to France than England, when the lairds far outshone the rude English barons. Instead, even rich lairds no longer enjoyed any splendour. They were strangers to luxuries like delicate furnishings, windows that opened, desserts, or fine clothes, and were rarely at all learned or refined. There was nothing anywhere to brighten the atmosphere of gloom and hopelessness in which the grimmest sort of religion flourished.

Paganism survived only in the form of superstitious fears, in the belief in charmers and sorcerers who thrived in remote places, and, above all, in the fear of Satan. He was never absent, and the acknowledged source of all carnal thoughts. A mysterious sound, an unexpected ailment, a spasm of doubt were proof of Satan's power, and civil and ecclesiastical authorities united to exorcise him by hunting witches with organized cruelty. Nor was there less to fear from God, whom pious Scotsmen regarded as an implacable despot to be served with unremitting devotion in a vain effort to escape His wrath. For the doctrine of election, which they held in all its severity, taught that Christ died only for the elect and left all the rest of mankind with no remedy against the fury of God. On earth, one could hope only for a commonwealth ruled by saints according to laws derived from studying the Bible.

The few humane and polite Moderate ministers had little following. Instead, the people flocked to hear the more terrifying preachers, especially the 'left-wing', ultra-Evangelicals, who gave them crude, but dramatic discourses on how they would spend eternity in the company of grisly devils, howling and roaring in everlasting torment. These preachers further endeared themselves to their audience by pursuing a number of worthy objects: the persecution of Episcopalians, the proscription of Roman Catholics, the extermination of witches, the re-establishment of a theocracy. And they were indefatigable inquisitors into higher matters. Nothing was too mysterious for them, be it the secret designs of the Deity before creation or the fate of man for all eternity. The most popular and influential preacher, Thomas Boston, sold his published sermons by the thousands to peasants, shepherds, pedlars, and lairds. His message was ever full of hell-fire and wrath:

> The Damned . . . must depart from God into everlasting Fire. I am not in a mind to dispute, what Kind of Fire it is. . . . Whether a material fire or not? Experience will more than satisfy the Curiosity of those, who are disposed rather to dispute about it, than to seek how to escape it. . . . Hell-fire will not only pierce into the Bodies, but directly into the Souls of the Damn'd. . . . How vehement must that Fire be that pierceth directly into the Soul, and makes an everlasting Burning in the Spirit, the most lively and tender Part of a Man, wherein Wounds or Pains are most intolerable. . . . When one is cast into a burning fiery Furnace, the Fire makes its way into the very Bowels, and leaves no Member untouch'd.[1]

Although he exhorted sinners to reform, Boston gave them little hope of success, and concentrated rather on their natural sinfulness. Professor Blackwell explained that it was an act of grace and benevolence for God to have made a covenant with Adam whereby he put all mankind's stock, so to speak, into one ship.[2] Everyone agreed that when Adam fell, man became a rank, stinking, corrupt creature; his physical beauty in the state of innocence was transformed into a monstrous body, so hideous and vile that it had to be kept under cover.

It was shown again and again that only faith, not morality, mattered. Besides, any hint that there might be natural virtue or light in a human soul was greeted with a charge of heresy. The total corruption of every man, woman, and child was beyond question; even a new-born infant was but a 'lump of wrath, a child of hell'. To the preachers it was obvious that the heart of man could harbour no good thought or desire, for the Creator would never let his image dwell so near the effigies of the devil. 'Hear O Sinner, what is thy case', Boston commanded, and explained lucidly:

> Innumerable Sins compass thee about; Mountains of Guilt are lying upon thee; Floods of Impurities overwhelm thee. Living Lusts, of all Sorts roll up and down in the dead Sea of thy Soul; where no Good can breathe because of the Corruption there. . . . The Thoughts and imaginations of thy Heart are only evil. . . . O sad Reckoning! As many Thoughts, Words, Actions, as many Sins. . . .[3]

The duty of ministers was to convince the people that 'unregenerate morality can never please God, and in this state of wrath and curse is

---

[1] Thomas Boston, *The Fourfold State* (1744), pp. 441, 443, 444, 445.
[2] Graham, *Social Life in Scotland*, vol. II, pp. 131–2.
[3] Boston, *The Fourfold State*, pp. 100–1.

loathed by Him'. It was blasphemy to preach that performing the ordinary duties made man less noxious to God, for while morality was desirable in its place, it was 'soul ruining', and led to perdition when it taught men to depend on their own merits. William Land, minister of Crimond about the beginning of the eighteenth century, was deposed for saying in a Synod sermon that virtue was more natural to the human race than vice.[1] Later in the century, the seceder Adam Gib could still protest that preaching moral duties called men to what 'was absolutely impracticable and leading to eternal perdition'.[2] Even in 1837, the new Principal of Edinburgh College was subjected to a prosecution in the Edinburgh Presbytery, on the charge of failing to preach the doctrine of original sin in its full rigour, denying the right of the civil power to punish heresy, denying that well-established doctrines should set the limits of enquiry, and showing undue charity to heathens and lapsed Christians.[3]

Nothing was allowed to escape the universal blight and the effect on morality was hardly salutary. Discourses on the true 'Scriptural and Rational way of preaching the Gospel' taught that the beasts also partook of sin and were therefore ferocious, repulsive, and carnivorous. That vegetables were just as cursed was evident from the weeds, brambles, thistles, and nettles that laid barren the ground. Lazy Scots farmers accordingly pleaded that they dared not clear the weeds for dread of interfering with the divine sentence on the soil. Some troubled sinners gave up in despair, others felt free to indulge in reckless vice, while those who felt assured of election were inspired to neglect conduct and duty. An English visitor to Scotland in the 'thirties protested: 'I wish these ministers would speak oftener and more civilly than they do, of morality'. Yet even when they did speak of it, not much was accomplished—'one would think there was no sin, according to them, but fornication; or other virtues besides keeping the Sabbath'.[4]

While eternal bliss was not to be had by moral conduct, any attempt to find pleasure in life on earth was strictly censured. Gratification of the senses, in whatever form, was ruled out. 'Since the Eyes of our first Parents were opened to the forbidden Fruit', Thomas Boston instructed the pious, 'Men's Eyes have been the Gates of Destruction to their Souls'.[5] All amusements were equally sinful—dancing, carnal; cards, dangerous; poetry, fanciful; tales, frivolous and untrue; dicing, an impious usurpation of the lots appointed by God. The world was not merely coupled with the flesh and the

[1] Graham, *Social Life in Scotland*, vol. II, p. 133 and n. 2.
[2] Adam Gib, *Sacred Contemplation*, p. 354 in Graham, *Social Life in Scotland*, vol. II, p. 144.
[3] J. Y. T. Greig, *David Hume* (London, 1931), p. 114.
[4] Edward Burt, *Letters from the North* (1815), vol. I, pp. 165 and 185.
[5] Boston, *The Fourfold State*, p. 38.

devil—it was the flesh and the devil. It was an enemy's country to be plundered, but never enjoyed, for enjoyment, like beauty, was a snare of the enemy. The good Presbyterian was always at war, or at most resting between battles, his only purpose in life being to fight against evil. He was affronted by everything—by a neighbour who was heard through the wall being amorous to his own wife, by a townsman who took the *Spectator*, or a friend who sent his daughter to a boarding school. He never indulged even in the pleasure of ordinary grief. Upon the death of a promising child, the proud and pious parent recorded only that, 'He was a pleasant child and desirable, grave and wise beyond his years, a reprover of sin among his comrades, frequent in his private devotions as he was capable'.[1]

No moment of life was outside the jurisdiction of the Church. It commanded that family exercises be held every day, and before communion, the minister inquired whether each household had complied. Every night, at nine or ten o'clock, elders went through the streets and taverns to dismiss any loiterers. The week was crowned by a sabbath more rigorous than anything enforced by the English Puritans, equal only to the New England Sabbath. No food was to be cooked, no fire lit; it was a crime to save a boat endangered by a storm, to whistle or walk in the roads, to grind snuff, feed the cattle, or bring water to a sick person. Children, as well as adults, submitted to endless sermons, instruction, and prayers, and were forbidden to go out of doors. The only amusement, open to all, was reporting on delinquents to the Kirk, or better still, hearing the minister enlarge on the doom of sinners who, clad in sackcloth, were made to stand on a platform or in front of the pulpit for as many as 26 Sundays until the minister was assured of their penitence. All offences, whether serious or trivial, were treated in the same way, and no one was safe from his neighbours' scrupulous oversight. When 'visitants' from the Presbytery arrived, accusations were most welcome, and not infrequently the minister found himself charged along with the rest for being wanting in reverence or for having broken the sabbath by setting up a fallen sheaf in the field. To compel a suspect to appear, or to stand at the pillar if he tried to take his rebuke from his seat, the Church could employ the sheriff. And a refusal to obey the orders of the Presbytery to 'stand rebuke' was punished by excommunication, 'being delivered over to Satan', banished from the Church, in short, being made an outcast from society, a sentence few could bear.

That David Hume escaped intimate acquaintance with this spirit is most unlikely. His parish, Chirnside, was distinguished for being a stronghold of fanaticism within a generally more tolerant area, the Merse. During the

---

[1] Turnbull's Diary, 1696, Scot. Hist. Society, p. 423 in Graham, *Social Life in Scotland*, vol. II, p. 88.

Episcopacy, in 1676, some 40 Covenanters, from Chirnside and its village persisted in worshipping at conventicles. After the defeat of Episcopacy the Presbyterianism that returned in 1689 with the Rev. Henry Erskine was un-compromising enough to win praise from Thomas Boston. It is doubtful that Erskine's influence can have worn off very soon after his death; that it lingered on is suggested by the fact that as late as 1873, Chirnside boasted of a Church belonging to the Cameronians, the most illiberal of Scottish sects. Most probably, Hume's uncle, George Home, the son of a covenanting father, was an Evangelical, 'godly minister', whose sermons in the Chirnside Kirk and weekly visits to the family did not much enhance the joys of the sabbath. There was, in any case, no lack of opportunity for David Hume to become well acquainted with religious enthusiasm.

As a boy, he seems to have been quite as pious as his uncle required. Although the book he read assiduously was condemned by the Covenanters of 1690 as superstitious and erroneous, the *Whole Duty of Man* seems austere enough by any other discerning standard. It did not lead him far astray, to judge by his amusements as a child—abstracting a list of the vices catalogued at the end of the *Whole Duty* and testing himself against them, 'for instance, to try if, notwithstanding his excelling his schoolfellows, he had no pride or vanity'. As Hume told Boswell, this soul-searching which was routine in the Kirk, was 'strange work'.[1] The catalogue of sins included such offences as 'not arranging any set of solemn rites for humiliation and confession, or too seldom', 'making pleasure, not health, the end of eating', 'wasting the time or estate in good fellowship'. In an old manuscript book, he recorded all his doubts, so as to expose and refute them. He tried again and again to dissipate them, to subdue his imagination and remain at peace with the common opinion. When at last he admitted failure, it was in a way against his will.

Exactly how he arrived at his aversion to Calvinist faith and morality, Hume never explained. But it seems clear that he had become an infidel well before he was twenty. His exposure to the university in Edinburgh, at the age of twelve, undoubtedly provided much of the stimulus. There the contrast between the Covenanting spirit and that of civilization was made very evident. At the same time, the college kept alive for him impressions of life under the Kirk: students not only had to attend church services and observe the sabbath in the usual way; they were examined on doctrinal questions and on the sermons they heard; they had to take turns at opening a class with a prayer, and their private devotions and opinions were overseen by censors and regents. But also another spirit was abroad. The course of study, though care-

---

[1] James Boswell, 'An Account of my last Interview with David Hume,' reprinted in *Dialogues concerning Natural Religion*, p. 76.

fully supervised, included the Latin classics, certainly Cicero, Horace, Virgil; the study of Greek; and very likely Locke and Newton. And the contrast between the secular authors and the Covenanters was underscored by the society at Edinburgh which had become a centre of cultural revival in Scotland.

By the time Hume came to the university, the effects of the union and the exposure to England had become marked, at least in Edinburgh. Some years before Hume had arrived there, a group of faculty and students of law and divinity had organized the Rankenian Club, to promote good English style and literary taste, and general freedom of thinking. The influence of the club did much to encourage literature and a more liberal culture in Scotland, a preference for metaphysical disquisitions over theological or political controversies which had until then absorbed all intellectual energies. When, after his first two years at Edinburgh Hume returned to study law, his literary ambitions led him to the more worldly and cultivated society available then. He became very friendly with Allan Ramsay, son of the bookseller poet, whose circulating library had become the centre of a literary circle and was often denounced by the authorities for spreading vice and obscenity. He also became attached to Henry Home of Kames, a man of wide learning, elegant tastes, and marked philosophic interests. And his closest friend was Michael Ramsay, described by some as 'a very debauched, licentious creature', in any case, an intellectual young man, far from puritan. In this company, Hume reread the Latin poets, orators, and philosophers, as well as Newton and Bacon; he became acquainted more intimately with Locke, Clarke, and Bayle; he learned French, and read the French classics, besides the more polished English writers, Milton, Dryden, Swift, Addison, Steele, Pope. Prodded on by their influence, Hume began to dig deeper, to ask himself just what he did or should believe.

From the emphasis in his adult invective, it seems likely that the taint of hypocrisy in religious enthusiasm first inspired him to doubt. There is an echo of a personal experience and excuse, a suggestion that he began by disliking the flavour of his own devotion in the line: 'Men dare not avow, even to their own hearts, the doubts which they entertain on such subjects. They make a merit of implicit faith; and disguise to themselves their real infidelity, by the strongest asserverations and the most positive bigotry'.[1] Once he had grown sensitive to his own dissembling, he began to detect the symptoms in others, and finally to see the whole of his religion in a new perspective. Thereafter, he could never speak about religion without heat. Whenever he referred to the

---

[1] *Essays, Moral, Political and Literary*, ed. by T. H. Green and T. H. Grose, 2 vols. (London, 1898), vol. II, p. 348. Cf. also Hume, *The History of England*, 6 vols. (London, 1841), vol. v, p. 550 Note D.

Puritans in England, Covenanters in Scotland, to zealots and enthusiasts of any kind, he betrayed the sort of animus that a strongly felt reaction against early beliefs often produces. Even when he guarded his expression, sensitive Christians could feel his deep-seated antipathy to them.

In whatever context he spoke on religion, his theme was always the same— the contrast between the bigotry and austerity of Christianity, particularly of abstract, Protestant Christianity, and the easy, tolerant, life-giving spirit of paganism. Pagan religions, Hume said more than once, 'contented themselves with divinising lust, incest, adultery; but the predestinarian doctors have divinised cruelty, wrath, fury, vengeance, and all the blackest vices'. All popular religions were varieties of 'daemonism', but those that exalted the Deity most, like Christianity, gave Him the most detestable character, and by forcing worshippers into pretending to adore what at heart they found reprehensible, compounded guilt with misery: 'The heart secretly detests such measures of cruel and implacable vengeance; but the judgement dares not but pronounce them perfect and adorable. And the additional misery of this inward struggle aggravates all the other terrors, by which the unhappy victims to superstition are forever haunted'.[1]

Certainly, there was a remarkable order and unity in nature—'All things are evidently of a piece'.[2] Every rational inquirer was disposed to look for a source of this order and to find good reason for believing in an intelligent author of nature. But he could not reasonably do more. For the Deity presented by natural religion was not an object of either sense or imagination; He was invisible and incomprehensible. He could not therefore be either understood or loved. As vulgar minds, however, found it difficult to believe in an abstract object, they soon began to give the Deity 'some sensible representation; such as either the more conspicuous parts of nature, or the statues, images, and pictures, which a more refined age forms of its divinities.'[3]

But in thinking that they could know God, or have some feeling for Him, men deceived themselves. They were agitated by hope and fear, or moved by vanity to esteem themselves the Deity's favourite objects; or at best, they were actuated by a 'forced and strained affection'. In fact, their religion merely degraded the Deity into a resemblance to themselves, in order to make Him something that they could understand and worship.[4] Thus religious belief invariably degenerated into idolatry (and superstition) or fanaticism (and enthusiasm). Of the two possibilities, idolatry was far preferable. It developed out of 'weakness, fear, melancholy', feelings that were favourable to priestly power, rites, and ceremonies. But this was the kindlier, less dangerous

---

[1] *Essays*, vol. II, p. 355. Cf. also *Dialogues*, pp. 224–6.
[2] *Ibid.* p. 314.
[3] *Letters*, vol. I, p. 51 and *Essays*, vol. II, p. 328. Cf. also *Essays*, vol. I, p. 220.
[4] *Letters*, vol. I, p. 51.

alternative. A ceremonial religion was more tolerant and sociable.[1] There was no exclusiveness about the old pagan religions. When the oracle of Delphi was asked to say what rites or forms of worship were most acceptable to the gods, it answered, 'Those which are legally established in each city'.[2] Besides, paganism sat lightly on men's minds, for it consisted only of a 'multitude of stories' that made no 'deep impression on the affections and understanding'. They were 'light, easy, and familiar', not at all terrifying—'Who could forbear smiling when he thought of the loves of Mars and Venus or the amorous frolics of Jupiter and Pan?'[3] Best of all, paganism confined religious duties to sacrifices in the temple, and left men, once outside the temple, free to think what they pleased.[4]

Far worse was an abstract theistic religion that required men to approach God directly, and gave them no 'sensible exterior observances' to occupy the mind during religious exercises and 'abate the violence of its disappointed efforts'. It arose out of presumption, along with hope, imagination, and ignorance, and inspired 'a fierce and gloomy spirit of devotion'. Laud should have been praised, rather than condemned for trying to revive some of the primitive popish institutions. They freed thought from concentration 'on that divine and mysterious essence so superior to the narrow capacities of mankind'; they let the mind 'relax itself in the contemplation of pictures, postures, vestments, buildings . . .',[5] and softened the spirit of proud worshippers. Christianity had enough of a disadvantage in its insistence on a single and universal God. A single God was so easily made a pretence for declaring the worship of all other Deities impious and absurd, and insisting that all men had to share the same faith and ceremonies. Monotheism always invited zeal and rancour, 'the most furious and implacable of all human passions'. The Jews were ever moved by an 'implacable narrow spirit'; the Mohammedans followed 'even more bloody principles . . .', and the inquisitors from Rome and Madrid, who invariably denounced virtue, knowledge, and love of liberty, offered up more human sacrifices than did barbarous nations. Indeed the

---

[1] In much the same vein, Hume said in a note intended to preface the second volume of his history (*John Hill Burton, Life and Correspondence of David Hume*, vol. II (Edinburgh, 1846), p. 12):

'When we have recourse to the aid of the senses and imagination in order to adapt our religion in some degree to human infirmity, it is very difficult and almost impossible to prevent altogether the intrusion of superstition, or keep men from laying too great stress on the ceremonial and ornamental parts of their worship. Of all the sects into which Christians have been divided, the Church of England seems to have chosen the most happy medium; . . .'

[2] *Essays*, vol. II, p. 337.
[3] *Ibid.* pp. 352, 349.
[4] *Ibid.* vol. II, p. 352.
[5] *History*, vol. V, pp. 195 f.

intolerance of religions that affirm the unity of God was as remarkable, Hume declared, as the tolerance of polytheism.[1]

There was, moreover, no escape from abstract, theistic religion. It invaded every moment, every feeling, thought, and action. It 'inspects our whole conduct, and prescribes a universal rule to our actions, to our words, to our very thoughts and inclinations; a rule so much the more austere, as it is guarded by infinite, though distant rewards and punishments, and no infraction of it can ever be concealed or disguised'.[2] And it did nothing to improve life on earth. Whereas pagans were inspired by their gods to live well and happily, to develop 'activity, spirit, courage, magnanimity, love of liberty, and all the virtues which aggrandize a people', belief in a single God, supposed to be infinitely superior to men, subjected men to terror and suffering, led them to believe that he required of them nothing but 'the monkish virtues of mortification, penance, humility and passive suffering'.[3]

The more profound spiritual effects were even worse. Whereas paganism emphasized ceremonies and idols, abstract theistic religion insisted on conformity in feelings and beliefs. But the ability to fulfil inner obligations, as it depends ultimately on grace, cannot be summoned at will. A worshipper can control only his profession of belief. If asked to do more, he must resort to hypocrisy, of which he himself will often be unaware. It is perhaps a less false hypocrisy than other kinds, but therefore all the more insidious. Men who dare not confess their doubts even to themselves, disguise their infidelity, in private too, by the 'strongest asseverations and most positive bigotry'.[4] The colder their hearts, the greater their fervour in religious exercises, and thus they become accustomed to fraud and falsehood and acquire a 'habit of dissimulation'. It is no wonder that the man who shows the highest zeal in religion is commonly distrusted and believed to be ready to deceive and cheat in everything.[5]

Having discovered the pretensions of the Kirk, and of religious enthusiasts in general, Hume bound himself to undermine them. The 'enemies to joy and pleasure' had to be exposed as 'hypocrites and deceivers'.[6] He would show that 'celibacy, fasting, penance, mortification, self-denial, humility, silence, solitude, and the whole train of monkish virtues' should rather be placed in the catalogue of vices, for they served no purpose but to 'stupefy the understanding and harden the heart, obscure the fancy, and sour the temper . . . .'.

---

[1] *Essays*, vol. II, pp. 337–8.
[2] *Ibid.* p. 304.
[3] *Ibid.* p. 339.
[4] *Ibid.* p. 348; *Dialogues*, p. 222.
[5] *Essays*, vol. II, pp. 359–60.
[6] David Hume, *An Enquiry concerning Human Understanding and an Enquiry concerning the Principles of Morals*, ed. by L. A. Selby-Bigge (Oxford, 1951), p. 279.

The man who lived by such rules—'a gloomy, harebrained enthusiast'—perhaps deserved after his death a place in the calendar of saints, but he should never in life, Hume was certain, be welcomed by anyone who was not 'as delirious and dismal as himself'.[1] One had only to remove the 'dismal dress' in which virtue had been clothed to reveal her true 'gentleness, humanity, beneficence, affability, nay even, at proper intervals, play, frolic, and gaiety'; then it would become clear that virtue did not require 'useless austerities and rigours, suffering and self-denial', but wished rather to make 'her votaries and all mankind, during every instant of their existence, if possible, cheerful and happy'.[2]

He began to question right down to the foundation, and there grew upon him 'a certain boldness of temper' which would not submit to any authority and led him to seek 'some new medium by which truth might be establisht'. He gave up all pretence of studying law, for which his family had destined him, and announced his intention of becoming a man of letters, 'a Scholar and Philosopher'.[3]

[1] *Ibid.* p. 270.
[2] *Ibid.* p. 279.
[3] *Letters*, vol. I, p. 13.

CHAPTER III

THE COMBAT OF REASON AND PASSION

WHEN he surveyed the scene, Hume found enemies of an affable virtue also outside the Kirk. There were many alternatives to Presbyterian theology, ranging from what seemed to be rank materialism to a theology that offered redemption and virtue to all men. They differed in purpose and form from the Kirk's doctrine, but not significantly, to Hume's mind, in moral spirit.

Hobbes, who had provoked the philosophical speculation that dominated England in Hume's time, did not attract Hume. By emphasizing man's egoism and brutishness, Hobbes seemed only to have accepted the Calvinist portrait of man in order to support a different, but equally unappealing, conclusion. Yet Hobbes' opponents, led by the Cambridge Platonists, were no more satisfactory. In trying to answer Hobbes by showing that morality was not arbitrary and variable, but eternal, objective, and demonstrative, they seemed just as bound to God's service and quite as certain that they knew God's purposes as any dogmatic Presbyterian.

Nevertheless, the Cambridge Platonists were reacting against Puritanism. Although many of them were connected with Emmanuel College, that 'seminary of Puritans', they had become impressed by an aspect of Calvinism that had for long been neglected in Scotland. Like the earlier Protestants, their feelings of closeness to God emboldened them to challenge and renounce whatever seemed to conflict with their duty to Him. When they found they could not accept the established interpretation of Calvinism, they transformed Emmanuel College from a haven for extreme puritans into the home of a vigorous, intellectual opposition to them. Against both Calvinism and Hobbes, the Cambridge Platonists argued that God had made man not a 'sorry worthless piece fit for no use',[1] but an image of Himself. They were repelled by the doctrine of predestination, and were convinced that man need believe only in his own power to perfect himself. Since God had written the moral law within the image He made, man had only to exercise his reason to discover it. Thus the Cambridge Platonists found in Scripture a gentler, more generous faith than the puritanism they had inherited. Far from disdaining anyone who professed somewhat different words, they insisted that character mattered more than creed. Their emphasis fell not on sin or on dogma, but on reason—the 'Light of Nature', and 'the Candle of the Lord'.

But from Hume's standpoint, this exaltation of reason was no great improvement on Presbyterian dogma. The doctrine of the Cambridge Platon-

---

[1] F. J. Powicke, *The Cambridge Platonists* (1926), p. 61.

ists implied that moral truth could be discovered with the same certainty and precision as mathematical truth. And there was no dearth of valiant philosophers who would undertake the task of showing how morals could actually be reduced to an exact science. The most outstanding was Samuel Clarke, regarded during Hume's youth as England's leading intellectual light. In some ways Clarke was attractive to a rebel against the Church. His rational arguments for religion had helped to undermine Hume's faith in the divinity of Christ, and he was in several circles suspected of heresy. He managed nevertheless to advance steadily up the ecclesiastical ladder until he became Rector of St James, and he gathered round him the most vigorous controversialists and promising young philosophers of the day. The public flocked to hear his lectures against 'those atheists Hobbes and Spinoza', as well as his sermons, full of logic and obscurity, which set forth in cumbrous periods the official morality of the day.

Clarke's success came partly of his ability to give a practical and popular form to the abstract, mathematical view of the universe that had been framed in the seventeenth century, under the inspiration of Descartes and Newton, and was now coming into its own. It was a view of the world that tried not to traffic with the textures, colours, and sounds of material things or the feelings of mortal beings, but emphasized quantity—'hard, cold, colourless, silent and dead'.[1] That this view might be extended to morals had been suggested by Locke, when he occasionally assimilated moral to mathematical truth. However much he differed from the Cambridge Platonists in metaphysics, he spoke their language about morality, about the 'eternal and unalterable nature of right and wrong'. But whereas the Platonists had stressed the objective reality of good and evil, Locke's emphasis fell on the possibility of demonstrating morality in the same way as mathematics. And Clarke went further. He undertook to demonstrate with mathematical exactitude the existence of God and the obligations of natural religion.

Although Clarke granted that there were many different moral relations, he was certain that they could all be classified and exactly described, and clear conclusions deduced from them. Some actions promoted the good of mankind, some made men miserable, others were neutral. But whatever the action, its tendency and results were always the same. The differences between good and bad actions were as clear and unvarying as the difference between black and white, or the magnitudes of numbers. To deny that I should do for another man what he in a like case should do for me was, according to Clarke, like asserting that 'though two and three are equal to five, yet five is not equal to two and three'.[2] Wickedness was 'the same absurdity and insolence in moral

[1] E. A. Burtt, *Metaphysical Foundations of Modern Science*, (London, 1932) pp. 236-7.
[2] Samuel Clarke, *A Discourse Concerning the Unalterable Obligations of Natural Religion* (6th edition, 1724), p. 54.

matters; as it would be in natural things', to try to alter the relations of numbers or the properties of geometrical figures.[1] If men sometimes found it difficult to distinguish between good and evil tendencies, it was not because the nature or results of actions were ambiguous, changeable, or questionable, but because the observers were ignorant or deluded.

Human uncertainty was due to the senses, which presented man with nothing more than a shifting 'phatasmagoria of unrealities', and indistinguishably confused the accidental and essential. Reason, however, saw the invariable relations between ultimate facts, and the man of reason could no more withhold his assent from the eternal rules of right, derived from unalterable relations, than a man instructed in mathematics could deny a geometrical demonstration he had understood. Circumstances were irrelevant for Clarke, and were never permitted to muddle the clarity and certainty of moral judgements. He saw no problem about deciding what cases were alike, and had no use for the dissenting opinions of men who were prejudiced by education, laws, customs, and evil practices. Indeed, he considered any attempt to examine how men really behaved a concession to Satan. The human being rightly understood was for him an anonymous unit whose duties could be determined in the abstract by formulae. He was, as Pope said, 'all seeing', and daunted by nothing on the 'high Priori road'.

This rational morality was made even more rigid by Clarke's follower, Wollaston, who, in his monastic retirement in the City, produced a theory that seemed to define sin as lying. It was wrong to kill a man, he argued, because by 'so doing I deny him to be a man', and his theory was hailed as a discovery in morals equal to Newton's discoveries in astronomy. Whereas Clarke was mainly interested in denying that morality was merely a matter of taste or power, Wollaston deliberately emphasized the uniformity of moral rules for all times and places. Following reason meant, Wollaston insisted, even more strongly than Clarke, following universal, abstract rules. What reason commanded in one case inevitably applied to all other cases: 'What is reasonable with respect to Quinctius, is so in respect of Naevius. Reason is performed in species. . . . The knowledge of a particular idea is only the particular knowledge of that idea or thing: there it ends. But *reason* is something universal, a kind of general instrument, applicable to particular things and cases as they occur'.[2]

In some ways, there was nothing so severe in the moral teaching of Clarke and Wollaston that it should have offended Hume. They encouraged men to endeavour to live well; they did not deny any possibility of happiness on earth; nor did they impose any austerities. It is indeed difficult to discover

[1] *Ibid.* p. 42.
[2] William Wollaston, *The Religion of Nature Delineated* (1759), p. 70.

from the exact science laid down by Clarke and Wollaston what their moral rules required, apart from commanding that a man should not 'desire to gain some small profit to himself by doing violence and damage to his Neighbour'[1] or that he should 'endeavour to appease with gentleness rather than exasperate with retaliation'.[2] But the assumption underlying their morality was the same as that of the Cambridge Platonists, and of the Kirk, that man was a divided nature, torn between holy reason and brutish passion. Their faith in reason was much higher than the Kirk's, but thopinion of their body or the passions no better.

The Cambridge Platonists had found Platonic and neo-Platonic doctrine attractive precisely because it taught that the spiritual world alone was real, that the soul was immortal and could ascend to heaven. It offered the metaphysical basis of Calvinism shorn of superstition and mystical dross, as well as the basis for a complete answer to Hobbes. When the Cambridge men and their followers departed from Plato, it was only to take a more, rather than less, doctrinaire view. They had none of Plato's sense for the texture and difficulty of truth; they were as certain as their Puritan ancestors had been that they had discovered in Scripture clear answers to all questions about the soul, heaven and hell, and the nature of God. What worried them was not how man could know what he ought to do, but only how he could acquire the will to do what they knew for certain he should.

Plato's latter-day followers learned from him mainly that spiritual man and carnal man saw very different worlds, that a true vision could be reached only by conquering fleshly lusts and unifying human nature with the Divine. The rational faculties, they believed, could come into their own only when the heart was purified and the will disciplined, when reason was not clouded over by a 'dark, filthy mist of sin'. The good life meant then endeavouring 'more and more to withdraw ourselves from these Bodily things, to set our soul as free as may be from its miserable slavery to this base Flesh'.[3] Imagination had to be transcended, and the 'eyes of sense' shut before reason would be left free to see the true permanent realities. Clarke described the passions as 'unbridled and furious', the appetites as 'inordinate', and regretted that some men were robust enough to escape the 'natural ill consequences of intemperance and debauchery'.[4] And Wollaston warned even more sternly against the corruption of human nature: 'Unless there be some strong limitation added as a fence for virtue, men will be apt to sink into voluptuousness, as in fact the generality of Epicurus's herd have done (notwithstanding all his talk of temperance, virtue, tranquillity, etc.), and the bridle will be usurped by those

---

[1] Clarke, *The Unalterable Obligations*, p. 54.

[2] *Ibid.* p. 60.

[3] John Smith, *Discourse I, Concerning the True Method of Attaining to Divine Knowledge* (1673), p. 16.

[4] Clarke, *The Unalterable Obligations*, pp. 104–5; cf. also pp. 125 ff.

appetites which it is a principal part of all religion, natural as well as any other, to curb and restrain'.[1]

Thus the rational moralists, however close they came to Deism, shared with Puritanism the traditional view of the passions as a source of falsehood and evil. Like all philosophers since Plato, and all Christians, they taught that the perfection of man consists in his union with God through his mind, that his imperfection comes of the mind's union with the body. Moreover, they made it just as difficult to question the moral law discovered by reason as it was to escape the commands of the Kirk. The advocates of rational morality were no more willing than the Predestinarian preachers to accept different interpretations of virtue. They, too, insisted that all men must live in the same way, and that this meant denying, or somehow overcoming, all that was not pure spirit. Their outlook was not much exaggerated by Steele's paraphrase, 'To love is a passion, 'Tis a desire, and we must have no desires'.

For Hume, the rational moralists underscored the fact that philosophy as well as religion, reason as easily as faith, could be used to subject all men to the same inflexible and unsuitable rules. Philosophy, he decided, had been bent to the uses of theology. Philosophers had become divines in disguise; they had 'warped' reasoning and even language 'from their natural course', and endeavoured to establish distinctions 'where the difference of the objects was, in a manner, imperceptible'; they disregarded nature and the 'unbiassed' sentiments of the mind in favour of unreal abstractions.[2] Not only superstition and enthusiasm had to be combated, but perhaps even more the philosophers' practice of discussing morality in the abstract, of deducing a 'variety of inferences and conclusions' from a few general abstract principles. This abstract method did not suit the 'imperfection of human nature'; it had been rejected in natural philosophy, and it had now to be abandoned by moral philosophy as well: 'Men are now cured of their passion for hypotheses and systems in natural philosophy and will hearken to no arguments but those which are derived from experience. It is full time they should attempt a like reformation in all moral disquisitions; and reject every system of ethics, however subtle or ingenious, which is not founded on fact and observation'.[3]

The direction Hume had to follow in order to construct a new view of man was suggested by a fellow Scotsman, Francis Hutcheson, probably the most outstanding and influential opponent of the Covenanters' creed. He led the Moderates in their attempt to strip Calvinist theology of its gloom and dogmatism, to describe God as a lawgiver and the source of morality, a Deity that reigned rather than governed. The problem, as Hutcheson saw it, was to show that man was not essentially depraved or egoistic, but benevolent.

[1] Wollaston, *The Religion of Nature Delineated*, pp. 37–8.
[2] Hume, *Enquiry*, p. 322.
[3] *Ibid.* p. 175.

The germ of his theory came from Shaftesbury, whose assimilation of morals to art and beauty readily attracted anyone in revolt against Puritanism. Although he, too, had been influenced by Plato, Shaftesbury emphasized another aspect of Platonic philosophy. He reaffirmed, against the scientific and mathematical current, the importance of beauty. He valued beauty more than logic, fought his opponents with ridicule rather than geometry, and tried to feel the harmony of the universe, not to reduce it to a barren system or set of formulae. The quality of a man's taste and the style of his life mattered more to Shaftesbury than his declared principles and reasonings. By saying that the moral perfection of man is akin to the perfection of a work of art, that a good man can arouse in a spectator a pleasure like that aroused by any beautiful object, Shaftesbury seemed to free life from the ugliness with which Puritanism had encased it. He placed the foundation for morality in the human constitution itself, not in a power to transcend it, and so removed from man the stigma of natural depravity.

On what Shaftesbury described as a 'rational affection' for goodness, Hutcheson built a more definite system. He traced morality to an internal sense, the moral sense, which he described as a passive power of receiving ideas of good and likened to the sense for beauty. Neither the exact relation between the moral sense and the sense of beauty, nor the character of motives, nor the ultimate end of moral behaviour was ever made perfectly clear by Hutcheson. But he did definitely distinguish the moral sense from reason, and rest moral judgements on feeling, rather than on any rational process. Nature had given man, he asserted, 'immediate monitors', independent of calculation and reflection, for distinguishing good from evil. Moral judgements were not then the results of ratiocination about, or of insights into the relations of things or ideas; they were an immediate feeling of approval or disapproval:

The Weakness of our Reason . . . [is] so great, that very few Men could ever have form'd those long Deductions of Reason which show some Actions to be on the whole advantageous to the Agent and their Contrary pernicious. The Author of Nature has much better furnish'd us for a virtuous Conduct, than our Moralists seem to imagine, by almost as quick and powerful Instructions as we have for the Preservation of our Bodys. He has given us strong Affections to be the Springs of each virtuous Action; and made Virtue a lovely Form, that we might easily distinguish it from its Contrary, and be made happy in the Pursuit of it.[1]

There could be no abstract, general rules, because 'everyone judges the affections of others by his own Sense, so that it seems not impossible that in these Senses men may differ as they do in Taste'.[2] Nevertheless, there was

---

[1] Francis Hutcheson, *Inquiry into the Original of Our Ideas of Beauty and Virtue* (1729), p. xiv.

[2] Francis Hutcheson, *Essay on the Passions* (1728), pp. 234–5.

order and universality in moral judgements. Although he never explained very satisfactorily how there could be variety amidst uniformity in morals, Hutcheson maintained firmly that morality was neither arbitrary, nor perfectly uniform in the sense of the rational moralists. Instead of proposing any single moral idea that all men had to follow, he affirmed simply that man was good.

What was most striking about Hutcheson's theory, certainly to someone in search of a new foundation for ethics, was that he reversed the roles of reason and passion.[1] As he used 'passion' to cover all types of feeling, it followed that the passions, far from being simply the source of human corruption, were the seat of man's best propensities. The function of reason was not to hold the passions in check, but rather to serve at least some of the passions, to adjust the general direction given by the passions to particular circumstances. Hutcheson himself stopped there; neither he nor Shaftesbury wished to deny the established view that human nature was divided between reason and passion, but merely to adjust it towards more amiable conclusions. Shaftesbury described reason as man's dignity, the source of virtue and happiness. Hutcheson frequently retreated altogether from the radical implications of his theory, and restored to reason much of its traditional importance, calling it a 'divine' faculty that 'frames the ideal of a truly good life'. He even tried to develop the relevance of mathematical calculation for morality, so much so that Sterne remarked: 'Hutcheson, in his philosophic treatise on beauty, harmony, and order, plus's and minus's you to heaven

---

[1] Cf. Norman Kemp Smith, *The Philosophy of David Hume*, (1949), ch. 2: Kemp Smith argues that Hume began thinking about the *Treatise* under the influence of Hutcheson, and arrived at his theory of knowledge by analogy with Hutcheson's moral theory. Insofar as Kemp Smith gives the inversion of reason and passion precedence, I have followed him. As every student of Hume must, I have found Kemp Smith's analysis invaluable. But I have put his insight into the moral character of Hume's first inspiration to the service of a more extreme thesis than his. As a result, whereas Kemp Smith has traced certain apparent oddities in the *Treatise* to a conflict between Hutcheson's and Newton's influences on him, I have denied that these were oddities when considered in terms of another interpretation. Hume's treatment of space and time, and of causation, with which Kemp Smith is especially concerned, are in my view not only consistent with the rest of the *Treatise*, but essential to Hume's purpose. Whereas Kemp Smith argues that Hume included a theory of passions and a system of ethics in the *Treatise* simply because he started his thinking there, I maintain that the whole system was designed to support the theory of passions. In other words, while I accept broadly Kemp Smith's account of the origins of Hume's theory of knowledge, I assign a moral objective to the whole enterprise. I have also found many suggestions in Kemp Smith's introduction to the *Dialogues* immensely helpful for developing my interpretation. On one question, my interpretation fails to resolve a difficulty about Hume's philosophy—that Kemp Smith can explain—the problem of personal identity. I have taken Hume literally at his word, and regarded the problem of personal identity as a failure in the system.

or hell, by algebraic equations—so that none but an expert mathematician can ever be able to settle his accounts with St Peter—and perhaps St Matthew, who had been an officer in the customs, must be called in to audit them'.[1]

After all, Hutcheson's system was linked with an optimistic theology. It was designed to demonstrate the wisdom and benevolence that ruled the universe. Besides, Hutcheson stressed the more ascetic of the Christian virtues—suffering, he said, gave opportunity for practising 'the most sublime virtues, such as resignation to the Will of God, forgiving of injuries, returning good for evil . . .'.[2] Despite his love for classical authors, Hutcheson was Christian, in just the sense that Hume wished to oppose. But he had planted a suggestion for a truly radical departure.

Where Hutcheson's suggestion might lead, Hume discovered through the French writers whom he began reading in Edinburgh. In Bayle, and in a number of writers of the seventeenth century—Fontenelle, l'Abbé de Saint-Pierre, Pascal, la Rochefoucauld, Malebranche—Hume found the view that man was in fact moved by his passions, and reason was but a passive onlooker. They did not deny the dichotomy between reason and passion, nor the holiness of one and the corruption of the other, but suggested that whatever he tried to be, man was after all nothing like God. Bayle said that reason did not always calm the passions, its decrees were not always executed, indeed reason often only increased the chaos within man. For since the Fall, man no longer inhabited the world of reason, but had become 'plunged into sense'.[3] Bayle even went so far as to say that the passions made the world go round, and prevented anarchy as well as caused it.

In Montaigne, however, Hume found more—a whole 'new scene of thought', a totally different estimate of man that denied the established picture of the hierarchy of being. Montaigne saw human life as Hume had hoped men could. His essays were a continuous lesson in moderation, opposed to every kind of extremism. He taught men to accept themselves for what they were, and to obey the law of their own nature rather than pretend to divinity. Only the subject of holiness and Christian zeal aroused him to severity. Like Hume, he was more offended by Protestantism than by Catholicism because he felt it was less mischievous to bend the knee than the reason. And he, too, warned men to beware of those who bore a sanctified appearance and imposed a burden of austerities. No zeal, he said, produced so much misery as Christian zeal, which moved men to hate and cruelty, never to benignity, goodness, or temperance.

Montaigne's descriptions of virtue could hardly have expressed better

---

[1] Laurence Sterne, *Works* (1803), vol. VIII, p. 161.
[2] Frances Hutcheson, *A System of Moral Philosophy* (1755), vol. I, pp. XXXIV–V.
[3] Bayle, Pierre, *Dictionary*, 2nd edition (London, 1738), vol. IV, p. 441 (2).

Hume's own thoughts, and were echoed again and again in Hume's work. Virtue was not, Montaigne said, 'pitched on the top of a high, steep, or inaccessible hill'; she held her mansion 'in a fair, flourishing, and pleasant plain'; she was 'lovely, equally delicious and courageous, protesting herself to be a professed and irreconcilable enemy to all sharpness, austerity, fear, and compulsion; having nature for her guide, fortune and voluptuousness for her companions'.[1] The priests had taught men to disdain the joys of life on earth and they had produced as a result nothing but mischief.

For if men tried to behave like angels, they succeeded only in becoming monsters—'instead of uplifting themselves, they degrade themselves'. They might as well renounce breathing as bodily pleasures. Nature has seen to it that satisfying our necessities should also be pleasurable to us—'it does wrong to the great and all powerful Donor to refuse His gift, to impair it and deface it'.[2] The most difficult and the first thing for a man to know was how to live the life proper to man:

It is an absolute perfection, and as it were divine for a man to know how to enjoy his existence loyally. We seek for other conditions because we understand not the use of our own and we go outside of ourselves because we know not what is happening there. Thus it is in vain that we mount upon stilts, for, if we walk upon them, yet must we walk with our own legs; and though we sit upon the highest throne in the world, yet we do but sit upon our own behind.[3]

There was a remarkable correspondence, too, between Hume's antipathy to the Kirk's commands and to 'the eternal and immutable relations' promulgated by the rational moralists, and Montaigne's dislike of fixity, of general rules, of any rigid schemes. For Montaigne denied that man could commune with the Divine Intellect, or discover any simple coherent theory that could explain or direct human activity. Diversity, Montaigne insisted, was the rule on earth; there were no clear, hard lines between good and bad, virtue and vice, for all virtues were not equally salutary, and some vices were worse than others. Nor did any single set of choices deserve supremacy—that way lay the opposite of life. 'We do not live, we only exist, if we hold ourselves bound and driven by necessity to follow one course alone. The finest spirits are those that show the largest choice, the greatest suppleness'.[4] Man's life was like the wind; and the wind, 'more wisely than we, loves to bluster, and to be in agitation and is content with its own functions, without desiring stability, solidity, qualities that are not its own'.[4]

[1] Montaigne, *Essais*, (Bibliotheque de La Pleiade, 1950), Bk. I, ch. 25, p. 195. (The translations of Montaigne are my own, adapted from Florio or Ives).

[2] *Ibid.* Bk. III, ch. 13, pp. 1256, 1252.

[3] *Ibid.* p. 1257.

[4] *Ibid.* Bk. III, ch. 3, p. 914.

[5] *Ibid.* Bk. III, ch. 13, p. 1245.

Man was and should be a bundle of contradictory things, a flux of impressions—'in everything and everywhere . . . but patchwork and motley'.[1] That was the moral of Montaigne's essays, where he tried to draw a true man, with all his vacillation and mixture, not a pure, abstract kind of creature. For such a being, ready-made rules of conduct were neither possible nor desirable. He had better rely on experience and example, than on the lofty and elaborate reasonings of philosophers.

All this in Montaigne showed him to be a kindred spirit. How striking it was then to find his view of human life associated with a unique description of the relation between reason and passion, mind and body. Montaigne did not merely say that passion ruled, or that reason followed more often than the divines admitted. He came near to denying altogether that man was a divided nature, an animal endowed with reason, whose highest affinity was with God. His radical insight was that nature was not split between brutes and spirits, with the uncomfortable human mixture in between, but a continuous line in which spirit or reason played its part at every stage.

Man as seen by Montaigne had much more in common with the animals than he liked to admit. There was a natural language common to children and animals, and there were many evidences of intelligence in the animals. Man was conceived, born, and fed, he moved, acted, lived and died like the beasts. Only vanity and presumption led him to suppose he had a special place in creation. His true condition was not that of a holy spirit unhappily sullied by its bond with matter; it was a mingled, homely condition, with its own pleasures and privileges, and its own kind of guidance.

There was no conflict between spirit and matter, indeed nothing more than a narrow seam between mind and body. It was wrong for the soul to draw apart, to despise and desert the body; indeed it could not really do so except through some 'ill-shaped, apish trick'. Instead the soul had better 'strike fresh alliance with the body, embrace it, cherish it, control and counsel it . . . marry the body and serve it as a husband to the end that their poverty should not appear to be different and contrary, but one and the same'.[2] Not only passion and desire needed to be controlled; spirit and mind could just as easily exceed their proper limits, and when they did, they produced wild dreams and chimeras. Virtue depended not on suppressing nature, nor on climbing higher and higher toward God, but on knowing how to judge and circumscribe one's ambitions. Whatever is sufficient is great—'There is nothing so fine and so justifiable as to play the man well and truly'.[3]

Thus Montaigne crystallized for Hume what others had suggested—the

---

[1] *Ibid.* Bk. II, ch. 21, p. 760.
[2] *Ibid.* Bk. II, ch. 17, pp. 721–2.
[3] *Ibid.* Bk. III, ch. 13, p. 1250.

need to formulate a philosophy based on new assumptions about human nature, a philosophy that would restore man's wholeness, and undo all the mischief wrought by a long tradition that had divided man between holy reason and brutish passion. Those who knew something more than hypotheses, who took the trouble to look at man as he really was, could see that the established formulas for human life had inflicted useless pain because they were not suited to the true human condition. There is no better statement of Hume's guiding motive in his philosophical enterprise than his statement opening Book II of the *Treatise*:

Nothing is more usual in philosophy and even in common life than to talk of the combat of passion and reason, to give the preference to reason, and to assert that men are only so far virtuous as they conform to its dictates. Every rational creature, 'tis said, is oblig'd to regulate his actions by reason; and if any other motive or principle challenge the direction of his conduct, he ought to oppose it, 'till it be entirely subdu'd or at least brought to conformity with that superior principle . . . nor is there an ampler field, as well for metaphysical arguments, and popular declamations, than this supposed preeminence of reason above passion. The eternity, invariableness, and divine origin of the former have been display'd to the best advantage: The blindness, unconstancy, and deceitfulness of the latter have been as strongly insisted on. In order to shew the fallacy of all this philosophy, I shall endeavour to prove first, that reason alone can never be a motive to any action of the will; and secondly, that it can never oppose passion in the direction of the will.[1]

In fact, Hume did more in the end. He established the principles of human nature on an entirely new foundation; not content with 'taking now and then a castle or village on the frontier', he marched up 'directly to the capital or centre' of the sciences.[2] He attacked the basis of all traditional notions on which children had been brought up and societies governed, men discussed, praised, and blamed. He did not care to deny the existence of God. What he proposed was far more radical than any declared atheism.

It was no wonder that he drove himself feverishly, and then suffered depression, illness, and doubt. Shortly before leaving for France he wrote to Dr Cheyne that at the age of eighteen,

there seem'd to be open'd up to me a new Scene of Thought which transported me beyond Measure, and made me, with an Ardor natural to young men, throw up every other Pleasure or Business to apply entirely to it. . . . I found that the moral Philosophy transmitted to us by Antiquity, labor'd under the same Inconvenience that has been found in their natural Philosophy, of being entirely Hypothetical, and depending more upon Invention than Experience. Every one consulted his Fancy in erecting Schemes of Virtue and of Happiness, without regarding human Nature,

---

[1] David Hume, *A Treatise of Human Nature*, ed. by L. A. Selby-Bigge (Oxford, 1955), p. 413.

[2] *Ibid.* p. xx.

upon which every moral Conclusion must depend. This therefore I resolved to make my principal Study, and the Source from which I wou'd derive every Truth in Criticism as well as Morality . . . within these three Years, I find I have scribled many a Quire of Paper, in which there is nothing contain'd but my own Inventions. This with the Reading most of the celebrated Books in Latin, French, and English, and acquiring the Italian, you may think a sufficient Business for one in perfect Health. . . . But my Disease was a cruel Incumbrance on me.

He found himself, Hume explained, unable to concentrate, strangely ill at ease, and generally incapable of delivering his opinions 'with such Elegance & Neatness as to draw to me the Attention of the World, & I wou'd rather live & dye in Obscurity than produce them maim'd & imperfect'.[1] It was fitting that Hume should have recovered the strength to complete his task in France.

[1] *Letters*, vol. I, pp. 15 ff.

CHAPTER IV

A NEW SCENE OF THOUGHT

To achieve his purpose, Hume had to show that man had no extraordinary powers like those claimed for him by others. Philosophers as well as the vulgar, Hume declared, felt obliged to assign 'some invisible intelligent principle' for anything that surprised them. As they could not understand the effect either of the mind on the body, or of the body on the mind, they asserted that 'the Deity is the immediate cause of the union between soul and body'. Sometimes philosophers felt impelled to go further, Hume continued boldly, and they extended 'the same inference to the mind itself, in its internal operation'. They described ideas as 'nothing but a revelation made to us by our maker'. Rather than trace an idea to the influence of human will, they spoke only of the 'universal creator, who discovers it to the mind, and renders it present to us. Thus, according to these philosophers, everything is full of God'.[1] Hume meant to cut the ties between man and God, and restore man to a purely human nature, such as the pagans found sufficient before Christianity removed man into a higher, more spiritual sphere.

It would seem that Hume's way had been well prepared by Hobbes and Locke, because they are commonly described as empiricists and iconoclasts who broke decisively with the Christian picture of man. Unlike continental philosophers, they were concerned not so much to satisfy purely intellectual curiosity, to discover the true constitution of knowledge or the essence of things, as to condemn certain prevailing intellectual fallacies and their unfortunate moral consequences. They wished in different ways to restrain human speculation within its proper confines, and to correct what Locke called the disposition of men to 'let loose their thoughts into the vast ocean of Being'. But from Hume's standpoint, neither of them provided anything more than a variation on the traditional view.

Hobbes spoke of reasoning, rather than of reason, and he described man as fundamentally a creature of passion, whose well-being was promoted by passion as much as by reasoning; and he was, in a sense, as persuaded of human fallibility as Montaigne. In this respect he belongs, as Hume does, to the sceptical late scholastic tradition.[2] But not only was his emphasis on man's brutishness uncongenial to Hume; Hobbes offered nothing useful to Hume because his attention was centred on the achievements of reasoning, rather than on exploring the implications of his view that reasoning was con-

---

[1] *Enquiry*, pp. 70–1.
[2] Cf. Michael Oakeshott, Introduction to Hobbes, *Leviathan* (Blackwell) pp. lii ff.

cerned solely with causes and effects. Although he defined philosophy modestly as 'the establishment by reasoning of true fictions', he retained unbounded confidence in the truths he allowed it to establish. Hume's concern was entirely with the nature and limits of reason, and it led him to reverse Hobbes' conclusions. It made him antagonistic to Hobbes' geometrical style of argument and to his whole dogmatic manner of dealing with human questions.

Locke's philosophy was more nearly to Hume's purpose. He was in the first place temperamentally more congenial, not so possessed as Hobbes was by the pursuit of system, and more inclined to emphasize the folly of human ambitions. Although his philosophy was used by Clarke and others to bolster systems that Hume equated with scholasticism, it was directed against the arrogant verbalism of the schools, the deism of Lord Herbert founded on innate principles, the sermons and political orations that elevated current prejudices into immutable truths. By attacking the belief in innate ideas and principles, and tracing human knowledge to its origins in sense, Locke's *Essay on Human Understanding* stripped away the protection enjoyed by a number of empty abstractions and inherited prejudices, and made it respectable to question elaborate systems. Thus it sanctioned the doubts of those beginning to grow restless under the rule of dogmatic theology, whether of the middle ages or of the Puritans. The disposition that Hume and Locke shared was perfectly expressed in Locke's statement:

proud man, not content with that knowledge he was capable of, and which was useful to him, would needs penetrate into the hidden cause of things, lay down principles and establish maxims to himself about the operations of nature, and then vainly expect that nature—or in truth God—should proceed according to those laws which *his* maxims had prescribed to him; whereas his narrow weak faculties could reach no further than the observation and memory of some few facts produced by visible external causes, but in a way utterly beyond the reach of his apprehension;—it being perhaps no absurdity to think that this great and curious fabric of the world, the workmanship of the Almighty, cannot be perfectly comprehended by any understanding but His that made it. Man, still affecting something of the Deity, laboured by his imagination to supply what his observation and experience failed him in; and when he could not discover the principles, causes, and methods of Nature's workmanship, he would needs fashion all those out of his own thought, and make a world to himself, framed and governed by his own intelligence. . . . They that are studiously busy in the cultivating and adorning such dry barren notions are vigorously employed to little purpose.[1]

Many of the practical conclusions that Locke drew from his philosophy were pleasing to Hume. Since human knowledge falls short of perfectly comprehending what exists, men ought not to think they were at the centre of the universe or try to capture a timeless insight into the whole. They

---

[1] Locke's Commonplace Book (in Alexander Carlyle Fraser, *Locke* (1890), pp. 37–8).

had better reconcile themselves to their more modest powers which vouchsafed them only very partial glimpses of truth. They should concentrate on what they could learn by experience and observation, in order to improve the useful arts, and not yearn to know more. For knowledge of the quality of things was beyond their reach, and served only to employ 'idle or overcurious brains. All our business lies at home'.[1]

But the other, positive purpose of Locke's philosophy was just what Hume set out to combat. For Locke intended also that his survey of human understanding and powers 'to see to what things they are adapted' would show that although men had not the full blaze of sun to light their way, yet 'the candle that is set up in us shines bright enough for all our purposes'.[2] He was concerned to defeat not only the pretensions of the scholastics, but also the apparent amorality of Hobbes. And against Hobbes, he argued that man was after all a rational creature, who could discern through his reason a certain and universal moral law. Human powers were not great enough to put any conclusion beyond rational criticism, but man could perfectly well rely on his own powers to guide him in ordinary life and particularly in moral questions. Thus Locke hoped, while clearing away false notions, 'to raise an edifice uniform and consistent'.

His new edifice, however much it seemed to depart from the established picture of man, still emphasized man's affinity to God. Locke made sensation the first and most primitive source of ideas, but not the sole source of knowledge. It was supplemented not only by another passive power, reflection—'the capacity of the mind to receive impressions made on it by its own operations', but also by an active power of the mind, intellect, which created ideas of relation—abstract, general, and universal ideas. Repeatedly, Locke reminded his readers that neither sensation nor reflection could produce general or abstract ideas, and that the power of producing them distinguished man from brutes: 'this, I think, I may be positive in, that the power of abstracting is not at all in them [brutes]; and that the having of general ideas is that which puts a perfect distinction betwixt man and brutes, and is an excellence which the faculties of brutes do by no means attain to . . .'.[3] The idea of cause, that is, of the power to cause change, he pointed out, could not be resolved into either sensation or reflection; the mind added to the materials supplied by sensation and reflection an idea of its own creation, the idea of cause and effect. The idea of substance was also admitted by Locke, and made equally independent of sensation and reflection. 'I never said that the general idea of substance comes in by sensation and reflection or that it is a simple idea of sensation or reflection', he replied sharply to the criticism of the Bishop of

[1] Memorandum of Studies at Montpelier and Paris, in Fraser, *Locke*, p. 50.
[2] *Essay on Human Understanding*, vol. I, pp. 1, 5.
[3] *Ibid.* vol. II, pp. 11, 10.

Worcester, 'for general ideas come not into the mind by sensation or reflection, but are the creatures or inventions of the understanding, as I think I have shown.'[1] For all his talk of the dependence of ideas on sensation, intuition was, after all, fundamental for Locke. It furnished all the basic principles of certainty and knowledge.[2]

Locke's moral theory, which Clarke took over, depended entirely on the assumption that man has a rational faculty linking him to God. Reason was declared to be 'natural revelation where the eternal Father of light and fountain of all knowledge communicates to mankind that portion of truth which he had laid within the reach of their natural faculties'.[3] For Locke, no less than for the Cambridge Platonists, reason was 'the Candle of the Lord' in man; it alone could discover the law by which he was to govern himself. As this law was nothing other than the rule God had set down for the governance of man, the nature of God and of virtue were one. Thus morality without God was unthinkable. That was why, despite his desire to extend toleration, Locke excluded atheists: 'The taking away of God, though but even in thought, dissolves all . . .'.[4] And for the same reasons, Locke counselled parents to teach their children how to make their irrational, sensual, animal natures submit to the rule of reason.

Locke nevertheless performed a most useful service for Hume. By distinguishing the creative, intuitive, synthetic powers of the mind from the passive, discursive, analytic powers of reflection and demonstration, Locke defined Hume's problem. 'Creative' reason was what the ancients called 'logos' or 'nous', that is, the faculty of apprehending necessary truths, of discovering the essence of things, the permanent causes or reasons for the existence of facts experienced by the senses. It enabled man to transcend both matter and mortality, and to deal with eternal things—first causes, human destiny, the relation between man and God. Reason was man's participation in the supreme rational power that shaped the universe, that imposed order on the chaos of matter and directed the world towards a rational end. Whereas the senses, memory, and imagination, which man shared with animals, enabled him to perceive individual things and to remember and collect his impressions, his intellect apprehended the principle of these things. It gave him knowledge of general truth that was not merely the sum of particular truths but a genuine insight into the nature of things, into final and formal causes.

In order to sever man from God, Hume saw that he needed only to deny 'creative' reason. He could then redefine reason as a more limited power to receive ideas, to compare and analyse them, a power that was impressive and

---

[1] Locke, *Works* (1892), vol. II, p. 348.

[2] *Essay on Human Understanding*, vol. IV, pp. 7, 19.

[3] *Ibid.* vol. IV, pp. 19, 4.

[4] Locke, 'A Letter Concerning Toleration' in *Of Civil Government* (Oxford, 1948), p. 156.

distinctive but did not carry man beyond nature. The result would be a 'compleat system of the sciences, built on a foundation almost entirely new, and the only one upon which they can stand with any security'.[1]

Since in the terms of Locke's analysis, the work of the creative intellect was to frame abstract ideas and discover relations, these operations absorbed Hume's attention. If he could trace them to some faculty other than intuitive reason, he would have destroyed the argument for placing man above the rest of nature and near to God.

At the height of his philosophic enthusiasm, Hume was moved by an ambition to follow the method of Newton, 'the greatest and rarest genius that ever rose for the ornament of the species', who had admitted 'no principles but such as were founded on experiment'.[2] He too would disdain any traffic with occult qualities and reduce all phenomena to the simplest causes without, however, probing too far. In this mood, he produced a largely mechanistic analysis of mental phenomena. He began by calling Locke's ideas 'perceptions', and resolved them into two kinds, 'impressions', and 'ideas'. Impressions included all the 'sensations, passions, and emotions as they make their first appearance in the soul'; ideas were the images of these perceptions in thinking and reasoning. Ideas and perceptions were analogous to physical atoms, simple and separable, but connected by association, 'a kind of attraction which in the mental world will be found to have as many extraordinary effects as in the natural, and to shew itself in as many and as various forms'.[3] The rest of the *Treatise* was devoted to showing that every activity of the mind could be explained without recourse to reason in the traditional sense. To this end, Hume occupied himself primarily with two topics, 'Space and Time', and 'Causation'.

The ideas of space and time had always been taken for a prime example of abstract ideas, for they included the notion of infinity and seemed more than any other idea to go beyond the natural capacities of the mind. The human mind was finite, and yet it seemed able to conceive of infinity; in many of its operations it depended on sensation, and yet it had an idea of a vacuum or space where there was nothing that could give rise to sensation. Thus the ideas of space and time had the 'air of a paradox', were 'contrary to the first and most unprejudic'd notions of mankind', and therefore, Hume explained, 'greedily embrac'd by philosophers', as showing the superiority of their science, 'which coul'd discover their opinions so remote from vulgar conceptions'.[4]

---

[1] Hume, *Treatise*, p. xx.

[2] *History of England* (1841), vol. VI, p. 341.

[3] *Treatise*, pp. 12–13.

[4] *Ibid.* p. 26. *Enquiry*, p. 156: 'The chief objection against all *abstract* reasonings is derived from the ideas of space and time; ideas, which, in common life and to a careless view, are very clear and intelligible, but when they pass through the scrutiny of the profound

Causation was crucial for Hume because it was the only idea of relation that seemed to involve a truly intellectual element. All the others Hume showed to be merely a comparison of ideas or impressions received through sensation. With these mental operations, he had no quarrel, as they implied no creative power of the mind to add something of its own, but merely a power to receive and manipulate ideas. Hume took pains to point out that mathematics was a case of the latter, that there was nothing remarkable in the ability to think of a triangle. Mathematicians liked to pretend that the objects they dealt with were 'of so refin'd and spiritual a nature', that they 'must be comprehended by a pure and intellectual view, of which the superior faculties of the soul are alone capable'.[1] Philosophers welcomed this notion, and used it to explain our abstract ideas. But to refute them, Hume declared, one need only remember 'that all our ideas are copy'd from our impressions'.[2] The mathematical idea of a triangle was derived from experience of real triangles, and made abstract in the usual way, which Hume hoped to illustrate by his treatment of space and time. He dismissed also relations of identity and of time and place, because they were comparisons that could be made merely by looking at the two objects. As they involved nothing more than 'a mere passive admission of the impressions thro' the organs of sensation', the mind had no need to go beyond what was immediately present to the senses.[3]

It was different, however, with causation. There something more seemed really to be involved and all our knowledge depended on it. For in making a causal inference, we go beyond direct experience to assert that what was true yesterday and today would also be true tomorrow. All our conclusions about matters of fact beyond observations of what is immediately present depend on assumptions about cause and effect. We assume that because such an object had always been attended with such an effect, other similar objects would be attended with similar effects, and thus regularly go beyond memory and sense: 'Should it be said that, from a number of uniform experiments, we infer a connexion between the sensible qualities and the secret powers; this, I must confess, seems the same difficulty couched in different terms. The question still recurs. . . . Where is the medium, the interposing ideas which

sciences (and they are the chief objects of these sciences) afford principles, which seem full of absurdity and contradiction. No priestly *dogmas* invented on purpose to tame and subdue the rebellious reason of mankind, ever shocked common sense more than the doctrine of infinite divisibility of extension, with its consequences; as they are pompously displayed by all geometricians and metaphysicians, with a kind of triumph and exultation.'

[1] 'The same notion runs thro' most parts of philosophy, and is principally made use of to explain our abstract ideas, and to show how we can form the idea of a triangle, for instance, which shall neither be an isosceles nor scalenum . . .'. (*A Treatise of Human Nature*, ed. by L. A. Selby-Bigge (Oxford, 1955), p. 72).

[2] *Ibid.* p. 72.

[3] *Ibid.* p. 73.

join propositions so very wide of each other?'[1] Or, in terms of traditional logic, what is the source of the middle term, the definition that makes our syllogisms about cause and effect possible? Rationalist philosophers explained that the intellect grasped intuitively the relation between cause and effect. Reason, by understanding the nature of the cause, they said, could see the necessity of the effect, or, it could see from the character of the event what had to be the nature of the cause. To make the causal inference, and arrive at knowledge beyond empirical verification, to discover the definitions of things was the acknowledged function of reason.

Hume was not alone in singling out the ideas of space and time and of causation as peculiarly significant. They had become subjects of general discussion among natural philosophers whose attention had been drawn to some of the same problems by the theory of gravitation. On the one hand, Newton seemed to have banished *a priori* explanation from natural philosophy, and established experiment as the sole basis for scientific truth; but on the other hand, he used concepts that seemed to have no foundation in sense experience. He had shown that gravitational force acted at a distance without any direct physical contact. But as the scientists of his day regarded 'natural' and 'mechanical' virtually as synonyms, and believed that a 'natural' explanation had to be in terms of particles of matter in motion, Newton seemed to have suggested that matter was moved by a non-material, supernatural force. Moreover, one of his central concepts in the *Principia* was 'absolute space and time' for which he gave no experimental evidence. Newton never discussed the metaphysical status of absolute space and time, but he suggested that it might be the sensorium of the Deity, and sometimes spoke as if it described a reality. Certainly, many of his followers took the reality for granted.

The continental admirers of the experimental method, Leibnitz, Huygens, Bernoulli, declared that Newton had left the straight and narrow path of empiricism and had taken refuge in scholastic, occult qualities to explain natural phenomena. As gravitational force was not given by experience, Newton had made a causal inference that was inadmissible in science. Their suspicions were confirmed by the defenders of religion, who eagerly claimed Newton's theory as evidence for the existence of an immaterial mind and welcomed the notions of 'absolute time and space' as proof of man's ability to discover realities beyond experience, to grasp 'occult qualities', and therefore to know God. Or else, like Clarke, the pious saw a direct relation between infinite space and infinite intelligence.[2] Newton himself preferred 'to avoid all questions about the nature or quality of this force', insisting that he had merely described what he had observed, and did not pretend to explain it.

[1] *Enquiry*, pp. 36–7.
[2] Clarke described infinite space and time as 'modes of an essence of substance incomprehensible to us' in *A Demonstration of the Being and Attributes of God*, 1725, p. 38.

He was sufficiently disturbed by the dangerous implications, however, to try, unsuccessfully, to explain gravitation by means of an ethereal fluid.

Certainly, in the context of mechanically oriented science, both of Newton's concepts carried intimations of divinity. They moved his contemporaries to consider whether science had to go beyond experience and have recourse to metaphysical realities to explain natural phenomena. They brought into question the whole nature and validity of the causal inference and of abstract ideas.

Hume's explanation of space and time followed the lines suggested by Newton's critics. Leibnitz, as well as Toland, argued that time and space were not absolute realities but were meaningful only in connection with objects either coexisting, or in succession. We do not understand the manner of the existence of objects in these two distinct ways, they said. We simply find ourselves aware of certain relations of situation or an order of objects. This solution was especially satisfactory for Hume because it enabled him also to reduce the notion of infinity to a similar status. For had he instead resolved space and time into sensation, it would have been at the cost of giving reality to the even more dangerous idea of an infinite being.

That he was mainly concerned to undermine the dependence of abstract ideas on creative reason, (without, however, denying their basis in reality), he made perfectly clear. In the first book of the *Treatise*, he had taken over Berkeley's criticism of abstract ideas and shown that they were 'in themselves individual, however they may become general in their representation. The image in the mind is only that of a particular object, tho' the application of it in our reasoning be the same as if it were universal'.[1] But he took Berkeley's analysis one step further and explained how a particular idea came to stand for other resembling particular ideas. This was, he said, the result of a custom of associating a whole number of objects with the name of one of them: 'The word raises up an individual idea, along with a certain custom; and that custom produces any other individual for which we may have occasion'.[2] His hypothesis, Hume declared, was utterly 'contrary to that, which has hitherto prevail'd in philosophy'. It was founded on the impossibility of general ideas, as usually understood.

We must certainly seek some new system on this head, and there plainly is none beside what I have propos'd. If ideas be particular in their nature, and at the same time finite in their number, 'tis only by custom they can become general in their representation, and contain an infinite number of other ideas under them.[3]

His analysis of space and time was entirely parallel to his analysis of abstract ideas, and he carefully underscored the connection. Space and time, as

[1] *Treatise*, p. 20.
[2] *Ibid.* p. 21.
[3] *Ibid.* p. 24.

separate realities, were conceived of, he explained, by the imagination. We perceive only patches or points of colour and touch. After experiencing many such coexistences, we can separate the space of these different perceptions from them and think of space in the abstract. The idea of time, because it was derived from a number of different kinds of impressions, afforded, he said, 'an instance of an abstract idea which comprehends a still greater variety than that of space, and yet is represented in the fancy by some particular idea of a determinate quantity and quality'.[1] The conception of space and time is exactly like the conception of relations, substances and universals. In all these cases, we are misled into turning the fixed names for relations into absolute entities. Such indefinite application of ideas which are originally relative to certain limited perceptions is characteristic of the human mind. It is the work of imagination, and is the result of custom.

As Hume came to recognize in the course of *Treatise*, the custom from which, he had said, abstract ideas arise must itself be dependent on a capacity to form general concepts and to make 'distinctions of reason' between, for instance, figure and colour, motion and the body moved. It was a difficulty that haunted his whole enterprise—in order to explain how a general term comes to be applied, or how it comes to be, he had to allow that the mind could recognize the identity of an object through time and could apprehend a resemblance between particular images. Indeed, if a particular idea becomes general by being annexed to a general term, the recognition of a resemblance between particulars must occur before that use of the general term upon which the custom rests. How these operations were possible to a mind whose every idea is derived from an impression, Hume never explained. He merely took the relation of resemblance for granted as an ultimate fact of experience. Philosophers have since suggested that he might have escaped these difficulties by acknowledging and developing a supplementing and synthetic activity of the imagination at which he hints. But he could not have gone much further than he did without running a danger he was most anxious to avoid, of letting in by another door the kind of power he was trying to exclude.

Custom played an even more remarkable role in Hume's theory of causation. And far from denying the radicalism of his theory, he made certain his readers noticed that the notion of causality was at the heart of all discussions of human intelligence and that his views were most unorthodox:

I doubt not but these consequences will at first sight be receiv'd without difficulty, as being evident deductions from principles, which we have already establish'd, and which we have often employ'd in our reasonings. This evidence . . . may seduce us unwarily into the conclusion, and make us imagine it contains nothing extra-

[1] *Ibid.* p. 35.

ordinary, nor worthy of our curiosity . . . for which reason I think it proper to give warning, that I have just now examin'd one of the most sublime questions in philosophy, viz., that concerning the power and efficacy of causes, or that quality which makes them be followed by their effects. . . .[1]

Hume had no wish to deny that there was a real connection between cause and effect or that all our reasoning depended on our being convinced that the connection was a necessary one. Quite the contrary, the very necessity of the causal relation was crucial for his purpose. That cause and effect were connected by contiguity and succession, Hume granted at once. But that did not explain, he pointed out, what was really distinctive about the causal relation, that it seemed to be a necessary connection: 'Shall we then rest contented with these two relations of contiguity and succession as affording a compleat idea of causation? By no means. An object may be contiguous and prior to another without being considered its cause. There is also a necessary connexion to be taken into consideration'.[2] We can see that the dog moves and that the stone does not; we see the facts and can conceive of their contrary; yet we say that the dog *must* move and the stone *can* not. In the same way, we do not say simply that every change has a cause, but that it *must* have a cause. What gives us assurance of that necessity?

If the traditional answer that the necessity is seen by reason, by an intuitive insight into the nature of the cause or of the effect were correct, Hume argued, we should be able to see causal necessity from one instance. We could then say that it was impossible for the one object not to follow, or be conceived not to follow. But in fact, we can conceive of causes and their effects as unconnected, and what is even more important, we never conclude that there is a causal connection until we have seen the same events related in the same way a number of times. As there is nothing in several instances repeated that there is not in any one of them, it cannot be that anything within the objects gives rise to the idea of necessity.[3] The cause must then lie in the mind, not in the objects:

Tho' the several resembling instances which give rise to the idea of power have no influence on each other, and can never produce any new quality *in the object* . . . yet the *observation* of this resemblance produces a new impression *in the mind*, which is its real model. . . . Necessity, then, is the effect of this observation, and is nothing but an internal impression of the mind, or a determination to carry our thoughts from one object to another.[4]

The necessity assumed is not, and cannot be, a necessity of reason (i.e.,

[1] *Treatise* p. 156.
[2] *Ibid.* p. 77.
[3] *Ibid.* p. 164.
[4] *Ibid.* pp. 164-5.

intuitively or demonstratively understood); it is only a necessity of feeling, in short, a *belief*, and it arises from custom.

Hume thus reduced what had formerly been described as an intuition about the essence of things to nothing more exalted than an experience of a customary conjunction between two objects. Again, he was involved in the difficulty that afflicted his analysis of abstract ideas. He did not explain what enabled the mind to recognize 'like' causes, or customary conjunctions. If, in fact, we can know only what we have already experienced, how can we depart from experience to recognize an object's similarity to the one we have experienced in the past? But Hume's attention was concentrated on what he was denying, that the causal inference was an operation of reason enabling man to discover the rational pattern imprinted on nature by the Divine Mind. Having shown that merely custom explained the feeling of necessary connection between cause and effect, Hume left 'those who delight in the discovery and contemplation of "final causes" ', to 'employ their wonder and admiration' elsewhere.[1] He had also eliminated the supposed difference between 'moral' and 'physical' necessity, for he had shown that all necessity lay in the mind, and arose from the influence of the repeated, constant conjunction of two objects. Instead of necessity there was only chance, reduced to order by custom.[2]

He had demonstrated, Hume felt, that reasoning never gives rise to 'a new original, simple idea',[3] that nowhere in man is there anything 'like this creative power, by which it raises from nothing a new idea, and with a kind of Fiat, imitates the omnipotence of its Maker . . .'.[4] It seemed that human thought possessed unbounded liberty and power, but closer examination revealed that it is 'confined within very narrow limits', and

that all this creative power of the mind amounts to no more than the faculty of compounding, transposing, augmenting, or diminishing the materials afforded us by the senses and experience. . . . In short, all the materials of thinking are derived either from an outward or inward sentiment; the mixture and composition of these belongs alone to the mind and will.[5]

The implications for the activity of philosophizing were not comfortable. By reducing reason to a combination of imagination and sense impressions, Hume had made it impossible to say why what we believe is true, or in any way to establish the certain validity of our beliefs. He had described the workings of the mind, but in doing so had merged logic with psychology; his description of the causal relationship had made it impossible to explain it.

[1] *Enquiry*, p. 55.
[2] *Treatise*, p. 171.
[3] *Enquiry*, p. 64 fn.
[4] *Ibid*. p. 69.
[5] *Ibid*. p. 19.

Most awkward of all, his method had not accounted for his own philosophizing. The picture he had drawn of the limitations of human knowledge ruled out his own ability to construct it. He had in fact disproved his title to prove or disprove anything. His *Treatise* could only be a miracle, unrelated to the rest.

It had not, however, been an interest in discovering the nature of knowing, for its own sake, that had driven him into philosophy. The point of his argument was moral, rather than epistemological, and this he made perfectly plain by concluding his analysis of human understanding with a section on the reason of animals.

Having demonstrated how the human operation that had hitherto been traced to a spiritual power, reason, was no such thing, he then turned the question round. He showed man to be standing closer to the animals than to God, not because, as Hobbes said, man was brutish but because animals were no less spiritual than he. At times Hume almost paraphrased Montaigne to argue that insofar as men reasoned, animals did too. It had long been observed, he said, that animals behaved very much as men did, and that they adapted means to ends in the same manner. It was only natural to assume that the causes of similar behaviour were similar:

> We are conscious that we ourselves in adapting means to ends are guided by reason[1] and design, and that 'tis not ignorantly nor casually we perform those actions, which tend to self-preservation, to the obtaining pleasure and avoiding pain. When therefore we see other creatures, in millions of instances perform like actions, and direct them to like ends, all our principles of reason and probability carry us with an invincible force to believe the existence of a like cause. . . . The resemblance betwixt the actions of animals and those of men is so entire in this respect, that the very first action of the first animal we shall please to pitch on, will afford us an incontestable argument for the present doctrine.[2]

Hume pointed out that this was not just a parenthetical observation but at the heart of his argument—'This doctrine is as useful as it is obvious, and furnishes us with a kind of touchstone, by which we may try every system in this species of philosophy'.[3] It is easy, he declared, to test any hypothesis advanced to explain a mental operation by asking whether it applied equally well to men and beasts. Other philosophical systems supposed 'a subtilty and refinement of thought' in a degree that exceeded the capacities not only of animals but also of most human beings. His own system, however, could 'equally account for the reasonings of beasts as well as for those of the

---

[1] Many of the difficulties about Hume's meaning arise from the ambiguity of 'reason'. Hume uses it frequently in the ordinary way, without making clear which meaning he is giving it.

[2] *Treatise*, p. 176.

[3] *Ibid.* p. 176.

human species'. And it was the only philosophical system that could. Since it is generally admitted that beasts do not perceive any real connection among objects, or form any general conclusions, yet learn from experience and adapt their behaviour accordingly, it is evident that 'rational' behaviour does not depend on reason in the sense given it by philosophers: 'I assert they [rational actions of animals] proceed from a reasoning, that is not in itself different, nor founded on different principles from that which appears in human nature.'[1]

Here perhaps Hume was more artful than candid. The force of his argument about animals is certainly that if we do not need to postulate a creative reason in order to explain the behaviour of animals, we need not do so for humans. But he avoided making an offensive statement by reversing the order, and declaring that, 'All this was sufficiently evident with respect to man. But with respect to beasts there cannot be the least suspicion of mistake; which must be own'd to be a strong confirmation, or rather an invincible proof of my system'.[2] Hume was tactful, but his meaning is clear. Was it not odd, he asked, that men took their own reason for granted, but were astonished by the instinct of animals? It was only because they had not been able to reduce animal instinct to the same principles. In the light of his new philosophy, however, the problem vanished, because it removed the apparent distinction between human reason and animal instinct. It discovered reason to be 'nothing but a wonderful and unintelligible instinct in our souls which carries us along a certain train of ideas, and endows them with particular qualities, according to their particular situations and relations'. It was an instinct that resulted from habit, and 'habit is nothing but one of the principles of nature and derives all its force from that origin'.[3] Man, then, was not outside or beyond nature, but part of it, merely a more elaborate animal: 'Everything is conducted by springs and principles, which are not peculiar to man, or any species of animals'.[4] Montaigne's essays had been given a metaphysical foundation.

That Hume had done something radical, all his contemporaries sensed. What the radicalism consisted in, however, they did not quite grasp. Only Kant recognized the full implications of Hume's theory. He saw the import of Hume's concentration on the 'necessity' of the causal relation, that he had denied not the reality of causation or the necessity of reasoning in the ordinary way, but rather the existence of 'pure reason'. As Hume had reduced reason to nature, Kant hoped to save reason by divorcing it from nature more thoroughly than anyone had yet dared. He purified reason of its traditional

---

[1] *Ibid.* p. 177.
[2] *Ibid.* p. 178.
[3] *Ibid.* p. 179.
[4] *Ibid.* p. 397.

character as pupil, receiving what nature chose to give, and transformed it into a judge, 'who compels the witnesses to reply to those questions which he himself thinks fit to propose'.[1] Thus Kant put the defence of creative reason on a totally new footing, which was, he hoped, not so vulnerable as Hume had shown the old one to be.

If one accepted Hume's picture of human nature, the whole hierarchy of being was rearranged. The *Treatise* proposed a metaphysics that was profoundly subversive of the Christian outlook. It was no wonder that Hume's friends wished him to withhold from publication his *Dialogue on Natural Religion*, and that he should have taken such great pains to insure its appearance after his death. For the *Dialogue* stated the postulate upon which the *Treatise* was based in its most general and simple form.

The general question of how mind and matter were related had interested Hume from the beginning. He had studied Bayle's account of Strato's atheism and Cicero's *Dialogue of the Nature of the Gods*, and was curious about the Cartesian philosophy of the brain. He had noticed throughout the history of philosophy that the most prevalent views had driven a sharp line between matter and spirit. Either they took up an atomistic, materialist position, like that of Epicurus, Democritus, Leucippus, and asserted that there was nothing but senseless matter and chance, or else they insisted that nature could not be explained without adding a spiritual, ordering force beyond matter. There was, however, a third possibility, suggested by Strato, and discussed by Cicero, that order is somehow inherent in matter. Strato's atheism was 'the most dangerous of the ancient, holding the origin of the world from nature or a matter endowed with activity', Hume remarked in his notes.[2] What he himself had decided, he made plain in the *Dialogues Concerning Natural Religion*.

Thought is not the only principle of order disclosed in experience, he pointed out. There are an infinite number of springs and principles which even our limited knowledge of nature shows her to possess—heat and cold, attraction and repulsion, instinct and generation. We know that every part of nature has its own life and motion, which not only operates it, but co-ordinates it with the whole. Our experience would seem to deny the possibility of matter utterly devoid of order, or, even spirit without matter. Certainly in all instances that we know, thought can influence matter only when it is joined to it, and it can be as easily influenced by matter. We have no reason to make 'this little agitation of the brain' the model of the universe.[3]

Besides, as we constantly see reason arise from generation, never genera-

---

[1] Immanuel Kant, *Critique of Pure Reason* (London, 1866), Preface to 2nd edition, p. xxvii.

[2] Hume, *Dialogues*, p. 35.

[3] *Ibid.* p. 148.

tion from reason, we might more easily make generation the principle of order than reason. It is no less intelligible or compatible with experience to say that the world arose by vegetation from a seed, than to say that it arose from a divine reason or contrivance.[1] An orderly system might as easily have been spun from the belly of an infinite spider as from a mind. Reason itself is no more intelligible than any other ordering principle: 'But reason, in its internal fabric and structure, is really as little known to us as instinct or vegetation; and perhaps even that vague, undeterminate word, nature, to which the vulgar refer everything is not at bottom more inexplicable'.[2]

In the *Dialogue*, no one of the disputants gains a victory, although no one really refutes Philo's statement:

For aught we can know *a priori*, matter may contain the source or spring of order originally within itself, as well as mind does; and there is no more difficulty in conceiving, that the several elements from an internal unknown cause, may fall into the most exquisite arrangement, than to conceive that their ideas, in the great universal mind, from a like internal unknown cause, fall into that arrangement. The equal possibility of both these suppositions is allowed.[3]

The emphasis falls not so much on any particular theory, as on denying the possibility of knowing what either matter or mind is, or precisely how the universe is arranged: 'These words, *generation, reason*, mark only certain powers and energies in nature, whose effects are known but whose essence is incomprehensible; and one of these principles, more than the other, has no privilege for being made a standard to the whole of nature'.[4] The sum of Hume's argument is that by experience we know that there is an order in nature, but we cannot know how it comes to be. It is therefore presumptuous to try to distinguish matter from mind, to say that one lacks order and the other imposes it. The very distinction is beyond our capacities. Even Father Malebranche, he pointed out, considered it blasphemous to call God a spirit, and argued that He was neither spirit nor matter, but simply, ' "He that is", or, in other words, Being without restriction, all Being, the Being infinite and universal'.[5] It was far better to rest with a more modest theory, and ascribe

---

[1] *Ibid.* p. 178.

[2] *Ibid.* p. 178. In the *Enquiry*, the same view is suggested when Hume says that we cannot pretend to understand the 'nature of the human soul and the nature of an idea, or the aptitude of the one to produce the other'. For this really implies a power 'beyond the reach of any being less than infinite. At least it must be owned that such a power is not felt, nor known, nor even conceivable by the mind. We only feel the event, namely the existence of an idea consequent to a command of the will: But the manner, in which this operation is performed, the power by which it is produced, is entirely beyond our comprehension'. (*Enquiry concerning Human Understanding*, p. 68).

[3] *Dialogues*, p. 146.

[4] *Ibid.* p. 178.

[5] *Ibid.* p. 142.

'an eternal inherent principle or order to the world, though attended with great and continual revolutions and alterations'. This, by being so general, solved all difficulties; it was perhaps 'not entirely complete and satisfactory', but it was at least a 'theory that we must sooner or later, have recourse to, whatever system we embrace'.[1] For we know only that 'everything is surely governed by steady inviolable laws'. If we could know the 'inmost essence of things', we would then 'discover a scene, of which, at present we can have no idea'.[2]

Hume preferred to leave the various arguments in his dialogue more or less in balance, not merely because he might thereby avoid offending popular opinion, but because, above all, he wanted to say that in the end we can but acknowledge a mystery. Neither spirit nor matter was to be made supreme. He had indeed attacked the argument from design, that argument for God's existence which the faithful regarded as the very heart of religion. And yet he was not an atheist strictly speaking, but a true defender of religion in its most generic meaning, as a sense of wonder. For he insisted that understanding the order of the universe was not within man's power:

The whole is a riddle, an aenigma, an inexplicable mystery. Doubt, uncertainty, suspence of judgement appear the only result of our most accurate scrutiny, concerning this subject. But such is the frailty of human reason, and such the irresistible

---

[1] *Ibid.* p. 174.

[2] *Ibid.* pp. 174–5. See also Hume's essay 'Of the Immortality of the Soul' (which he did not publish during his life): 'Matter, therefore, and spirit, are at bottom equally unknown; and we cannot determine what qualities inhere in the one or in the other.

They likewise teach us, that nothing can be decided *a priori* concerning any cause or effect; and that experience, being the only source of our judgements of this nature, we cannot know from any other principle, whether matter, by its structure or arrangement, may not be the cause of thought. Abstract reasonings cannot decide any question of fact or existence'. (*Essays, Moral, Political and Literary*, ed by T. H. Green and T. H. Grose, (London, 1898), vol. II, p. 399) and 'Everything is in common betwixt soul and body. The organs of the one are all of them the organs of the other'. (*Essays*, vol. II, p. 404).

In *The Natural History of Religion*, Hume says: 'We are placed in this world, as in a great theatre, where the true springs and causes of every event are entirely concealed from us; nor have we either sufficient wisdom to foresee, or power to prevent those ills, with which we are continually threatened. We hang in perpetual suspense between life and death, health and sickness, plenty and want; which are distributed amongst the human species by secret and unknown causes, whose operation is oft unexpected, and always unaccountable. These unknown causes then become the constant object of our hope and fear; and while the passions are kept in perpetual alarm by an anxious expectation of the events, the imagination is equally employed in forming ideas of those powers, on which we have so entire a dependence. Could men anatomize nature, according to the most probable, at least the most intelligible, philosophy, they would find, that these causes are nothing but the particular fabric and structure of the minute parts of their own bodies and of external objects; and that, by a regular and constant machinery, all the events are produced, about which they are so much concerned'. (*Essays*, vol. II, p. 316).

contagion of opinion, that even this deliberate doubt could scarcely be upheld; did we not enlarge our view, and opposing one species of superstition to another, set them a quarrelling; while we ourselves, during their fury and contention, happily make our escape into the calm, though obscure regions of philosophy.[1]

Hume had used the 'experimental method' not to confirm but to thwart the scientific spirit. For the scientist, however much he may assert that he wishes merely to observe the phenomena of this world, however much he denies the possibility of explaining them, is driven by the momentum of his own work into attempting to discover all or believing he could. He may say that his general laws describe nothing real, but even if he himself refrains from doing so, his disciples, as Newton's did, will take the reality of his scientific laws for granted. But Hume not only insisted on a fundamental, impenetrable mystery; he not only disintegrated the very power that was supposed to give men access to certain and undeniable truth. He denied also the sort of world that the scientists, from Copernicus on, had been creating.

Although insofar as he expelled formal and final causes Hume spoke for the new experimental science, in another way he was behind his time. On the one hand, he admired Newton for the wrong reasons: 'While Newton seemed to draw off the veil from some of the mysteries of nature, he showed at the same time the imperfections of the mechanical philosophy; and thereby restored her ultimate secrets to that obscurity in which they ever did and ever will remain'.[2] On the other hand, despite his criticism of 'the mechanical philosophy', Hume had taken his stand with Newton's opponents who refused to accept a mathematical force. He used Newton's own method to declare himself against the timeless world of immaterial forces that Newton, in completing the world view of the new science, proposed to substitute for a simpler, mechanical world, where men did not venture beyond everyday experience. The effect of Newtonism was to abolish the world of more or less, of qualities and sense perception, of concentration on our daily life, and to replace it by an Archimedean universe of precision, of quantity, and rest, where there is a place for everything but humanity. It substituted a mathematical nature for a physical nature, a world of being for a world of becoming and change. It reduced motion from a process of change that affected bodies and differed from rest to a status as permanent and indestructible as rest. Motion became a changeless change in a timeless time. It was no longer the motion of daily experience.

But Hume, as a philosopher of becoming, not of being, preferred the world he could feel about him to the Platonic idea of a mathematical world. His standpoint was more nearly that of the artist than of the philosopher—he was

---

[1] *Essays*, vol. II, p. 363.
[2] *History of England* (1841), vol. VI, p. 341.

more concerned to remember the particular experiences behind abstract ideas than to organize experience under concepts. In the world as he saw it, all qualities are mixed and confused; there are no distinctions of kind, but only of degree: 'Nothing in this world is perpetual; Every thing, however seemingly firm, is in continual flux and change'.[1]

[1] *Essays*, vol. II, p. 404.

CHAPTER V

VIRTUE IN A BUNDLE OF PERCEPTIONS

HAVING tumbled reason from her high throne to set her on earth judging facts and thus removed the divine imprint from man's soul, Hume used the same means to show that man bore no mark of Satan. For man restored to nature, he described a virtue that required no struggle with sin, no repression, no divine intervention, nothing but what could come naturally to human beings.

The passions, in which Hume casually included animal instincts and passions, along with moral sentiments and natural beliefs, were reduced, like everything else, to a form of sensation. Instead of being the unruly elements of the soul, opposed to reason, they became innocuous 'reflective impressions'. They arose, Hume said, as internal responses to 'original impressions', that is, to sensations caused by external objects or operations of the body. In other words, they were responses to bodily pleasures and pains. Some, like the sense of beauty and deformity, were calm; others, like love and hatred, grief, joy, pride and humility, were violent; all were equally natural and capable of being beneficial. They were secondary, internal, reflective impressions and neither good nor evil. They were the results of causes that 'operated after the same *manner* thro' the whole animal creation'[1] and were therefore, like reason, common to man and animals.

By describing passions as responses to impressions, Hume made it impossible for them to be ruled by reason. Reason, in Hume's sense, could only judge abstract relations between ideas, or the relations between ideas and matters of fact. With neither of these judgements could reason excite desire or aversion, that is, give rise to passion or influence it.[2] Passions themselves

---

[1] *Treatise*, p. 328.

[2] A passion is complete in itself. Unlike ideas, but like all other sensations, it bears no correspondence to something outside itself. The anger of an angry man is merely a fact, like illness or thirst, or the blackness of his hair. A passion can be neither true nor false nor inconsistent. Reason, however, can only pronounce things true or false or inconsistent; it discovers whether ideas correspond to other ideas or to matters of fact. A passion may seem to be opposed to truth and reason when it is founded on a false or insufficient judgement. But then it is really the judgement, not the passion, that is false or insufficient. As long as a passion is neither founded on a false supposition, nor chooses inadequate means, reason can offer nothing to oppose it: ' 'Tis not contrary to reason to prefer the destruction of the whole world to the scratching of my finger. . . . 'Tis as little contrary to reason to prefer even my own acknowledg'd lesser good to my greater, and have a more ardent affection for the former than the latter.' (*A Treatise of Human Nature*, p. 416). As he had in his analysis of reason denied the possibility of knowing final causes, Hume had in effect

are called into being by nothing but impressions, and they can be opposed only by contrary passions. What is taken for the combat between reason and passion, Hume explained, is in reality a 'calm' passion opposing a 'violent' one: 'Thus it appears that the principle which opposes our passions cannot be the same with reason, and is only call'd so in an improper sense. Reason is, and ought only to be the slave of the passions, and can never pretend to any other office than to serve and obey them'.[1] Man is not then a divided nature but all one, and he is moved, not by two opposing principles, but by a variety of sensations.[2]

Thus Hume denied the basis for the traditional account of virtue. He had ruled out even the possibility of giving reason ascendancy in Spinoza's manner. Spinoza, too, had reversed the order of reason and passion, but in his account the master governing passion is the passion to act rationally for its own sake. In the end, Spinoza differentiated man from beast, and the free man from the slave, by his power of making reason and judgement control action and passion. For the only passion reason could not examine was the passion to reason. According to Hume, however, reason is always controlled by passion, by any and every desire which may happen to employ reason as a means to its fulfilment. Reason could never make an all-inclusive survey of all passions or desires.

Yet Hume was very far from wishing to conclude that therefore virtue and vice could or should be confounded. He ranked those who 'denied the reality of moral distinctions' among 'disingenuous disputants'.[3] Although he appreciated Mandeville's 'spirit of satire',[4] and felt considerable sympathy with his attack on the hypocritical enemies of joy and pleasure, who asked men to forswear wants that supported society, Hume could not be so irreverent. He would not for a moment, even in jest, argue that all moral distinctions arise from education, as Mandeville said, and were 'at first, invented, and

---

denied that there was any way of discovering a natural direction or hierarchy of the passions; each passion, each desire was as real and as valid as any other. Reason could at most affect passion indirectly, by discovering a fact that arouses passion, or by indicating the means for satisfying a passion.

[1] *Ibid.* p. 415.

[2] Hume continued to use 'passion', 'appetite', and 'instinct' to describe inclinations somehow different from 'reason', and even to suggest that reason controls or ought to control passion. In each case, a careful reading will show that he is in fact thinking of a 'calm' passion off-setting a 'violent' one, and has not departed from his basic view. But as he had explained in his philosophical works what we really mean when we speak of the 'combat between reason and passion', and was not disposed to coin jargon, he felt free to use the ordinary expressions. In his terminology, as in all other things, he was not disposed to wipe out tradition, but rather to bend it somewhat.

[3] *Enquiry*, p. 169.

[4] *Essays*, vol. II, p. 247.

afterwards encouraged by the art of politics in order to render man tractable'.[1] Morality is certain, and there is a clear distinction between virtue and vice, Hume affirmed; he denied only that it was absolute.

He managed to preserve the certainty of morals without letting it become absolute by founding it on sentiment. Virtue and vice were not matters of fact whose existence could be discovered by reason. In wilful murder, for instance, no one can observe anything that could be called vice. The only fact in the case that makes us call it vicious is a feeling in some person: 'In whichever way you take it, you find only certain passions, motives, volitions, and thoughts. There is no other matter of fact in the case. The vice entirely escapes you, as long as you consider the object'.[2] Vice and virtue are not then qualities in objects, not anything outside human beings, but perceptions within them:

When you pronounce any Action or character to be vicious, you mean nothing but that from the particular Constitution of your nature, you have a Feeling or Sentiment of Blame from the Contemplation of it. Vice and Virtue, therefore may be compar'd to sounds, colours, heat and cold, which, according to modern Philosophy are not Qualitys in Objects but Perceptions in the Mind.'[3]

That his moral theory was a great advance in speculative science, Hume readily claimed. But he denied that it had any radical consequences for practice.[4] Prudence alone perhaps required him to say so at a time when the arbiters of morality cried down any modification of their theories as a challenge to all established notions of good and bad. And in one sense, it was perfectly true that Hume's theory left practice unaffected. It did not sanction murder or incest, or deny the value of honesty and gratitude. It did, however, radically change the manner in which these standards were to be applied.

This was inevitable once Hume traced virtue to a basic principle that made it impossible to think of morality in the old way as a divine command. Instead, Hume showed that virtuous behaviour is simply useful to mankind,

---

[1] *Ibid.* p. 203.

[2] *Treatise*, p. 468.

[3] *Ibid.* p. 469. While reason does not determine morality, it does provide the materials for moral judgements: 'One principal foundation of moral praise being supposed to lie in the usefulness of any quality or action, it is evident that reason must enter for a considerable share in all decisions of this kind; since nothing but that faculty can instruct us in the tendency of qualities and actions, and point out their beneficial consequences to society and to their possessor. . . . The various circumstances of society; the various consequences of any practice; the various interests which may be proposed; these, on many occasions, are doubtful, and subject to great discussion and inquiry. . . . And a very accurate reason or judgement is often requisite to give the true determination, amidst such intricate doubts arising from obscure or opposite utilities'. (*Enquiry concerning Human Understanding*, p. 285).

[4] *Letters*, vol. I, p. 39.

that it conforms to, rather than violates, what is natural to men. The utility of an action or character, he explained, arouses a natural sentiment of approval. Because of the sympathy between men, this approval becomes general, that is, attached to other things and men and to whatever contributes to the happiness of society. All men can feel a sympathy with the possessor of a useful quality. So men come to approve what benefits not only themselves but also others. And what is useful to men generally is called a virtue.

Virtue does not then require men either to discern super-human purposes, or to deny their human needs and wants. Quite the contrary, it shows how best to satisfy them. To be virtuous, men need not struggle with or repress their natural inclinations—'all morality depends on the natural course of our passions and actions'.[1] The virtuous man is drawn to his duty 'without an effort or endeavour'. Virtue therefore is congenial to men and only superstition is 'odious and burthensome'.[2] Moral conflict is not a combat between divine reason and brute passion, but a purely human balancing of the calm against the violent passions. Thus Hume removed the dismal dress with which divines and philosophers had disguised virtue, and demonstrated that a happy life spent in festivals, mirth, philosophizing, and singing was, as the ancient Strabo had taught, the best way for man to imitate divine perfection.

Although a large part of traditional morality was unaffected by Hume's denial of super-human perfection, his account of virtue did imply some important changes. He did not, for instance, accept the Christian view of suicide. Since man is not unique but an intimate part of the natural order, whatever he wishes to do with his life, Hume argued, cannot be contrary to nature or God. The life of man 'is of no greater importance to the universe than the life of an oyster',[3] and therefore suicide is no more impious than agriculture. When life becomes a burden, when we can do but small good to society at the expense of great suffering to ourselves, there is no obligation to go on living. On the contrary, by committing suicide, we may be doing society a service; and certainly no man would have recourse to such a remedy frivolously.

In much the same spirit, Hume insisted that pride is not a vice but a virtue. All heroic virtue, he pointed out, all that we admire as greatness of mind— courage, intrepidity, ambition, love of glory, magnanimity—'is either nothing but a steady and well establish'd pride and self-esteem or partakes largely of that passion'.[4] The pagans never decried pride, and those who are anxious to improve life in this world invariably esteem it. They believe that

[1] *Treatise*, p. 532.
[2] *Essays*, vol. II, pp. 359, 358.
[3] *Ibid.* p. 410.
[4] *Treatise*, p. 599.

'a genuine and hearty pride, or self-esteem, if well conceal'd and well founded, is essential to the character of a man of honour, and that there is no quality of the mind, which is more indispensably requisite to procure the esteem and approbation of mankind'.[1] Only the 'religious declaimers' make pride a vice; they denounce it as 'purely pagan and natural and represent to us the excellency of the *Christian* religion, which places humility in the rank of virtues and corrects the judgement of the world, and even of philosophers who so generally admire all the efforts of pride and ambition . . .'.[2] But humility, beyond what good breeding and decency require of us, is merely one of that 'whole train of monkish virtues' which men of sense reject because they 'neither advance a man's fortune in the world, nor render him a valuable member of society; neither qualify him for the entertainment of company nor increase his power of self-enjoyment . . .'.[3]

Nevertheless, in some other ways Hume insisted on an obligation to depart from nature, and submit to reason. For he found in reason the source of general rules without which social relations were impossible. Even good breeding depended, he pointed out, on neglecting natural sentiments in favour of certain established forms. The rule that we must never praise ourselves but should rather underrate our true qualities, for instance, had become established because men tend to be conceited and cannot judge when they have given too free expression to their exaggerated self-esteem. As such conceit annoys others and destroys easy relations, it seems best to observe a general rule forbidding any self praise, for thus we are assured that neither our own conceit, nor that of others, will disrupt conversation and conviviality.

The rules of justice are of the same character. Without them, each case would be decided on its own merits, as each man judged them. We would grant a friend the property he claimed from our enemy; the tall boy who had only a short coat would appropriate the long coat from the short boy. We would conduct ourselves entirely by particular judgements that considered only the characters and circumstances of the moment. However much this might accord with our natural sentiments, Hume reminds us, ' 'tis easy to observe that this would produce an infinite convulsion in human society, and that the avidity and partiality of men would quickly bring disorder into the world. . .'.[4] In order to bring peace and stability into social life, men set up general and inflexible rules, which ensure that they will always view certain issues from the same standpoint, regardless of the particular situation. They agree to judge some matters not as the different circumstances surrounding each dictate, but from a common standpoint accepted by all.

The rules of justice are as a result both natural and artificial. They are

---

[1] *Ibid.* p. 598.
[2] *Ibid.* p. 560.
[3] *Ibid.* p. 598; cf. also *Enquiry*, p. 270.
[4] *Treatise*, p. 532.

natural because the need for them is inseparable from the nature of the human species; they do not arise from humour and caprice, and could not one day be dispensed with as if they were a mere matter of fashion:

The interest on which justice is founded is the greatest imaginable, and extends to all times and places. It cannot possibly be serv'd by any other invention. It is obvious and discovers itself on the very formation of society. All these causes render the rules of justice stedfast and immutable; at least as immutable as human nature.[1]

They might even Hume said, be called 'Laws of Nature'.[2] Yet at the same time, the rules of justice are artificial. For they engage men to act contrary to their natural sentiments. They extend what is felt in one set of circumstances to cover many others. They are 'contrary to the common principles of human nature, which accommodate themselves to circumstances and have no stated invariable method of operation'.[3]

The distinction between natural judgements and artificial rules was all important for Hume. It not only explains the origin of justice, but is at the heart of his moral attitude and defines his disagreement with conventional views of morality. It determines as well his attitude to politics. It arises from his sensitivity to the contrast between impersonal and personal judgements, between abstract, general, unyielding rules and particular judgements conforming to the conditions and needs of the moment. What is generally regarded as Hume's defence of nature may be better described as a defence of the personal against the impersonal, the concrete against the abstract.

Hume stressed the deficiencies of impersonal judgements as no other philosopher had. Virtue and vice, indeed all natural qualities, he reminds us, 'run insensibly into each other'; they approach one another 'by such insensible degrees' that it is exceedingly difficult, 'if not absolutely impossible to determine when the one ends and the other begins'.[4] But general rules make exact definitions, and admit of no degree. They treat cases similar in some respects as if they were similar in all without considering what tangle of circumstances and motives may excuse one but not another.[5] Even when

---

[1] *Ibid.* p. 620. In a letter to Hutcheson, Hume emphasized the empirical character of nature as he used it: 'I cannot agree to your sense of natural. 'Tis founded on final causes, which is a consideration that appears to me pretty uncertain and unphilosophical. For, pray, what is the end of man? Is he created for happiness or for virtue? for this life, or for the next? for himself, or for his Maker? Your definition of natural depends upon solving these questions, which are endless and quite wide of my purpose. I have never called justice unnatural, but only artificial'. (*Letters of David Hume*, ed. by J. Y. T. Greig (Oxford, 1932), vol. I, p. 33).

[2] *Treatise*, p. 484.

[3] *Ibid.* p. 533.

[4] *Ibid.* p. 529.

[5] *Ibid.* p. 551.

rules admit of exceptions, it is only according to a rule. The false distinctions imposed by a general rule give it an air of clarity, but in reality it is much more obscure than a particular judgement. It covers many particulars, and as any one of them may be thought to represent it, a general rule usually means different things to different people.

Besides, a general rule never allows us to dispense with judgement and experience. No matter how perfect in itself, it still needs to be applied properly. One must recognize first of all which general rule is relevant. Then one must know how to take account of the special circumstances in which the rule is being applied. Neither reasoning nor knowledge is enough; prudence is essential:

In every situation or incident there are many particular and seemingly minute circumstances, which the man of greatest talents is, at first, apt to overlook though on them the justness of his conclusions, and consequently the prudence of his conduct entirely depend. Not to mention, that, to a young beginner, the general observations and maxims occur not always on the proper occasions, nor can be immediately applied with due calmness and distinction.[1]

However good the laws of a society, they cannot then be perfectly just. As a general idea is a bundle of particular ones, so a general law covers a wide range of particulars, but necessarily singles out some for attention. What the law commands is therefore inevitably more suitable for some cases than for others equally under its jurisdiction. It cannot allow for the character, situation, or connections of every person affected. It may deprive a good industrious man of all possessions just because his title is not in perfect order, only 'to bestow them on a selfish miser who has already heaped up immense stores of superfluous riches'.[2] It makes distinctions where none exist, and judges, who are obliged to decide for one side or the other, are forced 'to proceed on the most frivolous reasons in the world', or 'to take half arguments for whole ones to terminate the affair one way or another'.[3] No law can escape these defects: 'Even the general laws of the universe, though planned by infinite wisdom, cannot exclude evil or inconvenience in every particular operation'.[4]

Nevertheless, Hume was equally anxious to point out that general rules and impartial laws are indispensable. Whatever their inconveniences, they are outweighed by the evil of allowing 'full discretionary powers' to any magistrate.[5] But as general rules have no intrinsic merit, wherever they

---

[1] *Enquiry*, p. 45 n.   [2] *Ibid.* p. 305.
[3] *Treatise*, p. 531.   [4] *Enquiry*, pp. 305–6.

[5] *Essays*, vol. I, p. 178. 'Now every particular act of justice is not beneficial to society, but the whole scheme or system: And it may not, perhaps, be any individual person, for whom we are concern'd, who receives benefit from justice, but the whole society alike.' (*Treatise of Human Nature*, p. 580).

are not essential, it is better to leave the natural variety of human life unhindered. One ought never to forget the necessity for general rules, while remembering that as they are after all artificial, it is best to limit their dominion. The style of Hume's thinking about moral and social questions is perhaps nowhere better illustrated than in his insistence on both the drawbacks of laws and the necessity for enduring them.

He insisted at least as much that following rules was not to be confused with morality. Whether a man is virtuous depends on his inner experience, not his outward actions, on why he decides, not what he decides: ' 'Tis evident, that when we praise any actions, we regard only the motives that produced them, and consider the actions as signs or indications of certain principles in the mind and temper. The external performance has no merit'.[1]

What the moral sentiment approves may vary enormously. And Hume shows us that we have tacitly recognized as much. We admire the Athenians, who permitted their best citizens to marry their sisters, murder their children, and forsake their wives in order to court young men. Brutus, whom we call a hero, conspired to assassinate his best friend. The French, commonly thought to be the most civilized of modern nations, praised adultery, took pride in their subjection to an absolute ruler, honoured men who killed to avenge lighthearted raillery, and applauded parents who sent off their children to be mistreated in holy jails. Indeed, wherever we look, if we judge by what is approved, morality seems to be a mass of contradictions: Fénelon's standards are not Homer's; the Koran is revered by Mohammedans for its sublime moral teachings but to Englishmen it seems to teach treachery, cruelty, and inhumanity; the luxuries valued in England and France for their benefits to art and industry are regarded in Switzerland as wanton and vicious.[2]

But in fact the disagreements are unimportant; they arise not from differences in morality, but in circumstances. The moral sentiment operating at different times and places dictates quite different conclusions. It is with morality as with rivers: 'The Rhine flows north, the Rhone south; yet both spring from the same mountain, and are also actuated, in their opposite directions, by the same principle of gravity. The different inclinations of the ground, on which they run cause all the difference of their courses'.[3] In almost everything he wrote, Hume emphasized that there was no reason for all men, even all creatures, to live in the same way:

What seems the most delicious food to one animal, appears loathsome to another; what affects the feeling of one with delight, procures uneasiness in another. This is confessedly the case with regard to all bodily senses: But if we examine the matter

[1] Hume, *Treatise*, p. 477.
[2] Cf. *Dialogue*, in *Essays*, vol. II, pp. 289–309.
[3] *Essays*, vol. II, p. 297.

more accurately, we shall find, that the same observation holds even where the mind concurs with the body, and mingles its sentiment with the exterior appetite.[1]

It is always difficult to understand that another man might enjoy what we are indifferent to. And depending on our inclinations, our temperament, mood, and circumstances, we ourselves will judge the same things differently: 'Man is a very variable being, and susceptible of many different opinions, principles, and rules of conduct. What may be true while he adheres to one way of thinking, will be found false, when he has embraced an opposite set of manners and opinions'.[2] We need neither admire nor condemn another man's preferences. It is foolish to stand staring at one another like the Capucin monk and the Ambassador from Tunisia who had never seen the like of each other before, and could not be persuaded that 'the turban of the African is just as good or bad a fashion as the cowl of the European'.[3]

Whereas other philosophers had taken great pains to draw the best or highest sort of man, to decide whether the practical man or the contemplative man was superior, Hume denied precedence to any sort. He said only that human happiness seems to consist of three ingredients, action, pleasure, and indolence, 'and tho' these ingredients ought to be mixed in different proportions, according to the particular disposition of the person, yet no one ingredient can be entirely wanting without destroying, in some measure, the relish of the whole composition'.[4] It seems to be true, he thought, that action and employment make men less vulnerable to the stings of fortune, moderate the affections, and provide entertaining thoughts. But not all men are fit for such pursuits; indeed men have very different aptitudes for happiness. They are governed by their native temper and constitution, over which 'general maxims have little influence'.[5] Those of great delicacy of passion have perhaps 'more lively enjoyments as well as more pungent sorrows than men of cool and sedate tempers', but they are more nearly at the mercy of fortune. Contentment can be courted best by developing a highly refined taste, which 'enlarges the sphere both of our happiness and misery, and makes us sensible to pains as well as pleasures, which escape the rest of mankind'.[6] But delicate taste is not as burdensome as sensitive passions, because, although we cannot control external circumstances, we can decide what books we shall read, what diversions we choose, what company we keep. Thus a man becomes more self-sufficient and less dependent on accident: 'When a man is possessed of that talent, he is more happy by what pleases his taste, than by what gratifies his appetites, and receives more enjoyment from a poem or a piece of reasoning than the most expensive luxury can afford'.[7] This was, however,

---

[1] *Ibid.* vol. I, p. 216.
[2] *Ibid.* p. 289.
[3] *Ibid.* vol. II, p. 344.
[4] *Ibid.* vol. I, p. 300.
[5] *Ibid.* p. 222.
[6] *Ibid.* p. 92.
[7] *Ibid.* p. 92.

merely homely advice to those seeking contentment. It did not impose anything on them in the name of virtue. There is no single set of virtuous choices. What matters with respect to virtue is only how well a man balances his passions, so that he never falls victim to one or the other, and never becomes obsessed by some enthusiasm that must torment him and his fellow men. 'If a man have a lively sense of honour and virtue, with moderate passions, his conduct will always be conformable to the rules of morality. . . .'[1]

Hume's only firm moral commandment was a negative one—that there is no *a priori* way of deciding for or against some kinds of gratification. He did not therefore share the attitude of most moralists to luxury, but insisted that it has a good as well as a bad sense. Whether it is vicious depends entirely on the circumstances: 'In general, it means great refinement in the gratification of the senses; and any degree of it may be innocent or blameable, according to the age or country, or condition of the person. The bounds between virtue and vice cannot here be exactly fixed more than in other moral subjects'.[2] Any form of asceticism outraged Hume. He could not see that any gratification, however sensual, could 'of itself be esteemed vicious'.[3] Only those whose minds are 'disordered by the frenzies of enthusiasm', he declared, could imagine anything vicious in enjoying meat, drink, or apparel. Such indulgences become vices only when they are 'pursued at the expense of some virtue'. But where they do not interfere with the needs of friends, family, 'and every proper object of generosity or compassion', they are perfectly 'innocent and have in every age been acknowledged by all moralists'.[4]

What this might mean in practice is admirably illustrated in Fielding's novels. In Fielding's mind, the philosophical problem about the relation between reason and passion, that impressed Hume, took the shape of a difference between Allworthy and Masters Thwackum and Square. Like Hume, though by a different route, Fielding became interested in the teachings of the divines; and his library was well stocked with theological treatises. He declared himself in the party of the rational Low Church which Clarke represented, but his pharisees, whether free thinkers or pious, all speak in Clarke's syllogisms. Not any particular belief, but simply the propensity to reduce every issue to a matter of good reasoning distinguished Fielding's villains. They are men who can justify anything. When Tom lies to protect Black George, Thwackum can demonstrate that he ought to be punished with texts from Solomon. And Square explains that although there was something resembling fortitude in the action, as fortitude was a virtue and falsehood a vice, they could not be united together, and since the pardoning of Tom would con-

---

[1] *Ibid.* p. 222.
[2] *Ibid.* p. 299.
[3] *Ibid.* p. 306.
[4] *Ibid.* p. 299.

found vice and virtue, his punishment should be even larger to keep the distinction clear. But within Allworthy's breast, there was something with which 'the invincible fidelity which that youth had preserved corresponded much better than it would have done with the religion of Thwackum or with the virtue of Square'.

It was those who 'utterly discarded all natural goodness of heart' that Fielding hunted. He had no use for the virtuous lady who despaired over the loss of a ribbon but ostentatiously affected contempt for things of the world; for the good man, who owed no one a shilling, entertained his neighbours lavishly, and gave charity to the poor, but had nothing beyond justice for suffering sinners; for anyone who shuffled with principles and combined the greatest primness of expression and regularity of behaviour with the least possible sacrifice of his own interests. He preferred Parson Adams, who lived with exuberance, absorbed vast quantities of beer, tobacco and gossip in Lady Booby's kitchen and settled disputes vigorously with a terrifying mutton fist.

Parson Adams perfectly represents the benevolent man Hume admired. He is a man of good heart whose virtue is instinctive, and the opposite of a formalist who compensates for his want of generous impulses by rigidly observing the law. That moral standards are not something apart from mankind, unyielding and impersonal, is the essence of Hume's moral teaching. It is the opposite of Kant's view that man's reason obliges him to set up rational goals that he must forever keep before himself and pursue. Hume preferred rather to have men work from day to day for immediate, limited objectives, guided by conscience and accumulated experience.

Whereas Hobbes and Locke, empiricists though they were, were still seeking a single, unifying vision of life, Hobbes in terms of will, Locke in terms of reason, Hume emphasized imagination, a receptive, passive power, not a creative, moulding power. What gives form to life, as Hume saw it, is not any ideal mould into which all men must fit, nor some distant overpowering end to be pursued throughout life, but felt principles that guide the manner of choosing without prescribing in advance what is to be chosen.

As an analysis of moral behaviour, Hume's account left something to be desired. He admitted the influence of reason in a number of ways but left its nature undefined. He described the calm passions as founded on a distant view or reflection. In his discussion of artificial virtues, the practical reason seems to determine the sense of moral obligation, and at times Hume even implied that unreasonable conduct may result not only from false judgements but from a failure to make certain judgements. He not only made it clear that judgements bring to our attention certain facts which affect our desires, but he distinguished sharply between mere liking and moral approval, which depended on being able to see a thing or action independently of its relation to one's own interests. Yet precisely how felt principles were related to judgements, or how from a judgement that a means is desirable we are moved to desire that means, whether practical judgements can prompt passions, or whether reason operating under the control of one passion had any power to control other passions, Hume did not say. He was after all less anxious to elaborate a complete psychology of moral behaviour than to liberate morality from the dominance of pure reason, and show up the deficiencies of both the puritanical antipathy to nature and the rationalist illusion that a code of moral conduct could be deduced from a few absolutely certain principles. In order to deny that moral action could be reduced to a set of impersonal universal rules, he tried to exclude reason as a source of moral conviction and to put feeling in its place, thus making it impossible for the moral reaction to be anything but concrete and personal.

Perhaps the best summary of the moral temper Hume was defending is to be found in his views on personal identity. The person, he said, is 'a bundle or collection of different perceptions which succeed one another with an inconceivable rapidity and are in a perpetual flux and movement'.[1] He described the mind not as an essence or permanent core, but as a 'kind of theatre, where several perceptions successively make their appearance; pass, re-pass, glide away, and mingle in an infinite variety of postures and situations. There is properly no simplicity in it at one time, nor identity in different; whatever natural propensity we may have to imagine that simplicity and identity'.[2] We like to think that there is a connecting principle, and we invent fictions like a soul or self or substance. But in fact there is nothing, Hume declared, beyond a succession of related sensations, an easy transition of ideas that produces the notion of personal identity, for we can have no notion of any existence or of any simple substance apart from particular perceptions.[3] Man cannot then escape doing what Spinoza described as 'willy-nilly things which he knows absolutely nothing about'. He cannot survey the whole of his life and decide which things he ought to desire most. Whereas Spinoza regarded men who remained at the mercy of circumstances as not properly free beings, both Hume's moral theory and his description of the self were designed to impress on men that they were necessarily at the mercy of circumstances and

---

[1] *Treatise*, p. 252. 'We may observe that what we call a *mind*, is nothing but a heap or collection of different perceptions, united together by certain relations, and suppos'd, though falsely, to be endowed with a perfect simplicity and identity'. (*Treatise*, p. 207).

[2] *Ibid.* p. 253.

[3] This is one of the most significant points of difference between Hume and Locke. For Locke, there remains a notion of a self, an inward substance, a substratum of ideas: 'Sensation convinces that there are solid extended substances and reflection that there are thinking ones'. (Bk. II, ch. xxiii, sec. 29, *Essay Concerning Human Understanding*). There are for Locke two facts of consciousness—a succession of ideas, and an idea of the self.

could never take account of all possible actions and their consequences. They could not hope to be perfectly self-conscious.

Hume recognized that his view of the self led him into inconsistency—he could not explain what it was that did the perceiving of distinct existences, nor could he see any other source of connection among them. But having raised the question, he was content to leave it unresolved. He had not constructed a perfect philosophical system, but he had succeeded in describing how the human person looked to a man of his moral temperament. Like everything else in the universe, it was not formed by an effort to make a unity or impose a pattern. It had no sharp outlines. It was an amorphous whole that came together out of assorted sensations, actions and ideas. It was a theatre, and a bundle.

CHAPTER VI

THE PHILOSOPHICAL ENTHUSIASM RENOUNCED

In the end, Hume's feeling for the complexity and uncertainty of everything human destroyed his faith in his own philosophy. All his painstaking inquiries led him to conclude that there were no grounds for being sure of anything, either in philosophy or common life. He had after all shown that the belief in truth was nothing more than experience and habit working on imagination to give some ideas more force than others. His philosophy seemed to require him to regard no opinion as more probable or likely than any others, and made it meaningless even to desire to know ultimate truth:[1] ' 'Tis impossible upon any system to defend either our understanding or senses; and we but expose them farther when we attempt to justify them in that manner'.[2]

This was in a way what Hume had set out to do. He had intended his philosophy to persuade men that there was no infallible truth about human behaviour and the world. Although men had to act in ordinary life as if they were certain, Hume wished them always to keep a reservation in their minds and hearts. In a sense, he was asking only for what truly reasonable men have always done, although there have never been many such men. For most people have to choose between doubting and believing, and can rarely understand the possibility of doing both at once. In fact, however, Hume had gone beyond characterizing the reasonable man. He had translated a state of mind, a disposition, into a philosophy.

As a result, he began to fancy himself 'in the most deplorable condition imaginable, inviron'd with the deepest darkness, and utterly depriv'd of the use of every member and faculty'. If once he left his study, to converse, dine, or play backgammon with his friends, when he returned, his speculations struck him as 'so cold, and strained, and ridiculous, that I cannot find it in my heart to enter into them any farther'.[3] The solitude which the pursuit of philosophy imposed upon him was nearly unbearable. He began to fancy himself some 'strange uncouth monster, who not being able to mingle and unite in society, has been expell'd all human commerce, and left utterly abandon'd and disconsolate'.[4] In short, philosophy, with all its 'subtleties and sophistries',[5] seemed hardly a reasonable occupation.

---

[1] *Ibid.* pp. 266–7.
[2] *Ibid.* p. 218.
[3] *Ibid.* p. 269.
[4] *Ibid.* p. 264.
[5] *Ibid.* p. 270.

Yet he could not give it up. While composing the *Treatise*, he was still wholly infatuated:

I cannot forbear having a curiosity to be acquainted with the principles of moral good and evil, the nature and foundation of government, and the cause of those several passions and inclinations which actuate and govern me. I am uneasy to think I approve of one object, and disapprove of another; call one thing beautiful and another deformed; decide concerning truth and falsehood, reason and folly, without knowing upon what principles I proceed.[1]

It was something after all, he decided, to have given a new turn to philosophical speculation and to have emphasized the importance of experience, of observing human nature, as against theorizing about it in the abstract. And he became reconciled to being more certain than his speculations warranted; he told himself that it was proper to 'yield to that propensity which inclines us to be positive and certain in particular points, according to the light in which we survey them in any particular instant'.[2] But before very long, he came to think differently.

The years after he returned with his *Treatise* from France, while he was marking time in London, in the worldly society of the coffee houses, at the Rainbow, or with other Scotsmen at the British in Cockspur Street, his doubts about philosophy grew upon him. The indifference with which his book had been greeted confirmed this mood. He began to suspect 'in a cool hour' that most of his reasonings would be 'more useful by furnishing Hints and exciting People's Curiosity than as containing any Principles that will augment the Stock of Knowledge that must pass to future Ages'.[3]

In the essays that he wrote during those years, he expressed odd sentiments for a philosopher. While discussing the sceptic, he took to task the philosopher who, having once laid hold of a favourite principle, extends it 'over the whole creation and reduces to it every phenomenon, though by the most violent and absurd reasoning'.[4] Philosophical devotion, he said, was like the enthusiasm of a poet, 'the transitory effect of high spirits',[5] as well as of leisure, genius, and study. The philosopher 'no sooner puts in his stake than he is transported'[6] by those passions he himself condemned. While he reasons about life, 'life is gone; and death, though *perhaps* they receive him differently, yet treats alike the fool and the philosopher'.[7] His great philosophical endeavour no longer appeared to be quite so amiable or important an under-

---

[1] *Ibid.* pp. 270–1.
[2] *Ibid.* p. 273.
[3] *Letters*, vol. I, p. 39.
[4] *Essays*, vol. I, p. 214.
[5] *Ibid.* vol. I, p. 220.
[6] *Ibid.* p. 228.
[7] *Ibid.* p. 213.

taking. Indeed, his devotion to philosophy looked much like any other fanaticism. He began to feel that by turning to philosophy, he had not after all exorcised the spirit of the Kirk.

There were good reasons for this feeling. After he became disenchanted with his Church, his character and outlook did not change at once. The young philosopher reflecting on the *Treatise* could easily be recognized as a son of the Kirk. The letter he wrote to Dr Cheyne shortly before leaving for France has a distinct air of piety about it, even of priggishness. He told the doctor how he had studied the 'books of morality' by Cicero, Seneca, and Plutarch, how smitten he had been with 'their beautiful representations of virtue and philosophy', and how he had tried to improve his temper and will, fortifying himself with 'reflections against death, and poverty, and shame, and pain, and all the other calamities of life'.[1] He observed his ailments minutely, dosed himself meticulously, and took to riding because it was good for his health. When he wrote from France to a school friend, he supplied statistics—Rheims has 40,000 inhabitants, 30 families keep coaches. And for his 'idle thoughts', he offered a pompous dissertation on the differences between French and English manners. He was no longer a fierce Presbyterian, but he was not at all like the favourite of Parisian salons that he later became.

Indeed the *Treatise* itself is very much the credo of a man who has found a faith to replace one he had lost. For the supreme philosopher, no less than a devout member of the Kirk, is obsessed, as Hume said, by a particular vision of truth, by the desire to demonstrate that it is the only truth, and that it can be reduced to some one or few principles. Even a philosopher who lets the reader see his perplexities is seduced by his own abstractions. Thus Hume, while he was composing his *Treatise* in La Flèche, was possessed by the philosophical enthusiasm. He proclaimed his to be the one real philosophy, a new revelation of the truth about human nature. His was a holy crusade against Satan, who had taken on the form of abstruse metaphysics, final causes, and substance, and his talisman against Satan was the 'experimental method'. While exposing the true nature of human reason, Hume was as relentless as a pious Presbyterian denouncing an adulteress. Although his *Treatise* is remarkable for his willingness to let loose ends hang without attempting to tie them up, he did try to make a whole creed. The urge to do so, hardly compatible with the moral message of his philosophy, was part of his puritan heritage, which had taught him the habit of encompassing all that he thought, felt, and did in one creed. Even when he set out to destroy this habit, he used its methods; and it was not until he had thoroughly disengaged himself from it, that he came to see his devotion to philosophy as the old enthusiasm in another form.

[1] *Letters*, vol. I, p. 14.

By the time he had recast the first book of the *Treatise of Human Nature*, eight years after it was published, he was ready to take leave of the philosophical mood altogether. He now modestly offered the world merely *Philosophical Essays Concerning Human Understanding*. The earlier work, 'which pretended to innovate in all the sublimest parts of philosophy', was, he declared, 'a mistake in conduct'. 'The positive air which prevails in that book, and which may be imputed to the ardour of youth, so much displeases me, that I have not the patience to review it'.[1] Hume, the man of moderation, was ready to take over. The Kirk's influence had really been undone, for he had come to accept the 'whimsical condition of mankind'.

The dispute between the dogmatists and the sceptics no longer seemed so profound. They disagreed really, he declared, only on the degrees of doubt and assurance that it is proper to indulge in:

No philosophical Dogmatist denies that there are difficulties both with regard to the senses and to all science; and that these difficulties are in a regular, logical method, absolutely insolvable. No sceptic denies that we lie under an absolute necessity, notwithstanding these difficulties, of thinking, and believing, and reasoning with regard to all kind of subjects, and even of frequently assenting with confidence and security.

The difference was only one of emphasis—'The Sceptic, from habit, caprice, or inclination insists most on difficulties; the Dogmatist, for like reasons, on the necessity'.[2] The problems of the sceptical philosopher were not unique to him, and what he taught was not all that extraordinary. He, too, was a dreamer, and when he awoke, he would be

the first to join in the laugh against himself, and to confess, that all his objections are mere amusement, and can have no other tendency than to show the whimsical condition of mankind, who must act and reason and believe; tho they are not able by their most diligent inquiry to satisfy themselves concerning the foundations of these operations, or to remove the objections which may be raised against them.[3]

Hume had learned to ridicule even his own pretensions. More and more, he came to hold the sentiments he expressed to a friend before leaving with General St Clair's expedition: 'I set out next week, as fully convinced as Seneca of the vanity of the world, and the insufficiency of riches to render us happy. I wish you had a little more of the philosophy of that great man, and I a little more of his riches'.[4]

In the *Enquiries*, he described philosophy not as the science of human nature, but as 'the reflections of common life methodized and corrected'.[5]

---

[1] *Ibid.* p. 187.
[2] *Dialogues*, p. 219 n.
[3] *Enquiry*, p. 160.
[4] *Letters*, vol. I, p. 101.
[5] *Enquiry*, p. 162.

Instead of displaying his confidence in the revolutionary truths that the experimental method would establish, he indulged in concessions to the 'easy philosophy', which any educated man could understand and read, and he disparaged 'the mere philosopher' who 'lives remote from communication with mankind and is wrapped up in principles and notions equally remote from their comprehension'. The most perfect character lay 'between the two extremes of the mere ignorant and the mere philosopher'.[1] He was critical of moralists who tried to reduce human phenomena to a single principle. His own aspirations had become much more humble—to enlarge the stock of knowledge 'on subjects of unspeakable importance'. He would be happy if, 'reasoning in this easy manner', he could undermine 'the foundations of an abstruse philosophy, which seems to have hitherto served only as a shelter to superstition, and a cover to absurdity and error'.[2]

Sceptical philosophy, he came to think, was not the whole truth, but in a more modest way useful. A small tincture of scepticism could soften the pride of men, by showing them that the few advantages they 'have attained over their fellows, are but inconsiderable, if compared with the universal perplexity and confusion, which is inherent in human nature'. Philosophy was not so much a revelation as a means of tempering the boldness of men. The greater part of mankind, who 'are apt to be affirmative and dogmatical in their opinions', and eager to escape from any hestitation or perplexity, tend to oppose one belief by violent affirmations to the contrary. But reflection on the infirmities of the human mind might 'inspire them with more modesty and reserve, and diminish their fond opinion of themselves, and their prejudice against antagonists.'[3]

Hume became less interested in metaphysical intricacies, and more anxious to press the moral of his philosophy, that the human condition allowed for no absolute purity, that men had better resign themselves to a measure of uncertainty and confusion, and a mixture of good and evil, true and false. All that he wrote after the *Treatise* was animated by the sentiment with which he ended his *History of Natural Religion:*

... good and ill are universally intermingled and confounded: happiness and misery, wisdom and folly, virtue and vice. Nothing is pure and entirely of a piece. All advantages are attended with disadvantages. An universal compensation prevails in all conditions of being and existence. And it is not possible for us, by our most chimerical wishes to form the idea of a station or situation altogether desirable. The draughts of life, according to the poet's fiction, are always mixed from the vessels of each hand of Jupiter: Or if any cup be presented altogether pure, it is drawn only, as the same poet tells us, from the left-handed vessel.

[1] *Ibid.* p. 8.
[2] *Ibid.* p. 16.
[3] *Ibid.* p. 161.

The more exquisite any good is, of which a small specimen is afforded to us, the sharper is the evil, allied to it; and few exceptions are found to this uniform law of nature. The most sprightly wit borders on madness, the highest effusions of joy produce the deepest melancholy, the most ravishing pleasures are attended with the most cruel lassitude and disgust, the most flattering hopes make way for the severest disappointments. And, in general, no course of life has such safety (for happiness is not to be dreamed of) as the temperate and moderate, which maintains as far as possible, a mediocrity, a kind of insensibility in everything.[1]

It was only natural that the author of such a statement should have ceased to write systematic treatises and turned his efforts to essays and history, so much better suited to saying that 'nothing is pure and entirely of a piece.'

Hume's retirement from philosophy strikes us as odd today partly because we no longer know the literary man, in the eighteenth century sense, who took all of knowledge for his province and felt no obligation to devote himself exclusively to one. But it is also because we know of no other philosopher who was both so completely enthralled by the philosophical mood and so able to free himself from it. Those who have called Hume a sceptical philosopher have described inaccurately something they sensed—his distrust of all systems, hence of philosophy. He was not sceptical about the existence of the external world, or about man's capacity for knowing something about it, but he was sceptical about man's ability to make all his notions coherent and consistent, or to perceive a permanent truth. While driven by his puritanical habits to make a systematic truth of his doubts, his essential purpose, though not yet evident to himself, showed through. It led his readers to feel, though they could not properly explain it, a destructive spirit. Perhaps there cannot be a philosophical system compatible with Hume's view of man—it may be no accident that systematic philosophy as we know it in the western world began with Plato, who first described man as a compound being. Any conception of man as one cannot perhaps be accounted for by philosophy, but only displayed in essays or history, aphorisms, poetry, or novels. In any case, Hume was the rare philosopher who remembered that there were more things in heaven and earth than philosophers dreamt of. He undermined philosophy with her own weapons, and then found even that not enough.

[1] *Essays*, vol. II, pp. 261–2.

CHAPTER VII

A MATTER OF DEGREE

WHAT Hume was really sceptical about is most obvious in his views on politics, with which he occupied himself in the years after he had recovered from his philosophical enthusiasm. He did not forget his philosophical interests, but let them take the more natural shape of a *History of Natural Religion*, a *Dialogue* on morals, and the *Dialogues on Natural Religion*. About politics, he never tried to construct a clearcut theory. There are a few sections on it in the *Treatise*, but essays and, even more, history were the appropriate vehicle. For Hume's politics follows no logical scheme and offers no formulas. Although it is consistent in itself and of a piece with the rest of his thought, its pattern lives only in particular judgements. One can discover it in the way one comes to know a man's character, by seeing him in many different moods and circumstances.

What is obvious at once is Hume's refusal to see political disputes as a struggle between good and evil. In the essays, where he commented on current issues, no side is presented as entirely wrong or wicked, and disagreement appears to be not only natural to the human condition, but, when properly conducted, useful. This was far from the prevailing tone in the political debates of his day, which circled around Walpole and Bolingbroke. Walpole, no longer at the height of his power, was being subjected to heated opposition of which Bolingbroke claimed to be the leader. Although both sides were really concerned with the details of party government and the developing cabinet system, each sought profound justification in Locke's principles.

The Whigs under Walpole paraded as the party that had defended the British constitution against Stuart usurpations. Charles I, they said, had deliberately violated the original contract between king and people; Charles II and James II had done the same, and attempted besides to impose Catholicism. William of Orange had restored the force of the original contract, and the Whigs were its devoted defenders. Bolingbroke argued that he and the Patriots were defending Old Whiggism against the party who, having overthrown the Stuarts, later deserted their principles. The liberty of the nation, he said, depended on preserving a perfect balance among the democratic, aristocratic, and monarchic elements of the constitution. But Walpole's policies had led the Crown to overwhelm the other parts of the government; its use of corruption had given it control of the standing army, appointments, elections, and administration; it had undermined the power of parliament and weakened the possibility of opposition. The true political division was no longer between Whig and Tory, but between the party of the court, Walpole's party, and the party of the country, who were protecting the British Constitution against a usurping minister. There was, Bolingbroke argued, room for only one party, of the true patriots, the party of the country. If a corrupt parliament refused to assert itself and demand the rights due to it, the people, led by the Patriots, should have recourse to their natural rights and restore the old constitution, or make a new one.

Hume refused in the first place to argue in these terms. The Whig doctrine of original contract annoyed him, not because it was used to justify the rebellion, but because it founded the right to rebel on an absurd notion—that government was first produced magically out of chaos by men who were at one moment capable of nothing but war and at another ready to agree on peace. Already in the *Treatise*, for all his philosophical enthusiasm, Hume had denied that there was any clear-cut origin of government, or any sharp division between a peaceful, social, and a warlike, pre-social state. Government, like all human things, had grown up over many years, somewhat haphazardly, as a consequence of a variety of events and influences. It was unlikely that men had ever lived as isolated individuals; they had always lived in families, and even if families warred with one another, within each there was peace. The association of families under a single government was brought about and has survived through a combination of force, habit, and rational assent. Tracing the origin of government to the consent of the people conflicted with experience which showed that consent counted relatively little in public affairs, especially when conditions were unsettled, as when a new government was being established, during 'the fury of revolutions, conquests, and public convulsions'.[1] Thus Hume deliberately blurred the distinction between governments founded by force and governments originating in a contract, a distinction that had become a cliché of political theory: 'The common situation of society is a medium amidst all these extremes'.[2]

Indeed no argument about government in terms of a right established in the distant past was acceptable. Even disputes about the claims of particular persons or families to the throne seemed utterly unreasonable to Hume. One had only to look into the history of various nations, to study 'their revolutions, conquests, increase, and diminution; the manner in which their particular governments are establish'd, and the successive right transmitted from one person to another', to realize that loyalty to some king or line of kings displayed more 'bigotry and superstition', than reason.[3] The sort of conservatism that made the past as such a standard was to Hume just a form of revolutionary enthusiasm: 'Those who form a pretended respect to anti-

[1] *Ibid.* vol. I, p. 450.
[2] *Enquiry*, p. 188.
[3] *Treatise*, p. 562.

79

quity, appeal at every turn to an original plan of the constitution, only cover their turbulent spirit and their private ambition under the appearance of venerable forms'.[1] It was anyway best not to inquire too meticulously into origins, for 'few governments will bear being examin'd so rigorously'.[2] More than anyone else the English should beware of appealing to the maxims of their ancestors or of remote, uncultivated ages. For the further back one goes, the more barbarous English governments grow: 'the only rule of government which is intelligible, or carries any authority with it, is the established practice of the age, and the maxims of administration, which are at that time prevalent and universally assented to'.[3]

It made no better sense to look for a clear rule by giving precedence either to liberty or to authority. Both inevitably have a part in every government. It is only a question of degree, of the proper proportions between them, and that question has to be answered anew each time it arises. Whatever may be said, the people always retain a right of resistance 'since 'tis impossible, even in the most despotic governments, to deprive them of it.' In a mixed government it must be so, since the whole point of a mixed government is to allow the parts of the constitution to resist one another. If the people are supposed to share in the power of the government, they must be able to defend their share: 'Those, therefore, who wou'd seem to respect our free government, and yet deny the right of resistance, have renounc'd all pretensions to common sense, and do not merit a serious answer'.[4]

In any case, opposing all attempts to alter a government is simply foolish because human institutions must constantly be mended. New laws must be passed to fit new circumstances; every law innovates somewhat; and it is not always easy to discover how much a law innovates, whether it merely reforms or makes a radical change. Sheer necessity makes it impossible to keep the balance between authority and liberty unchanged. Under every government, there must then be a 'perpetual intestine struggle, open or secret, between Authority and Liberty' in which neither can absolutely win.[5]

No exalted matter of principle is involved in disagreements over the propriety of resisting the established government. Everyone agrees that where obedience brings on public ruin, it is right to oppose the government with force. On the other hand, no one defends the use of violence in any but extreme circumstances. The disagreement then is only 'on the degree of necessity which can justify resistance and render it lawful and commendable'.[6] And there is no escaping such disagreement because men have different temperaments. Men of 'mild tempers, who love peace and order, and detest

[1] *History*, vol. II, p. 496.
[2] *Treatise*, p. 558.
[3] *History*, vol. II, p. 496.
[4] *Treatise*, p. 564.
[5] *Essays*, vol. I, p. 116.
[6] *Ibid.* p. 461.

sedition and civil wars', are more inclined to favour the established government, while 'men of bold and generous spirits, who are passionate lovers of
liberty, and think no evil comparable to subjection and slavery, more willingly risk revolutions'.[1] The only way out is to find the proper medium between
extremes, and that is difficult to do because the very words used in the discussion are bound to be ambiguous and confusing, and because good and
ill 'run so gradually into another as even to render our sentiments doubtful
and uncertain'.[2]

Hume refused to argue unequivocally, as Locke had, for a right of resistance. But he also declared Hobbes' politics 'fitted only to promote tyranny,
and his ethics to encourage licentiousness'.[3] No one but utopians of the
worst sort argued, as he believed Hobbes had, that anything short of absolute
government would sentence men to endless wars. They thought it possible to
stop the tides; they refused to accept the conditions of life which meant to
Hume accepting the inevitability of struggle, of unrest, of something less than
perfect peace. The Civil War, for instance, ought not to be blamed on the
failure of the king's power to maintain order, nor on anyone's weakness, but
on the unwillingness of both sides to recognize that neither liberty nor
authority could prevail absolutely, that they had to be incessantly adjusted.
Judicious men, Hume was sure, were always reluctant to consider a conflict
inevitable or to pronounce one side good and the other evil. If such men had
had the sway of their respective parties, the war might have been avoided. For,
'Even at present, many men of sense and knowledge are disposed to think
that the question with regard to the justice of the quarrel may be regarded as
very doubtful and ambiguous'.[4]

A desire to halt the natural movement of life or to escape the necessity of
solving problems over and over again never tempted Hume. He modestly
wished only to confine the struggle somewhat. To this end he hoped to persuade his fellows that perfect peace was impossible and struggle eternal. One
should try to define and limit the conditions of the struggle. But nothing
could be settled for all times.

On all other questions that divided his contemporaries, Hume's attitude
was similar. He considered them only in connection with particular circumstances; he credited neither side with a monopoly of truth or virtue; and he
reduced the disagreement to a matter of degree.

Even in a matter like corruption, there could be no verdict in the abstract.
Hume was no admirer of Newcastle's practices, and he condemned corruption as ignoble. Some forms of it, he declared, such as pensions or bribes,

[1] *Ibid.* pp. 133–4.
[2] *Ibid.* p. 121.
[3] *History*, vol. v, p. 459.
[4] *Ibid.* p. 410.

'cannot be too carefully guarded against, nor too vehemently decried, by everyone who has a regard for the virtue and liberty of a nation'.[1] Nevertheless, he insisted that the influence acquired by the monarchy from the disposal of places, honours, and preferments, from a form of corruption, was the only means available under the British constitution for checking the power of the Commons. The very nature of parliamentary liberty made it impossible to limit it by law; 'for who can foretell how frequently grievances may occur, or what part of the administration may be affected by them?' Yet it was natural that parliament should try to exercise its power to the fullest extent. Accident had provided, at different times, 'irregular checks to this privilege of Parliament', thus preserving 'in some tolerable degree, the dignity and authority of the crown'.[2] During the eighteenth century, this irregular check took the form of selling offices and distinctions to the king's supporters.

If members of parliament were entirely dependent on the Crown, or derived their property wholly from the king's gifts, they would be slavish. But an interest in obtaining offices from the Crown only made them reluctant to oppose the king hastily or violently. It was easy to attach invidious names to the Crown's use of its favours, 'but some degree and some kind of it are inseparable from the very nature of the constitution, and necessary to the preservation of our mixed government'.[3] Under other circumstances, like those of a century later, Hume might have found that such practices had grown too harmful, or too useless, to be tolerated. He had not argued for letting the Crown buy support at all times and places, but only for recognizing that under some circumstances it was more useful than harmful.

Problems that inspired others to enunciate noble principles were simply dismissed by Hume. He had nothing very grand to offer on the question: are members of parliament obliged to obey instructions from their constituents? Yet the question attracted much attention later in the century and moved both Burke and Bentham to make some of their most impressive statements. Hume, however, said that the issue was not really about 'obligation', but merely about how seriously instructions should be taken. For whatever anyone might prefer, in fact constituents would always exert some influence on their representatives. And there could be no general decision about how far it should extend. Its character would vary in each case, depending on whether the electors were rebellious and sophisticated like those of London or more like those of Totnes, and whether the issue was foreign affairs or taxes. In each case the question had to be answered differently. And as always, Hume underscored the difficulties of putting sufficiently refined answers into

[1] *Ibid.* vol. VI, p. 146.
[2] *Ibid.* p. 563, note 3A.
[3] *Essays*, vol. I, p. 121.

words—'But such is the nature of language that it is impossible for it to express distinctly these different degrees; and if men will carry on a controversy on this head, it may well happen that they differ in their language and yet agree in their sentiments; or differ in their sentiments and yet agree in their language'.[1]

It was only natural that Hume should have been denounced by both parties. He refused even to see much distinction between them. He separated what he called personal parties from real parties, and divided real parties into three kinds, parties of interest, of principle and of affection. But having made these distinctions, he proceeded to show that any actual party was not one of these: even where the parties were personal, that is, united by friendship and divided by animosity, a split in the government would not occur without some real differences of principle. Conversely, even in those factions founded on differences of principle, 'there is always observed a great deal of personal animosity and affection'.[2] The Court and Country parties were perhaps opposed on principle, as Bolingbroke alleged, but not altogether. Their disagreements on principles were, after all, very much heightened by differences of interest. Those who were receiving favours from the Crown were not anxious to antagonize their patron. The others were not perhaps indifferent to the benefits they were deprived of.

Anyway, the principles themselves were never perfectly clear. The Whigs, although they had loved liberty more than the Hanovers, had betrayed liberty, chiefly through 'ignorance, frailty, or the interests of their leaders'. The Tories had once loved both monarchy and Stuarts, but the latter more, and in order to 'depress' the Hanovers, they had embraced principles close to republicanism. The Tories 'have been so long obliged to talk in the republican style', Hume explained, 'that they seem to have made converts of themselves by their hypocrisy'.[3] Besides, no party could be all white or black because 'to tell the truth', men become associated with a particular party for a variety of reasons, of which they are not always aware, 'from example, from passion, from idleness'.[4]

And yet, although Hume disagreed with both sides, and found their quarrels somewhat tiresome, he did not wish to eliminate parties. They encouraged fierce animosities among men who should be assisting one another and weakened the government.[5] Still, they were inevitable and even beneficial. As the exact balance between the republican and monarchical part of the English constitution was delicate and uncertain, there were bound to be

[1] *Ibid.* p. 113, fn. 1.
[2] *Ibid.* p. 128.
[3] *Ibid.* p. 143.
[4] *Ibid.* p. 135 fn.
[5] *Ibid.* p. 127.

different opinions about what it ought to be. There was no way of settling the question forever because the power of the king varies with the character of the king, and what might suffice to counterbalance the Crown in one case might be too little or too much in another.[1] Most reasonable men might agree to preserve a mixed government, but they were bound to disagree on the particulars. Therefore, 'However the nation may fluctuate between them the parties themselves will always subsist, so long as we are governed by a limited monarchy.'[2] There were inconveniences to parties, but they had to be endured in order to enjoy the blessings of a mixed government.

Instead of endorsing Bolingbroke's call for a single party, Hume suggested that party conflicts might be softened. He even praised the growing interest in a coalition because it tended 'to prevent all unreasonable insult and triumph of the one party over the other, to encourage moderate opinions, to find the proper medium in all disputes, to persuade each that its antagonists may possibly be sometimes in the right, and to keep a balance in the praise and blame which we bestow on either side'.[3] But if a coalition had been likely, Hume might have been found on the other side, stirring up party differences. He looked for a moderation of disagreement, not for its disappearance. A balance between evils was the best one could hope for.

[1] *Ibid.* p. 121.
[2] *Ibid.* p. 134.
[3] *Ibid.* p. 464.

CHAPTER VIII

THE SCIENCE OF POLITICS

It is disconcerting then to find that on other questions Hume takes a stand, even lays down general rules, as if for all men and all times. But he is speaking with the authority of prudence, not science, as a man who has learned wisdom more than truth. And his notion of prudence implied that any attempt to settle political questions scientifically was chimerical and dangerous. The all-important but subtle difference between the rules of a prudent man and the laws of a social scientist never concerned Hume,[1] because the possibility of social science in the twentieth-century sense was not an issue in his day. He was thinking of other opponents.

He was arguing against three sorts of people: those, like Clarke or Hobbes, who tried to deduce rules for human conduct from what Hume regarded as metaphysical absurdities; those, like Berkeley, who denied a natural order because they affirmed man's direct dependence on God (the appearance of gravitation in some instances did not justify, Berkeley said, concluding it was universal, because God might act sometimes in one way, and sometimes in another, 'just as He sees convenient'); those, like Bolingbroke, who, in order to undo Walpole, argued that a government should stand or fall on the merits of the governors. Against the first, Hume was anxious to show that views about politics and morals must be drawn from what men are really like, not from imaginary pictures of human nature; against the second, he wished to establish the existence of a natural order that is safe from divine interference; the last he wished to persuade that violent abuse of a minister is both unnecessary and dangerous because the nature of a government depends mainly on constitutional arrangements and laws which should not be lightly challenged. He argued, therefore, for experimental knowledge, that is, for experience against 'hypotheses' in the sense of metaphysical or *a priori* principles. And he tried to show that experience revealed the persistence of certain regularities that did not conform to the abstract principles preferred by philosophers, and could not be destroyed by either human or divine will.

[1] He has as a result been credited, especially by Frederick Watkins (*Hume: Theory of Politics*) and also, somewhat, by J. A. Passmore (*Hume's Intentions*) with being an inchoate social scientist (although Passmore sees a conflict between Hume's interest in science and other aspects of his philosophy). This interpretation, however, misunderstands the nature of his generalizations and the purpose of his anti-metaphysical arguments. It reflects also the current tendency to regard prudence as a primitive form of science. If Hume has anything to tell the social scientist, it is rather to remind him of how delicate is the process of formulating and using general rules about human beings.

Yet when he spoke of an experimental science of man, Hume did not mean it strictly. In fact, he sharply distinguished between the 'experimental' and the 'scientific' methods, and regarded them as opposed to one another. In speaking of the correct method in morals, he says,

we can only expect success, by following the experimental method, and deducing general maxims from a comparison of particular instances. The other scientific method, where a general abstract principle is first established, and is afterwards branched out into a variety of inferences and conclusions, may be more perfect in itself, but suits less the imperfection of human nature, and is a common source of illusion and mistake in this as well as in other subjects.[1]

He was not proposing to 'explain' the causes of human phenomena, but only to gather correct observations of human nature and arrange them in some orderly fashion. Even in the *Treatise*, he intended not to explain why men thought as they did, but only to describe what occurred when they thought. For despite his admiration for Newton, and his adaptation of Newton's method for his psychology, Hume had a simpler and more consistent view of science.

Newton held that science was incomplete as long as it remained purely descriptive; science had to discover causes, which could, Newton suggested, be seen in phenomena. And he sometimes spoke about gravity as if it were a force implied by the phenomena observed, thus justifying those disciples who persisted in treating gravitation as an explanatory principle. Newton, of course, had no wish to deny, as Hume did, a human capacity for understanding the nature of things. This led him at other times to insist that the theory of gravitation was purely descriptive, so as to avoid any dangerous suggestion that God was unnecessary. But Hume was anxious to restrict science to description, for the opposite reason, because he wished to deny any link to God, which would be implied in a human power to discover causes in the strict sense. Science to Hume meant an orderly body of knowledge disclosing that things in fact behave in certain ways; why they do so must remain an eternal mystery because knowledge of causes, in the sense of seeing the inner nature from which effects flow, is beyond man. Nor was Hume any readier to accept scientific explanation in the later sense of a hypothesis or 'leap' beyond experience. He was content to forego explanation altogether and to stay with experience. He would confine himself to observing the appearance of effects in different circumstances:

For to me it seems evident, that the essence of the mind being equally unknown to us with that of external bodies, it must be equally impossible to form any notion of its powers and qualities otherwise than from careful and exact experiments, and the observation of those particular effects, which result from its different circumstances

[1] *Enquiry*, p. 174.

and situations. And tho' we must endeavour to render all our principles as universal as possible, by tracing up our experiments to the utmost, and explaining all effects from the simplest and fewest causes, 'tis still certain we cannot go beyond experience; and any hypothesis, that pretends to discover the ultimate original qualities of human nature, ought at first to be rejected as presumptuous and chimerical.[1]

In the *Treatise*, where Hume was arguing against the philosophers and theologians, he defended generalizations about human affairs in order to deny free will. He did this, however, not because he wished to advocate determinism, but because the belief in free will was part of the prevailing theological dogma that separated man from the natural world. To say that man had free will was, Hume thought, tantamount to declaring that human behaviour was uncaused, and that every common sense notion about human behaviour was unfounded. It implied that there was no regularity in human life, and knowledge about it had to be independent of experience. Against those who removed man from nature in this way, Hume pointed out that 'It is at least possible' that 'the contrariety of events may not proceed from any contingency in the cause, but from the secret operation of contrary causes'.[2] Moreover, he reminded them, politics, war, commerce, indeed everything in human life, depended on the belief in a certain regularity. The prince who imposed taxes expected his subjects to pay; the general who commanded an army counted on a certain courage; the master who ordered his dinner assumed his servants would obey. Anyone who lived in the ordinary way, whatever he said, believed in some regular conjunction of cause and effect in human affairs, as in all others.[3]

In the essays, Hume's defence of general rules arose out of his concern with immediate political issues. Even under the title 'That Politics may be Reduced to a Science', he was arguing against Bolingbroke. The essay opens with a pointed reference to the criticisms that were being made of Walpole: 'It is a question with several whether there be any essential difference between one form of government and another? and whether every form may not become good or bad, according as it is well or ill administered?' If it were true that all governments were alike, he continues, and that the differences arise only from

---

[1] *Treatise*, p. xxi.

[2] *Enquiry*, p. 87.

[3] *Treatise*, p. 405. Hume used the term 'necessity' when he meant 'cause', because he was denying that human actions were 'random'. That his emphasis on 'necessity' did not mean he was a determinist is evident from his treatment of particular questions. Moreover, he insisted that all causes of human character were moral causes, and denied the influence of physical causes even on national character. (Cf. 'Of National Character,' *Essays*, vol. I, p. 249). Today we are apt to forget that the doctrine of free will has often, and certainly in Hume's time, been interpreted as a denial of causality in human affairs. The objections raised by Hume, and by others since, have led the defenders of free will to suggest ways of reconciling it with causality.

'the conduct and character of the governors', all political disputes could end. It would follow that a bad minister must at once be replaced by a better one. But in fact that is not the case, as even the critics of the government had confessed in accusing it of subverting an excellent constitution. If the constitution were really excellent, Hume pointed out, it would provide a remedy against mal-administration. The state of affairs could not then be as bad as it was painted. If a minister proved to be as destructive as his critics alleged, then the constitution needed revising, and its subversion was quite desirable.

Hume agreed with Bolingbroke that the British constitution was admirable, but this meant, he pointed out, that it provided some check even on the worst rulers. Those who abused the government so violently ran the risk of undermining a good constitution. And so he concluded the essay, 'That Politics may be Reduced to a Science', with a plea for moderation:

Let us therefore try, if it be possible from the foregoing doctrine, to draw a lesson of moderation with regard to the parties into which our country is at present divided. . . . Those who either attack or defend a minister in such a government as ours, where the utmost liberty is allowed, always carry matters to an extreme, and exaggerate his merit or demerit with regard to the public. . . . Would men be moderate and consistent their claims might be admitted; at least might be examined. . . . I would only persuade men not to contend, as if they were fighting *pro aris & focis*, and change a good constitution into a bad one, by the violence of their factions.[1]

At the same time, Hume had a more general purpose, to convince his readers that it was important to frame laws carefully, that the welfare of a country depended on more than the virtue of its rulers. His contemporaries, being inclined to emphasize persons rather than institutions, were reluctant to use their critical powers on the laws. To encourage more attention to institutions, Hume emphasized that some kinds of laws and constitutions had more desirable effects than others, whatever the character of the ruler. So he declared it a universal maxim in politics, 'That an hereditary prince, a nobility without vassals, and a people voting by their representatives, form the best monarchy, aristocracy, and democracy'.[2] Quite regularly, also, free governments made their own citizens happier than any other, but in their colonies were more ruinous and oppressive than monarchies. Hume reviewed a number of different constitutions, and in each case pointed out the connection between the laws and the conditions of the country—Venice was stable, Athens and Rome were tumultuous, all because of the differences in their laws. It was therefore of first importance to devise laws carefully, for 'effects will always correspond to causes; and wise regulations in any commonwealth are the most valuable legacy that can be left to future ages'.[3]

[1] *Essays*, vol. I, pp. 107, 109.   [2] *Ibid.* p. 101.
[3] *Ibid.* p. 105.

By insisting that there were better and worse constitutions, Hume was not, however, supporting any particular form of government. Although he gave one essay the ambitious title of 'The Ideal Commonwealth', it contains merely some innocuous observations on an administrative machine, representative and republican in form. Nothing Hume says there could inspire revolutionaries. His models are not, he makes it plain, Plato or More: 'The idea . . . of a perfect and immortal commonwealth will always be found as chimerical as that of perfect and immortal man'.[1] It was amusing to see if one could sketch a better model than Harrington's. Perhaps it might even prove useful one day. But forms of government were not like engines, which could be tried out and discarded when found useless. Although one could imagine a republic superior to the British constitution, what guarantee was there that it would actually be established once the monarchy was dissolved? Any man able to destroy the existing constitution must have the power of an absolute monarch, and history had shown the folly of expecting such a man ever to relinquish his power:[2]

To tamper, therefore, in this affair, or try experiments merely upon the credit of supposed argument and philosophy, can never be the part of a wise magistrate, who will bear a reverence to what carries the marks of age; and though he may attempt some improvement for the public good, yet will he adjust his innovations as much as possible, to the ancient fabric, and preserve entire the chief pillars and supports of the constitution.[3]

Anyway, there was much less difference between forms of government than it seemed. In an absolute government, the monarch may be so confident of his power that he permits a number of liberties. In a republican government, where there is little distrust of the chief magistrate, he may be granted very broad discretionary powers, which become greater than those of an absolute ruler. So there may be 'a species of liberty in monarchies, and of arbitrary power in republics', which make the two governments strongly resemble each other. Similar results may thus be produced by governments seemingly very different. Besides, all governments tend to move toward the same equilibrium: 'In monarchical government there is a source of improvement, in popular government, a source of degeneracy which in time will bring these species of civil polity still nearer equality'.[4]

But even in their pure state, the drawbacks of the different governments, Hume felt, may easily be in balance. Free and absolute governments were, history showed, equally hospitable to art and science, but commerce tended to decay under absolute government because in a monarchy birth, title, and

<hr>

[1] *History*, vol. v, p. 460.
[2] *Essays*, vol. i, p. 126.
[3] *Ibid.* p. 480.
[4] *Ibid.* pp. 95, 162.

place are esteemed above industry and riches.[1] Neither one was clearly superior even on purely political grounds. The elaborate checks in a mixed government made it less vulnerable to abuse. On the other hand, as Hume reminded Montesquieu, mixed governments, like all complicated machines, are more subject to disturbances arising from the contrast and opposition of the parts.[2] In the case of the British monarchy, the danger from the monarchical part was more imminent, but the threat from the popular part was more terrible. While Hume was not in the least inclined to denigrate England's mixed government, under other circumstances he might equally well have accepted a republic. Glorious consequences were not to be expected from any form of government. All that really mattered was whether power was distributed among the various social orders and governing bodies so as to make an unchecked concentration of power impossible:

> When there offers, therefore, to our censure and examination, any plan of government, real or imaginary, where the power is distributed among several courts, and several orders of men, we should always consider the separate interest of each court, and each order; and if we find that, by the skilful division of power this interest must necessarily in its operation, concur with the public, we may pronounce that government to be wise and happy.[3]

This could be achieved, Hume was convinced, in more than one way and under different sorts of government.

In short, in politics as in morals, merit does not lie in outward conformity to a general standard. No one form of government is necessarily preferable. What counts is how well the dangers potential in every government, whatever its form, are guarded against. Just as in the good man the passions are in balance, so in the good government, the various powers and interests are arranged to prevent any one from becoming excessive. The moral is: do not seek an ideal polity, but seek to safeguard the existing form of government against the weaknesses inherent in it.

In the realm of economics, however, Hume approved of more substantive general observations. He made a number of definite recommendations, along the lines developed later by his friend, Adam Smith. Not the quantity of money, but men and commodities, he insisted, determined the strength of a community. Its economic condition benefited more from a love of refinements than from simple living. He denied that the lowness of the interest rate indicated that the country was flourishing; he opposed the notion that a balance of trade had to be maintained; he argued against a large public debt, and warned that it would go on growing because it enabled a minister to make

---

[1] *Ibid.* pp. 159–60.
[2] *Letters*, vol. I, p. 138.
[3] *Essays*, vol. I, p. 119.

a great figure without antagonizing the public. He defended free trade against protectionism, and condemned those who urged a 'narrow and malignant' politics for trying to destroy the productive powers of colonies.[1] He urged the magistrate in general to trust the encouragement of an art or profession to those who would benefit from it, opposed restrictions on the internal market, and cautioned against high taxes. Such general observations on economics were valid, Hume explained, because in that realm the public good 'depends on a concurrence of a multitude of causes'. Economics was very different from foreign affairs, for instance, where it was folly to make such general recommendations, because foreign politics depended 'on accidents and chance and the caprices of a few persons'.[2] It was equally inappropriate to try to account in general terms for phenomena like the rise of learning. But it was proper to speak generally on the rise and progress of commerce, because the desire for gain operated more uniformly than the desire for learning.[3] In economic affairs, the same causes operated in much the same way on a multitude, and not merely on odd individuals; they were gross and stubborn causes, not readily affected by private whim and fancy, and therefore amenable to generalization.

Yet even these 'general reasonings', or as Hume sometimes said, his reasonings on 'general subjects', were regarded by him simply as observations that comprehended a great number of individuals. They were merely 'general facts', or descriptions of 'the general course of things'. They were concerned with probabilities not necessities, and had the logical status of maxims (a term often used by Hume) not laws. They were statements about what is likely to happen because it usually happens, and although for practical purposes they might be assumed to hold always, they could not be proved. This meant that Hume was always conscious of the possibility that his general conclusions 'may fail in particular cases',[4] and exceptions invariably occurred to him. When he showed that the greatness of a state and the happiness of its subjects were 'inseparable with regard to commerce', although not in other respects, Adam Smith commended his observations. But Hume himself added: 'This maxim is true in general; though I cannot forbear thinking, that it may possibly admit of exceptions, and that we often establish it with too little reserve and limitation'.[5]

In fact, not even Hume's economic recommendations were totally abstract. They were drawn from and supported by historical examples, and directed against particular, current misconceptions. Besides, Hume took care to point

[1] *Ibid.* p. 348.
[2] *Ibid.* p. 288.
[3] *Ibid.* p. 176.
[4] *Ibid.* p. 288.
[5] *Ibid.* p. 289.

out how difficult it was to discover the right policy, and that what was beneficial one moment might easily be harmful the next:

Though a resolution should be formed by the legislature never to impose any tax which hurts commerce and discourages industry, it will be impossible for men, in subjects of such extreme delicacy, to reason so justly as never to be mistaken, or amidst difficulties so urgent, never to be seduced from their resolution. The continual fluctuations in commerce require continual alterations in the nature of taxes; which exposes the legislature every moment to the danger both of wilful and involuntary error. And any great blow given to trade, whether by injudicious taxes or by other accidents, throws the whole system of government into confusion.[1]

In other fields, while Hume was certain that: 'History informs us of nothing new or strange',[2] some of the uniformities he pointed out are hardly more than truisms: 'A man who at noon leaves his purse full of gold on the pavement at Charing Cross may as well expect that it will fly away like a feather as that he will find it untouched an hour after'.[3] No abstruse scientific truth is revealed by the observation that: 'Ambition, avarice, self-love, vanity, friendship, generosity, public spirit, these passions mixed in various degrees and distributed through society have been from the beginning of the world, and still are, the source of all the actions and enterprise which have ever been observed among mankind'.[4] Any man who had studied history and seen men might know that: 'Mankind are, in all ages, caught by the same baits: The same tricks played over and over again, still trepan them. The heights of popularity and patriotism are still the beaten road to power and tyranny; flattery to treachery; standing armies to arbitrary governments; and the glory of God to the temporal interest of the clergy'.[5]

Yet Hume was even more anxious to remind his readers that the basic uniformity did not rule out a great 'diversity of characters, prejudices, and opinions'.[6] He condemned unqualified laws such as those Hobbes laid down. One could not deny absolutely the wisdom of resistance because rulers, like other men, may suddenly become so transported by violent passions as to be unendurable: 'Our general knowledge of human nature, our observation of the past history of mankind, our experience of present times; all these causes must induce us to open the door to exceptions. . . .'[7] We can learn something about the sentiments and inclinations of the Greeks and Romans by studying the temper and actions of the French and English, but we must not simply transfer all observations from one nation to another.[8] Men can live together because they can to some degree predict each other's behaviour, but they also may differ unexpectedly not only from one another, but even from them-

[1] *Ibid.* p. 368.
[2] *Enquiry*, p. 83.
[3] *Ibid.* p. 91.
[4] *Ibid.* p. 83.
[5] *Essays*, vol. I, p. 372.
[6] *Enquiry*, p. 83.
[7] *Treatise*, p. 552.
[8] *Enquiry* p. 83.

selves at other moments. The characters of men are bound to be 'to a certain degree, inconstant and irregular.'[1] This is the only constant character of human nature.

General reflections, or philosophy, can therefore account only 'for a few of the greater and more sensible events; but must leave all the smaller and more delicate revolutions, as dependent on principles too fine and minute for her comprehension'.[2] After all, Hume was still firmly addicted to the distinction he had made in the *Treatise* between artificial rules and natural judgements. He was, if anything, even more conscious of the inadequacies of impersonal dicta. In everything but mathematics, a general truth ought never to be more than a guide. Men of sense, unlike the vulgar, can recognize a general fact without concluding that it covers every individual, or forgetting its tentative character. They remember that 'no prudent man, however sure of his principles, dares prophesy concerning any event, or foretell the remote consequences of things'.[3]

About the science of politics one had to be especially cautious, for its generalizations are very prone to mislead. It is true that, 'So great is the force of laws, and of particular forms of government, and so little dependence have they on the humours and tempers of men, that consequences almost as general and certain may sometimes be deduced from them, as any which mathematical sciences afford us'.[4] This must be pointed out especially when there arises an immoderate zeal for overthrowing a minister, or when law makers are indolent. At other times, however, it might be more pertinent to recall that 'the science of politics affords few rules, which may not sometimes be controlled by fortune and accident'.[5] For men are placed in the world like an audience in the theatre. They can see the show, and speculate on how the actors perform; but the 'true springs and causes of every event' remain entirely concealed.[6]

---

[1] *Ibid.* p. 88.
[2] *Treatise*, p. 438.
[3] *Essays*, vol. I, p. 122.
[4] *Ibid.* p. 99.
[5] *Ibid.* pp. 452–3.
[6] *Ibid.* vol. II, p. 316.

CHAPTER IX

THE PROPER POLITICAL DISPOSITION

HOWEVER reserved Hume was about the possibility of discovering, or the usefulness of acting on general laws in politics, and however impartial he was between political parties, he was altogether committed to a particular style of politics. Whenever he found instances of it, he was ready with praise; when it was absent, he could not be sympathetic. To what he called 'the vulgar', who judged by ordinary party criteria, he seemed inconsistent. For it was not any political principle or doctrine, but his preference for a disposition that gave form to his politics.

It is a disposition, first of all, that considers visions of another, better world, or indeed any desire to impose some ideal pattern of life or government on all men, irrelevant to politics. Hume was convinced that such attempts were futile; he would have agreed with Dr Johnson that there is nothing 'too little for so little a creature as man'. The ideals men pursued rarely, if ever, had the influence so often attributed to them. The shape of politics, like the shape of a personality, could not be imposed by a single act or idea; it was the consequence of many particular events, men, and circumstances, each in itself often insignificant or even petty. Men prated of glory and heavenly cities, but what in fact happened had little relation to such pronouncements.

This mundane attitude determined Hume's view of the Civil War. He chose to write about it because he thought it 'the most curious, interesting, and instructive part of our history'.[1] He did not see it as an occasion when the armies of God and Satan met. It was a time when certain ambiguities and contradictions in the Constitution could no longer be tolerated, and an unfortunate congruence of events and passions had produced a catastrophe instead of the peaceful adjustment that might have been. What had happened then, as always, was determined by a series of small decisions and actions in which, perhaps, ideals played a part. The king's failure to answer parliament's petition immediately, Buckingham's rivalry with Richelieu, the abilities of Pym, the king's personal deficiencies, the ambitions of Cromwell, were at least as important as the imposition of ship money and the fear of Catholicism.

Hume therefore blamed no man, not even any group of men: 'the truth is, there is so much reason to blame, and praise, alternately, king and parliament, that I am afraid the mixture of both in my composition being so equal, may

[1] *Letters*, vol. I, p. 168.

pass sometimes for an affectation, and not the result of judgement and evidence'.[1] He defended the Stuarts against those who charged them with having precipitated the Civil War, not because he considered their policies faultless, but because he believed that they had played a relatively small part in the whole picture. He could not cast the king as the villain of the piece because he saw even a king as one of many men harnessed together by circumstances, passions, personal and legal ties. This refusal to believe that any man or conviction can alone determine the course of history, and the tendency to reduce great historical events to so many ordinary occurrences and unforeseen consequences gave Hume's history its air of calm, which, as he lacked the novelist's talents, amounted almost to dullness. For what grandeur is there left in a decision of state when one has been told that the king threw himself on the bed and cried, 'I told you this before'? It is the same standpoint that led Tolstoy to describe Napoleon's pudgy hands and Montaigne to commend Tacitus for attending to private manners and tendencies rather than to 'universal battles and commotions'. It was a standpoint that made Hume's history admired for its civilized tone in the salons of Paris, and moved Victorians to condemn him, at the very least, for frivolity.

Insofar as the grand ideals men professed had any influence, they were always, Hume felt certain, pernicious. Worldly interests paraded as high-minded patriotism, religious enthusiasm masked crude ambition. Cromwell and Pym and their followers fared badly in Hume's hands because he was certain that: 'Equally full of fraud and ardour, these pious patriots talked perpetually of seeking the Lord, yet still pursued their own purposes'.[2] He attributed the calmer spirit under the later Stuarts to the fact that cant and hypocrisy had been detected, and pretensions to greater purity had become suspect. It was significant, he pointed out, that whereas the patriots of the '40's called themselves the 'godly party', the anti-papists of '79 were content to describe themselves as the 'good' and the 'honest' party, 'a sure prognostic that their measures were not to be so furious, nor their pretensions so exorbitant'.[3]

Yet the genuine or sincere idealist worried Hume even more than the spurious one. For once the cause became sacred, it could be made to sanctify anything. As ultimate benefits grow more inspiring, benevolence here and now seems less needful, and thus holy purposes beget a 'narrow contracted selfishness'.[4] Religious enthusiasm was a species of such idealism, and Hume blamed it for the worst evils of the Civil War. He considered the conduct of the parliamentary party laudable, he said, 'till they push'd their Advantages

[1] *Ibid.* p. 179.
[2] *History*, vol. v, p. 550 note D.
[3] *Ibid.* vol. vi, p. 159.
[4] *Dialogues*, p. 222.

95

so far as to excite a Civil War . . . and to this Extremity nothing carry'd them but their furious Zeal for Presbytery: a low Bigotry, with which they sully'd a noble Cause'.[1] Religious enthusiasm was a delusion that made men think they were 'above ordinances', and 'unlimited and unrestrained by any rules which govern inferior mortals'. It led astray even men as noted for 'temper, insinuation, address, and profound judgement' as Henry Vane, whose excellent understanding was so corrupted by such 'whimsies, mingling with pride, . . . that sometimes he thought himself the person deputed to reign on earth for a thousand years over the whole congregation of the faithful'.[2] It had converted the truly noble principles which had inspired the constitutional struggle into 'the most virulent poison'.[3] Destruction was ever the result of religious enthusiasm because 'popular rage . . . must be attended with the most pernicious consequences, when it arises from a principle which disclaims all control by human law, reason, or authority'.[4]

In later times, when idealism was no longer linked to God, and the danger was not of religious enthusiasm, Hume would have spoken against its modern equivalents—faith in the master race, the class struggle, progress, or equality. For they, too, have inspired men to 'disclaim all control by human law, reason, or authority' in the name of a higher glory. His remarks on a species of egalitarianism are a fair illustration of what he might have said in our time: In a perfect theocracy, governed by infinitely intelligent beings, distribution of honours and goods according to virtue might perhaps work. But if ordinary men try as much, 'the total dissolution of society must be the immediate consequence'. For the 'uncertainty of merit' and the 'self-conceit' of each man would make it impossible to establish any 'determinate rule of conduct'. It is all very well for fanatics to suppose 'that dominion was founded on grace, and that saints alone inherit the earth'; reasonable men, and the civil magistrate, put such 'sublime theorists on the same footing with common robbers', and maintain firmly that 'a rule, which, in speculation may seem the most advantageous to society, may yet be found, in practice totally pernicious and destructive'.[5]

Whatever its shape or form, glory had no place in Hume's politics. He had little tolerance for grandiose schemes—the old Romans were, he declared, 'the general robbers of the world, whose ambition and avarice made desolate the earth, and reduced opulent nations to want and beggary'.[6] What struck him about Pericles was not what he did for the glory of Athens but that when

[1] *Letters*, vol. I, p. 222.
[2] *History*, vol. V, pp. 431–2.
[3] *Ibid.* p. 108.
[4] *Essays*, vol. I, p. 469.
[5] *Enquiry*, p. 193.
[6] *Essays*, vol. II, p. 357.

he lay dying, and his friends began enumerating 'his great qualities and successes, his conquests and victories, and his nine trophies erected over the enemies of the republic', the dying hero suddenly interrupted them to say, 'You forget the most eminent of my praises, while you dwell so much on those vulgar advantages in which fortune had a principal share. You have not observed that no citizen has ever yet worne mourning on my account'.[1] And in the *Treatise*, Hume concluded his discussion of pride and courage with an admonition against heroism. Of course, in a way, one had to admire the hero's dazzling character, and so mankind generally sang his praises. But 'men of cool reflexion', who think not only of the hero himself, more readily disparage heroism. They remember: 'The infinite confusions and disorder which it has caused in the world, . . . the subversion of empires, the devastation of provinces, the sack of cities . . .'.[2] Heroism destroys peace and liberty, and is therefore a plague.

Any government that attempts to reform its subjects is no less dangerous. The function of government is not to change men. That is better left to time and accident:

Sovereigns must take mankind as they find them, and cannot pretend to introduce any violent change in their principles and ways of thinking. A long course of time with a variety of accidents and circumstances, are requisite to produce those great revolutions, which so much diversify the face of human affairs. And the less natural any set of principles are, which support a particular society, the more difficulty will a legislator meet with in raising and cultivating them. It is his best policy to comply with the common bent of mankind and give it all the improvements of which it is susceptible.[3]

Radical or violent action rarely brings the improvement it promises. Although tyrannicide was much approved of in ancient times because it freed mankind from 'many of these monsters, and seemed to keep the others in awe, whom the sword or poniard could not reach', experience has taught modern men that such means do not usually achieve their ends. On the same grounds, Hume opposed war against France, whatever her ambitions. The best protection against the danger that the French might establish a universal monarchy was to maintain steady resistance through a balance of power, and to hope that 'the natural revolutions of human affairs, together with unforeseen events and accidents, may guard us against universal monarchy and preserve the world from so great an evil'.[4]

Nothing like a belief in providence lay behind Hume's conservatism. He was only certain that crusades brought destruction and evil, and that less

---

[1] *Enquiry*, p. 177.
[2] *Treatise*, pp. 600–01.
[3] *Essays*, vol. I, p. 292.
[4] *Ibid.* p. 353 fn.

drastic, but firm resistance was often aided in unforeseen ways by the 'natural revolution of human affairs', that in general 'human life is more governed by fortune than by reason'.[1] Even the excellence of the British constitution, he often pointed out, was mainly the work of fortune; history teaches us what a 'great mixture of accident . . . commonly concurs with a small ingredient of wisdom and foresight in erecting the complicated fabric of the most perfect government'.[2] It was not out of faith in a beneficent natural order, but because he was sceptical of any human attempt to see and control all, that Hume trusted to chance more than radical remedies. His affinity was not with Burke, but with Montaigne, who said: 'It seems that our opinions and deliberations depend quite as much upon fortune, and that it involves our judgement also in its confusion and uncertainty.'[3]

Since men could so much more readily do damage than good, it was best in politics to aim too low rather than too high. It was safest to assume that every man was thoroughly selfish although in fact many men were not:

Political writers have established it as a maxim that in contriving any system of government, and fixing the several checks and controuls of the constitution, every man ought to be supposed a knave, and to have no other end in all his actions, than private interests. . . . Without this, say they, we shall . . . find, in the end, that we have no security for our liberties or possessions, except the good-will of our rulers; that is, we shall have no security at all.[4]

Insofar as the magistrate set out to make men better than they are, he must not try to substitute a virtue for every vice. He must not hope to free men from every defect—'this concerns not the magistrate who aims only at possibilities. . . .' Very often a vice could be cured effectively and safely only by being replaced with another vice, and in that case, the magistrate had to decide only which was least pernicious to society. Hume accordingly argued that luxury, even when it may become excessive and give rise to many ills, should be tolerated because it was preferable to the idleness that would commonly replace it.[5]

The man of the proper political disposition would confine government to profane tasks. He would expect it to mediate collisions of interest, to enforce and sometimes impose agreements between parties, either to keep out of each other's way or to engage in some common endeavour, and generally to protect members of society while they engage in their private activities. Where it had to interfere was fairly obvious. The government need not intervene between two neighbours who wish to drain a meadow which they possess in

[1] *Ibid.* p. 231.
[2] *History*, vol. II, p. 497.
[3] Montaigne, *Essais*, Bk. I, ch. 47, p. 323.
[4] Hume, *Essays*, vol. I, pp. 118–19.
[5] *Ibid.* p. 309.

common, because each will know the other's mind, and both must perceive that if either fails in his part, the whole project will collapse. But it is different where large numbers are involved. A thousand persons could not agree in any such action—'it being difficult for them to concert so complicated a design, and still more difficult for them to execute it; while each seeks a pretext to free himself of the trouble and expense, and woul'd lay the whole burden on others. Political society easily remedies both these inconveniences'.[1] In addition, the government might be expected to look after morals in the most rudimentary sense, by encouraging men to be honest and industrious. The magistrate must subdue anti-social inclinations and stimulate industry; and he must check extravagance, corruption, or inefficiency in government. But these are all mundane duties.

An ideal minister, by Hume's standards, would not then be behaving amiss if, like Plantagenet Palliser, he 'passed his days and nights in thinking how he may take a halfpenny in the pound off the taxes of the people without robbing the revenue'. He would generally support whatever furthered tranquillity in society. What that might be, one could not say in general. He might even favour an established religion, but only because without it the country would be plagued by a too diligent clergy—'each ghostly practitioner, in order to render himself more precious and sacred in the eyes of his retainers will inspire them with the most violent abhorrence of all other sects. . . . Customers will be drawn to each conventicle by new industry and address in practising on the passions and credulity of the populace'.[2] By giving the clergy fixed salaries, a government might make exertion superfluous and thus bribe them into indolence.

However it goes about it, government must preserve liberty and peace. The two were not really distinct for Hume, because he equated liberty with freedom from arbitrary interference. Liberty was wholly dependent on law and could never be reconciled with 'illegal violence'. On this point Hume allowed no qualifications—a people governed by a tyrant without law 'are slaves in the full and proper sense of the word; and it is impossible they can ever aspire to any refinements of taste or reason. They dare not so much as pretend to enjoy the necessaries of life in plenty or security'.[3] The extent of a ruler's power mattered far less than its legal status. For a power granted by law could never be so dangerous to liberty as a lesser authority acquired through violence.[4]

In fact, the proper political disposition is summed up for Hume in the belief that ruling is above all the activity of enforcing stable rules of conduct.

[1] *Treatise*, p. 538.
[2] *History*, vol. III, pp. 26 f.
[3] *Essays*, vol. I, p. 179.
[4] *Ibid.* pp. 379–80.

The true mark of public spirit is not an urge to pursue exalted ends or to make men better, but a devotion to the rule of law. This is prescribed neither by the divine right of kings nor by any contract between ruler and ruled, but by a simple and universal interest in preserving internal peace. Images of mob disorders and the tyranny they brought on were always before Hume's eyes. He never forgot the unruly Roman populace and how it was used to support a succession of military tyrants. The lessons of Roman history were reinforced by the record of the Civil War in England. And they were brought to life by the chronic mob disorders in his own time: when Walpole proposed his Excise Tax, the noise of the mob outside parliament nearly drowned the debate indoors; there were violent disturbances when French actors were employed at the Haymarket Theatre, when the malt tax was imposed in Scotland, when cheap Irish labour was imported, when gin was taxed; a mob of two thousand stoned to death a witness for an unpopular cause; a mob rioted at the execution of a well-known smuggler, and when the queen pardoned the commander of the guard for firing on the rioters, the mob stormed the prison, released the prisoners, and lynched the commander. Such disdain of the rule of law may gratify the passions of arrogant men, but only, Hume was convinced, at the cost of exposing society to arbitrary rule and chaos. Liberty may all too easily be destroyed in the name of liberty.

Still, one could not categorically rule out revolution. The grounds on which Hume would judge whether revolution was justified were far more complicated and difficult than those defended or opposed by Whigs and Tories. They provided no easy rule of thumb, yet they were perfectly clear:

But tho', on some occasions, it may be justifiable, both in sound politics and morality, to resist supreme power, 'tis certain, that in the ordinary course of affairs nothing can be more pernicious and criminal; and that besides the convulsions, which always attend revolutions, such a practice tends directly to the subversion of all government, and the causing an universal anarchy and confusion among mankind. As numerous and civiliz'd societies cannot subsist without government, so government is entirely useless without an exact obedience. We ought always to weigh the advantages, which we reap from authority against the disadvantages; and by this means we shall become more scrupulous of putting in practice the doctrine of resistance. The common rule requires submission; and 'tis only in cases of grievous tyranny and oppression, that the exception can take place.[1]

The burden of proof was on those demanding a change—' 'tis certain that the concurrence of all those titles, original contract, long possession, present possession, succession, and positive laws, forms the strongest title to sovereignty, and is justly regarded as sacred and inviolable'. A break was unavoidable only when custom itself became confused, when the titles to power became so 'mingled and opposed in different degrees' that clear possession

[1] *Treatise*, pp. 553–4.

could be given to none. Then the problem became 'less capable of solution from the arguments of lawyers and philosophers, than from the swords of the soldiery'.[1]

Whether he found a disposition to observe custom determined many of Hume's judgements in the history. He regarded the king's prerogative as a species of arbitrary power and was not in the least disposed to defend it as such. But he excused the first two Stuart kings because he believed there were good precedents for the powers they claimed, and that they had not therefore violated the established legal order. If the limitations on prerogative had been fixed and certain, the character of Charles I was such, Hume believed, that he would have observed them. But in fact there were many precedents for arbitrariness, while, at the same time, the people were wanting more liberty.[2] As a result, the 'throne perpetually tottered'[3] and the smallest mistake was bound to be fatal; even after the event, it was difficult to say what should have been done. A king deficient in political prudence had not a chance. There were many parallel instances in history. Much the same sort of circumstances had brought down Edward II. His father, despite his violent invasions of liberty, had met with few difficulties. But the son lacked the skill to manage under a constitution that depended mainly on the king's personal character. When custom was uncertain the king ought not to be held responsible for all the misfortunes that followed. Kings should be judged only on their willingness to be ruled by custom:

it is a shameful delusion in modern historians, to imagine that all the ancient princes who were unfortunate in their government, were also tyrannical in their conduct, and that the seditions of the people always proceeded from some invasion of their privileges by the monarch . . . always to throw, without distinction, the blame of all disorders upon the sovereign, would introduce a fatal error in politics, and serve as a perpetual apology for treason and rebellion; as if the turbulence of the great, and madness of the people, were not equally with the tyranny of princes, evils incident to human society, and no less carefully to be guarded against in every well-regulated constitution.[4]

For Charles II, however, Hume had no sympathy. The monarchy, when he ascended the throne, was definitely limited, and the prerogatives he and his successor claimed were well beyond the law as it had by then been defined. But the docile parliament of James II, with its 'violent aversion' to opposition which kept it for so long from displaying 'some small remains of English spirit and generosity',[5] was also censured. Indeed Hume generally condemned any

[1] *Ibid.* p. 562.
[2] *Letters*, vol. I, p. 264.
[3] *History*, vol. IV, p. 563, note 3A.
[4] *Ibid.* vol. II, pp. 111–12.
[5] *Ibid.* vol. VI, pp. 260–1.

disposition in the people to resign their inherited privileges. It was the people's duty, as well as the king's, to protect the established order, or in other words, to use every legal means available to them to resist a king's subversion of the constitution. Respect for custom required an active readiness to use custom in defence of custom.

In the same spirit, Hume criticized the Commonwealth men for disregarding the established laws and procedures in order to gain their ends. He located the beginning of the despotism that they imposed in the trial of Strafford, when the Commons discovered a species of treason 'entirely new and unknown to the laws' and invented 'a kind of accumulated or constructive evidence', by which an unguarded word or action, 'assisted by the malevolent fancy of the accuser, and tortured by doubtful constructions is transmuted into the deepest guilt'. Such procedures soon left the kingdom in a condition where, as Strafford had predicted, 'no man shall know by what rule to govern his words and actions'.[1] For liberty existed only when no one could be accused of a crime that the law had not defined, or sentenced without due process.

A true lover of liberty was ready to endure injustice under law rather than try to set things right by destroying the laws. It did not matter so much whether the established limits and forms of authority were the wisest possible; if they were not outrageous it was much more important that they remained stable. For they became established only after a long and painful process, and their overthrow put liberty in the greatest danger. The rule of law must never be lightly cast away for someone's presumptuous or dishonest conviction that he had found a better route to an obscure destination. Liberty that deserved the name was never exclusive or illiberal. It gave no licence to some haughty individual or potent group, but belonged impartially to all citizens.

To keep men from wildly pursuing distant glories, Hume wished to bind them not only by law and authority, but by all the gross and narrow ties of custom, private and local attachments. He considered a respect for the traditional forms and methods of conducting business in the smallest court or office part of the rule of law, because every governmental action involved an exercise of power, and law could define the limits of power only generally. An exact regulation of power had to rest on example and precedent.

For the same reason, Hume considered integrity the basic political virtue. Nowhere else, except in Montaigne, does one find such an emphasis on integrity combined with so worldly an appreciation of political subtlety. Like all virtues, the integrity Hume valued is a quality of character, not of particular acts. It means a basic disposition to remain true to standards and pledges regardless of immediate advantage, and an antipathy to deceit. It is founded on a disdain of force and an unqualified preference for humanity and modera-

---

[1] *Ibid.* vol. v, pp. 36, 38.

tion in dealing with men. For Hume regarded every use of deceit and treachery as a use of force, and obedience induced by force as a most detestable last resort, unavoidable among barbarians, but intolerable among civilized men. Respect for integrity was the mark of civilization. Deceit was therefore an 'infamous art'; treachery like cruelty was one of the most 'pernicious and most odious of vices', and 'peculiar to uncivilized ages';[1] and Machiavelli's reasonings were 'extremely defective'. There 'scarcely is any maxim in his *Prince*', which has not been 'entirely refuted' by experience, Hume declared. Machiavelli's errors were perhaps due to his having studied only the 'furious and tyrannical governments of ancient times', or the 'little disorderly principalities of Italy'.[2] Even so, Hume pointed out, when Machiavelli came to write history, he was forced to acknowledge the superiority of virtue in politics; then, as all historians did, he denied that poisoning, assassination, and perjury were 'lawful arts of power', and showed a 'keen indignation against vice'.[3] Those who were really skilled in the arts of government repudiated force. They recognized the advantages of 'mildness and moderation', of humane maxims over severity that forces rebellion and makes compromise impossible. In a civilized age 'the tempers of men are softened', and they have no fear of being honest and humane.[4]

Whether a king had integrity and kept faith with his subjects was as crucial for Hume as whether he was loyal to custom. The two qualities were indeed but different aspects of the same general disposition to respect the rule of law, and to refrain from using force. It was important for Hume that Charles I had not only sincerely believed in the legitimacy of his claims, but had made no secret of his belief. His 'good faith' was beyond question. Even in the midst of great difficulties, his professions continued to be sincere. He could never be persuaded to make concessions that he thought 'he could not in conscience maintain'. That his violations of the petition of right were due to his conception of royal prerogative[5] was the more plausible explanation of his conduct, Hume insisted, because he was free from insincerity in his private life—'he was reserved, distant, stately; cold in his address, plain in his discourse, inflexible in his principles; wide of the carressing insinuating manners of his son, or the professing, talkative humour of his father'. He lacked the qualities that his circumstances demanded of a king, but he was 'candid, sincere, upright, as much as any man whom we meet with in history'.[6]

Unlike him, the two later Stuarts had hypocritically conspired against their subjects' wishes. Charles II 'pawned his regal word'. He imposed on the people of England when, in spite of their obviously strong feelings against France and for Holland, he allied England to the former and waged war

---

[1] *Essays*, vol. I, p. 307.
[2] *Ibid.* p. 156.
[3] *Ibid.* vol. II, p. 391.
[4] *Ibid.* vol. I, p. 303.
[5] *History*, vol. V, p. 887.
[6] *Ibid.* p. 557, note O.

against the latter. He was, Hume declared, a 'dexterous dissembler', who lacked the 'integrity and strict principles of his father'.[1] Had he, at the very least, remained loyal to the cause of France, Hume would have found him somewhat less contemptible even if more arbitrary and inept. James II, although he had a certain courage in his convictions, violated even explicit pledges. 'Almost the whole of this short regime', Hume says, 'consists of attempts, always imprudent, often illegal, sometimes both, against whatever was most loved and revered by the nation'.[2] When James II declared that he would observe the laws, the people trusted him because they believed in the word of a king. But in the first exercise of authority, the king 'showed that either he was not sincere in his professions of attachment to the laws, or that he had entertained so lofty an idea of his own legal power, that even his utmost sincerity would tend very little to secure the liberties of the people'. He had, however, every reason to know the limits of his power. His open adherence to Catholicism violated his pledge to protect the religion of his people while his covert attempts to strengthen Catholicism lost by their deceit what they gained in tact. If James II had openly tried to win his subjects to absolute monarchy, he might have done more harm, but by Hume's standards, he would have been less ignoble. It added to his infamy in Hume's eyes that he universally passed for a man of great sincerity and great honour.[3]

Nevertheless, the Stuarts had threatened liberty less than Elizabeth had. Hume admired her skill and her public policy, but thought her a dangerous monarch because she had the personal force to make her subjects welcome her power. The much less attractive Stuarts, who used more direct methods, made the public recognize the true character of those arbitrary measures that Elizabeth had imposed with ease. Rulers who never outraged their subjects but seduced them into foregoing their liberties did not bring on revolutions, but they more easily destroyed liberty.

A like danger attended the politician who could dissimulate successfully. Hume's greatest fear was not of a man like Buckingham, the favourite whom James I raised from obscurity to a dukedom, who was imprudent, 'headstrong in his passions', and 'utterly destitute of every talent of a minister', but also incapable of dissimulation.[4] Buckingham's sort might mislead men like James I, but generally his defects soon became obvious. Far more sinister was Shaftesbury, whose mastery of the Machiavellian arts earned him a place very close to Cromwell in Hume's gallery of scoundrels. A man who changed party twice, who was so skilful that he could always maintain 'the character of never betraying those friends whom he deserted',[5]

[1] *Ibid.* vol. vi, p. 159.
[2] *Ibid.* p. 274.
[3] *Ibid.* pp. 240–1.
[4] *Ibid.* vol. iv, p. 334.
[5] *Ibid.* vol. vi, pp. 8–9.

who soon worked his way into the leadership of his new party, was to be feared as well as despised. Hume attributed Shaftesbury's success to the fact that minds had been debauched, and the sense of honour and decorum in public conduct had been destroyed by the many factions and sudden revolutions.

Parties were no more excused than men from observing truth and honour. The Whigs were censured for having often paid 'more regard to political than to moral considerations', even while parading their principles. Because they were obliged to court the populace, Hume explained, they complied with popular rage and fear by 'propagating calumnies, and by promoting violence which served to infatuate as well as corrupt that people to whom they made a tender of liberty and justice'. The arts of demagogues were, he granted, often useful in a free constitution, but 'men of probity and honour' shunned them.[1]

There was no invitation to martyrdom in Hume's insistence that kings be candid. He coupled the 'most settled maxims of honour and policy'[2] because he was certain that once a man came to be distrusted, he lost the foundation of his power.[3] Policy alone required that Charles II should have taken every means to regain his subjects' confidence which 'by his rash conduct' he had betrayed. He should have put himself entirely at the mercy of the parliament to demonstrate his good faith, for the parliament had given him no cause for suspicion, while the king's past conduct had excited 'very reasonable jealousies'.[4]

The same principles applied also to foreign relations. Hume thought England had neglected both interest and honour when she deserted the Dutch. Sir William Temple had been one of England's most successful diplomats because he had an unblemished record for integrity.[5] But Grafton was no more brilliant than honest and he satisfied no one when he assured the French invaders of Corsica that England would not intervene, and then, to appease English public opinion, sent the Corsicans several thousand obsolete muskets that arrived after the French invaded.

Since morality, as Hume understood it, was not ordained by heaven to make men miserable on earth, but a means to human happiness, there was no conflict between morality and expediency, only between the dictates of violent

---

[1] *Ibid.* p. 331.

[2] *Ibid.* p. 113.

[3] Montaigne spoke out just as emphatically against considering deception part of worldliness: 'Our intelligence being conducted solely by the way of the word, he who falsifies that betrays all society.... If it deceives us, it severs all our intercourse and dissolves all the ties of our government'. (*Essais*, Bk. II, ch. 18, pp. 752-3).

[4] *Ibid.* p. 81.

[5] *Ibid.* p. 15.

and of calm passions. Puritans and enthusiasts were invariably torn between what they described as public causes and private honour. But that was only because their private honour was not fit for humans, and their public causes were divorced from the wellbeing of men here and now. For those who sought only peace and liberty, and did not pretend to be pure spirits rather than fallible humans, integrity was also expedient. When political ends are modest and mundane, politics may be moral. It is only when the end is glory that political violations of moral rules are granted dispensations. Some great movement, an overwhelming purpose, or a noble principle makes everything else shrink out of sight. Before Pericles' vision of Athens, it is profane to feel for the sorrows of bereaved mothers. Then only the cause counts, and what matters is a man's valiance in defence of it, not his character. But for Hume there was no cause other than peace and liberty, which, he believed, were protected best by truth and honour. Integrity was expedient and there was no distinction between political and private morals.[1]

Hume was expressing the creed of the worldly eighteenth century, which, for all its sophistication, or rather because of it, placed its faith in honour. If politicians were in some ways corrupt, in others they were exceedingly correct, and they never claimed a right to be immoral.[2] Even the cynical Horace Walpole attributed Sandwich's failure to his intrigues: 'He loved subtlety and tricks and indirect paths, qualities repugnant to genious'. The divorce of politics from morality was more characteristic of the Civil War, and of the nineteenth century, when men looked for glory.

The integrity that Hume admired is not, however, for innocents. It does not give absolution from worldly wisdom. It requires discretion:

The quality, the most necessary for the execution of any useful enterprise, is DISCRETION; by which we carry on a safe intercourse with others, give due attention to our own and to their character, weigh each circumstance of the business which we undertake, and employ the surest and safest means for the attainment of any end or purpose. To a Cromwell perhaps, or a De Retz, discretion may appear an alder-

---

[1] For Montaigne as well, 'the public interest' could never excuse a breach of decency: 'Let us not fear ... to decide that there is something not lawful, even against enemies, that public interest ought not to require everything from all men contrary to private interest ... and that all things are not permissible to a right-minded man in the service of his king or of the general cause and of the laws. ... If it be highheartedness and the result of a rare and surpassing virtue to despise friendship, private bonds, one's plighted word, and the ties of kindred, in favour of the common welfare and of obedience to authority, it is enough surely to excuse us from it, that this is a sort of loftiness that can find no place in the highheartedness of Epaminondas. ... Let us deprive of this pretext of rightness those who are by nature wicked and blood-thirsty and treacherous; let us turn our backs on this heinous and insane justice, and hold fast to more human copies'. (*Essais*, Bk. 3, ch. 1, p. 898).

[2] Cf. John Carswell, *The South Sea Bubble and The Old Cause*, (London, 1954) where this aspect of eighteenth-century politics is especially well illustrated.

manlike virtue, as Dr Swift calls it; and being incompatible with those vast designs, to which their courage and ambition prompted them, it might really, in them, be a fault or imperfection. But in the conduct of ordinary life, no virtue is more requisite, not only to obtain success, but to avoid the most fatal miscarriages and disappointments.[1]

Discretion requires us to 'curb and conceal' our arrogance, to appear to have agreeable sentiments especially when they have to be feigned. And it takes discretion to know how discreet one may be without violating integrity.

When a young man asked Hume whether, as he lacked true religious feelings, it would be immoral for him to stay in orders, Hume replied:

It is putting too great a respect on the vulgar, and on their superstitions to pique one's self on sincerity with regard to them. Did ever one make it a point of honour to speak truth to children or madmen? . . . The common duties of society usually require [hypocrisy]; and the ecclesiastical profession only adds a little more to an innocent dissimulation, or rather simulation without which it is impossible to pass through the world. Am I a liar, because I order my servant to say, I am not at home, when I do not desire to see company?[2]

Victorians, like John Morley, found this shocking advice. But Hume was saying only that Church positions were generally taken up merely as a means of livelihood. They carried certain duties, which had to be performed carefully, and it would be improper to preach Deism from the pulpit. But one's sermons were not supposed to be a perfect expression of one's inner convictions. Anyway, few people in the world were sensitive enough to understand another man's inner convictions, even when they were made plain. As long as taking the office was not interpreted as a strict pledge about one's beliefs, which in the current state of society it was not, and one's outward actions did not violate the duties of the office, one could play the game according to the accepted rules with a clear conscience. Sincerity had to be tempered with discretion.

Without discretion, Hume's whole structure of political behaviour would topple. It made it reasonable for him not to deny, as Hobbes had, a right to revolution, despite his devotion to peace and order. For he could argue that the absolute exclusion of resistance in all possible cases was founded on false principles, and yet, that one had sometimes to avoid expressly admitting a right to resistance when that might 'be attended with dangerous consequences'.[3] Here again, Hume was not asking any man to betray his convictions, but only to consider the consequences of his public acts and utterances, to remember that the same words had not the same effect in different circumstances. To discuss the right of resistance in a book was not the same as to declaim it in parliament. And at a time when peace was precarious and

---

[1] *Enquiry*, p. 236. [2] *Letters*, vol. I, pp. 439 f.
[3] *History*, vol. VI, p. 66.

the people given to hysteria, as under Charles I, it was perhaps hardly permissible to mention the right of resistance:

> If ever, on any occasion, it were laudable to conceal the truth from the populace, it must be confessed that the doctrine of resistance affords such an example; and that all speculative reasoners ought to observe with regard to this principle, the same cautious silence which the laws in every species of government have ever prescribed to themselves.[1]

Hume allowed for the same sort of discretion when he pardoned General Monk for having pretended to favour the Commonwealth while working for the king's restoration. He explained that Monk had never, while employed by Cromwell, participated in violent measures against the opposite party. Because of his connection with Oliver Cromwell, it was right that at first he should have remained faithful to Richard Cromwell. But once he saw that Richard could not maintain order, he violated no pledge when he decided that the only hope for peace lay in a Restoration. Conditions were such that he could not have told anyone of his change of party without destroying all possibility of success. His dissimulation grew out of fixed convictions, and it was limited and temporary. It mattered too that in the last moment Monk had not betrayed any explicit orders, because none had been sent to him, and that he had never taken an oath of objuration against the king: 'His temper was naturally reserved; his circumstances required dissimulation; the king, he knew, was surrounded with spies and traitors; and, upon the whole, it seems hard to interpret that conduct, which ought to exalt our idea of his prudence, as a disparagement of his probity'.[2] Nevertheless, Hume regretted that Monk should have at one point made a false declaration of enthusiasm for the Commonwealth.[3] It was probably in a similar spirit that Robert Walpole warned the public against the South Sea Bubble, but when his warnings were ignored, felt free to make his profits along with everyone else. So, too, a member of parliament in Hume's time could honourably accept rewards for having remained loyal to the leader of his group, but he was considered corrupt if he changed sides at a critical moment to further his private interests. The line between worldly judgement and dissimulation might sometimes be very fine, yet it was, Hume felt certain, a sharp line and one that every good and prudent man must draw.

But exact knowledge of how he ought to behave, or whether he had behaved properly would never be vouchsafed the man of integrity. There was no handbook for him to follow, no simple answer dictated by either grand principles or clearcut rules, nothing but his own sense of decency and

[1] *Ibid.* vol. v, p. 288.
[2] *Ibid.* p. 428.
[3] *Ibid.* vol. vi, p. 16 n.

moderation. He was denied assurance not only of rightness, but also of success, and he could not abjure success.

He could, however, be proud of certain failures. Indeed a willingness to accept failure rather than be false to one's commitments was part of political honour.[1] Thus Hume praised Algernon Sidney, even though Sidney 'had entered deeply into the war against the king', had been invited to join the court which condemned Charles I, had worked against the Restoration, and joined the popular party during the excitement about the popish plots. For Sidney's integrity was beyond question. He was willing to go as far as his principles permitted, but no further—he refused to sit on the court that condemned the king, and he 'opposed Cromwell's usurpation with zeal and courage', but also, at the Restoration, he chose banishment 'rather than submit to a government and family which he abhorred'.[2] In the end he was executed for maintaining principles favourable to liberty 'such as the best and most dutiful subjects of all ages have been known to embrace . . .'. He complained of the injustice of the sentence but 'had too much greatness of mind' to deny that he had engaged in conspiracies.[3] By some standards he was a failure. To Hume, he was a man of judgement and honour, the sort of man on whom in the last resort liberty depended. Hume had no tolerance for the vices of devils, for tyrannical, rebellious, spiritual pride, but he accepted and generously forgave the fallibility of men.

While integrity was all important, genius hardly mattered. Hume even preferred to entrust government to mediocre men who would be content to occupy themselves with the plodding detail work that is the essence of peaceful government. Few men of great gifts, he felt, would imitate Sulla and retire when there were no more great deeds to accomplish. Heroes wanted victories, states to be destroyed, conspiracies or usurpers to be overthrown; they were not suited for the slow execution of the laws. The ideal politician, therefore, was not likely to be very inspiring, but that was not, to Hume's way of thinking, a calamity. He would have remained unmoved by Horace Walpole's statement that, 'to a man without ambition or interested-

---

[1] Montaigne summed up this balance between integrity and self-preservation as follows: 'I will follow the best side to the point of danger, but no further, if I can help it. Let Montaigne be swallowed up in the public ruin if it be necessary; but if it be not necessary, I shall thank fortune if he escapes; and all means that my duty allows me I shall employ for his preservation. Was it not Atticus who, while holding to the right side, and to the side that lost, escaped by his moderation in that universal shipwreck of the world, amidst so many mutations and diversities? . . . To maintain a wavering attitude, half this and half that, to keep one's feelings unstirred and without preference amidst the troubles of one's country and public divisions, this seems to me neither seemly nor honourable'. (*Essais*, Bk. III, ch. I, p. 886).

[2] *Ibid.* p. 224.
[3] *Ibid.* p. 225.

ness, politicians are canaille. Nothing appears to me more ridiculous in my life than my ever having loved their squabbles, and at an age when I loved other things too'. Politicians had, after all, to busy themselves with inglorious things.

It was right for the politician to think of politics as a part of social life, not the purpose or consummation of existence. Political divisions should always be subordinate to social ties, and it was a sign of bigotry to Hume when opposing parties broke off social intercourse and contracted no marriages. It was well for a politician to regard parliament as the nation's best club, to find, as Gibbon did, that a seat in parliament was an 'agreeable improvement' in one's life, 'just the mixture of business, of study, and of society, which I always imagined I should and now I find I do like'. The old-fashioned advice that Chatham's grandfather gave to his son was, by Hume's standards, high-minded enough: 'If you are in Parliament show yourself on all occasions a good Englishman and a faithful servant to your country. If you aspire to fame in the House, you must make yourself master of its precedents and orders. Avoid faction, and never enter the House pre-possessed; but attend diligently to the debate and vote according to your conscience and not for any sinister end whatever'.

But if the politician had to be in a way mediocre, he had also to be thoroughly civilized. Civilization was not the same as morality. Hume refused to divide men into good and bad; in the history he rounded off each portrait with a neat balance of virtues and vices, that fails utterly to give a picture of a living man, but makes it clear that he was neither saint nor villain. For Hume would allow no character to be 'wholly bad or good; tho' the prejudices of party make writers run easily into the extremes of both panegyric and of satire'.[1] It was quite otherwise, however, with the distinction between the vulgar and civilized. That division Hume made readily and emphatically.

He considered the plebeian thoughts, inelegant speech, lack of magnanimity of the Commonwealth men part and parcel of their fanaticism and imprudence. Trouble-World Lilburne, Praise-God Barebones, the weird and impracticable William Prynne, with their long psalms, long sermons, and long faces were such a rude contrast to the patriots of antiquity, Cato, Brutus, Cassius:

What a difference when the discourse, conduct, conversation, and private as well as public behaviour of both are inspected! . . . The Leisure of those noble ancients was totally employed in the study of Grecian eloquence and philosophy; in the cultivation of polite letters and civilized society; the whole discourse and language of the moderns were polluted with mysterious jargon and full of the lowest and most vulgar hypocrisy.[2]

[1] *Ibid.* p. 24.   [2] *Ibid.* vol. v, p. 24.

On the king's side, it was the generosity, refinement, and courage of many of the aristocracy that Hume admired. But for a man like Laud, who for all his learning and elevation was intemperate and ill-behaved, he had harsh words:

This man was virtuous, if severity of manners alone, and abstinence from pleasure, could deserve that name. . . . In prosecution of his holy purpose, he overlooked every human consideration; or, in other words, the heat and indiscretion of his temper made him neglect the views of prudence and the rules of good manners. . . . All his enemies were also imagined by him the declared enemies to loyalty and true piety, and . . . every exercise of his anger by that means, became in his eyes a merit and a virtue.[1]

Something more than a frivolous love of fine rhetoric or graceful manners inspired these judgements. For politics, as Hume understood it, is an art not a science. It is the art of choosing the least evil. It is guided by a sense for what civilization at its best can produce, and depends on a capacity for making fine discriminations, for seeing differences of degree where the vulgar only roughly distinguish kinds, for recognizing the connotations of things without losing sight of their true proportions. It requires sureness about rules and great delicacy in applying them. It is above all an activity of judging. And how a politician judges will be determined in the end by the sort of man he is. Knowledge and morality are therefore not enough; they must be supplemented by taste. The political disposition Hume admired was inseparable from civilized taste.[2]

[1] *Ibid.* vol. IV, p. 467.
[2] In our day, the only attempt to express such a political disposition has been made by Michael Oakeshott, *Rationalism in Politics*. As his viewpoint demanded, Prof. Oakeshott has presented his attitude towards politics in a series of essays on diverse subjects, which, very like Hume's essays, have been misinterpreted by reviewers attempting to discover in them a doctrine quite foreign to the author's intention.

CHAPTER X

THE END OF PROFANE POLITICS

THE same considerations perfectly consistently determined Hume's reactions to the political events of his last years. When Wilkes became the cause of a public furore that threatened a revolution, and for what Hume regarded as frivolous reasons, he was bound to be against Wilkes. His response was that of a man devoted to the rule of law, and above all, to moderate, civilized behaviour in politics:

This madness about Wilkes excited first indignation, then apprehension; but has gone to such a height that all other sentiments with me are buried in ridicule. This exceeds the absurdity of Titus Oates and the Popish plot: and is so much more disgraceful to the nation, as the former folly, being derived from religion, flowed from a source which has from uniform prescription acquired a right to impose nonsense on all nations and all ages. But the present extravagance is peculiar to ourselves, and quite risible.[1]

The refusal of parliament to seat Wilkes may have been ill-judged, but it did not, Hume felt, put the liberties of the nation in extreme danger. In any case, the way to resolve constitutional issues was not through mob violence, but, when at all possible, through the 'ordinary parliamentary Arts of Opposition'.[2] Wilkes, whatever his rights, was behaving as an agitator, and wantonly encouraging disorder, which alone showed him unfit for public office. It was an opinion shared by many, including Chatham.

Neither was Hume alone in his fears of revolution during 1769 and 1770. Many believed an outbreak was imminent—Horace Walpole, upon arriving from France in October, 1769 reported that, 'It [England] approaches by fast strides to some great crisis, and to me never wore so serious an air, except in the Rebellion'. Hume who was always remembering Roman history was anyway inclined to discover a danger of military dictatorship: 'Are we sure, that the popular Discontent may not reach the Army, who have a Pretence for Discontents of their own?' It would be fortunate, he felt, if England, possessed as she was by 'licentiousness, or rather the frenzy of liberty', escaped from the confusion without 'falling into a military Government, such as Algiers or Tunis'.[3]

As he was concerned most with the characters of politicians, Hume was not disposed to let affection for a disputable principle override his distrust of

[1] *Letters*, vol. II, p. 197.
[2] *Ibid.* pp. 212–13.
[3] *Ibid.* p. 210.

I   DAVID HUME

Wilkes. And since it was the first function of government to maintain peace, Hume favoured the king and the ministers when they seemed ready to restore order, and condemned them when they permitted the government to be insulted by mobs. It was equally in keeping with his outlook that he should have revised his writings under the influence of public events. As an author of books that were being widely read, he was, by his own standards, bound to think of the circumstances under which he published. He altered the history to remove any seeming approval of licentiousness. In the essays, he dropped his unguarded and extremely enthusiastic expressions in favour of freedom of the press. Yet, although he now insisted that such liberty was attended with grave disadvantages, he did not suggest suppression. And indeed he never altogether lost his sense of balance. Even while reporting his worst fears, he could laugh at himself:

You say I am of a desponding Character: On the contrary, I am of a very sanguine Disposition. Notwithstanding my Age, I hope to see a public Bankruptcy, the total Revolt of America, the expulsion of the English from the East Indies, the Diminution of London to less than half, and the Restoration of the Government to the King, Nobility, and Gentry of the Realm. To adorn the Scene, I hope also that some hundreds of Patriots will make their Exit at Tyburn, and improve English Eloquence by their dying Speeches.[1]

While Hume criticized the government for being weak at home, where it should have exerted its strength, he had even less sympathy for its courage abroad. In both cases, he saw policies that made for violence and disorder. It was Lord North's duty to take firm action against the mobs of London, but, by the same token, North was 'rash, insolent, and unjust', guilty of 'unpardonable temerity' when he ran the danger of a war with Spain 'which would have thrown all Europe, and almost the whole Globe into a Ferment'.[2] And it was foolhardy of the government to think it could subdue the distant and rebellious American colonies, when it could not do as much at home. As early as 1771, Hume doubted that England could keep America. The American issue was never for him, as it was for Burke, a matter of lofty principle but of ordinary practicalities. In 1774, he argued that the colonies, like a grown boy, were too old for the birch, but perhaps not yet ready for full independence—'Dr Franklyn wishes to emancipate them too soon from their Mother Country'.[3] But by 1775, he was ready to go further than Chatham; he declared himself an American in his 'principles', and urged that the colonies be left alone to govern or misgovern themselves as they saw fit. The rumoured proposal to withdraw the fleet and army drew from him enthusiastic approval:

[1] *Ibid.* p. 210.　　　　　　　　　　[2] *Ibid.* pp. 236–7.
[3] *Ibid.* p. 288.

I should have said that this Measure only anticipates the necessary course of Events a few Years; that a forced and every day more precarious Monopoly of about 6 or 700,000 pounds a year of Manufactures, was not worth contending for; that we should preserve the greater part of this Trade even if the Ports of America were open to all Nations; that it was very likely, in our method of proceeding, that we should be disappointed in our scheme of conquering the Colonies; and that we ought to think beforehand how we were to govern them after they were con-quer'd.

Nothing less than extreme violence and oppression could subdue the colonies, and no civilized man would countenance that: 'Let us, therefore, lay aside all Anger; shake hands, and part Friends'.[1] [2]

---

[1] *Ibid.* p. 301.

[2] It would be hard to find a better example of the subtle but irrelevant and wrong-headed explanations to which Hume's way of thinking about politics is subjected than the comments of his biographer, Greig: 'How could the same man, and at the same time, be both, Edmund Burke and George III? How could he defend the Colonists in North America for their resistance to the arbitrary power of king, ministers, and venal House of Commons and yet attack the Old Whigs, and Patriots, and Wilkites, and democratic radicals of every sort, for trying to resist the same agencies at home?

'... In metaphysics, theory of knowledge, economics, ethics, and religion, and in politics as far as they concerned Americans, he deserved rather to be dubbed a Radical: he de-pended, not upon authority, but upon his own reasonings; ... he disintegrated and destroyed many settled notions by an acid logic of his own. Why therefore did he fail to bring the same acid logic to the politics of Charles I and Cromwell, George II, and John Wilkes?

'The paradox may be accounted for by means of unresolved antipathies, rooted, though perhaps not completely buried, in his past life. . . . One might almost say that two David Humes inhabited the same body. One, the main personality, composed the *Treatise*, the *Political Discourses*, and the *Dialogues concerning Natural Religion*; befriended Thomas Blacklock; adopted Jean-Jacques; loved Adam Smith; encouraged Gibbon; and desired the Colonists to be allowed to go their own way. But the other David Hume, who queru-lously raged against the English Whigs and John Wilkes, formed a partially dissociated personality, the product of his early inconclusive struggles to escape from Christian super-stitioners and Calvinist enthusiasts.' (Greig, *Life of Hume*, pp. 375–6). Another sort of explanation, no more discerning, is well represented by a reviewer of Hume's letters to Strahan in *The Nation*, of Feb. 7, 1889—'It is difficult to understand exactly what Hume meant when, with his high Tory notions and his fondness for kings and lords, he professed himself an "American in his principles." Can it be true, as Dr Johnson once snarlingly said, that Hume was "a Tory by chance, as being a Scotchman", and not at all a Tory "upon principle", as being "upon principle a Hobbist"? How could he write to Strahan that "it is a pleasure to hear that the Bill-of-Rights men have fallen into total and deserved contempt", when a little later he is found writing to his nephew that "the republican form of government is by far the best?" Was it the personal influence of Lord Hertford which made him re-actionary in his home politics, or was it the conservatism inspired by historical studies? Was it the personal influence of Gen. Conway (Lord Hertford's brother) which made him hope for the successful revolt of the American colonies, or was it his mad hatred of the English . . . ?'

Vexing as these issues were, Hume was nevertheless peculiarly irascible. In 1768 he told Turgot that the events of the past few years had made it clear that not only was the belief in progress unfounded, but retrogression seemed to be in order. The people, he said, 'roar Liberty, tho' they have apparently more Liberty than any People in the World; a great deal more than they deserve; and perhaps more than any men ought to have'. He explained, rather oddly for him, that good men refused to become ministers because they could expect nothing but obloquy from their office, that the rich were too indolent to acquire knowledge, and the poor too occupied with their daily labour.[1] Two years later, he wrote to his friend, Gilbert Elliot, 'Our Government has become a Chimera; and is too perfect in point of Liberty, for so vile a Beast as an Englishman, who is a Man, a bad Animal too, corrupted by above a Century of Licentiousness. The Misfortune is, that this Liberty can scarcely be retrench'd without Danger of being entirely lost; . . . ' He was revising his history and hoped that his 'Indignation at the present Madness, encourag'd by Lyes, Calumnies, Imposture, and every Infamous Art usual among popular Leaders, may not throw me into the opposite Extreme'.[2] Hume seems to be speaking against liberty generally, but he had in mind a particular aspect of liberty—the influence of the mob urged on by 'the infamous art' of 'popular leaders'.

What really disturbed him was the growing prominence of a new style of politics connected with the rise of Chatham and the end of Walpole's era. This lay behind his violent expressions of antipathy to the English, which grew stronger during the years of Bute's ministry, when the mobs showed their disapproval of his policies by attacking all Scotsmen. It was not so much Hume's feelings as a Scotsman that were aroused, as his more profound horror of mob prejudice and violence, in whatever form. He had been frightened away from London in the 'fifties when this tendency became pronounced; he now lost all patience with it. And he associated all these signs of barbarism in England with Chatham.

Earlier, he had not altogether approved of Walpole. His first essays included a fairly hostile 'character' of Walpole, criticizing him for the civil list, the notes of credit, the large standing army, and blaming him even for the absence of great literary figures. Nevertheless, Hume had found some virtues to offset the failings, and had praised Walpole for maintaining peace and encouraging a flourishing trade. When he saw that Walpole was on the decline, he called him a 'great man', and was 'inclin'd to think more favourably of him, and to suspect, that the Antipathy, which every true born Briton naturally bears to Ministers of State, inspir'd me with some Prejudice against him'.[3]

---

[1] *Ibid.* p. 180.   [2] *Ibid.* p. 216.

[3] E. C. Mossner, *The Life of David Hume* (Edinburgh, 1954), p. 143.

But to Chatham, Hume was consistently and immoderately hostile: 'Think of the Impudence of that Fellow and his Quackery; and his Cunning; and his Audaciousness, and judge of the Influence he will have over such a deluded Multitude'.[1] Chatham's imaginative strategy in the Seven Years War, his American policy which came closer than any other to Hume's views, his general superiority to other politicians of his day, none of these was ever commended or even mentioned. Instead, he was 'that wicked madman, Pitt, who has reduced us to our present condition'.[2] Hume was convinced that when Chatham, in 1766, roused the Commons with his demand that the Stamp Act be repealed, he was only manoeuvring for power. He was inclined to suspect that Chatham's retirements were not really due to illness. Indeed there was nothing Chatham could do to please Hume:

I think that Mr Johnson is a great deal too favourable to Pitt, in comparing him to Cardinal Richelieu. The Cardinal had certainly great Talents besides his Audacity: The other is totally destitute of Literature, Sense, or the Knowledge of any one Branch of public Business. What other Talent indeed has he, but that of reciting with tolerable Action and great Impudence a long Discourse in which there is neither Argument, Order, Instruction, Propriety, or even Grammar? Not to mention, that the Cardinal, with his inveterate Enmities, was also capable of Friendship: While our Cutthroat never felt either the one Sentiment or the other.[3]

For Chatham represented the sort of politician and a style of politics that Hume abhorred.

Chatham was a man of strong passions, seeking forgetfulness in action. Hate and violence came more easily to him than love and moderation; his language was rash and uninhibited; he was ostentatious to the point of being theatrical. There was about him always an edge of frenzy, that, while it made his oratory great, prevented him from ever being modest or quiet. Working with other men as equals was almost impossible for him, and he treated even his closest associates as 'a parcel of schoolchildren'. He was arrogant, remote, a man who walked alone.

For he was a statesman with a mission. He was the heir of the revolutionary leaders of the seventeenth century. His language was that of Pym, not of Newcastle, Townshend, or even Fox. He despised the jealousies, vanities, and ambitions of office seekers, and could never be either adroit or accommodating; his talents showed best in opposition when he could threaten ministers and frighten governments. When, occasionally, he tried to play the game of politics in the style of Walpole, he was clumsy. He never thought to discuss with his colleagues the political implications of accepting marks of favour from the king. When he tried to placate the king, he became almost slavish.

[1] *Letters*, vol. II, pp. 197–8.
[2] *Ibid.* p. 301.
[3] *Ibid.* p. 242.

He generally made the wrong offers at the wrong times, threatened when threats carried no weight, complied too easily and too late, and was always out-manoeuvred by dull-witted men. He detested legal arguments mainly because he had no respect for custom or precedent: 'Talk not of precedents!' he declared—'I boast a sovereign contempt for them'. He wished to be a 'scarecrow of violence to the gentle warblers of the grove, the moderate Whigs and temperate statesmen'. For he saw no place for old rules in a new world.

Not peace, but wealth, grandeur, and an empire greater than any the world had seen since Rome was what Chatham offered England. He set himself to destroy Spain and France and seize the commerce of the world for England. 'I know that I can save the country and that I alone can', he told the king, and this madly arrogant statement was, in a sense, justified. Chatham was, Burke said, the first statesman by whom 'commerce was united with and made to flourish by war', and the 'principal instrument' raised up by providence 'in His memorable work'. The French Abbé Raynal, in his *History of Indian Commerce* (of 1780) declared that Chatham 'raised the heart of England so high, that his administration was nothing but a chain of conquests'. Whereas Walpole had been a minister of peace, Pitt was indignant when Walpole's ministry managed, through a combination of firmness and tact, to deal with Spanish claims without going to war. Compromise was not, he thundered, the way to glory for England. Through war and audacity, risk and violence, he laid a foundation for imperial greatness that survived both the loss of America and Napoleon.

The 'Great Commoner' could do without Walpole's skill in intimate politics, because he relied on his appeal to the populace, on his ability to fill their imaginations—'he considered Mobs in the light of a raw material which might be manufactured to a proper stuff for their own Happiness in the end'.[1] His policies, he made it seem, had no connection with personal power and party manoeuvres; they were part of the drama of mankind. He spoke as the mouthpiece of destiny and could be heard in large crowds and by distant audiences: 'When Trade is at Stake . . . you must defend it or perish'. Every one of his gestures was sweeping enough to be seen round the country, and even round the world. He alone therefore was able to influence the Americans, along with the mobs of London.

All these qualities made him a great statesman and the epitome of what Hume considered dangerous in politics. Hume, who saw nothing but imprudence in the ambitions of Athens, and chastised Britain for her 'ancient Greek spirit of jealous emulation', was impressed only by the costs, the burdens, the calamities of empire building:

---

[1] Mrs Crewe, *Table Talk*, in *Miscellanies of the Philobiblion Society*, vol. 7, no. 5, (London, 1862-3) p. 13.

When I reflect that, from 1740 to 1761, during the Course of no more than 21 Years, while a most pacific Monarch sat on the Throne of France, the Nation ran in Debt about a hundred Millions; that the wise and virtuous Minister, Pitt, could contract more Incumbrances, in six months of an unnecessary War, than we have been able to discharge during Eight Years of Peace; and that we persevere in the same frantic Maxims. . . . In other Respects the Kingdom may be thriving. . . . But all this is nothing in comparison of the continual Encrease of our Debts, in every idle War, into which, it seems the Mob of London are to rush every Minister.[1]

Chatham's speeches sounded to Hume, as to Chatham's old-fashioned colleagues, like 'formidable sounds and furious declamations'. To fight, or to perish were never, Hume was convinced, the only alternatives. Even if Horace Walpole was right in saying that Pitt 'gave reverberation to the councils of England, banished despondence, infused spirit into the country, humiliated France, and carried the glory of Britain to a pitch at which it never had arrived', Hume liked him all the less for it. Spiritual uplift was not the proper function of a statesman. Chatham went outside his proper bounds—under his direction, government was not merely a referee who enforced the rules; it was not orderly and economical, but over-active and capricious. Instead of moderating the passions of men, it inflamed them.

But Chatham's style was eminently suited to the new conditions of politics that began to develop more rapidly towards the end of the eighteenth century, conditions in which Hume's style had little chance of surviving. For his profane politics is so earthbound that it is utopian. Neither Hume's moral nor his political ideas are acceptable to those striving for the impossible, for saints and heroes. He emphasizes the virtue of staying within reasonable bounds rather than trying to overreach them; his moderation might seem to be made for mediocrity. And yet Hume's outlook, in politics perhaps even more than in morals, will not come easily to ordinary men. The qualities it demands are not often widely diffused among the public: patience, moderation, endurance, a willingness to compromise and to tolerate differences of opinion, a love of order combined with an acceptance of inevitable disorder, dislike of change for its own sake but a readiness to see the necessity for change, a distrust of ideal theories and speculative politics while admiring loyalty to civilized standards. The political morality Hume demanded is in a way far more difficult to observe than the extremest puritan austerity. For it is easy either to follow some set of rules absolutely or to ignore moral qualms altogether. It is easy also to try to establish a perfect city, come what may. But the man who tries to adapt himself to circumstances and yet preserve his integrity, to recognize new problems without destroying law and order, has an endless task. He is eternally obliged to balance one thing against another, to distinguish and compromise, and all this without falling into moral indiff-

[1] *Letters*, vol. II, p. 237.

erence. Perhaps most difficult of all, Hume's politics assumes great personal resources, an ability to find meaning in life for oneself, and to require from the state nothing more than a convenient setting for private enthusiasms.

These requirements could more easily be satisfied in the conditions of politics under Walpole. Then politics was still the affair of a small group who were intimates and decided affairs of state over port. They were selected for their skill in manoeuvring amidst opposing ambitions and policies. Most of them had been brought up to expect a life of leisure, and regarded politics as one of several diversions. Even apart from the politicians, the people influential in politics (as opposed to the mob) generally had better things to do, and looked upon politicians much as they did upon the bailiffs of their estates. They were in any case close enough to the scene of decision to be aware of the emotions and purposes that entered at every stage, and to see politics as a personal drama, not a dreary mechanism. The invective was sharp, and the pamphleteering scurrilous, but there was life to the political scene.

For the large masses of the people, however, who saw none of the letters that circulated and never dined with a minister, something more was required. They were far from the council tables, and could not easily feel that they had helped to decide what happened. Perhaps even more than participation, the mass of people wanted relief from the grimness, or perhaps only from the tedium, of their lives, something to colour their days and give them stuff for dreams. But what inspiration could they find in Walpole's slow negotiations with Spain, which from the distance, were difficult to distinguish from aimless or dishonorable intrigue? Peace and prosperity are never interesting. Politicians who seek only to influence other politicians and have not learned to exploit public opinion to their advantage, provide no amusement for the public. Subtle conversations on stage escape the audience in the uppermost gallery of the theatre; they can hear only rousing declamations. The London mob, as Hume lamented, was accordingly always eager for violent action and pressed for war. As the mob grew bigger, more widespread, and shoved closer to the doors of parliament, heroic figures like Chatham were bound to win out over boring men of moderation. It was not only the demands of manufacturers and workmen that, from the end of the eighteenth century on, inspired great arguments on Equality, the Rights of Man, the Principle of Utility, Trade, Empire. Grand topics and grand visions were needed for a public that was large and growing more dependent on politics to give meaning to their lives. The wish of public opinion to be engaged by politics produced in turn an awareness among politicians of how public opinion could be exploited even for ordinary political issues, an awareness that brought profane politics to an end. Chatham was the first non-revolutionary example of the new sort of politician in England.

Theoretically, the breakdown of profane politics was expressed in two different ways, by Burke and by Bentham. Burke's difference from Hume is the more profound, although he contributed very little to the development of a new view of political activity. For he belonged to an older tradition that was due for a temporary eclipse, partly as a result of Hume's work.

Yet, at first sight, Hume and Burke appear to be in agreement. Burke, too, detested Chatham. And often he seems to be voicing Hume's very sentiments and opinions, only more eloquently and forcefully. It is from Burke, rather than from Hume, that we have learned about the folly of neglecting all but reason in politics; that politics ought to be adjusted not to human reasoning, but to human nature; of which reason is but a small part. The importance of custom, tradition, and precedent are associated with Burke, who in so many different contexts emphasized that man is a creature of habit and that the mass of the people live by prejudice and custom. Veneration for the rule of law, for temperance and humility, the dependence of schemes of government and policy on the men who frame and execute them, the primacy of the feelings and desires of each individual, these tenets are as central for Burke as for Hume. When we think of them, it is difficult to believe that Burke told Boswell that he spoke to Hume only because the liberal state of society required it.[1]

Nevertheless, we can sense also in Burke's phrases not merely different talents, but the presence of another spirit. However much importance he attached to custom, Hume would never have called custom 'the standing Wisdom of the country'. Although he believed strongly that men of violent passion were a menace to liberty, he could never have exhorted them, as Burke did, to put 'moral chains on their appetites'. Hume said party divisions were inseparable from mixed government; but Burke implied that a man who was less than zealous in support of his party was immoral. The difference was described by Johnson when he replied to Boswell's report that Burke was thought mad: 'if a man will appear extravagant, as he does, can he wonder that he is represented as mad?' By extravagant, Johnson meant, 'roving beyond just limits or prescribed methods, outrageous vehemence, unnatural humour'.[2] Certainly Burke overstepped what Hume considered just limits.

First of all, the man himself was even by standards other than Hume's 'extravagant'. Both in private and public life, he often verged on desperate courses. He almost always spoke with vehemence, he lost his temper, he was the first man whom Mrs Thrale saw drunk and heard using bad language. His speeches, like Chatham's, had an air of frenzy. But Burke was even worse than Chatham in that he spoke not to the House of Commons at all, but to humanity, to eternity, to God. His orations rarely convinced the

---

[1] Robert Binet, *Life of Edmund Burke* (London, 1798), vol. II, pp. 425–8.
[2] Cf. G. M. Young, *Burke* (British Academy, 1943).

members of parliament to vote as he wished, but they came close to furnishing politics with a sacred text.

This was not merely because Burke was a great orator and political philosopher, but because he was speaking of sacred matters. Politics was, for Burke, more than an activity governed by ethical standards; it was itself ethical. It linked the life of man to the higher moral law. For Burke's belief in the higher reason that governed the universe was at the centre of all his thoughts and feelings, and the manner in which he understood the higher reason to be revealed to man shaped his politics.

It is out of the encounters of each generation and of each individual with the universal moral order, Burke believed, that the social heritage grows. The traditions and customs of a country are the products of the separate efforts of individual reasons throughout the years to reach the higher reason, and they accordingly embody whatever success men have had in the past in achieving moral wisdom. But they are more as well. They reflect, in addition to what men have chosen, the operation of the providential order in human affairs. History is the march of God's Providence, as well as of human efforts to reach God.[1]

His belief that the social order was intimately linked in this way to Divine Reason led Burke to stress the value of instinctive passionate nature. But he understood moral perfection very differently from Hume, as conformity to the rational order of the universe. Only he was convinced that the moral law of the universe could not be grasped by an abstract vision, or by ratiocination of any kind. Its complicated and various character could be discovered only through submission to a way of life, to the established social order. This meant that man had to rely on his instinct and prejudice as well as on his reason. Thus, for Burke, man's passionate nature was just like his reason, a means of becoming attuned to the rational moral law of the universe. For all his praise of instinct and passion, Burke belongs to the rational-natural tradition of political thought that stems from Plato, whereas Hume belongs to the tradition that founds political order on will, artifice, and imagination.[2] For Hume, justice was artificial, and law consisted of rules imposed by man to achieve certain purposes. For Burke, law was a discovery of the highest reason of the universe, and obedience to law was not merely convenient, or a condition for achieving moral perfection, but itself part of moral perfection. Hume's politics is built on convenience, Burke's on truth. It is only natural then that whereas the emotions Hume considered appropriate to political institutions were loyalty, obedience, respect, or scepticism, Burke saw in political institutions objects of love and veneration.

[1] Cf. Charles Parkin, *The Moral Basis of Burke's Thought* (Cambridge, 1956).
[2] M. Oakeshott, Introduction to Hobbes' *Leviathan*.

The difference between Hume and Burke is one of atmosphere and emphasis, and had little practical consequence during Hume's lifetime. Still it implies a totally different view of political activity. Society becomes the Temple of God, and the state, along with the Church, is its guardian. Although Burke remained thoroughly convinced that the only safe criterion in politics is the happiness of the individual, that expedience is 'that which is good for the community, and good for every individual in it', he placed social activity of every kind on a much higher plane than Hume did. There is an intimation that each man may find not only meaning in his earthly existence, but also immortality through the life of the whole, an aspiration very remote from Hume's robust pagan insistence that he knew nothing beyond this life and declined to hope for more.

Burke's urge to immortality is associated with an antipathy to scepticism of any kind. He did not attribute the difficulties of politics, as Hume did, to a mixture of good and evil in all things human, but to Original Sin, to pride in self, to lust after innovation. Whereas Hume's humility is purely secular, an admission of man's smallness and fallibility, Burke's humility is religious, the humility of the created being before his Maker. Hume was never certain of anything but the wrongness of certainty and zeal, and his tone is always sceptical. Burke spoke with the assurance of a man who had recognized the eternal order of things and felt that his allegiance to it empowered, even enjoined him, to instruct and chastise those who denied it. He not only infused a cosmic spirit into politics, he made government responsible for the highest morality.

It is the conviction that politics has to do with good and evil that imparted the air of extravagance to Burke's arguments, even those that echo Hume. And it allied him to Chatham, who had no thought for the Higher Reason. For both differed from Hume in their readiness to see politics as a means to glory. Neither would think of discussing the value of England's empire in terms of costs and immediate advantages. To Chatham, who thought only of temporal glory, empire was an end itself. For Burke, the halo around empire was celestial. He could therefore commend Chatham's style of politics to posterity, especially to a righteous posterity, better than Chatham himself.

Burke did not advocate independence for America when Hume did because he did not wish England simply to withdraw from a troublesome entanglement and let America govern herself. He hoped rather to inspire his countrymen into recognizing the grandeur of their duties. When he railed against Hastings, he was not in a way extravagant, because he was denouncing not merely an erring magistrate but a man who had blotted the record of England's dominion over a great empire which had been given into her hands by 'an incomprehensible dispensation of the Divine Providence'. Misgovernment was far more than a crime against certain individuals or nations; it was an impious neglect of a God-given duty.

The most obvious practical consequence of the difference between Hume and Burke appears in connection with war.[1] Whereas for Hume war was always the greatest evil, and to be avoided by every workable negotiation and compromise, for Burke war was the ultimate means of securing justice in the world. It could not, and should not, Burke believed, be banished. Although he entertained an ideal of a commonwealth of Europe, it did not exclude war; also he disapproved of the principle of balance of power uncorrected by some other principle allowing moral intervention. It was typical of a 'voluptuous and frivolous age', he said in the *Annual Register* for 1772, to suppose that while a state is 'flourishing within itself, and suffers no immediate injury from others, it has no concern in the quarrels, interests, or misfortunes of its neighbours'. Far from a militarist, he was well aware of what a war cost, but his conception of justice and of politics implied a readiness to fight for a holy cause. Some kinds of bloodshed were a crime; but every man was duty-bound to shed blood 'to redeem the blood of man. It is well shed for our family, for our friends, for our God, for our country, for our kind'. There was for him no possibility of tolerating the French Revolution, of merely containing France, of bargaining or compromising with her, of waiting for the 'natural revolution of fortune', because he saw in France not merely sedition and rebellion, or a growing threat, but the eruption of evil. Britain, as the champion of good, had no choice but to fight.

This disposition to translate political questions into moral crusades was what Hume called fanaticism and feared above all in politics. It led, as he believed it must, to what Shelburne called a 'metaphysical war', fought with the conviction that nothing but total victory would do. Yet Burke was very much more in step with the times than Hume might have been in his place. He was wiser even than the younger Pitt who only later recognized the expansionist tendencies of the French Revolution (although it is also possible that Burke's prophecy helped to bring about the events he prophesied). His own cosmic view of politics made him able to understand the power of revolutionary fanaticism. He would never have made Hume's mistake about Rousseau. He saw, too, the importance of appealing to patriotism to rouse Britain against France. Indeed the notions that became common in nineteenth century politics—patriotism, wars of liberation, the white man's burden, and the rich man's sin—so alien to Hume, were native to Burke.

Burke was a portent of things to come. But the resurrection of politics into a sacred activity came not in the form that Burke gave it, not under the auspices of religion, but of science. This development began with Bentham.

[1] Cf. Alfred Cobban, *Burke and the Revolt Against the Eighteenth Century* (London, 1960).

PART II

JEREMY BENTHAM: LIBERTY AND LOGIC

CHAPTER XI

BLACKSTONE'S CHALLENGER

The death of Hume was but one of several omens that 1776 marked the end of an era. The list of great monuments to Whig civilization was completed with the publication of Gibbon's *Decline and Fall* and Smith's *Wealth of Nations*. The Americans declared their independence in terms that gave intimations of something new to come. And not least among the signs announcing another era was the appearance of a small book, called *A Fragment on Government*, by an anonymous author.

At first glance, it was simply a tirade against Blackstone's *Commentaries*, which had become the canonical interpretation of law in England. But there was much more to the *Fragment on Government*. In the opening lines, it declared a new spirit: 'The age we live in is a busy age; in which knowledge is rapidly advancing towards perfection. In the natural world, in particular, every thing teems with discovery and with improvement'. It had become recognized besides, the author declared, that if discovery and improvement were possible in the natural world, there could be 'reformation' in the moral realm. But this, he felt, was too modest a hope, for why should there not be discovery and improvement in the moral as well as in the physical world? Men already had available to them an axiom which, if explored with method and precision, might produce far-reaching improvement in the moral realm—the axiom that 'the greatest happiness of the greatest number' was the measure of right and wrong. However, for the moment the author would content himself with denouncing and exposing Blackstone, in whose work he found 'scarce a syllable . . . by which a man would be led to suspect that the affair in hand was an affair that happiness or unhappiness was at all concerned'.[1]

Until Blackstone's works lost the esteem they had acquired, there would be no hope for the interests of 'true science' and 'liberal improvement'.[2] For Blackstone deluded the public with an elegant style and spurious reasoning into accepting whatever was established. He spoke the language of a gentleman, using metaphor and allusion, instead of writing as a scientist, with pure precision. Yet the only reason he gave for unquestioning submission to the existing laws was that they were issued by a government whom men had promised to obey, thus resting his argument on the fiction of an original contract already thoroughly demolished by Hume. Moreover, Blackstone

---

[1] Jeremy Bentham, *A Fragment on Government*, ed. W. Harrison (Oxford, 1948), p. 28.
[2] *Ibid.* p. 7.

asked men to obey a law that was no law, the common law, which was nothing but a large and muddled mass of judicial opinions from which lawyers could draw whatever they liked.

The only ground for obeying any law or for observing any promise, the anonymous author asserted, was its utility. Indeed whatever the practice, there was but one all-sufficient reason for it, the principle of utility. 'Accurately apprehended and steadily applied',[1] utility could give the clue to distinguishing good from bad without useless disputes about words. It rested every case on a 'matter of fact; that is future fact—the probability of certain future contingencies',[2] so that debates about politics and legislation could be settled by judgement, not passion, by bringing evidence of 'such *past* matters of fact as appear to be analogous to those contingent *future* ones'.[3] Utility gave clarity and certainty, unlike Blackstone's haphazard method of 'cross and pile'[4] that made all governments equally good or bad and freed legislators from any possibility of doing wrong.

There was no longer any need for the law to remain an obscure matter of conjecture that left the public a prey to unscrupulous lawyers. On the principle of utility, it could be made perfectly explicit and settled. For once the law was arranged on a natural basis, such as the principle of utility provided, and not according to some irrelevant technical nomenclature, it would be easy to see at once the mischief in a bad law, or at the least, the doubtfulness of its utility, simply because no bad law could fit into such an arrangement.[5] There was no need for any of the law to remain hidden in the form of unwritten or common law, whose false halo must go. Above all, legal fictions had to go, for a fiction was nothing but an artful falsehood that made it possible for judges and lawyers to usurp legislative power—'the pestilential breath of fiction poisons every instrument it comes near'.[6] All law could and should be reduced to statute, organized rationally, available for all to see. Once written and arranged in this manner, the laws of one country could with little variation serve any other.

In sum, the author of the *Fragment on Government* charged that Blackstone had spread confusion, defended arbitrary power usurped by judges and lawyers, and obstructed progress. Against Blackstone he argued that law rightly understood was the product of deliberate enactment by a legislative body, that it was possible, in the light of natural reason, to frame a body of law that could be universally applicable and so complete that it would reduce the task of judge and jurist to the mechanical application of its terms. He quoted Hume with great approbation, describing himself as a disciple of Hume, and with some reason, insofar as he adopted Hume's views on the

[1] *Ibid.* p. 93. [2] *Ibid.* p. 101.
[3] *Ibid.* p. 102. [4] *Ibid.* p. 64.
[5] *Ibid.* p. 25. [6] *Ibid.* p. 20 fn.

II   JEREMY BENTHAM

original contract. But in fact he had thrown out a challenge to the view that was Hume's even more than Blackstone's, that politics was necessarily a haphazard affair, in which a variety of beliefs and procedures, irregularities, fictions, and inconsistencies all had their place, in which not very much could, or even should, be made perfectly clear and fixed. The *Fragment on Government* asserted that it was possible and desirable to define the right and wrong of every political practice exactly, and that any failure to do so was inexcusable.

The assurance and daring of the author led his readers to suspect a great name in law—Johnson attributed it to the retired solicitor-general, Dunning; others suspected the chief justice of the Court of Common Pleas, Lord Camden, and even the great judge who presided over the King's Bench, Lord Mansfield—and the speculation gave the anonymous little book a certain vogue. But the interest died quickly when the author's father, who was unable to contain his pride, revealed that it was the work of Jeremy Bentham, an unsuccessful lawyer of twenty-eight.

Bentham was at that time supposed to be studying law and building up a law practice. His father had set him up some ten years before in modest yet fitting chambers in Elm Court fronting the Inner Temple lane, and had given him property yielding an income of about one hundred pounds a year. But in fact the young lawyer devoted most of his time to writing a theory of punishments and rewards, and for diversion read philosophy and jurisprudence, or made experiments—chemical, mechanical, and physical—in a laboratory fitted into a closet. When the Archbishop of York called on him to solicit his vote for a candidate, the young Bentham was reading Montesquieu and evaporating urine in order to obtain phosphorus. His father, who did not suspect so great a truancy, disapproved of any extracurricular interests and often admonished him to attend strictly to worldly things. But his words were wasted on a son who had from an early age been inclined in another direction.

Jeremy Bentham's temperament was such that even the ordinary education of an eighteenth century gentleman had not the usual effect on him. He had spent a painful period at Westminster, and at twelve had gone up to Oxford. At Queen's College, his library included Voltaire's 'Essay on General History', 'Paradise Lost', Molière's plays, and a large selection of classics— Juvenal, Horace, Terence, Cicero, Virgil, Pliny, Demosthenes, Sallust, Lucian, and Homer. He learned Greek and Latin well enough to become adept at verses and to remember passages until the end of his life. But unlike his eminent contemporaries, he never submitted either his mind or style to these ancient authors. Socrates struck him as insipid—'I could find in him nothing that distinguished him from other people, except for his manner of putting questions. This would have been good, had it been explained why,

9   129   L P C

but the devil of a bit of an explanation was there'.[1] Although he admired the moral loftiness of Télémaque and was reduced to tears by Clarissa, characters and images generally left him untouched. Impersonal facts interested him more; besides, they were comforting.

He had been a lonely, timid child, afraid of ghosts and indeed of anything tainted with mystery, easily persecuted by mischievous servants or schoolboys. Fairly early he learned to protect himself against the terrors produced by his imagination by concentrating on 'facts'. When shown a sampler picturing the temptation of Adam, he was struck first of all by the disproportionate size of the apple: 'It was larger than that species of the genus Orangeum which goes by the name of the forbidden fruit in some of our West India settlements'.[2] Gay's Fables neither amused nor instructed him because the stories about cocks and bulls were untrue.[3] The cousin who found most favour with him had a mind full of 'knicknackery and conceit' and vast stores of miscellaneous information. As he learned more, this love of facts was transformed into a faith in science, above all, in physics. The remedy for all the mischief perpetrated by blind belief in the occult was to be found, he came to feel, in physical science:

It is from physical science alone that a man is capable of deriving that mental strength and that well-grounded confidence which renders him proof against so many groundless terrors flowing from that prolific source [perverted religion], which, by enabling him to see how prone to error the mind is on this ground, and thence how free such error is from all moral blame, disposes him to that forbearance towards supposed error, which men are so ready to preach and so reluctant to practice.[4]

The other leading strain in his character was unwittingly encouraged by his father. Jeremiah Bentham was ambitious and commonplace. Although his family had for three generations been citizens of substance, they had never been distinguished—his grandfather was a prosperous pawnbroker, his father and he were attorneys. His first son, who was clearly a prodigy, had to be Lord Chancellor. After the death of his wife when Jeremy was twelve, all his hopes were concentrated on his sons, but especially on the elder. Convinced that he was being a devoted and generous father, he did everything in his power to push Jeremy up. But neither his ambition nor his anxiety to have his son recognize his benevolence sat very well with the Lord Chancellor to be.

Jeremy Bentham no sooner began to study law than he conceived a great

[1] The Works of Jeremy Bentham, ed. by J. Bowring, 11 vols. (Edinburgh, 1843), vol. x, p. 583.
[2] Ibid. p. 18.
[3] Ibid. p. 22.
[4] Ibid. vol. VIII, p. 13.

distaste for it. At sixteen, he took his Bachelor's degree from Oxford, and in November, 1763 dutifully began to dine in Lincoln's Inn and attend the Court of King's Bench. But when a month later he returned to Oxford to hear Blackstone's lectures, he was inspired mainly to reflect on the illogicality, indeed frivolity, of the established notions of law. Although he continued his studies, by the time he was admitted to the bar, in 1769, he had become wholly indifferent to his practice which anyway never came to anything. He dismissed one case by advising settlement out of court, and lost another through ignorance of a precedent. He was absorbed not in law books but in Hume, Priestley, Hartley, Beccaria, Helvetius, Montesquieu. Barrington's *Observations on the Statutes* confirmed his own low opinion of the existing body of law, and his interest in natural science, especially in Newton, directed his plans. Instead of joining the mean herd of lawyers and judges, he preferred to become a legislator who would make their low chicanery impossible. Locke and Helvetius, he was convinced, had prepared the way for a digest of the laws:

the first establishing a test of perspicuity for ideas; the latter establishing a standard of rectitude for actions. The idea annexed to a word is a perspicuous one, when the simple ideas included under it are assignable. This is what we owe to Locke. A sort of action is a right one, when the tendency of it is to augment the mass of happiness in the community. This is what we are indebted for to Helvetius. The matter of the Law is to be governed by Helvetius. For the form and expression of it we must resort to Locke.[1]

The philosophical issues and subtleties were of no interest; he looked only for useful contributions to his work.

But his work, which from 1769 on was an analysis of the penal law, had not the sort of practicality that Jeremiah Bentham could appreciate. He saw his son's energies being wasted on 'abstruse' writings, which would never obtain high office for him. When, in addition, at the age of twenty-six Jeremy fell in love and wanted to marry a penniless girl, he was made to feel the full force of his father's benevolent intentions. His friend, Lind, urged that he try to support a family by writing—party pamphlets, for instance, were generously rewarded—but Bentham was convinced that this would make his work on law reform impossible. His only hope, he felt, lay with his father, who could well afford to make a sufficient marriage settlement. Although, to his surprise, even his stepmother supported his suit, Jeremiah Bentham could see in the marriage nothing but a rash and criminal act, a kind of suicide. He hoped that, at least, his son's desire to marry would push him into law practice, and he let Bentham know that his marriage might be looked upon with greater favour if he withdrew his verdict against the law. There were

[1] *Ibid.* vol. x, pp. 70–1.

besides hints that if Jeremy pursued both the objects of his heart, he would be disinherited in favour of his younger brother, Samuel, who was likewise subjected to painful tirades and scenes. What was the best course for his son to follow was perfectly clear to Jeremiah Bentham, and his son's wishes were irrelevant.

Bentham's ambition to be a legislator won out; he would do nothing to endanger his freedom to continue his work; his father was intransigent and the girl grew weary of waiting. The affair had greatly agitated and depressed him, and he wrote bitterly to his brother, Sam: 'Don't wonder if some time or other he should be the death of me . . . How happy it is for Man, that Tyranny extends not beyond the Grave!'[1] In the midst of his dejection, he even broke off his friendship with Lind. His course, however, was set. By the time the *Fragment on Government* was published, he had committed himself to an independent life as a law reformer. In the next few years, he dallied for a bit with the part of a cynical man of the world, and feebly courted a young lady of fortune discovered by his father. When the lady decided against him, he was happy to forget the enterprise. What he never forgot was the effect of his father's benevolence.

From then on the course of his life, even his daily routine, never varied. He rose at six, walked two or three hours, sometimes across Hampstead Heath as far as Caen Wood, the residence of Lord Mansfield, to whom Bentham paid silent homage as a fellow reformer of the common law. After breakfasting, he worked until four, then dined. His small income made it difficult for him to live up to middle class standards of dress and entertaining, much less to go into society, but he had no wish to do so. He had his own amusements—the harpsichord and violin, and he loved the theatre.

Although he belonged to one of Dr Johnson's clubs, St Paul's Churchyard Club, he rarely attended, and never became part of the literary or political society of his day. The celebrated men and books did not interest him. About Johnson, he said only that like Godwin, he 'infused a tinge of melancholy' into all his books, was obsessed by religion, and provided in his writing 'no facts'.[2] Goldsmith's *Deserted Village* was too dismal, and untrue besides. Burke he had once respected, thinking him highminded and noble, but upon meeting him just as the French Revolution broke out, he was repelled, and decided that Burke was insincere and shallow, indifferent to the happiness of the people, a mere deviser of imagery and deceit. For Fox, he had felt a brief admiration, but later judged him deficient in true virtue, debauched by gaming and trickery, and redeemed only by his lately acquired fondness for botany. The one circle in which Bentham felt at home, and with whom he

[1] Add. Mss. BM, 33,537, p. 366b.
[2] Bentham, *Works*, vol. x, p. 13.

met fairly regularly was distinguished by a different sort of membership—a physician, an architect, an instrument-maker, and a watchmaker.

His need for companionship was mainly satisfied by his brother, Samuel, nine years his junior, for whose education he made himself responsible, and by John Lind, whom Bentham met through his father. When, after being unofficial minister to the king of Poland, Lind returned to England in 1773 as tutor to the Polish king's nephew, he and Bentham became intimate friends. It was through Lind that Bentham came to write the *Fragment*. Lind, who was gaining some reputation as a political writer, had sent Bentham his essay on Blackstone's *Commentaries*. In the course of criticizing his friend's effort, Bentham in effect rewrote it, and Lind, acknowledging his superiority, gave the whole project over to him. A digression in Bentham's comment on the *Commentaries* grew into the *Fragment*.

After his estrangement from Lind, Bentham's closest friend became George Wilson, a Scots barrister, who tried hard to push him into publishing. Soon after, he also met a German, Swediaur, who, knowing what intellectual work was being done on the Continent, was impressed by Bentham's originality and offered to translate his work. Through Swediaur, Bentham became acquainted with Benjamin Franklin, and was delighted to discover that Franklin kept Helvetius on his table. With these new friends, Bentham was encouraged to feel that he was gathering around him something like a band of disciples.

But his best chance for influence during these early years came through Lord Shelburne, who hoped to find in the author of the *Fragment* a useful party pamphleteer. When he came to visit at Bowood in 1781, Bentham was able to show Shelburne the introduction to his code, which had by then been printed, although not published, under the title, 'An Introduction to the Principles of Morals and Legislation'. It was read out to the ladies, and Bentham was much esteemed and even petted by them. He also met a number of great men—the lords of the law, Camden and Dunning, who failed to show any interest in his projects which Bentham, for his part, proudly disdained to put forward; when Pitt came, Bentham found him 'good natured' and 'raw', but could not think of any ideas they might have in common.[1] On the whole, he only joined in the conversation by 'a word now and then to keep the ball rolling' and to show he 'was not a perfect ninny'.[2] Although Bentham declined the role of party pamphleteer, Shelburne remained friendly and tried to put his work into circulation, but nothing came of it. In sum, while Bentham had a pleasant holiday amidst the aristocracy, neither he nor they were in the least affected by it.

[1] *Ibid.* p. 100.
[2] *Ibid.* p. 104.

His hopes became centred rather on the monarchs of Europe, who all seemed to be interested in codification—he sent his introduction to the Grand Duke of Tuscany, to Voltaire, to the prime minister of the Two Sicilies, to Gustavus of Sweden and Frederick of Prussia. The most promising candidate, he thought, was the ruler of Russia, Catherine the Great, and he was soon given an opportunity to serve her. Samuel, who had become a master shipwright and had been well trained in science and mathematics by his brother, had gone to Russia in 1779, where he was engaged for Prince Potemkin's projects to build a navy in the Black Sea and to set up model farms, indeed a model civilization, in the steppes. Samuel appealed to his brother for assistance, and finally, in 1786, Jeremy Bentham agreed to come, complete with treatises on agriculture, commerce, and manufacturing, two experienced dairy-women, and a general manager for a dairy.

After a five months' journey, full of discomfort and some bizarre experiences at the hands of the manager and dairy maids, Bentham arrived at Potemkin's headquarters in the Ukraine to find anything but an ideal community. He soon saw that there was nothing for him to do there, but he stayed on, working steadily, since the aim of his journey had been to present the Empress with a comprehensive code for Russia. The great day was, however, steadily delayed, partly because Bentham failed to use occasions for meeting the Empress, partly because his code was not ready. This was hardly surprising as he was busy on a number of other projects—a plan for a model prison, the Panopticon, and a pamphlet on the 'Defence of Usury'. In November, 1787, he left Russia without having met the Empress. Nor did he bring himself to call on King Stanislaus in Warsaw, with whom he had corresponded when Lind was the king's agent in England. In Berlin he did succeed in presenting a gift of asbestos to a chemist he greatly admired.

It was only upon his return from Russia, in 1788, through a dinner at Lansdowne House, that Bentham came to have any real influence. Samuel Romilly, whom he had met earlier, introduced him to Dumont, a Swiss writer and former clergyman. Dumont became what Macaulay called Bentham's 'interpreter to mankind'; he translated and edited the voluminous manuscripts, and, in his edition of the *Traités*, gave the world the first fairly complete and readable text of Bentham's legal theory. Thanks to Dumont, Bentham became famous on the Continent even while he remained insignificant in England. For it was not until twenty years later that he met James Mill, who made him the influential figure in England he had hoped to be.

Regardless of success or failure, Bentham all the time worked on in seclusion, at first in the farmhouse near Hendon where he took lodgings after his return from Russia. Then in 1791, when his father died, he moved to Queen Square Place in Westminster where he remained to the end of his life, except for eight years in the luxurious Ford Abbey which he rented in 1810. The folios, nearly illegible, piled up on his desk at the rate of ten or fifteen a day; the green curtain was pinned over with bits of paper on which he scribbled stray thoughts; and the routine never varied—he always spent six or eight hours of the day writing, with interruptions only for meals, walks in the garden, playing the organ or perhaps a game of battledore and shuttlecock. Composing civil and criminal codes was his life.

Instead of Lord Chancellor, Bentham became the 'hermit of Queen Square Place', an eccentric figure in a brown Quaker coat, white ribbed stockings drawn over his trousers, and white hair falling to his shoulders, with a striking resemblance to Benjamin Franklin. He lived in his 'hermitage' like a castaway on his island, seeing nobody, reading nothing, and writing books which no one read. Even his walks in the garden, though he might stop to admire the flowers or point out a slab 'sacred to Milton, prince of poets', were not quite ordinary, for he called them 'antejentacular' or 'postprandial trots'. Indoors, his desk and bookcase were placed on a raised platform which was surrounded by 'a vibratory ditch' for walking; the room was furnished besides with an organ, and an arm-chair for the single visitor he allowed at any time. The household included his stick, 'Dapple', the sacred teapot, 'Dickey', and the distinguished Lanborne, a cat, who was first baptized Sir John then the Rev. Dr.

Well before he died, Bentham became a legend. In 1821, a young admirer, invited to visit the renowned code maker, came filled with apprehension by the stories of strange goings-on at Queen Square Place. Nor was he reassured when upon arriving there he was told to await the master in an extraordinarily hot room, filled with weird noises, as of ghosts clanking their chains. He was greeted by Bentham's voice coming, it seemed, from nowhere. The noises turned out to be nothing worse than the central heating system which Bentham had devised for himself, and the voice had come through a pipe that connected the study upstairs with the waiting room below. Although the household was somewhat monastic, the heat at dinner even more overpowering, and the master's eating habits a little disconcerting, Bentham was after all kindly and engaging. He himself ate sparingly, and took his sweet course first, but he saw to it that his guests had a conventional and ample meal, complete with wine, and generally was careful not to impose on them any of his eccentricities. Towards the end of the evening, in the presence of the guests, one of the disciples tied on his night cap and bathed his eyes, while the old man ran on in a 'shrill chatter' of somewhat heavy-handed jokes. A series of well-established rituals ended the day.

Bentham's regular court included a confidential friend (for many years this was Bowring, whom we have to thank for a most unreadable and garbled edition), and two young secretaries, who were called 'reprobates'. Besides there was usually some visitor whom Bentham had invited or who had come to pay homage. James Mill and Romilly were often there; Brougham was occasionally granted an invitation; Francis Place and Ricardo came, as well as a number of distinguished foreign visitors. Others tried to lure Bentham to their houses but he went out only to Romilly's. Only once he dined with George Grote. In 1825, he paid a brief visit to Paris, which proved well worth the effort, for this time he was everywhere honoured as a distinguished jurist. But mostly he stayed at home, living quietly and serenely, wonderfully content. He died calmly, at the age of eighty-four, without any pain or struggle, having requested that only one friend remain with him to the end, and that servants and the younger men be spared the sight, so as to 'minimize pain'. He directed that his body should be made available for dissection. For he never neglected to observe the principle of utility.

CHAPTER XII

UTILITARIANISM—A SYSTEM OF TOLERANCE

Nature has placed mankind under the governance of two sovereign masters, *pain* and *pleasure*. It is for them alone to point out what we ought to do, as well as to determine what we shall do. On the one hand the standard of right and wrong, on the other the chain of causes and effects, are fastened to their throne. They govern us in all we do, in all we say, in all we think: every effort we can make to throw off our subjection, will serve but to demonstrate and confirm it. In words a man may pretend to abjure their empire: but in reality he will remain subject to it all the while. The *principle of utility* recognizes this subjection, and assumes it for the foundation of that system, the object of which is to rear the fabric of felicity by the hands of reason and law. Systems which attempt to question it, deal in sounds instead of sense, in caprice instead of reason, in darkness instead of light.[1]

Thus Bentham opened his introduction to the *Principles of Morals and Legislation*. The principle that he so confidently placed beyond question was an unusual sort of principle, certainly if it were meant to serve as the foundation of a moral system. It simply approved or disapproved of every action 'according to the tendency which it appears to have to augment or diminish the happiness of the party whose interest is in question'.[2] As happiness, according to Bentham, was the sum of pleasures, the principle of utility was nothing but an injunction to maximize pleasure. Since Bentham himself emphasized that this was what every man anyway tried to do, the principle of utility did not impose anything on anyone. At most, it was a counsel of prudence. It told men to count alternatives and future consequences against the immediate satisfaction before them, to make certain that they were not sacrificing a greater to a lesser pleasure, but nothing more. It did not even sanction hedonism, for Bentham made it plain that when he advocated maximizing pleasure, he did not mean by pleasure anything more than the satisfaction of whatever desires one might feel. His list of pleasures included fourteen varieties, ranging from pleasures of sense to those of wealth, malevolence and piety,[3] and if any were excluded, it was an oversight, for Bentham meant his list to be exhaustive.

Yet it was precisely this lack of ethical content that made the principle of utility, or, as he later called it, the greatest happiness principle, so appealing

---

[1] Bentham, *An Introduction to the Principles of Morals and Legislation*, ed. by W. Harrison (Oxford, 1948), p. 125.

[2] *Ibid.* p. 126.

[3] *Ibid.* pp. 155 ff.

to Bentham. As a result of its emptiness, it was perfectly objective. It was the only sort of moral principle that could satisfy his desire to prevent any man from imposing his judgement on another. For he was acutely aware of the paradox that once we have made our fellow men the objects of our enlightened interest, we go on to make them the objects not only of our pity and of our wisdom but ultimately of our coercion.

The moral foundation of Bentham's system was not the principle of utility but his conviction that to deny a normal adult the right to determine his own life was to treat him as a child and to derogate from his dignity as a rational being. He felt strongly that to reason about the happiness of other men 'otherwise than with a reference to their own desires and feelings'[1] was at the least absurd. Nothing but folly and impertinence impelled one man to direct another man's view of his interests, to decide for him what constituted pleasure and pain. For it was quite impossible to understand other men sufficiently well to know what their interests or needs were. Men did not react in the same way to the same circumstances: 'In the same mind such and such causes of pain or pleasure will produce more pain or pleasure than such or such other causes of pain or pleasure: and this proportion will in different minds be different'.[2]

The predilection to do good to others could be even more dangerous than direct attempts to tyrannize over them. No one was more objectionable to Bentham than the philanthropic fanatic who, inspired only by kindness, produced endless misery. Even hypocrites, he was sure, were less harmful than sincere do-gooders: 'If the benevolence be but in their mouths, it is bad: if it be in their hearts, it is worse, still worse'. There was hope for release from the hypocrite who, being moved by some specific interest, might end his persecution once that interest ceased; but the really well-meaning benefactor could never be diverted; his zeal made his persecution interminable: 'With intentions very commonly of the purest kind, a man becomes a torment either to himself or his fellow creatures'.[3] Religious fanatics were, of course, in the first ranks of such benevolent tyrants. But any moral system that issued positive commands could serve 'as a cloke, and pretence, and aliment, to despotism; if not despotism in practice, a despotism however in disposition: which is but too apt, when pretence and power offer, to show itself in practice'.[4] If no one admitted the justice of 'doing good', despotism under the guise of morality would be less likely. There might still be despots, but they would be readily recognized for what they were—tyrants using others to promote their own self-interest decked out in the language of benevolence.

---

[1] *Works*, vol. I, p. 344.
[2] *Principles of Morals*, p. 164.
[3] *Ibid.* p. 142 fn.
[4] *Ibid.* p. 142 fn.

But even if they were not misused, conventional moral principles were a covert way of imposing one man's opinion on the rest. They consisted 'in so many contrivances for avoiding the obligation of appealing to any external standard, and for prevailing upon the reader to accept of the author's sentiment or opinion as a reason for itself'.[1] Anyone disposed to defend one of these moral principles should ask himself, Bentham suggested, whether it is not

a kind of phrase which at bottom expresses neither more nor less than the mere averment of his unfounded sentiments; that is, what in another person he might be apt to call caprice? . . . whether his sentiment is to be a standard of right and wrong, with respect to every other man, or whether every man's sentiment has the same privilege of being a standard to itself? . . . whether his principle is not despotical and hostile to all the rest of the human race?[2]

Indeed, the only honest way to hold such moral principles was to say, 'I am of the number of the Elect. . . . If therefore a man wants to know what is right and what is wrong, he has nothing to do but come to me. . . .'.[3]

Bentham found a way of escaping this difficulty through the principle of utility. It had been suggested to him by everyone, or at any rate, he attributed his inspiration to different authors—Beccaria, Helvetius, Bacon, Hume. In fact, from each of them Bentham drew only what he was looking for. He borrowed phrases, but the principle of utility as he came to understand and use it was entirely his own invention.

When applied to private behaviour, it imposed nothing but tolerance. It said that men who sought the greatest happiness would live better and be kinder to their neighbours than those who did not. But since it defined happiness as the fulfilment of whatever desires a man had, it required those who followed it only to avoid interfering with other men's search for happiness as they understood it.

What utility might do to improve the moral state of mankind did not concern Bentham. If pressed, he would have revealed no very shocking moral beliefs—he generally accepted the standards of his society, and valued honesty, loyalty, industry, temperance as much as any decent man. In his notorious remark that pushpin was as good as poetry he merely left out a phrase, 'for the purposes of ethical theory and law'. He himself in practice ranked pleasures in a hierarchy, and it was a perfectly conventional hierarchy. Nor did he feel any discomfort about saying, on the one hand, that malice was a 'wretched pleasure',[4] or that the philanthropist John Howard made the 'truly Christian choice' and 'died a martyr after living our apostle',[5] while

---

[1] *Ibid.* p. 140.
[2] *Ibid.* p. 130.
[3] *Ibid.* p. 141 fn.
[4] *Ibid.* p. 218 fn.
[5] *Works*, vol. IV, p. 121.

insisting, on the other hand, that all motives should be given neutral names and that Christian values constituted a vicious dogma. Bentham took for granted a stable system of values, and concentrated on the problem of keeping it from being enforced too rigorously by troublesome do-gooders.

About philosophical problems, of the sort that worried Hume, he refused to think. When George Wilson sent him a book by Dr Gregory on liberty and necessity, Bentham regretted that 'a practical professional should stand forth as an author on subjects purely speculative'. 'Entre nous', he replied, 'I don't care two straws about liberty and necessity at any time. I do not expect any new truths on the subject and were I to see any lying at my feet, I should hardly think it worth while to stoop to pick them up.[1] He continued to speak, as so many of his contemporaries did, of the 'irascible' appetite, opposed to reason, yet declared that 'curbing the irascible appetite is as good a subject of exercise and boasting as extraordinary walking, running, donkey-racing, chess-playing, etc.' For all his indifference to the philosophical issues, asceticism or puritanism in any form repelled him, simply because they granted dominion to the self-righteous and their desire to make all men conform to their own code. Men would be improved quite enough, Bentham felt, if only they refrained from making one another miserable in the name of morality.

In politics the principle of utility gave more direct support to tolerance. It declared the 'right and proper end' of government to be 'the greatest happiness of all the individuals of which it is composed, say, in other words, the greatest happiness of the greatest number'.[2] The rationale of Bentham's utilitarian politics may be summed up as follows: Governments pretend to rule for the happiness of the governed. Governors abuse their power by defining the happiness of the governed so as to include what they find most beneficial to themselves. The abuse is not recognized as such because most men are inclined to believe that everyone should be his brother's keeper, and accordingly that the rulers are properly the 'keepers' of the ruled. If a government is allowed to judge what happiness should mean to the ruled, its policies are practically unassailable, since it can always retort that the objector does not properly understand what is 'good'. But if happiness is defined as whatever a man desires, then a government committed to promoting the happiness of the governed can justify only policies that accord with the wishes of the governed. The latter will be able to object clearly and forcefully when the government is ignoring their wishes, and the government will not be able to excuse discriminating against some tastes on the grounds that they do not accord with a 'true' view of happiness.

But the principle of the 'greatest happiness of the greatest number' was not

[1] *Ibid.* vol. X, p. 216.
[2] *Ibid.* vol. IX, p. 5.

enough to guide politics. It had to be supplemented by the 'principle of self-preference', according to which, 'in the general tenor of life, in every human breast, self-regarding interest is predominant over all other interests put together'.[1] This meant that every human being would choose that line of conduct which seemed to him at the moment most likely to increase his own happiness. Again, like the principle of utility, in a way it said nothing much. Macaulay's observation that the principle of self-preference when explained means only 'that men if they can, will do as they choose . . .'[2] was not as damning as he believed. Or, at least, Bentham would have agreed. For he did not mean to say that men were incapable of sympathy or benevolence; nor did he doubt that there were noble men. But political reasoning, he was certain, should not assume that such men existed:

admitting, as perhaps it may be admitted, that in a highly matured state of society, in here and there a highly cultivated and expanded mind, under the stimulus of some extraordinary excitement, a sacrifice of self-regarding interest to social interest upon a national scale has not been without example—public virtue in this shape cannot reasonably be regarded as being so frequently exemplified as insanity.[3]

Even if the probability of evil were ever so faint, Bentham was anxious to guard against it, for by minor precautions, great evils could be prevented. By trusting to the benevolence of men in power one took great and unnecessary risks; to assume that they were malevolent was not perhaps accurate, but much safer.

There was another implication of the self-preference principle that interested Bentham quite as much. It emphasized that whether or not men were selfish, they could not but see one another through alien eyes. The purest of motives could not do away with an ultimate barrier between individual men. In short, the self-preference principle expressed, in an unusual, technical form, Bentham's awareness of an ultimate mystery and privacy about every man's view of life.

By basing political thinking on these principles, Bentham hoped to eliminate from politics vague, mystical notions like natural law. Authors who opposed natural laws to enacted legislation, he declared, were simply trying to substitute laws of their own invention for established laws. If that were not the case, there could not be so much disagreement about the substance of natural laws. Because all systems of natural law were imaginary, anyone could make them what he pleased. It was not disagreement with what natural law theorists advocated that inspired Bentham's objections, but dislike of any language that had no clear reference to something concrete.

[1] *Ibid.* p. 5.
[2] Macaulay, *Essays and Biographies* (London, 1906), vol. I, p. 365.
[3] *Works*, vol. IX, p. 61.

If any supplement to utility were necessary, he preferred to speak of 'securities against misrule', because, 'When instead of the word "securities" and "misrule", you employ such a word as "right", a cloud, and that of a black hue, overshadows the whole field'.[1] In fact, 'securities against misrule' served much the same function for Bentham as 'natural rights' do for others. Thus Bentham could explain that, 'if no demand for security against misrule can have place, until and except in so far as some law is violated, no such security can possibly be obtained in the case in which it is most needed'.[2] Much the same sort of consideration, led him to deplore constitutional prohibitions because they enabled past generations to impose their will on the future, and yet to insist that a proper legal code must begin with a general law of liberty—'a law which should restrain delegated powers, and limit their exercise to certain particular occasions, for certain specific causes'.[3]

Occasionally, and indirectly, he even admitted an affinity with natural law writers. His criticism of Grotius and Pufendorf was that while they recognized utility as 'the mother of Justice and Equity',[4] they did not sufficiently disentangle it from all the vague generalities to which they were addicted. Grotius, he said, 'enters into an investigation which is not altogether of the clearest, but the result of which is that utility, though not the parent of natural law, is however a distant relation to it, being first cousin to its Great-Grandmother'.[5]

But anything like the French Declaration of Rights was useless. 'I am sorry that you have undertaken to publish a Declaration of Rights', Bentham wrote to Brissot-'It is a metaphysical work—the *ne plus ultra* of metaphysics. . . . You can never make a law against which it may not be averred, that by it you have abrogated the Declaration of Rights, and the averment will be unanswerable'.[6] For the same reason he considered the American Declaration of Independence 'a hodge-podge of confusion and absurdity, in which the thing to be proved is all along taken for granted'.[7]

Those who chose to criticize what they considered a bad law by denying that it was a law were indulging in idle talk. A command of the legislature continued to be law until it was repealed by the legislature. To demonstrate that it was a bad law one had to point out its defects and the superiority of a new rule to be put in its place. The only way to show the defects of a law

---

[1] *Ibid.* vol. VIII, p. 557.

[2] *Ibid.* p. 557.

[3] *Ibid.* vol. I, p. 576.

[4] Bentham, *The Limits of Jurisprudence Defined*, ed. by C. W. Everett (New York, 1945), p. 117.

[5] *Ibid.* p. 118.

[6] *Works*, vol. X, pp. 214–15.

[7] *Ibid.* p. 63.

was by considering how it was related to the feelings and actions of men living here and now. That was what the principles of utility and of self-preference forced one to do. As long as the discussion used the language of utility, Bentham was more than willing to make the same sort of judgements that natural law theorists made, to declare some positive laws good and others bad according to a standard outside them.

Yet the language of utility did more than impose a way of speaking and thinking about politics. It defined certain conditions of good government.

In the first place, the principle of utility forbade any sort of paternalism in politics. This meant for Bentham that it was important to preserve not only liberty of conscience, of the press, or of opinion—they were in any case 'in one place or another established'—but also liberty of taste. This liberty was 'the last that remained to be established', and was as yet 'scarcely so much as advocated'.[1] Paternal government, which encouraged a member of parliament to decide what another man, whom he had never met, felt and needed, was at the least presumptuous, but even more an insult to adults. Grown men were not to be treated as children—'pupillage being a state of dependence is an evil which ought to cease as soon as it is possible without occasioning a greater evil'.[2] Only infancy and insanity justified paternalism. Of course, all men had somehow to be restrained for the good of others—society must put 'bridles in our mouths' to prevent 'our doing mischief to one another'—but to direct a man for his own good was another matter: 'The tacking of leading strings upon the backs of grown persons in order to prevent their doing themselves a mischief is not necessary either to the being or tranquility of society however conducive to its well being'.[3]

Morality and legislation had the same centre, but not the same circumference; whereas morality guided the individual throughout his life, in all his relations with his fellows, legislation could not, and anyway should not. There were many injurious actions which it ought not to forbid, although morality did. For legislation could influence behaviour only by punishments, and in many attempts to cure some lapse from morality the evil of the punishment would be greater than the evil of the offence. Moreover, it was too difficult to define some offences precisely enough so that the innocent would not be caught in attempts to punish the guilty—'Instead of suppressing one vice, the laws would produce other vices, new and more dangerous'.[4] Legislators who would not trust to the prudence of individuals, but tried to trace for their subjects, day by day, moment by moment, all the petty details of their life,

[1] *Ibid.* p. 530.
[2] *Ibid.* vol. I, p. 348.
[3] *Ibid.* vol. III, p. 5.
[4] Bentham, *The Theory of Legislation*, ed. C. K. Ogden, (London, 1950), p. 62.

were possessed by the same passion and littleness of spirit that characterized founders of religious orders.

In opposing any right of the state to enforce virtue, Bentham did not deny society a role in helping individuals to live well. For society is not, in his view, synonymous with the state. There were after all a multitude of non-political institutions—the family, the school, the church—that could look after social wants other than the narrowly political. Admittedly the most necessary and powerful single part of society was the political community, but it was by no means the whole, and the function of government, Bentham insisted, was not to make men lead the best possible life:

The principal business of the laws, the only business which is evidently and incontestibly necessary, is the preventing of individuals from pursuing their own happiness, by the destruction of a greater portion of the happiness of others. To impose restraints upon the individual for his own welfare, is the business of education; the duty of the old towards the young; of the keeper towards the madman: it is rarely the duty of the legislator towards the people.[1]

The only legitimate way for governments to reason about the happiness of their subjects was with 'reference to their own desires and feelings',[2] for the purpose of gratifying as many desires as were compatible with the equal right of all men to happiness. This is what the principle of utility enabled legislators to do. It provided a clear criterion for their decisions.

But it was not enough for Bentham to state the general principle. He was anxious to guard against any intrusion of mystery, against any cover of tyranny, to make reasoning about desires and feelings precise and objective. The value of a pleasure, he explained carefully, depended on four circumstances—intensity, duration, certainty, proximity. But as pleasures and pains often produced others, one must take into account also the productiveness and purity of a pleasure or pain, and where many individuals were concerned, its extent, that is, the number of persons likely to be affected. In addition, Bentham devoted many pages to analyzing the 'circumstances influencing sensibility', to classifying motives and dispositions, in a great many divisions and subdivisions full of numbers and italics. He recognized that to list all the circumstances influencing sensibility would 'be a work of great labour as well as nicety: history and biography would need to be ransacked: a vast course of reading would need to be travelled through'.[3] So he confined himself regretfully to 'dry and general instructions'. He wished that psychology were more like temperature in physics, so that one could measure degrees of trustworthiness by some simple device like a thermometer. For the present, he

---

[1] *Works*, vol. I, p. 163.
[2] *Ibid.* p. 344.
[3] *Principles of Morals*, p. 166 n.

knew of only two sorts of pleasures and pains that could be measured—pecuniary interest and aversion to labour.[1] But for the rest he could provide tables of factors that legislators ought to take into account.

If the principle of utility ruled out paternalism, it also made it clear that whatever his intentions, the legislator could not avoid imposing his will on others whenever he passed a law. For laws are general, and however carefully framed, they have to overlook many differences among men and circumstances. The legislator is forced to 'make use of general terms or names', so that persons, things, and acts are considered 'in parcels'.[2] A general law assumes a perfectly smooth and flat surface where there are in fact many ridges and furrows. It treats large numbers of men as if they were grains of sand. Although certain uniformities and regular connections between outward signs and inward dispositions gain for the legislator 'the suffrage of opinion', they never make government action preferable to private. Thus the principle of utility made it clear that 'every man is the best judge of his own interests', or, more exactly, that the legislator was likely to be a worse judge because he could not, indeed should not, know individuals. Apart then from ruling out deliberate paternalism in politics, the principle of utility added to the debit side of every government action the impossibility of accommodating law to differences of temperament and circumstance.

Finally, the principle of utility made it impossible to forget that a government acted only through inflicting pain. If one considered every action in terms of pleasures and pains in individuals, it became clear that even when government did not punish, even when it merely offered rewards, it still coerced, and inflicted pain. For money bestowed upon one man could come only from taxes on others, and therefore represented the pain of loss that they suffered; rewards of honour were similarly costly to someone, for honour meant pre-eminence and if one man was elevated another suffered from being made the lower of the two. Every law, then, whatever its nature, imposed 'the evil of coercion or restraint; or the pain which it gives a man not to be able to do that whatever it be, which by the apprehension of the punishment he is deterred from doing'.[3] Even when a law required a man to act as he would generally, it forced him to ignore any temporary dislike he might feel for such action, and added to his deliberations the possibility of punishment. Therefore the legislator must never forget that whatever good a law might do in the long run, it was certain 'in the first instance to produce mischief. . . . No law can ever be made but what trenches upon liberty. . . . To make a law is to do evil that good may come'.[4] It was not enough to find something in favour of

---

[1] *Works*, vol. VII, p. 568.
[2] *Limits of Jurisprudence*, p. 167.
[3] *Principles of Morals*, p. 286.
[4] *Limits of Jurisprudence*, p. 139.

a law; it had to be shown that its benefits outweighed the general reasons against every law. The business of government was essentially to choose among evils. The whole art of politics consisted in combatting one evil with another, just as the doctor employed poisons to cure pain. Again, Bentham did not let the matter rest there, but provided the legislator with means for analysing and weighing carefully the evils between which he had to choose—evils of the first, second, or third order, primitive or immediate evils, permanent or evanescent evils, and so on.

From these principles, it followed that it could not be desirable for a government to manage all economic affairs directly. In the first place, a government would require unlimited prerogative just in order to gather the necessary information about what was wanted and what could be made available. Futhermore, to match human desires, the laws would have to be discriminatory and changeable rather than general and stable, and even so, they would fail to secure a workable economy. A competitive system was free of such difficulties. For competition operated by bargains and exchanges between individuals in which each had to give up something, and yet received something he wanted in return—and all exchanges are founded on reciprocal advantages. By these means, men were given as good an opportunity as society could contrive to decide for themselves what they wished to make and consume.

Competition held no mysterious virtues.[1] Bentham thought it was a good

---

[1] Halévy's diagnosis (in *The Growth of Philosophic Radicalism*) of a conflict in Bentham between the principle of the natural identity of interests which governs his economics and the principle of the artificial identification of interests which governs his law reform has encouraged a gross misinterpretation of Bentham, as well as of Adam Smith and his followers. Neither Bentham nor Smith believed in a natural harmony or a natural identity of interests. Smith's metaphor, the 'invisible hand', was designed to emphasize the possibility of achieving certain social effects indirectly—'By preferring the support of domestic to that of foreign industry, he intends only his own security; and by directing that industry in such a manner as its product may be of the greatest value, he intends only his own gain, and he is in this, as in many other cases, led by an invisible hand to promote an end which was *no part of his intention*'. [My italics; *Wealth of Nations* (Modern Library), p. 423]. It is the last part of the sentence that is most significant. The whole of the *Wealth of Nations*, just as Bentham's economic writings, is designed to show how the unintended consequences of certain individual actions may work out to be of social value. So-called *laissez-faire* economics advocates not that certain desired social effects should be left to nature, but that they are best aimed for *indirectly*. The action of government is neither unnecessary nor peripheral, as Halévy assumes; only it should be used not to achieve certain desired results directly, but to encourage them to follow upon individual actions.

Those who cannot believe that order can be achieved without having been purposely designed by someone will inevitably assume, as Halévy did, that any willingness to rely on unintended consequences reflects a belief in a natural harmony. If that were true, however, neither the *Wealth of Nations* nor any of Bentham's economic essays need have been

146

system because he believed men wanted very different things and should be permitted the greatest possible liberty of taste. Although the variety of human desires made government control inefficient and unjust, in free arrangements between members of the community this variety of desires made possible mutually satisfactory exchanges. Thus competition was likely to coerce less and waste less than attempts by government officials to run things from the centre.

The government had to make certain that the exchanges were truly free, that no coercion was used by one of the parties. Its main task in the realm of economics was to prevent any substitution of force for bargaining. There were besides some areas where other considerations had to take precedence over freedom of choice, and there the government had to supplement or supplant private enterprise. The government should provide, for instance, against indigence. The same objections did not apply here, Bentham argued, for the pain of hunger could be relieved in all men by fairly uniform methods, and was undoubtedly greater than any pain inflicted by the taxes imposed to provide for the indigent. Infancy could not look after itself; neither could old age. If the care and protection of relatives was precarious even for children, it was especially so for old people. And even capable adults might sometimes need to be protected by the government. In the highest state of social prosperity, many men might have no resource other than their daily industry, so that accidents, such as revolutions of commerce, natural calamities, and above all, illness, could throw them into indigence.

If savings and voluntary contributions sufficed to provide for such extremities they would be preferable to aid given by law, for such provision discouraged industry, or at least, frugality, by seeming to reward idleness and dissipation. But in fact savings and voluntary contributions could not do the job. Even if some of those reduced to indigence might have provided for themselves,

written since their purpose is to examine in detail the process by which certain social effects are produced by certain sorts of individual behaviour.

Halévy's dichotomy between the two principles in Bentham's thought is valuable insofar as it draws attention to some sort of break, but it wrongly describes its nature. The real conflict in Bentham's thought is between a willingness to accept one sort of social process in economic matters and a conviction that it is chaotic when allowed to prevail in other areas such as law. Bentham's attitude to the common law is understandable in terms of his antipathy to anything that cannot be subjected to logical analysis. Since the common law could be understood only historically, to Bentham's mind, it was an unforgiveable haven to mystery. His acceptance of unintended consequences in economics is understandable since he believed that there they could be explained by a fairly adequate and simple theory which removed any appearance of mystery. But Halévy's thesis leaves Bentham incomprehensively addicted to a mystical notion such as 'natural harmony' or 'a natural identity of interests', just the sort of notion he abhorred and most violently denounced. Neither does it explain the peculiar character of Bentham's opposition to the common law.

and failed through neglect or sloth, they did not constitute an argument against government protection, for vengeance is not a proper object of law:

Vengeance is condemned by the principle of utility, as an impure motive founded upon antipathy. What will be the fruit of these evils, this neglect and this indigence, which you regard in your anger as a just punishment of prodigality. . . . The distress, the death of some prodigals, of those unhappy persons who have not been able to refuse themselves the infinitely little enjoyments of their condition, who have not known the painful art of striving by reflection against the temptations of every moment—their distress, I say, even their death itself, would have little influence, as instruction, upon the laborious classes of society.[1]

The legislator ought then to establish a regular contribution for the wants of the indigent, but only those in need of absolute necessities should be regarded as indigent.

National security had likewise to be provided for by the government. This did not include, Bentham made it clear, protection for struggling industries, because subsidies inevitably involved injustice—they meant taking funds and privileges from some members of the community in order to distribute them to others. But the Navigation Act was necessary, even though it granted the shipping industry advantages denied to other members of the community. In this case, the injustice was less important than the common need for a strong navy, and the national benefits secured through a Navigation Act were sufficiently great to override the drawbacks.

It was always proper for the government to assist in the spread of information. Bentham urged that the government require clear labelling of poisonous substances, and establish brands or marks for quantity and quality. Such activities were justifiable because, without coercing, they helped the individual to satisfy his wants more effectively. They were not at all like the government's undertaking enterprises on its own account, for a government official could neither know nor care as much as the private entrepreneur about how capital could best be employed. But if a minister received special information, he would do well to make it available to the public. Then, whether a project was desirable or not would be decided by whether it satisfied the wants of individuals. This would be known best by those immediately concerned with the matter, by those who stood to lose by judging wrongly. In any case, the mistakes of some could be corrected by others.

It was important to let individuals bear the responsibility for their decisions, for otherwise the system could not work. Bentham objected therefore to 'sentimental' protection against loss, such as the Roman practice of abolishing debts, so admired by generous souls. It was not, he insisted, an act of benevolence but quite the contrary, and it had unfortunate economic effects even on debtors:

[1] *Works*, vol. I, p. 315.

I cannot refrain from noticing here the ill effects of one branch of classical education. Youth are accustomed from their earliest days to see, in the history of the Roman people, public acts of injustice, atrocious in themselves always coloured under specious names, always accompanied by a pompous eulogium respecting Roman virtues. The abolition of debts occupies a conspicuous place in the early transactions of the Republic . . . .. The historian excites all our interest in favour of the fraudulent debtors who discharged their debts by a bankruptcy and does not fail to render those odious who were thus despoiled by an act of violence. What end was answered by this iniquity? The usury which had served as a pretext for this theft, was only augmented on the morrow by this catastrophe; for the exorbitant rate of interest was only the price paid for the risks attached to the uncertainty of engagements.[1]

Bentham's attitude to the activities of government abroad was governed by the same principle. Colonization, for instance, was not to be justified by the glories of empire. It was worth considering under some circumstances when it yielded benefits both to the home country and to the colonial possession. Although he added a few suggestions, Bentham held basically the same views as Adam Smith. Colonization could be used to relieve the pressure of too great a population. Besides, colonies might add to the wealth of the world by working unused lands, often very rich in raw materials. When a colony was well conducted and free of regulations that might hinder its prosperity, 'there may result from it a new people with whom we shall possess all the connections of language, of social habits, of natural and political ties'.[2] But in fact most colonies seemed to Bentham undesirable.

They were mainly a burden to the mother country. They required a great investment of capital which never yielded as much as it might have at home. Markets and new products could be had more cheaply by free trade; there was no need to govern or possess a land in order to sell merchandise there. The advantages of monopolies cherished by mother countries were all illusory: the monopoly might produce a forced reduction of prices for a time, but the colonist would not continue to cultivate sugar if he lost by its cultivation. The monopoly that obliged colonists to buy from the mother country was equally unnecessary: If the products were actually superior to and cheaper than those of other countries they would be bought anyway; if inferior products were forced on the colonies, the monopoly was in effect a subsidy to home industries which ought to die. Moreover, the mother country might suffer by being obliged in return to buy only from her colonies when she might do better elsewhere. To all this was added the cost of preserving colonies—'When you have made a prison of your colonies, it is necessary to keep all doors carefully shut'. A single war could wipe out even the greatest benefits, and above all, considerations of justice and humanity told against colonies:

[1] *Ibid.* p. 318.
[2] *Ibid.* vol. III, p. 56.

149

The evils suffered in these establishments from the ignorance, the weakness, or the insensibility of European governments, exceed everything which can be imagined. When we consider the multitudes of men destroyed, the fleets lost, the treasures swallowed up, the establishments pillaged—we are astonished to hear colonies spoken of as a means of enrichment. The natural development of their fruitfulness, and of their industry, has been retarded for ages . . . nations have impoverished themselves, that they might hold them in servitude, when they might have been sharers in their wealth by leaving to them the enjoyment of the benefits of liberty.[1]

Still, Bentham did not advocate rash emancipation: 'It is necessary to examine what is due to colonial establishments—to a family which has been created and which ought not to be abandonned'. Certain questions had to be considered before emancipating any colony:

Can they maintain themselves? Will not their internal tranquility be interrupted? Will not one class of the inhabitants be sacrificed to another? for example, the free men to the slaves, or the slaves to the free men? Is it not necessary that they should be protected and directed in their condition of comparative weakness and ignorance? Is not their present state of dependence their safeguard against anarchy, murder and pillage?[2]

As in all questions, pleasures and pains had to be carefully weighed. Vague sentimentality inevitably corrupted thinking about public questions. The only way to judge good and bad in politics was to reduce every policy to concrete acts and feelings.

But above all, Bentham was anxious to make governments realize and remember that all other ends were subordinate to the greatest happiness. It was not that rulers deliberately sought evil, but they were easily seduced into it by false views of greatness and power, or by private passions. Morality, equality, liberty, justice, power, commerce, religion—all these were objects respectable in themselves, which ought to enter into the views of the legislator, but they were means, not ends as they were so often taken to be. Thus a government 'entirely occupied with wealth and commerce, looks upon society as a workshop, regards men only as productive machines, and cares little how much it torments them, provided it makes them rich'. Such governments were indifferent to a multitude of evils that could be cured; while looking for greater production of the means of enjoyment, they constantly put obstacles in the way of enjoying. Equally harmful were governments that sought only power and glory, that disdained peaceful security, and lost themselves in intrigues, negotiations, wars, and conquests: 'They do not consider of what misfortunes this glory is composed, and how many victims these bloody triumphs require. The "eclat" of victory, the acquisition of a province, conceal from

[1] *Ibid.* p. 56.
[2] *Ibid.* p. 56.

them the desolation of their country, and make them mistake the true end of government'.[1] It was a mistake as well to think only of the equal distribution of political power or to think that all but one form of government necessarily imposed slavery, to care nothing about whether a state was well administered, whether the laws protected property and persons, whether the people were happy. Fanatics 'are always ready to stake all the happiness of a nation upon a civil war, for the sake of transporting power into the hands of those whom an invincible ignorance will not permit to use it, except for their own destruction'. Such fantasies all grew out of the same error—'A small part of the plan of utility is seized upon; an exclusive attachment is evinced for the small part; in the pursuit of some particular branch of the public good, the general happiness is disregarded . . .'.[2] Only the happiness of the greatest number deserved such unqualified devotion.

As to the form of government, that was simply a matter of making the actual end coincide with the proper end of government. The best solution, Bentham came to believe, was to place the ultimate power in the hands of all. Although he did not write on the question until fairly late in life, and was quite willing at all times to deal with absolute monarchs, occasionally even to favour them, the principles on which his theory of democracy was based were those he put forward in his earliest writings. He had never been an admirer of the aristocracy, and in the *Fragment*, he had disputed Blackstone's confidence in their superior wisdom: 'The fact is, as everybody sees, that either the members of the House of Commons are as much at leisure as those of the House of Lords, or, if occupied, occupied in such a way as tends to give them more than ordinary insight into some particular object of government'.[3] Moreover, Bentham pointed out, members of the House of Commons who had yet to make their fortunes, had a greater interest in acquiring wisdom than those peers who were already at the top. It did not, however, follow that the people possessed all virtues—they were 'a set of masters whom it is not in a man's power in every instance fully to please and at the same time faithfully to serve'.[4] Bentham's preference for democracy did not stem from a love or hatred of any class; it followed logically from his principles.

A monarchy could not satisfy the requirements of good government because, like any other man, a king invariably sought his own interest, and nothing constrained him to seek the greatest happiness of the greatest number. In a limited monarchy, where a small privileged class shared power with the king, the government aimed at the happiness of those few. Only in a democracy, where power was in the hands of all, would the government

[1] *Theory of Legislation*, pp. 14–15.
[2] *Ibid.* p. 15.
[3] *Fragment*, p. 75.
[4] *Ibid.* p. 30.

necessarily seek the happiness of all. Ideally, there ought therefore to be universal suffrage, annual parliaments, vote by ballot, no king, no house of peers, no established church. Members of parliament should never be given two consecutive terms and should be made to attend to business conscientiously by elaborate rules. Every four years, they should elect a prime minister. By all these devices, Bentham hoped to make it impossible for the government to neglect or to sacrifice the public interest to some private interest. Although he did not advocate revolution to establish a perfect government, in reflecting on what made a government work well, he was not inclined to weigh in the influence of tradition or custom. That was the sort of intangible, mystical factor with which he preferred not to traffic.

To the relationship between the member of parliament and his constituents, Bentham gave careful thought. The member of parliament ought to act, he believed, as a deputy rather than as a representative. But he must not bind himself to any particular policy beforehand, for that would require disavowing his conscience. If upon reflection he found that his constituents' opinions were contrary to his own view of what the greatest happiness required, he had to do one of two things: resign his seat or speak on the measure as his judgement directed, while voting as his constituents demanded. He might hope that his arguments would convince his constituents or that his vote in accordance with their wishes would not lessen the greatest happiness, but he had no other recourse.[1] Among his odd papers, Bentham left a sketch of an address to a constituency, written probably when he hoped for a seat from Shelburne:

I cannot engage to give silent votes or to argue in favour of what are not my opinions, and import into the senate the disingenuity of the bar. This only I will say, and I say it truly, that, to find myself in contradiction to the sentiments of a clear and permanent majority among you, would ever be matter to me of the most poignant concern, and the most mortifying disgrace.[2]

It was not a very lofty declaration, but it testified to the orator's awareness of the need to flatter, to persuade, and yet remain honest.

For all his hard-headedness, Bentham was inclined to be optimistic about democracy, mainly because of his faith in progress, in the efficacy of new knowledge. He was certain that the Athenian outrages need not be repeated by modern democracy. After all, the influence of Montesquieu, of Bacon and Newton, had made modern political speculation much superior to the ancient; past generations laboured under disadvantages from which modern men were free. The people were no worse than any other class:

I have not that horror of the people. I do not see in them that savage monster which their detractors dream of. The injustices of the Athenians, had they been ten

[1] *Works*, vol. IX, p. 161.
[2] *Ibid.* vol. X, p. 245.

times as frequent as they were, would not, in my view of things, be much to the present purpose . . . had they the light of two thousand years of history to guide them? or the art of printing to diffuse it? When the Athenians were cruel and unjust, were the Dionysiuses and Artaxerxeses less so?[1]

In later years, the success of America seemed to Bentham to have demonstrated that a democracy could work.

Yet Bentham had no mystical faith in democracy either. He resolutely rejected 'the imposture of collective wisdom'. Terms like 'the community', 'public interest', and 'public good' offended him. They were fictions, wilful falsehoods that allowed unauthorized persons to steal power. A word like 'community' was all too easily shrouded in mystery and used to mislead the untutored, or apt to encourage even the best-willed men to forget the realities to which it referred. 'The public interest', Bentham declared, 'is only an abstract term: it represents only the mass of the interests of individuals'. It made no sense to talk of sacrificing 'individual interests' to the 'public interest'; such a statement was either a tautology or it meant giving the interests of some individuals pre-eminence over those of others—'they ought all to be taken account of, instead of considering some as everything, and the rest as nothing'. A government that justified itself by appealing to the 'public interest' covered 'a question in itself simple', with 'an air of profundity and political mystery' in order to frighten timid citizens out of questioning its policies.[2]

Democracy was simply a mechanism that effectively muzzled power. It was not predicated on a belief in the virtue or wisdom of any class. If Bentham preferred to leave the day-to-day work of governing in the hands of men who might be described as belonging to the middle classes, it was only because unlike the ordinary labourer they more often had time and a basic education, and unlike the leisured aristocrats, they had some experience of affairs. It was their personal qualifications, not any aura about their class, that mattered to Bentham. When he came to advocate universal suffrage, it did not mean that he had transferred his allegiance from one class to another. He never renounced his statement of 1795 made in criticism of America: 'What then shall we say of that system of government of which the professed object is to call upon the untaught and unlettered multitude whose existence depends on their devoting their whole time to the acquisition of the means of supporting it, to occupy themselves without ceasing upon all questions of government?'[3] The essence of democracy was that it made it impossible for any man to have his way without the concurrence of at least many others; no one then could find supporters unless his interests coincided with theirs. A democracy did not rely on greater purity of morals; quite the contrary, it assumed that

[1] *Ibid.* vol. IV, p. 363. [2] *Ibid.* vol. I, p. 321.
[3] *Ibid.* vol. II, p. 522.

because every man would pursue his own interests, everyone would check everyone else: 'The principle of self-preference has for its regulator in the breast of each, the consciousness of the existence and power of the same principle in the breasts of all the rest: and thus it is that the whole mechanism is at all times kept in a state of perfect order'.[1]

In the same spirit, Bentham favoured freedom of the press. He never argued that given freedom, truth would prevail, but rather:

If the liberty of the press may have its inconveniences arising from pamphlets and loose sheets being spread among the public, addressed to the ignorant as well as to the enlightened part of the nation, the same reason need not be applied to serious works of greater length—to books which can only have a certain class of readers, and which cannot produce any immediate effect but which allow time to prepare an antidote.[2]

Liberty of the press had its drawbacks, but 'the evil that might result from it was not to be compared with the evil of censorship'.[3] Like all things, it was a mixed blessing, to be preferred because in the end it made for the least possible interference with the freedom of individuals to pursue their own ends.

[1] *Ibid.* vol. IX, p. 63.
[2] *Ibid.* vol. I, p. 575.
[3] *Ibid.* p. 538.

CHAPTER XIII

A PERFECT SYSTEM OF LEGISLATION

THE IMPORTANCE OF LOGIC

AT first sight, then, nothing very striking distinguishes Bentham's general view of politics from Hume's. His concern for tolerance was perhaps more nearly a ruling interest, but it was one that Hume would have found congenial. Hume might have been amused by Bentham's painstakingly detailed discussions of questions that he mentioned only in passing, but he would have considered Bentham's arguments reasonable and valuable. Bentham was more suspicious of the aristocracy, perhaps less so of the lower classes, certainly more critical of the existing British government. But it is not any difference of opinion that divides Bentham from Hume so much as the style of his thinking, which belongs to another world.

The difference is partly a matter of syntax and vocabulary. Bentham's distinctive way of using the English language appeared even in his earliest work, but it became more pronounced with the years. All sentences, Bentham came to think, should have the same structure; they should have only one leading idea, placed as close as possible to the beginning, to be followed at once by the qualifying clauses. Repetition in a complex sentence was highly desirable because it revived and strengthened impressions.[1] While he occasionally failed to write as he preached, either because he was more anxious to make converts than to increase scientific knowledge, or because he let himself lapse into informality, in his serious work he observed his rules meticulously. He outlawed verbs in favour of substantives and would never write 'to move' if he could use 'to give motion': 'Where a substantive is employed, the idea is stationed as it were upon a rock; where no substantive is employed but only a verb, the idea is as it were a twig or leaf floating on a stream, and hurried down out of view along with it'.[2] He coined new words, some of which are now common—maximize, minimize, international, codify, eulogistic, dislogistic—along with others which have not yet been accepted—maleficence, filiality, impossibilized, interessees, archetypation, phraseoplerosis, noology, thelematology, nomography, deography, and pathography. His insistence on imbedding all qualifications within each sentence led Hazlitt to declare that high treason wrapped up in one of his inextricable periods 'would never find its way into Westminster Hall'. The wrappings not infrequently made sentences like the following:

[1] *Works*, vol. VIII, p. 316.   [2] *Ibid.* vol. III, p. 267.

But so far as concerns acquisition, finding that operation, necessary as it is to human existence, loaded notwithstanding, to wit, by the influence of the above-mentioned causes, with the sort of reproach involved in the import of the several articles, in the long list of dyslogistic appellatives exhibited in the Table—and at the same time not provided with eulogistic, nor so much as with neutral appellatives—thence, in their endeavours to obtain the approbation of their hearers or readers—and for that purpose to elude the force of the dyslogistic appellatives, which in a manner lie in wait for it, unable to find for the desire in question any appellative, which by its eulogistic quality, would be rendered applicable to their purpose—men put aside that species of desire, and look out for some other, which, being furnished with eulogistic appellatives, shall, at the same time, be nearly enough resembling to it, or connected with it, to be made to pass instead of it.[1]

In other words, men try to avoid being called acquisitive.

Yet more than complicated or clumsy language was involved. For even when Bentham meant to be supporting the same conclusions as Hume drew, the difference in expression affected the substance of the argument. When he argued against the theory of the original contract, he was not content to show the defects of abstractions or how easily they could be confounded with one another. He had to replace the old abstractions with better ones. Instead of saying, as Hume had, that political society in fact arose haphazardly out of a variety of circumstances, many of them accidental, Bentham felt obliged to define political society exactly: 'When a number of persons (whom we may style subjects) are supposed to be in the habit of paying obedience to a person, or an assemblage of persons, of a known and certain description (whom we may call governor or governors), such persons altogether (subjects and governors) are said to be in a state of political society'.[2] Similarly, he could not rest with ridiculing Blackstone's phrases about natural law and their effect on government. He had to explain

that the authority of the supreme body cannot, unless where limited by express convention, be said to have any assignable, any certain bounds—That is to say, there is any act they cannot do—to speak of anything of their's as being illegal—as being void;—to speak of their exceeding their authority (whatever be the phrase), —their power, their right—is, however common, an abuse of language.[3]

To demarcate the limits of law, Bentham was never inclined to confess as Burke did: 'It is one of the finest problems in legislation, and what has often engaged my thoughts whilst I followed that profession—What the state ought to take upon itself to direct by the public wisdom, and what it ought to leave, with as little interference as possible to individual discretion . . .'. Nor would he confine himself to any general statement about public peace, safety, order and prosperity; not even a list of activities fit for government would do.

[1] *Ibid.* vol. I, p. 214.
[2] *Fragment*, p. 38.
[3] *Ibid.* p. 95.

Instead, Bentham devoted to this problem twenty sections of a difficult chapter. After defining ethics—'Ethics in as far as it is the art of directing a man's actions, may be styled the art of self-government, or private ethics',[1] he moves on to the question: 'What other agents are under human influence and susceptible of happiness?' And he answers: 'Other human beings who are styled persons, and animals which on account of their interests having been neglected by the sensibility of the ancient jurists, stand degraded into the class of things'.[2] Finally, after a similar long preamble on legislation, he produces a definition of legislation, as 'the art of government: which in as far as the measures it displays itself in are of a permanent nature is generally distinguished by the name of legislation: as it is by that of administration, when they are of a temporary nature, determined by the occurrences of the day'.

But since human beings are of two classes, non-adult and adult, Bentham continues, there is in the art of government a sub-class called education, which also has two divisions—private and public. After further discourse on the three categories of ethical rules, Bentham arrives at the conclusion that while both ethics and legislation have happiness for their end, while 'the very acts which they ought to be conversant about, are even in a great measure the same', they 'are not perfectly and throughout the same'.[3] After five more pages, the line is at last drawn. Although some amplification is saved by a reference to an earlier chapter on 'Cases Unmeet for Punishment', we are told that there are four cases where legislation should not, while ethics should, interfere: '1. Where punishment would be groundless. 2. Where it would be inefficacious. 3. Where it would be unprofitable. 4. Where it would be needless'.[4] Half a dozen more pages produce the relatively short statement: 'It is only with respect to those broad lines of conduct in which all persons, or very large and permanent descriptions of persons, may be in a way to engage, that he [the legislator] can have any pretence for interfering; and even here, the propriety of his interference will, in most instances, lie very open to dispute'.[5] After several more pages of elaboration, the whole is concluded with a recapitulation:

Private ethics teaches how each man may dispose himself to pursue the course most conducive to his own happiness, by means of such motives as offer of themselves; the art of legislation (which may be considered as one branch of the science of jurisprudence) teaches how a multitude of men, composing a community, may be disposed to pursue that course which upon the whole is the most conducive to the happiness of the whole community, by means of motives to be applied by the legislator.[6]

[1] *Principles of Morals*, p. 411.　　[2] *Ibid.* p. 411.
[3] *Ibid.* p. 414.　　[4] *Ibid.* p. 415.
[5] *Ibid.* p. 420.　　[6] *Ibid.* p. 423.

It is hardly surprising that Dumont, who had taken on the task of popularizing Bentham's work, complained, with exemplary mildness, that the forms were 'too scientific, the subdivisions too multifarious, the analyses too abstract'.

Bentham knew he was not easy to read; he did not mean to be. For he was convinced that truths in the political and moral sciences could not be 'forced into detached general propositions, unincumbered with explanations and exceptions'. All those writers who read so easily had cared only to hit upon some 'cant word or short form of words, such as should serve as a sort of hook on which to hang the opinions of which their prejudices and passions have been productive . . .'.[1] There was consequently nothing in the celebrated philosophers but 'delusive falsehood, as many sheet anchors to error, corroboratives to obstinacy, provocatives to violence, bars to true instruction, masks to ignorance'.[2] The so-called classics derived their influence mainly from misunderstandings arising from their abundant use of elliptical, metaphorical, and fictional expressions. Occasionally Aristotle was exempted from the general condemnation, for his method was more nearly to Bentham's taste. Plato, on the other hand, was the worst of all—'a whimsical, cracked-brained, but smooth-tongued journeyman [of Aristotle's] who begat on her [philosophy] a race of Chimaeras'.[3]

Political truths could not be stated so simply. They could not 'compress themselves into epigrams. They recoil from the tongue and pen of the declaimer. They flourish not in the same soil with sentiment. They grow among thorns; and are not to be plucked like daisies, by infants as they run'.[4] Bentham preferred to teach the reader to 'distinguish between showy language and sound sense—to warn him not to pay himself with words—to shew him that what may tickle the ear or dazzle the imagination, will not always inform the judgement . . .'.[5] The only way to avoid all the confusion and perversion was to 'lay aside the old phraseology and invent a new one',[6] though, perhaps in some cases, instead of wholly fabricating words one could put together two old words. But however one did it, the established canons of language had to be violated and a great many readers had to be offended, if one were to escape the seductions of imagination.

Above all, it was essential to define every term exactly, for 'proportioned, therefore, to the fixity given to words, will be the degree of security for good

---

[1] Letter to Dumont, May 11, 1802, Bentham-Dumont Mss., Library of Geneva University, in C. K. Ogden, *Bentham's Theory of Fictions* (London, 1932), p. xxvi.

[2] *Ibid.* p. xxvii.

[3] Mss., University College, London, Portfolio 69, f. 61, p. 199.

[4] *Principles of Morals*, p. 124.

[5] *Fragment*, p. 112.

[6] *Principles of Morals*, p. 221.

in every shape, and against evil in every shape. Until, therefore, the nomenclature and language of law shall be improved, the great end of good government cannot be fully attained'.[1] To rid human life of all the fictitious entities that plagued it, Bentham contemplated tracing out 'throughout the whole of their extent, the principal relations between the field of thought and the field of language—comprising of necessity the leading principles of the art and science of universal grammar'.[2] But even without such a grand map, he proposed to make the language of law exact by shaping it exclusively to its purpose. For as long as words carried associations connected with other contexts, they became treacherous invitations to imagining. Properly understood, any given tongue was not one language, but many languages, each an instrument fashioned for the needs of the particular environment in which it was to be employed. Every word had to be adapted strictly to the operation it helped to perform; it was like a part of a clock, nothing in itself, meaningful only in its appropriate context. Thus the language suitable for history could never be appropriate for law. Precise language was technical language.[3]

Bentham was certain that in every case it was possible explicitly to show how the import of a word was related to the fundamental ideas of pain and pleasure, and thus a 'distinct and fixed' meaning would be given to a 'numerous tribe of words of which, till that time, the meaning has been floating in the clouds and blown about by every blast of doctrine—words to which, in the mind of many a writer, no assignable ideas, no fixed, no real import, had been annexed'.[4] Only a rigorous application of logic was needed to make the references of words perfectly clear. The method of 'bipartition', exemplified by the Porphyrian tree, could solve all problems. The recipe was simple: Take any genus, divide it into two classes, one of which possesses, while the other lacks a certain mark. The two classes must be mutually exclusive and together exhaustive. Repeat the operation upon each of the classes.

THE STATE OF ENGLISH LAW

Nothing could violate these requirements more than English law in the eighteenth century. It had developed, much as languages do, out of a variety of customs and modes of thought. As it had had a continuous history of more than seven centuries, hardly a rule remained unaltered, and yet the body of the law was the same as that administered by the court of judges in the middle

---

[1] *Works*, vol. III, pp. 270-1.

[2] *Ibid.* vol. VIII, p. 120.

[3] Although Bentham called the kind of law he condemned 'technical', in that context he meant by it law that had grown rather than been created according to a logical system. See ch. I.   [4] *Ibid.* vol. III, p. 286.

of the twelfth century. There were records in Westminster (which are still there today), that bore testimony to this very real continuity.

The law of England had not been enacted on any guiding principle; there was no code, not even an authoritative statement of principle enacted in some superlative piece of legislation. Isolated examples of consolidating statutes collected and recapitulated the principles of some particular branch of law. But mainly, one had to look for English law not only, or even primarily, to acts of parliament, but to the reports of cases decided in the courts. Conceptions as fundamental as the sanctity of human life and the validity of contract depended not upon any legislative act, but upon judicial exposition.

Moreover, there were two independent streams of English judicial law, the common law and equity. The latter had grown out of the king's special authority and duty to supplement the defects of the ordinary law and correct the weaknesses of its procedure. It reflected an anxiety to make the system of law not only uniform but also able to recognize and adjust to the infinite variety of character and circumstance. Although the rules had to be firm and applied impartially, at times it was thought desirable to soften the rigid application of the law. Whereas the common law embodied those 'general customs which are the common rule of the whole kingdom', equity provided 'the cancellation and shutting up of the rigour of the law'. Victims of technicality in the courts of common law could petition the chancellor, the 'keeper of the King's conscience', and out of this there developed an independent Court of Chancery, where the appeal was not to authority, but to 'reason and good conscience'.

But the Court of Chancery, having passed through its early stage of doing battle with obstinate oppressors of the poor, with correcting the anomalies of feudal law and supporting the obligations of good faith, began spreading the most ingenious nets to catch any form of fraud. The court's operations became excessively refined, the natural reason of just men was overlaid with elaborate artifices and safeguards multiplied at a cost out of all proportion to the substance of what was being preserved. The court ceased to give fairly good working decisions within a moderate time; instead it imposed a standard of vigilance beyond the powers of ordinary mortals, barely compatible with the ordinary conduct of business, in which the intricacies swallowed up the litigants. The fact that the court operated on separate rules meant besides that on the same case judgement might be given for the plaintiff by the common law justices at Westminster Hall, and for the defendant by the chancellor at Lincoln's Inn.

Even within the common law itself, however, the logic of the law was not easy to follow. In the first place, it conceived of litigation essentially as a combat, a game between two parties in which the court was only umpire. The parties were wholly answerable for the conduct of their cases. The rules of the game were declared and applied by the court as was required, but it was for the parties to learn the rules and play the game correctly at their peril. The umpire would only declare his judgement and it was not his business if the players threw away any opportunities for scoring. If there was a relevant point to which the attention of the court was not called, the court could not be expected to take account of it. For its business was not to inquire, but to hear and determine between parties according to the proof which the parties brought forward.

Secondly, and worst of all by Bentham's standards, the law was not a collection of fixed propositions. The rules emerged out of litigation, and had to be extracted from the material facts of any particular case. Instead of deducing his decision from a fixed set of principles as Bentham would have wished, the judge reasoned by example, that is, he reasoned from case to case. Since he was bound by the doctrine of precedent, he was obliged to make his decision consistent with rulings in previous cases or in higher courts. In effect, he reasoned that since two cases were alike in one respect, they were alike in another respect. But he never compared only two cases, for the lawyers on the opposing sides stressed different sets of similarities. The judge had to decide which was the more pertinent resemblance and summed up his decision in a rule of law, that is, in a statement that certain facts would be normally followed by certain consequences. In giving judgement he was not bound by the statement of a rule of law made by the prior judge even in a case considered relevant. And he could rule out facts which had been considered important in the preceding case. His only obligation was to see the law as a fairly consistent whole.

What made this system so annoying to Bentham was that each time a decision was made, despite the emphasis on consistency, the rule of law necessarily changed somewhat. For it was at the very least extended to include new particulars, and as the new examples were added, the classification covering all of them became slightly different, until in time a new concept grew up. Each decision was in effect a reclassification of all the cases that went before. The classification changed as the classification was made.

The movement of the law was not produced only by the appearance of new conjunctions of circumstances. As people's wants and ideas changed, the words in a rule of law came to have new meanings, or notions once uncommon came to be widely held. Whereas in one case an argument for a similarity between cases might be refused by the court, later, when the idea had become accepted in society, the court might adopt it. In subsequent cases, the idea might be further defined and tied to other ideas already accepted by the courts. New concepts were thus always being gradually accepted, and pushing an old category out of the system or converting it into something else. Sometimes the accommodation was made by attaching new meanings to old concepts, so that while the legal category remained the same in form, its content was altered. In this way fictions became common, for they made it possible to stretch the law to fit new circumstances without breaking the fabric.

The law consequently fluctuated between legal concepts in the process of being built up and concepts which were breaking down. It was a continuous process—the new concept would have been suggested by the old, and the new instances were always being weighed with the old. The process expressed itself in a tension between ambiguity and clarity that testified to the living quality of the law. It was a system that had grown out of the varying policies of different ages, out of the contentions, successes, interests, and opportunities of different orders and parties of men. It resembled one of those old mansions, constructed in parts over the years, altered, repaired and added to according to the taste, fortune, or convenience of successive proprietors. To anyone who looked for a regular plan that he could comprehend at a glance, for a building constructed according to some set rules of architecture, it was something of a monster.

Yet to those who defended the common law system, then as now, it did not seem essentially different from a system that relied more on statutes or codes. They argued that the latter was also uncertain. In the first place, there was always the problem of discovering what the meaning of a statute was—one had to inquire into the intent of the legislature, the circumstances or actions which it might have had in mind, and so on. In the second place, even in statute law there was no escaping the problem of applying a general law to particular circumstances, or of discovering which of several possible laws was most applicable to the case in hand. To enunciate a general principle in an act was one thing, to apply it to a complicated set of facts was another; and in the process many carefully worded clauses suffered a strange metamorphosis. However well parliament did its work, the courts had always to bring order out of confusion. Thirdly, no code of law, however providential, could do more than reflect the opinion of competent observers upon the needs of a given moment. It was no sooner issued than it had to be twisted and strained, curtailed and extended, to cover cases which were inconceivable at the time of its promulgation. The law of negligence, for example, had to be different before and after the introduction of the railroad or the motor car; the law of contract had continuously to cover an ever greater variety of commercial conditions. Parallel with the process of legislation, there always had to be a steady growth of judge-made law, interpreting and adapting its rules to meet changing needs. For in a variable world, laws could get no patent of exemption. Men were innovating creatures and whatever belonged to them could not escape the rule of fashion.

But above all the defenders of the common law have pointed out that its complexity was intimately related to English liberties. 'Doubtless, all arbitrary powers, well executed, are the most convenient', Blackstone said, 'yet let it again be remembered that delays and little inconveniences in the forms of justice, are the price that all free nations must pay for their liberty in more substantial matters . . .'.[1] Simplicity, he warned, was a dangerous watchword. One should not 'mistake variety for confusion'. It was misleading to oppose to 'the number of our municipal constitutions, and the multitude of our judicial decisions' the examples of 'arbitrary governments of Denmark, Muscovy, and Prussia; of wild and uncultivated nations, the savages of Africa and America; or of narrow domestic republics, in ancient Greece and modern Switzerland', and to expect the same 'paucity of laws, the same conciseness of practice' to work for 'a nation of freemen, a polite and commercial people, and a populous extent of territory'.[2] The complexity of English laws had arisen out of an anxiety to safeguard the liberty and property of the subject.

Besides, it permitted a salutary combination of elasticity and firmness. In ages when legislation was regarded as abnormal, as something occasioned only by the perversity of mankind, the system of common law had made it easy to adapt law to changing needs—continuously, gradually, and without crisis. Englishmen owed the steady development of their liberties amidst an unusual degree of political stability to this capacity of the common law to move imperceptibly with the times. The fictions which accumulated in the process were something to be grateful for, not scorned, for they gave England with a phrase what elsewhere had to be wrested by the sword.

On the other hand, there was a special toughness about the common law which made it able to withstand the efforts of the Tudors and Stuarts to subvert it. A simpler, more rational and elegant system would have lent itself more easily to arbitrary purposes. Although there were times when the judges were subservient, when the king could dismiss them from their offices at a moment's notice, the clumsy cumbrous system would never break, however much it was made to bend. It was forever rebounding, and it confounded the strongest king, the ablest minister, the rudest Lord-Protector. The most despotic will could do little with its 'ungodly jumble'.

None of these arguments made, or could have made, any impression on Bentham. He saw in the common law nothing but 'An assemblage of fictitious regulations feigned after the image of those real ones that compose the Statute Law'.[3] For a rule of law, in his view, could be predicated only of some assemblage of words and never of a 'bare assemblage of naked ideas'.[4] The common law could be understood only by imagining some corresponding article of statute law: 'The Common Law is but the shadow of the Statute

---

[1] William Blackstone, *Commentaries* (1787, 10th edition), vol. IV, p. 350.
[2] *Ibid.* vol. III, pp. 325–6.
[3] *A Comment on the Commentaries*, ed. C. W. Everett (Oxford, 1928), p. 126.
[4] *Ibid.* p. 244 n.

Law although it came before it. Before the appearance of the Statute Law even the word "Law" could hardly have been mentioned . . .'.[1] Common law was 'imaginary law' made up for each occasion—it had not 'so much as a shape to appear in—not so much as a word which anybody can say belongs to it—which is everywhere and nowhere—which comes from nobody and is addressed to nobody'. It was dog law—'When your dog does anything you want to break him of, you wait till he does it, and then beat him for it . . . this is the way judges make law for you and me'.[2]

Bentham's charges against the common law were always vehement but not all of one kind or even consistent. Reformer and enemy of tradition though he was, he sometimes opposed the common law because it was too adaptable to circumstances. Whereas the line of utility was straight and inflexible, he declared, the line of analogy 'takes on throughout inflexions from the influence of circumstances it meets within its course'.[3] Yet in the next breath he could accuse the common law of being too rigid, and complain that the judges could not make any exception to a rule of law that was not deducible from some other.[4] About fictions, of course, he was never temperate. Fiction was both 'an engine, for the accumulation of undue profit and illegal power', and a source of 'nonsense, by which the eye of the understanding, being blinded or bewildered, is thus prevented from seeing the absurdity and wickedness which is at the bottom of it'.[5]

Equity also received its share of vitriolic condemnation. That the Court of Chancery should have been criticized was not surprising, for, under the chancellorship of Eldon, it had become a notorious scandal. But Bentham made no distinction between the procedure of equity, the expense and delay, and its substance, which was generally admired. Nor would he for a moment grant that it might have once served a laudable purpose: 'This is a finer sort of law they call equity, a distinction as unheard of out of England as it is useless here to every purpose but that of delaying justice, and plundering those who sue for it'.[6] Equity was, quite simply, an abomination because like common law it was case law. In that sort of system Bentham could find no virtues.

Nevertheless, he disapproved just as vigorously of Roman law, even though it was codified law. In Roman law, he declared, 'there is no method, no connection, no consistency: no idea of a whole: no extensive and commanding views. It has no more pretensions to the title of a system, than the contents of

---

[1] *Ibid.* p. 125.

[2] *Works*, vol. v, p. 235.

[3] *Jeremy Bentham and the Law*, ed. by George W. Keeton (London, 1948), p. 107.

[4] *Ibid.* p. 107.

[5] *Works*, vol. v, p. 92.

[6] *Ibid.* p. 234.

a quarry or a mason's yard have to that of a palace. There are some good things in it, because amongst such an immense quantity of matter of all sorts it could not be otherwise . . .'.[1] Some of the particular criticisms he made of Roman law were inaccurate. But that was anyway of no real concern for Bentham. His real quarrel with Roman law was on another ground.

Although it had been reduced to codes, Roman law was in effect a compilation of opinions. And the great jurists—Ulpian, Papinian, or Paulus—continually moved back and forth between theory and practice, between principles and application, between general rules and particular cases. If a new form was framed, it was immediately bound up with an old fashioned one and thus it participated in the fixity of the old. In sum, Roman law was an organic development like the common law. As such, it could not stand up to Bentham's challenge: if anyone doubted his verdict on Roman law, he declared, let him 'make the experiment and try whether it will bear any one test of merit: let him choose any one standard and observe how it comes up to it'.[2]

A rational system of law, as of politics, meant only one thing to Bentham, a system in which every piece was derived from a single principle and its corollaries. Law-making was for him essentially like geometry. From a leading axiom or axioms, the whole system had to be constructed. By comparison, anything like the English law, which was hardly built upon what Bentham would regard as an immovable basis of sensations and experience, inevitably seemed to be founded upon the quicksands of instinct and prejudice:

Legislators have been hitherto directed upon the most important points by a species of instinct; they have felt an evil; they have confusedly sought for a remedy. Laws have been made nearly in the same manner as the first towns were built. To look for a plan among these heaps of ordinances, would be like searching for an order of architecture amidst the huts of a village.[3]

The famous English blessings were by Bentham's standards necessarily insecure, because they had grown up by accident, and often were not guaranteed or supported by any clear and definite apparatus. The liberty of the press, for instance, could be no true liberty since it had grown up 'under favour of the contest between Whigs and Tories'. It was 'not the work of institutions, . . . not the work of law: what there is of it that exists, exists not by means but in spite of law . . . it is the weakness of the law that we have to thank for it'.[4] It did not matter to Bentham how well a system of

[1] Mss., University College, Portfolio 27, f. 27, p. 131.
[2] *Ibid.* Portfolio 27, f. 27, p. 131.
[3] *Works*, vol. I, p. 159.
[4] *Ibid.* vol. II, p. 443.

law had served in times of crisis. Neither was mere codification of any use The sort of code advocated by Savigny, who admired the organic quality of Roman law and insisted that codifiers must have accurate historical knowledge, was as distasteful to Bentham as the common law. Law that was not a logical system, deduced from one principle, was not properly law.

For the same reasons, Bentham was critical of Montesquieu's views on legislation, despite his great admiration for him. Montesquieu was not critical enough of law as it existed—although he begins with a 'censorial plan', long before he concludes 'he throws off the censor and puts on the antiquarian'.[1] Montesquieu employed his wits to discover good reasons for chaotic laws, because he did not realize how very simple the science of legislation was: 'the principle of utility directs all reasons to a single centre: the reasons which apply to the detail of arrangements are only subordinate views of utility'.[2] Even Bacon came in for criticism, on account of his argument that assigning reasons to laws would only lead to disputes. But this was probably because, Bentham explained charitably, the principles of laws were not yet fully known in Bacon's time and therefore the reasons assigned for laws were bound to be inadequate. A code of laws founded on utility, however, would be beyond criticism—'should all the lawyers in the world attack it with keenest appetites, what would be the result? They would be like vipers biting at a file'.[3]

A code framed in this way would require neither schools to explain it, nor casuists to unravel its subtleties: 'It would speak a language familiar to everybody; each one might consult it at his need'. It would be distinguished from all other books by its greater simplicity and clarity. The father of a family could, by reaching for the code on his bookshelves, dispense justice without any assistance. He would need only to turn to the chapter on the relevant subject and discover the answer to any problem.[4] Nothing more than the code was needed, for on the 'grand principle of utility', one could form a 'precise notion of a perfect system of legislation'.[5]

Once the code was prepared, no interpretations or unwritten laws were to be permitted: 'Whatever is not in the code of laws ought not to be law'. Judges would not be allowed to make new law. Commentaries, if written, could not be cited: 'If a judge or advocate thinks he sees an error or omission, let him certify his opinion and the correction he would propose'.[6] Indeed, a code could be so perfect that no revision would be needed more than once in a

---

[1] *Principles of Morals*, p. 428 n.
[2] *Works*, vol. I, p. 162.
[3] *Ibid*. p. 160.
[4] *Ibid*. vol. III, p. 209.
[5] *Ibid*. vol. I, p. 194.
[6] *Ibid*. vol. III, p. 210.

hundred years, 'for the sake of changing such terms and expressions as by that time may have become obsolete'.[1] And as it would embody all that was most admirable in the civilization, the code ought to become one of the first objects of instruction in all schools, parts of it to be committed to memory and recited as a catechism.[2]

One codifier could do the work for all countries. The legislator anyway made laws for many more persons that he ever saw, and there was no need for him to see them all: 'The same motives attract and repel: the same passions agitate . . . the convent and the camp, the cottage and palace. . . . It is not by the multitude of the objects of any kind that pass in review before him that a man becomes intelligent, but by the attention which he bestows on them'.[3] Montesquieu had taught legislators that they could not ignore the 'influence of time and place', but this could easily be arranged for. The legislator would simply have to be given information on the present laws of a country, its geography, the manners of the people, their religion, and so forth. He would have to observe certain rules 'respecting the method of transplanting laws',[4] and carefully calculate the dissatisfaction a change in laws might arouse. He should prefer indirect legislation to direct, gentle to violent means, and arrange for instruction and exhortation to precede, or in some cases to replace, new laws. He should introduce more familiar laws first, and not lose his temper if the people show strong prejudice against his laws.[5] Yet, when all is said and done, the problem of transplanting laws arises mainly where the new laws are irrational, as when the jumble of English law was introduced into India. Had it been true law, the Indians would have been able to see its salutary effects at once.

The laws of nations differ so widely mainly because they have been 'thrown together at hazard, without connection, and without arrangement. There is no common measure among them'. The cases demanding diversity are few, much fewer than is supposed, and even then the difference will often be only temporary. A truly rational system of law will bring nations together: 'The free communication of knowledge will propagate this system in all directions the instant it is created: such a system of legislation will prepare for itself a universal dominion'.[6] That such a system is possible could no longer be doubted:

The idea of its perfection is no longer a chimera. A universal system of laws is accessible to him who knows how to appreciate it; he may trace the whole of its horizon and though no one now living may be permitted to enter this land of

---

[1] *Ibid.* p. 210.
[2] *Ibid.* vol. I, p. 158.
[3] Mss., University College, Portfolio 27, f. 17, p. 154.
[4] *Works,* vol. I, p. 180.
[5] *Ibid.* pp. 181 f.
[6] *Ibid.* p. 162.

promise, yet he who shall contemplate it in its vastness and its beauty may rejoice, as did Moses, when, on the verge of the desert, from the mountain top, he saw the length and breadth of the good land into which he was not permitted to enter and take possession.[1]

RATIONAL LAW

Bentham's insistence on rationality affected the procedure and substance of the law even more than its form. Nothing was permitted to interfere with the achievement of simplicity.

He had in the first place no patience with the indirectness of a legal process in which justice depended on the efforts of both sides to present the best possible case. The most nearly perfect tribunal, according to Bentham's standards, was to be found in the domestic forum, the father inquiring into the wrong-doing of a child, and Bentham often justified his recommendations by arguing that they were perfectly acceptable in domestic proceedings. Nothing more than the correct general principles was needed to give a judge alone, or a judge and jury, both ability and detachment sufficient to decide everything.

The efforts of lawyers to present the best possible case for every client seemed to him merely efforts to perpetrate fraud. The counsel employed his superior knowledge to discover subterfuges for saving the guilty or for concealing his client's dishonesty and this, Bentham protested, was proclaimed a judicial triumph. In reality, the lawyer was an accomplice after the fact, more clear-headed than the obvious accomplice and more skilled in managing weapons of offence and defence with impunity, but just as indifferent to good and evil. The privilege of lawyers not to disclose facts revealed to them by their clients was still another part of the conspiracy to uphold fraud. Lawyers exploited their promise of secrecy to become confidants and assistants of criminals, or else they conspired with the judge to oppress the innocent and save the guilty. The reasons usually given for the privilege of non-disclosure—that the legal adviser might have the fullest knowledge of the facts, or that the prosecution be forced to prove its case 'of its own'—were meaningless to Bentham.

He did not even worry about the danger of brow-beating witnesses—it could never be done, he declared, unless the lawyer and the judge conspired together. The privilege of a witness to refuse to answer incriminating questions was designed to protect Englishmen against arbitrary proceedings such as those of the courts of Star Chamber and High Commission. Since such courts no longer existed, there was no longer any need for the privilege, no need to fear that the judge might harass the accused or a witness. Bentham ridiculed

---

[1] *Ibid.* p. 194.

even the privilege of husbands and wives not to testify against each other. There should be no asylum for criminals, not even within their own families. Indeed Bentham would have eliminated the basic principle—that no one should be compelled to incriminate himself—which lay behind so many of the privileges he opposed. For this principle, by permitting criminals to escape and making their discovery more difficult, rendered justice less efficient. Dumont, whose experience of continental law made him more sensitive to abuses that were relatively unknown in England, commented that if Bentham's suggestions were adopted the accused would be surrounded by agents of justice and the police, and left with no means of defending himself.

When he turned to the law of evidence, Bentham deserted his general preference for doing things by rule, and argued against rules. His main concern was as always to catch the criminal, and he was certain that the elaborate procedures established over the centuries were merely sources of gain to the lawyers. It was impossible to find infallible rules for evidence which would insure perfectly just decisions; therefore it was best not to have any rules, but simply to put legislators and judges on their guard. No evidence or testimony should be excluded merely from fear of being deceived.

Bentham accordingly advocated removing most restrictions on evidence from witnesses who could not be heard in court, that is, hearsay evidence. Instead of excluding hearsay, he would have merely labelled such testimony 'suspicious'. He was not the only one in his day to attack the traditional hearsay rule, and since his time the advantages of relaxing some part of it have been generally accepted. He recognized also the force of cross-examination and the drawbacks of not being able to interrogate an absent witness. But he took an extreme position against excluding hearsay because the danger of what he called 'misdecision' for want of information was to his mind far greater than the danger of misdecision arising from false information. Although he had little regard for the wisdom of juries, he considered the argument that they should be employed but not trusted to evaluate hearsay to be a 'gross and palpable' absurdity.[1] The dangers of admitting hearsay evidence were not the sort that impressed him. Instead of rules for admitting evidence, he preferred to rely on what he described as a scale of belief, which would enable the judge to gauge the significance of testimony. The scale would be divided into ten degrees. One side would be positive, inscribed with the degrees of positive belief (that is, affirmative of the fact in question), and the other negative, inscribed with the degrees of negative belief (that is, denying the same fact); the bottom of the scale would be marked by o, denoting the absence of all belief either for or against the fact in quesion. 'Such is the simplicity of this mode of expression, that no material image representative

---

[1] *Ibid.* vol. VII, p. 160.

of the scale seems necessary to the employment of it'.[1] The witness could then say 'my belief is ten or five degrees on the positive side', or 'ten or five degrees on the negative side', just as, in speaking of the temperature indicated by the thermometer, we say that the mercury is ten degrees above zero. All difficulty and confusion could thus be excluded.

His impatience with any inefficiency made Bentham anxious to dispense even with the jury. He admitted that a jury could sometimes protect the liberty of the individual, but he could not tolerate the additional inconvenience, delay, and expense it involved. In any case, he insisted, it was not a very effective protection for liberty, since the jurors (whom he called 'guinea men, or guinea corps')[2] were often intimidated and dependent on the judge. If anything, it would be better to substitute a quasi-jury, to consist of three or five men, who would not pronounce a verdict, but simply keep watch on the judge, interrogate if necessary, and in case of need, demand a rehearing.

The general effect of Bentham's recommendations was, as the *Edinburgh Review* remarked, that by a strange twist he had come to agree with a defender of absolute monarchy—his radical designs for judicial procedure and organization restored the patriarchal system advocated by Filmer.[3] In fact, Bentham's code of evidence was hardly a code at all—it was written in general terms, abounded in many general warnings to judges to be 'suspicious' of certain evidence and to legislators to beware of certain dangers, though the precautions were never specified. Only incidentally did Bentham ever mention a specific rule of English law, and his criticism was invariably aimed at complete abolition rather than at amending the existing rules.

Nevertheless, Bentham suggested, even to those who did not accept his general view, how useless technicalities could be swept away, how others might be modified, and the system as a whole made simpler and more coherent. When Fitzjames Stephen drafted his code of evidence in 1872, he adopted many of Bentham's suggestions. But he incorporated them into a code that was really a digest, an organized and revised summary of the law of England as it existed in his day. For Stephen considered the English system of prosecution and trial an unsurpassed way of reaching a correct verdict. Whereas Bentham would have brought the English system close to the Continental one, Stephen not only doubted that the French system permitted less impunity, but argued that it was always pernicious to increase the odds against crime by endangering the essential liberties of the subject. The procedure of accusation and trial, he declared, should be conducted so as to assure the rights of individuals as well as to protect society against criminals. A certain degree of impunity was but a small price to pay for safeguarding higher

---

[1] *Ibid.* vol. VI, p. 225.   [2] *Ibid.* vol. V, p. 79.
[3] *Edinburgh Review*, March, 1824, p. 172.

constitutional interests. Stephen could not agree with those, like John Stuart Mill, who praised Bentham for treating the law 'as no peculiar mystery, but a simple piece of practical business, wherein means were to be adopted to ends, as in any of the other arts of life'.[1] Stephen saw in this businesslike attitude a threat to the safeguards of English liberties, and found Bentham guilty of having ignored the vital principle that one of the great objects of the law of judicial evidence 'is to prevent fraud and oppression in their worst form, to keep out prejudices which would be fatal to the administration of justice'. For criminal justice may easily be administered so as 'to make it a subject of universal horror, and to cause people to fear any connection with it like the plague. Rules of evidence which prevent these evils are not to be lightly tampered with'.[2]

As Bentham never concerned himself with history, he was not inclined to consider why laws had become established. Many of his suggestions on procedure would at once have reminded Hume of the outrages during the Civil War, the perjuries, spying, false accusations and evidence. Bentham's only comment on that period was a eulogy of Cromwell, whom he called a hero, a 'wonderful man', who wielded an 'honest pen', an enemy of lawyers, clergy, and aristocracy, an advocate of codification.[3]

On the substance of penal law, Bentham had even more suggestions than on evidence. Again, simplification and efficiency were his overriding concerns, and his faith in the efficacy of rational laws knew no bounds—'by all good laws almost all crimes may be reduced to acts which may be repaired by a simple pecuniary compensation; and . . . when this is the case, the evil arising from crimes may be made almost entirely to cease'.[4] It was this faith, and not just a readiness to criticize the criminal law, that distinguished him. Even Blackstone had been far from complacent about the state of penal law. He had also been influenced by Montesquieu and even more by Beccaria, and was the first legal author to treat the subject of criminal law separately and at some length. He rejected the notion that the object of punishment was expiation, and unlike most reformers, emphasized rather the reforming function of punishment. In full agreement with Beccaria, he stressed 'preventive' as against 'punishing' justice. He pointed out that 'the quantity of punishment can never be absolutely determined by any standing invariable rule', but had to be varied according to the circumstances of the case. While he considered a scale of offences with a corresponding scale of punishments too romantic an idea, he recommended that the principal divisions could be marked so that penalties of the first degree would not be assigned to offences

---

[1] John Stuart Mill, Appendix in E. L. Bulwer, *England and the English* (New York, 1833), vol. II, p. 206.

[2] J. F. Stephen, *A General View of the Criminal Law of England* (1890), p. 207.

[3] *Works*, vol. IV, pp. 501–2.   [4] *Ibid.* vol. I, p. 580.

of an inferior rank. In general, Blackstone denounced repressing crime at all costs and advocated a more flexible adjustment of punishment to crime.

Bentham, however, wanted more than reform of criminal law. Indeed in many respects he was at odds with Beccaria even though he professed to follow him. He disagreed with Beccaria's opposition to giving rewards for securing the conviction of offenders, or to granting impunity to accomplices who had betrayed their associates, and above all, he did not accept Beccaria's assumption that 'it is impossible to reduce the turbulent activity of men to absolute regularity'. He was seeking a degree of order that Beccaria had described as 'a chimera of weak men when invested with authority'.[1]

Bentham would have preferred to start from a complete classification of offences and punishments, all defined in terms of pleasures and pains, arranged by genus and species. Once this was done, he felt, the rest would be simple, for then one would merely have to classify an offence to discover the punishment suitable to it. Although at one point he acknowledged that a complete classification of offences was not yet attainable, this did not keep him from proposing to make a 'map of universal delinquency, laid down upon the principle of utility'.[2] He made a detailed analysis of the circumstances that should be considered in judging criminal liability; he argued that all offences were not equally mischievous and that it was important to differentiate the extent and nature of the mischief caused by offences; and in striking contrast to Montesquieu and Beccaria, he insisted that the same offence did not always deserve the same punishment, for the offence might be mitigated by special circumstances, and the same punishment had not always the same effect. The result was a strange mixture that in some respects greatly humanized the law and in others made it a more brutal instrument.

In one way his proposals allowed much more discretion in punishment, and thus somewhat destroyed fixity in rules. But Bentham did not fear that such flexibility would lead to uncertainty in the law because at the same time he hoped to eliminate subjective judgements. He was especially anxious to provide 'objective' criteria for judging intention and to eliminate any personal element in such judgements. Why a man behaved as he did was a mystery even to himself, and no answer could be proved wrong; but what he did, his acts and their consequences, were objective facts about which there need be no mistake or doubt. One need not then enter into a man's feelings to judge him, and to 'objective' judgements one could permit great latitude.

Nevertheless, despite the liberal room for discretion, and refinements in Bentham's classification of offences as compared with the fairly rudimentary outline of criminal acts accepted by Montesquieu and Beccaria, his system

---

[1] Beccaria, *Crimes and Punishments* (Edinburgh, 1778), p. 156.
[2] *Principles of Morals*, p. 403.

would have made criminal law more rigid. Because it was derived strictly from one principle, it necessarily ignored many complexities in motives, many differences in degrees of guilt and danger, many social and individual interests for which a less clean-cut system left room. Despite his emphasis on the variety of human life, the possibility that even the most detailed analysis could not completely account for actual human conditions did not worry Bentham.

Yet at other times he was carried away by a concern with psychological effects. He suggested, for instance, that perhaps instead of capital punishment, which he opposed, there might be mock executions, carefully planned to terrify spectators: the scaffold should be painted black, the officers dressed in crepe, the executioner in a mask, the emblems of the crime placed above the head of the criminal (who would be, unknown to the spectators, a dummy), with the whole dreadful spectacle moving in solemn procession through the city to religious and awesome music. Or, a man who murdered with poison might be compelled to drink a dose of the poison he had used, with proper remedies for 'the producing an evacuation being at hand to be administered after a certain interval'.[1]

In the same spirit, Bentham suggested that it might be well to make an abridgement of the penal code with prints representing the characteristic punishment for each crime, so as to provide a sensible and speaking image of the law. To encourage repentance in prisoners, he urged periods of solitude, darkness, and a hard diet, a regime that might be varied in duration according to the strength or obstinacy of the prisoner. The food should be, he thought, both inadequate and unpalatable, for otherwise the recurring gratification afforded to the palate might neutralize the pain caused by the loss of other pleasures. And some prisoners might be made to wear masks, rendered 'more or less tragical, in proportion to the enormity of the crimes of those who wear them', so as to impress upon their minds the infamy of their acts.[2] Or, on a smaller scale, Bentham suggested that anyone who apprehended a highwayman should be rewarded with the horse ridden by the highwayman. Simple arrangements of this sort, he was certain, would do away with the 'timid caution' of British policy, and enliven it with 'strong and masterly touches which strike the imagination, and fill the mind with the idea of the sublime'.[3]

While some of his recommendations, such as eliminating capital punishment, transportation, and whipping, made the law more humane, on the whole Bentham favoured greater rather than less severity in the penal laws. He even retained certain mutilations as forms of punishment. Whatever effectively deterred crime was acceptable.

[1] Mss., University College, Portfolio 96, f. 10, p. 190.
[2] *Works*, vol. I, p. 431.
[3] *Ibid.* vol. II, pp. 217–18.

Bentham had no fear of any risks involved in emphasizing efficiency. It was possible, he was certain, both to protect the innocent and eliminate all loopholes for the criminal, and he was not one to indulge in idle talk about preferring to have ten guilty persons escape rather than make one innocent man suffer. For he saw no eternal incompatibility, as Beccaria did, between the different ends of justice:

> I shall only observe that all precautions which are not absolutely necessary for the protection of innocence offer a dangerous protection to crime. I know no maxim in procedure more dangerous than that which places justice in opposition to itself— which establishes a kind of incompatibility among its duties. When it is said, for example, that it is better to allow one hundred guilty persons to escape, than to condemn one that is innocent—this supposes a dilemma which does not exist. The security of the innocent may be complete, without favouring the impunity of crime. . . .[1]

Administrative arrangements that other reformers laboured to eliminate were unhesitatingly advocated by Bentham. On the Continent, where police had long been in existence, Beccaria and others warned that extending the power of the police was an invitation to tyranny. They cited England's traditional hostility to police as an important source of her liberty. But Bentham favoured strengthening the police in a number of ways. He advocated a centralized, permanent Ministry of Police who would have use of the defensive forces of land or sea, and could invade every part of the country. Apprehending criminals was not the most important work of the police, Bentham insisted; preventing crime should be its main function and prevention, to be efficient, had to be all-pervading.[2] To this end Bentham would have divided England into administrative divisions like those of France, where he saw simplicity and uniformity in place of the chaos that prevailed in England, Scotland, and Ireland.[3] The country could thus be covered by a swarm of officials, whom Bentham called 'local headmen', who were to link the central preventive service to the smaller units.

In addition, Bentham favoured encouraging common informers, and opposed the traditional suspicion of them embodied in English law. He appealed to the public to recognize the advantages of using informers: 'The informers who would require to be paid, need have only a small salary; and a hundred gratuitous informers would present themselves for one who required to be paid. . . . Informers, animated by public spirit, rejecting all pecuniary recompense, would be listened to with the respect and confidence which is their due'.[4] Neither could Bentham see why spies should not be employed, and impatiently dismissed the usual objections:

[1] *Ibid.* vol. I, p. 558.
[3] *Ibid.* pp. 147 ff.
[2] *Ibid.* vol. IX, pp. 439–40.
[4] *Ibid.* vol. I, p. 559.

To the word espionage, a stigma is attached: let us substitute the word inspection which is unconnected. . . . If this inspection consist in the maintenance of a system of police, for the preservation of the public tranquility and the execution of good laws, all its inspectors and all its guardians, act as a useful and salutary part; it is the vicious only who will have reason to complain: it will be formidable to them alone.[1]

Even Romilly, who generally accepted Bentham's suggestions with readiness, could not agree.

The work of the police would be further facilitated, Bentham thought, if pardons were granted to accomplices who had helped bring others to justice, and if the custom adopted by English sailors, of carrying their family and Christian names upon their wrists, were made universal. Such a device would be 'a new spring for morality, a new source of power for the laws, an almost infallible precaution against a multitude of offences, especially against every kind of fraud in which confidence is requisite for success. Who are you, with whom have I to deal? The answer to this important question would no longer be liable to evasion'.[2] While Bentham conceded that there might be objections to such a practice, and that during the French Revolution many people owed their survival to disguises impossible under such a system of identification, he nevertheless hoped public opinion would come to accept it: 'if it were the custom to imprint the titles of the nobility upon their foreheads, these marks would become associated with the ideas of honour and power'.[3]

That he was giving the police far-reaching powers to interfere, powers that resembled what he himself deplored as 'ante-judicial' methods, Bentham realized. But he was confident that the dangers could be avoided. The law had to define very exactly the circumstances in which police action could be taken and how it was to be carried out, and the public had to be informed that these were the only grounds for interference with their security, property, and honour. The police would be directed by law not to issue too many or too vexatious regulations, to remember that precautions necessary in periods of danger should not be continued in periods of quiet, 'as the regimen suited to disease ought not to be followed in a state of health'.[4] Their conduct, they would know, had to be such as would not offend the 'national spirit', for one nation [would] not bear what is borne by another'.[5] Then all would be well. There was no need to fear precisely worded laws based on the principle of utility.

[1] *Ibid.* vol. II, p. 222.
[2] *Ibid.* vol. I, p. 557.
[3] *Ibid.* p. 557.
[4] *Ibid.* p. 557.
[5] *Ibid.* p. 557.

CHAPTER XIV

GADGETS FOR HAPPINESS

BENTHAM offered his services as codifier to everyone—Russia, Bavaria, Spain, Venezuela, France, Portugal, the United States, the state of Pennsylvania; his papers even include an essay on *Securities against Misrule adapted to Mohammedan states*. But in fact, he never wrote a code. Whenever he was invited to do so, he became strangely intransigent. The Greeks requested him in 1823 to give them some suggestions, and he sent them his instructions for drafting a constitutional code in English, saying that the Greeks had better learn English as it was 'the only language from which tolerably adequate views of justice can at present be imbibed'. An influential Greek newspaper publisher, who had advised Bentham to prepare a code with a more native cast, nevertheless urged him to send any code he had ready. Instead, Bentham sent an ordinance in Spanish on the *Tactics of Legislation of the Republic of Buenos Aires*.[1] In the end, a Bavarian lawyer framed the Greek legal system.

With Spain his negotiations were equally strange. When asked about the value of a jury system, he declined to commit himself, yet suggested that Spain adopt the English expedient of common and special jurors. When he was reminded that Spain needed a legal system suited to her special circumstances, Bentham reprimanded his adviser for suggesting that the Spanish Code had to be unlike any other. Anyway, he refused to concern himself with only a part of the laws—he was interested in complete codification, or nothing at all. As in the case of Greece, although Bentham probably had some influence on the Spanish legal system through his pupil, Nuniz, he himself took no part in the Spanish codification.[2] In similar fashion, for the newly instituted dictatorship of Venezuela, he drew up a code on the liberty of the press, and later he sent plans for prison reform. To this, Col. Hall, an Englishman in the service of the Venezuelan government, replied that the revolutionary government was at the moment occupied by more pressing matters.[3] When Alexander invited Bentham to help with the codification for Russia, Bentham first returned the Czar's gift that came with the invitation, and then discovered that the Russian legislative commission was too inept for him to work with it.[4] When the French Revolution broke out, the Abbé Morellet entreated him to write a

---

[1] Cf. Mss., University College, Portfolio 12, ff. 16, 18, 19. *Works*, vol. x, pp. 534-7; vol. iv, pp. 580-8.

[2] Cf. Mss., Portfolios 13 (ff. 13, 3), 12 (f. 7). *Works*, vol. x, pp. 433 f., 438 f.

[3] *Works*, vol. x, pp. 457 f., 500, 513. Cf. Mss., Portfolio 12, ff. 7, 15.

[4] *Works*, vol. x, pp. 406 ff., 478; vol. iv, pp. 514-28.

constitutional code; Bentham ignored Morellet's request and wrote instead a small piece, *On Political Tactics*, advising the French how to proceed in their legislature.[1] In short, he never took full advantage of an opportunity to exercise his vocation.

Nor did Bentham do much more for England. He left many odd fragments of codes, outlines, and unfinished drafts. None of them had the essentials of a workable code; their classifications were complicated and impractical, and they were full of sweeping generalizations. He was inclined to produce definitions such as the one he gave for insanity—loss of reason—a definition that would have released nine-tenths of the certified lunatics in England, and caused nearly all those who had escaped punishment on grounds of insanity to be convicted. Yet at the same time, Bentham allowed hallucination to be an extenuation or even a complete defence, because it was like any other belief honestly held. By defining defamation as an accusation of an act, he left out any charges referring to a man's character, or competence. In another field, the same sort of nonchalance permitted Bentham to include crime and tort in a single category.[2]

In the end, Bentham served English law not by constructing any grand system or even part of a system, but by making an extraordinary number of ingenious detailed suggestions, many of which now seem commonplace. Hardly any part of English law fails to show his influence and, to this day, would-be reformers of law can find many useful proposals in Bentham's work. Although his ambition was to make a grand synthesis, his contribution was to particulars. In practice, Bentham's addiction to the scientific method led him to concentrate always on the detail. To the despair of his friends and admirers, he was always being distracted from his large projects by an interest in some current problem. And the solutions he offered were not those of a moralist or a philosopher, but of an engineer or inventor.

An astonishing list of gadgets was the result. He devised a new method for preparing tea, installed a central heating system in his house, and planned a Frigidarium (a sort of ice-house for preserving fermentable substances, which he hoped to put on a commercial basis in the form of a 'frustum of a globe mounted on a cylinder, about sixteen feet diameter clear in the inside'). He suggested that by entrusting the census to the minister of each parish, and paying by the number of heads counted, with penalties for omissions or false reports, the census would at once be made more accurate and more economical. He wrote a treatise called *A Plan for saving all trouble and expense in the transfer of stock and for enabling the proprietors to receive their dividends without powers of attorney or attendance at the Bank of England by conversion of Stock into Note Annuities.* He invented a method for preventing forgery of

[1] *Works*, vol. x, pp. 98-201.
[2] *Bentham and the Law*, pp. 230–1.

bank notes. He suggested that the friction between England and Ireland might be cured by renaming the United Kingdom 'Brithibernia', but unhappily, Lord Holland, who received the suggestion, felt that while names had a great influence upon mankind, princes had not perhaps the same power to change them. Even drunkenness and disorderliness among Irish immigrants to America inspired Bentham to devise a solution—a programme of evening classes.

Political difficulties were treated in the same spirit. Since, if a procedure or an institution worked, the minutest details would bear inspection, it must follow, Bentham seemed to conclude, that wherever the minutest detail was exhibited, the system was workable. He was therefore careful to say in his Radical Reform Bill just how the voting box was to be constructed. It was to be a double cube of cast-iron, with a slit in the lid into which the voting cards, two inches by one, white on one side and black on the other, could be inserted.[1]

While absorbed in his gadgets, he remained curiously unmoved by what seemed to others very stirring events. The Gordon Riots, which had been set off by a petition against the Relief Act then before parliament, took place while he was visiting at Bowood. For close on a week, houses, chapels, bridges and prisons were attacked and burned; the mob was often so drunk as to fall into the flames it had kindled; a party attempted to capture and burn the Bank of England; and the forces of the government seemed incapable of doing anything effective. All of England was shocked. Bentham, however, alluded to the riots only in passing: 'Talking with Lord B. yesterday (nobody else in the room) about the riots, he took notice, that in the Scotch Assembly . . . there were but two voices against the toleration'.[2] The outrages were repeated on a smaller scale in Birmingham, this time against the pro-French society of which Priestley was a member. Yet, but a few years later, Bentham could write in his *Essay on Political Tactics* that in a free state 'the multitude' would be 'more secure from the tricks of demagogues—the passions accustomed to a public struggle will learn reciprocally to restrain themselves . . . the signs of uneasiness will not be signs of revolt; the nation will rely upon those trustworthy individuals whom long use has taught them to know'.[3] He could be sanguine because he had thought of a way to handle riots: 'At the moment of disorder, the presence of the magistrate ought to be announced by some extraordinary sign'—a red flag, perhaps, might do, since it had worked well in the French Revolution. 'A multitude can only use their eyes: their eyes should therefore be addressed'. If it became absolutely necessary to add words to signs, a speaking trumpet should be used because

[1] *Works*, vol. III, p. 573.
[2] *Ibid.* vol. X, p. 95.
[3] *Ibid.* vol. II, p. 311.

'even the singularity of this instrument would contribute to give more eclat and dignity to the orders of justice, by removing all idea of familiar conversation, by impressing the conviction that it was not the simple individual himself who was heard, but a privileged minister, the herald of the laws'. And he went on to elaborate on the speaking trumpet. It had often been used at sea, he explained, and, 'Poets have often compared a people in commotion to the sea in a storm'. The analogy must not be wasted on poets—'it would be of much greater importance in the hands of justice'. Even the words to be spoken through the trumpet were prescribed—'The orders should be in few words— nothing which appears like ordinary discourse or discussion—no reference to the king, but to justice alone'.[1]

Bentham provided against another sort of danger from riots in his plans for a prison, where he made meticulous recommendations on how to protect it from attacks: there should be only one approach, the building should be recessed away from the streets, the walls rounded off at the corners so that they could not be climbed easily; the protecting wall should be eight or nine feet, and behind the wall a protecting road where those who did not wish to take part in the riots could be sheltered. His was the first plan, he declared proudly, in which 'the peaceable protection of passengers is made a part—the first in which the discrimination of the innocent from the guilty was ever provided for or thought of'.[2] Any attack could then be opposed by firearms from the building. Even if a great many people were slaughtered, it was better than that the prison be destroyed or the prisoners turned loose. But in fact nothing of the sort would happen, because 'the more plainly impracticable you make the enterprise, the surer you may be it will never be attempted'.[3]

He reacted to the French Revolution in much the same way. When it haunted all of England, and the country gave Pitt and Liverpool extraordinary majorities largely out of panic, Bentham could express sympathy with the revolution. Yet he was not pleased by the revolutionaries' methods. The Declaration of Rights drew the most emphatic expressions of disapproval, and certainly the 'delirium' and 'passionate eloquence' of the orators in the Constituent Assembly annoyed him. He pronounced the confiscation of church property and the restoration of their ancestors' goods to descendants of Protestants persecuted under Louis XIV an attack on security; he referred to the French as Pandemonians; his house became a refuge for emigrés; and he nearly joined a society to counteract the Republican propaganda. Yet when he was made a French citizen along with Paine, Priestley, Wilberforce, and Mackintosh, he made no great objection, but merely responded that he was quite willing to become a republican in Paris provided that he could remain

---

[1] *Ibid.* vol. I, p. 370.
[2] *Ibid.* vol. IV, p. 108.
[3] *Ibid.* p. 108.

a royalist in London. Mainly, he was just curious to see what the great cleansing done by the revolution would accomplish, and this led him to praise it unreservedly at the beginning: 'The National Assembly of France has been charged with madness for pulling down establishments [but] . . . if you would have a good house in the site of a bad one, you must pull down your bad one'.[1] When the French Assembly substituted the election of judges for appointment, and Bentham was asked to comment, he applauded the suggestion— it was a 'bold experiment' and since the committee had the courage to face the idea, it should be 'fairly tried in its simplest form'.[2] Later, he thought better of it and said his opinion had been a concession 'against the grain', a concession extorted by circumstances. On the whole, however, he was inclined to let the French experiments run their course. He would not have initiated them, but it was not often that a legislator was handed such a good laboratory.

In time he found a more satisfactory proving ground for his theories in the United States. When the Americans first declared their independence, he sided with the government, not because he admired North or his policy, but because the Americans had founded their case on 'natural rights'—'If government be only the representative of rights, for which there is no standard and about which there will be an infinite variety of opinions, the right to which the mother country laid claim would seem to stand on an older and firmer foundation than the rights pretended by the colonies'.[3] But as the United States flourished, Bentham began to see in it a confirmation of his ideas. Its success, he was sure, was due to its democracy and its freedom from outworn traditions. It was perhaps fortunate that he never came to know the United States directly, for he might have been profoundly disturbed. Many of those virtues that he attributed to the perfection of the American democratic machinery were secured then, as now, by an irrational admixture of confusion and corruption. In a sense, the United States confirmed Bentham's belief that democracy works by the opposition of interests. But the play of interests took place in just the sort of muddled and complicated manner that Bentham abhorred. For he was convinced that complexity harboured tyranny, that the secret of good government lay in simplicity.

His most concentrated effort to demonstrate the virtues of rational simplicity was expended on the panopticon. It became his pet gadget and absorbed more than a decade of time, expense, and anxiety. When in 1784, parliament made a plan for administrative deportation to Australia, Bentham announced that he had a better alternative: he had a method that made it

[1] *Ibid.* p. 338.
[2] *Ibid.* p. 309.
[3] *Ibid.* vol. x, p. 57.

possible to become master of all that might happen to a certain number of men, to dispose of everything around them so as to produce on them the desired impression, and allow nothing to escape, nor to oppose the desired effect. All this could be accomplished by 'a simple idea in architecture'—a prison constructed and administered on his new plan. Moreover, it would be applicable,

without exception, to all establishments whatsoever, in which, within a space not too large to be covered or commanded by buildings, a number of persons are meant to be kept under inspection. No matter how different, or even opposite the purpose: whether it be that of punishing the incorrigible, guarding the insane, reforming the vicious, confining the suspected, employing the idle, maintaining the helpless, curing the sick, instructing the willing in any branch of industry, or training the rising race in the path of education: in a word, whether it be applied to the purposes of per-petual prisons in the room of death, or prisons for confinement before trial, or penitentiary-houses or houses of correction, or work-houses, or manufactories, or mad-houses, or hospitals, or schools.[1]

Whatever the panopticon may have lacked as a model for prison reform, it perfectly embodied Bentham's 'gadgeteering' spirit. An ideal prison, Bentham decided, had to provide for complete inspection and achieve all its objectives with the maximum economy. Inspection was made certain by a circular plan of a perimeter of cells facing the centre and separated by a ring-like open space from an inner block or tower from which all parts of the prison were visible. This was to house the inspector and his family, the more numerous the better, as they could all share in the watching. As the prisoners would never be free from observation, they would not only be prevented from escaping, but also more effectively reformed by the pressure of constant surveillance.

The features introduced to insure economy were more surprising. Bentham's own injunctions about the dangers of unrestrained power, which dominated his economic and political proposals, were forgotten. The panopticon was to be farmed out to a keeper who offered the best terms and was otherwise pro-perly qualified. He would hold his position for life unless flagrant abuses were discovered. Virtually omni-competent, his only obligation was to make his prison pay for itself, and his incentive would be the right to keep the larger part of the profits (instead of a salary), while the rest was distributed among the prisoners. By learning to extract as much labour as possible from his charges, the keeper would discipline the prisoners, reward himself, and benefit society as a whole.

On details, Bentham's ingenuity was boundless. The suggestion for a visitors' gallery to replace the usual medical supervision and official inspection

[1] *Ibid.* vol. IV, p. 40.

was typical. This had the great advantage, in Bentham's eyes, of securing superintendence by unknown, miscellaneous inspectors who would therefore be incorruptible. At the same time, the visitors would provide not only inspection, but a good source of income. (If they proved too great a burden for the prisoners, masks could be provided, made so as to illustrate the exact nature of the prisoner's crime while shielding him from the public state.) Indeed, every activity, Bentham showed, could be made to serve several purposes.

When he discovered that the panopticon would be more expensive than he had supposed, Bentham altered his first plan radically to insure greater economy. He gave up his original proposal for housing the prisoners in solitude, and discovered that it was better to double, triple, even quadruple the number of prisoners in a cell; besides, the beds could be hammocks, and the mattresses, straw sacks; there was no need for stockings, shirts, and hats, while a coat, waistcoat, and breeches could double at night as a blanket. Food ought to be unlimited but unvaried, and consequently cheap—its unpalatability was desirable to avoid unnecessary gratification. But whatever changes Bentham made in the panopticon scheme, he remained as certain as ever that he had constructed a perfect prison.

The glorious prospects were infinite—morals would be 'reformed—health preserved—industry invigorated—instruction diffused. Economy seated, as it were upon a rock—the gordian knot of the Poor Laws not cut but untied, all by a simple idea in Architecture'.[1] In his enthusiasm, Bentham went so far as to say: 'Call them soldiers, call them monks, call them machines, so they were but happy ones, I should not care'.[2] His mind was on the gadget before him, and as its purpose was to house prisoners efficiently, for the moment, he forgot everything else.

[1] *Ibid.* p. 39.
[2] *Ibid.* p. 64.

CHAPTER XV

A MODEST UTOPIAN

YET for all his single-mindedness, Bentham cannot be summed up by any simple, uncompounded idea. He seems rather to be one of those divided natures which lend themselves to two quite opposite portraits.

One shows a man, very much of the eighteenth century, of unusual benevolence and disinterestedness, morbidly sensitive to the variety and transience of all things human. His efforts were directed to reminding men how different were their characters and needs, and how difficult it was for an outsider to know them. In politics, he emphasized that no good was pure, that whatever benefits a government bestowed had to be weighed against attendant evils. He would not prescribe the specific laws that should govern any society or the ultimate ends that should inspire men's lives; he wished merely to teach men how to think about laws in order that they might avoid the greatest perils of political life:

Were I to choose to what I would (most truly and readily) attribute these magnificent prerogatives of universality and immutability, it should rather be to certain grounds of law, than to the laws themselves; to the principles upon which they should be founded; to the subordinate reasons deducible from those principles and to the best plan upon which they can be put together; to the considerations by which it is expedient the legislator should suffer himself to be governed, rather than to any laws which it is expedient he should make for the government of those who stand committed to his care.[1]

But there is also another portrait—of the hermit of Queen Square Place, sitting on his platform in the dining room, dreaming of a world that had adopted his code and canonized him as High Codifier and Grand Benefactor of all mankind. He wrote uninterruptedly, and every paragraph had its preordained place in a grand system. Whatever community adopted his constitutional code, he was confident, would have no further need of any of its former institutions, and whoever opposed the code was an enemy of the people. For the good produced would be pure from evil, and the government perfectly directed to the interests of the governed:

Now for the first time is the invitation given to examine and discuss the most interesting of temporal subjects, on the ground of a set of determinate and throughout mutually connected, and it is hoped, consistent principles. Now for the first time is to the subject matter . . . given the form and method of the matter of a distinctive branch of art and corresponding science.[2]

[1] *Ibid.* vol. I, p. 193.   [2] *Ibid.* vol. IX, p. 2.

Neither portrait is false, and yet neither is wholly true. His concern with tolerance and liberty of taste was too central in his life and thought to allow the second portrait to represent him. And yet the whole of Bentham will not fit into the image of an eighteenth century gentleman, certainly not one of those whom Shaftesbury called 'lovers of Art and Ingenuity; such as have seen the world and have informed themselves of the Manners and Customs of the several Nations of Europe . . .'. When Bentham travelled, he sent Shelburne plant and animal specimens, but rarely a word about the people, their land, their architecture or arts. Although he wrote to Arthur Young for information about the people and land, he asked questions like, 'What may be regarded as the average annual value of the gross produce in the form of a per centage for every 100 pounds laid out in the improvement of land not yet in culture, upon an average of articles of culture, soils, situations, etc., and quantities of capital applied per acre, according to the usage of the present time, and in farms of the average size . . .'.[1] If Hume belongs pre-eminently to the eighteenth century, Bentham would seem to be excluded. All that was so important for Hume and for his contemporaries steeped in the traditions of their country—instinct, custom, and imagination—were nothing but the devil's work for Bentham. Whereas Hume's arguments were always directed against looking at institutions only by the light of reason, Bentham insisted that reason alone, in the narrowest sense of logical analysis, was relevant. He would never have written as complacently as Hume did about property law: 'there are no doubt motives of public interest for most of the rules which determine property; but still I suspect that these rules are principally fix'd by the imagination, and the more frivolous properties of our thought and conception'.[2] Although he borrowed a key word from Hume, he set himself against what Hume most respected. For he ostracized metaphor and excluded imagination from the art of politics.

Was Bentham then more nearly an heir of the seventeenth century, of those men who wished to prevent 'the gross dew of the imagination' from staining 'the pure glass of judgement'? Did Spratt not describe Bentham's own credo when he stated that of the Royal Society: 'To separate the knowledge of Nature from the colours of Rhetorick, the devices of fancy or the delightful deceit of Fables', 'to make faithful records of all the works of Nature or art, . . . so the present Age and posterity may be able to put a mark on the Errors which have been strengthened by long prescription; to restore the Truths that have lain neglected: to push on those, which are already known, to more various uses, and to make the way more passable to what remains unrevealed'. Certainly Bentham would have agreed. And with some members of the Royal Society, with someone like Sir William Petty, he would

[1] *Ibid.* vol. x, p. 373.
[2] David Hume, *Treatise of Human Nature*, p. 504 n.

184

have felt completely at home. He not only believed in the efficacy of facts and numbers; he even invoked the same patron saints—Locke, Newton, and Bacon. Nevertheless, the resemblances are less important than the differences. The patron saints had some eccentricities that Bentham ignored.

Locke and Newton were both profoundly concerned with matters that had no meaning for him. While Locke assures us that 'our business here is not to know all things, but those which concern our conduct', he still felt driven 'to examine our abilities and see what objects our understandings were not fitted to deal with', to see the whole and give man his place in the universe. All those philosophical questions that Bentham disdainfully dismissed were central for Locke. This was true also of Newton. He neither ignored the bearing of his scientific theories on the rest of human life, nor wished to suggest that nothing else should concern men. For all his animadversions on the mystical hypotheses of his forbears, he insisted that his theories were hypotheses not facts, and nothing would have horrified him more than an attempt to order human life solely by logic and mathematics.

Bacon, however, would seem to fit perfectly into the role of Bentham's mentor. After all, Bentham praised him as 'that resplendent genius' who had shed 'the true light . . . upon the field of thought and action, and hence upon the field of art and science'.[1] His ambition, like Bentham's, was to find a set of fixed rules that would allow the business of interpreting nature to be done 'as if by machinery', rendering the excellence of the inquirer's wit irrelevant, indeed placing 'all wits and understandings nearly on a level'.[2] Where his procedure was applicable, Bacon had no use for anything beyond it; he, too, was convinced that 'it is vain to expect a great increase in knowledge from the superinducing and ingrafting of new things upon the old'.[3]

Still, in an important way, Bacon's temperament differed from Bentham's. On the one hand, he was more truly empirical. Whereas Bentham sat in his study and drew elaborate plans for a great refrigerating machine, Bacon caught his last chill while stuffing a chicken with ice. He believed that one had to go out, and see, and do, not sit at home and project. For all his talk of procedure and induction, his emphasis fell on actually observing, whereas Bentham's attention was fixed entirely on the method. On the other hand, although Bacon declared, 'I have taken all knowledge to be my province', although he separated the truth of science from the truth of religion, he retained both. We are obliged, he said, to believe the Word of God, though our reason be shocked at it—'For if we should believe only that which is agree-

---

[1] Bentham, *Works*, vol. VIII, p. 99.
[2] Francis Bacon, *Novum Organum* (London, 1859), p. 4, and p. 36 [Bk. I, Preface and lxi].
[3] *Ibid.* p. 19 (I, xxxi).

able to our sense, we give assent to the matter and not to the author'.[1] In Bacon's universe 'the upper link of Nature's chain' remained fastened to Jupiter's throne.[2] Any attempt to make reason the sole support of human life struck him as grossly arrogant. If he condemned the philosophy of the schoolmen, it was not for dealing in mysteries, but for being a presumptuous effort to read the secret purpose of God and to force His works into a conformity with the human mind. Whereas Bentham's faith rested ultimately on logic, Bacon's praise of observation and his absorption in studying particulars stemmed from a distrust of logic. Traditional logic, he felt, did not take into account the innate weakness of the human mind, that gave credence to 'idols and phantoms'. It jumped from particular sense-impressions to propositions of the highest generality. The advantage of inductive reasoning was that it would rise *gradually* from specific cases; it would add 'leaden weights' to the intellect 'so as to keep it from leaping and flying'.[3] 'Anticipation of the mind' would be superseded by an unprejudiced 'interpretation of nature'. Thus he wrote essays and aphorisms, not treatises setting forth a system of logically organized principles. For all his absorption in technique, Bacon kept something of the 'marvelling temper', of that 'negative capability' of remaining 'in uncertainties, mysteries, doubts, without any irritable reaching after fact and Reason'.

But Bentham had none of it. He deliberately blocked out from his view the larger part of knowledge. He built for himself high barriers between the world of 'fact' and the world of mystery, shut himself up behind them, and denied that anything lay beyond. The central problem of the seventeenth century, 'Can I know anything of reality?' had no meaning for him. He was content with a simple distinction between sense and nonsense. And he meant by sense never straying from the objectives and facts immediately before him.

He had set himself to bringing order out of chaos. And the only means of accomplishing his purpose, he had decided, was to submit wholly to a rigorous discipline and let nothing distract him. He not only refused to discuss certain questions, but trained himself to think only about what was strictly relevant to his purpose. He outlawed intuition and sank all contraband thoughts. Neither history nor literature, not even experience, could influence him because he picked out only what was pertinent to the problem uppermost in his mind and ignored the rest.

Yet he adopted his method not because he was indifferent to human feelings, or denied the complexity of human life, but because he could not accept the ordinary risks of living. Thus he could not reconcile himself to the ambiguity of words, to believing that however well or honestly men tried

[1] Francis Bacon, *The Advancement of Learning* (Oxford, 1920), p. 253 [II, xxv (1)].
[2] Bacon, *Novum Organum*, p. 10 [I, 1 (3)].
[3] *Ibid*, p. 98 [I, civ].

to communicate with one another, something would be misunderstood, or perhaps discovered without being said. His horror of the pains suffered by human beings impelled him to construct a system that was proof against human frailty.

He had to make certain that the business of government could never run any danger of being perverted, that it would always be administered perfectly. He felt no need to consider, as Hume did, whether there was any point in dwelling on constitutional arrangements. He would as soon have thought of discussing whether the sun rose. For otherwise there was nothing left but to rely on personalities, on personal judgements, on inherited institutions. And that way lay the perils of the undefinable and mysterious. If politics was to be made absolutely safe, personality could play no part in it. For those ancients whose political fortunes were swayed by their attachments to personalities, Bentham had nothing but scorn and pity—he could not approve of the Solons and Lycurguses who derived their title, as he put it, from their popularity: 'In those days men seem to have been more under the government of opinion than at present. The word of this or that man, whom they knew and reverenced, would go further with them than at present. Not that their passions as it should seem were more obsequious to reason; but their reason was more obsequious to the reason of a single man . . .'. All defenders of liberty have hoped to free men from arbitrary personal authority. But Bentham was seeking more. He hoped to eliminate altogether the need to depend on judgement; he wished to replace practical wisdom with a technique.

Nevertheless he had misgivings and inhibitions about putting his grand schemes into practice. He declared the principles on which they were to be made, he prepared all sorts of instructions for how they should be made, but he himself never made them. His original purpose, his regard for men living here and now, for what each man felt he desired, came to haunt him. It prevented him in the end from becoming the Grand Codifier who produced a set of perfect laws for all men and all times. On the pretext that a few more details remained to be worked out before the great code could be completed, he became rather a maker of gadgets, who concentrated on discovering the device that had gone wrong. He divided the world into small, sealed-off cells, and tried to establish perfect order in one after another, without worrying about the whole. In his workshop, pounding out his gadgets, he found refuge from his ambitions, and took comfort in the thought that the more one learned about mechanics, the easier it would be to fix things. If the right screw were turned, or the leverage shifted, all would be well. In the end his utopianism took the form of believing that by analysing precisely each problem in turn, one could make error and tyranny vanish.

Bentham's was a modest sort of utopianism. It never let him indulge in the glorious visions that his heirs made commonplace. He never suggested that politics should attempt to explain and direct the whole of human life. When he advocated annual elections and universal suffrage, or argued that the representative should be purely a delegate and the House of Lords eliminated, he was concerned only with increasing public control over the government. If he often overlooked a number of problems that might arise from his proposals, he never paraded democracy as a cure for mankind's spiritual ills. He had great faith in his devices, but merely as means for achieving particular objectives. For he thought of himself neither as a prophet nor as a philosopher in the usual sense. He was, he said, 'a hard-working, painstaking man; a lawmaker by trade—a shoemaker is a better one by half'. The fall of man was outside his province—it was sufficient for him to investigate the species of the apple. Instead of exploring either widely or profoundly, he turned his natural inventiveness to elaborating the details of social and mechanical contrivances, many of which have proved very useful or, at the least, suggestive; all that he cared about after all was that his labours should make it easier for men to live as they liked. In this reluctance to give his contrivances spiritual significance, he remained very much an eighteenth-century Englishman.

Yet his dream of reducing politics to an impersonal, foolproof system made him the first of those who tried to move politics into the high and dry barracks of what they supposed was science. With Bentham, we leave the time when political writing is at one with literature, when it is distinguished either by the loftiness of philosophy, the irony of the pamphlet, or the elegance and easy good sense of the essay. In the end, however, the very precision on which Bentham rested his faith defeated his purpose. The colourless treatises, so completely shorn of deceitful metaphors, were interpreted by disciples moved by different experiences and aims. For all the care Bentham had taken with his definitions, he could not prevent his readers from adding their own connotations; he succeeded only in eliminating from his technical words, endless categories and qualifications, anything that might readily suggest the moral spirit behind the logic. By ruthlessly ignoring the refractions of ideas and emotions, he produced devices of a monstrous efficiency that left no room for humanity. In his ardour for reform, Bentham prepared the way for what he feared.

PART III
JOHN STUART MILL: FROM
PURITANISM TO SOCIOLOGY

CHAPTER XVI

JAMES MILL

IT was a triumph of conviction over temperament when James Mill became associated with Bentham. For the two men could hardly have had more different dispositions or more opposed notions about the way to live.

James Mill was a Northerner, a son of the Kirk, who had never known ease of any kind. His family, being both humble and ambitious, were as immune to pleasure as the strictest interpreter of the Kirk's dour views might require. And his mother, who felt she had been dragged down in the world by her marriage to a shoemaker, was determined to restore her son to what she regarded as his rightful heritage. Fortune favoured her with a son who shared her hopes. From childhood on, he endeavoured, with all the determined discipline of a hard-working Calvinist tradesman, to improve himself and to rise in the world; his chosen way up, however, was learning rather than commerce. In due course, he was licensed to preach, and took up his duties willingly enough; but for all his efforts, success as a preacher did not come. He was not given a parish, and in 1802, at the age of twenty-nine, he was driven to try his luck in London as a journalist.

At first London seemed to him a land of boundless freedom and opportunity. 'You get an ardour and a spirit of adventurousness, which you never can get any idea of among our own overcautious countrymen at home', he wrote back in his first letter.[1] There, it seemed, the most romantic schemes were welcome, unlike Scotland, where the slightest oddity was at once repressed. It was encouraging to see how little talent there was. He attended parliament regularly, and found the ministers and most of the members, with but a few distinguished exceptions like Fox, far inferior to the orators in the General Assembly of Scotland. They had nothing to say, no notion of how to say it with order and distinction, and were in fact 'more like boys in an evening society at college, than senators carrying on the business of a great nation'.[2] With so little competition, the possibilities seemed most promising. He was ready to 'labour hard and live penuriously', and once started, he was certain that 'It will be devilish hard, if a man, good for anything, cannot keep himself alive here on such terms'.[3]

Anyone who might be of use to him was carefully cultivated, and by the end of the first year, Mill had succeeded remarkably well. He was to edit as

---

[1] Alexander Bain, *James Mill* (London, 1882), p. 37.
[2] *Ibid.* p. 39.
[3] *Ibid.* p. 42.

well as contribute to a new literary review, the *Literary Journal*; he also became editor of the *St. James Chronicle*, and a frequent contributor to other reviews. As his income seemed very substantial, he became engaged to the daughter of a well-to-do widow and married her in 1805.

But the prosperity did not continue. By the end of 1806, when he was already the father of a son, John Stuart, the *Literary Journal* ceased publication; having before that given up the *Chronicle*, he was left with nothing but the income from reviews, amounting to hardly anything. He decided to stake his savings on a history of India, which was to be completed in three years, and establish him both financially and professionally. His spirits were not high, and early in 1807, he wrote sadly to his friend, Barclay, 'Have you no good kirk yet in your neighbourhood, which you could give me, and free me from this life of toil and anxiety which I lead here? This London is a place in which it is far easier to spend a fortune than to make one. I know not how it is; but I toil hard, spend little, and yet am never the more forward'.[1] The history, which was distinguished by its contempt for almost every feature of Indian life, Hindu and Moslem, and became a manual for all the more humane and enlightened administrators of India, was not published until twelve years later. During that time Mill became the father of nine, a man very much harassed by financial difficulties, and Bentham's leading apostle.

He met Bentham in 1808, and it would seem from the effusive admiration in his letters of the following year that he may already have been converted, at least to Bentham's legal theories. There is little to indicate how his complete conversion came about. In his first years in London he was critical of the government, but not hostile. Though the *St. James Chronicle* was a highly conservative and clerical journal, he had no doubts about becoming its editor. The articles that can be traced to him show him to be still very much a son of the Kirk.

He summarily executed disbelievers, and tolerated no frivolity about religion. Though he read Voltaire, he had little to say in his favour—for Voltaire used 'poisoned arms against religion and liberty', and 'anything that would abate the admiration so long attached to his works would be a public benefit'.[2] Though careful not to make loose accusations of infidelity, Mill severely scolded Villers (whose book on the Reformation Mill had translated), for describing the Bible as mere scraps of literature from distant ages— 'These books comprise the extraordinary code of laws communicated by a benevolent divinity to man',[3] Mill retorted. Hume and Gibbon were pronounced 'the two most celebrated infidels of our time' and their opinions

[1] *Ibid.* p. 63.
[2] *Ibid.* p. 52.
[3] *Ibid.* p. 52.

attributed to their having spent their youth in France and become 'intoxicated with the vanity of imitating Frenchmen'.[1] Mill himself went to Church regularly for some time after his marriage, and had all his children baptized. As he believed his religion was confirmed by reason, he was not tempted to soften its rigours. In a paper produced in 1804, he declared that 'Religion without reason may be feeling, it may be the tremors of the religious nerve, but it cannot be piety toward God, or love towards man'.[2] On all other matters, he was no less anxious than a pious Presbyterian should have been to censor and improve the morals of his fellow men. In the year that he met Bentham, he wrote an article in the *Annual Register* on a fragment of a projected history by Fox. The great merit of the work, Mill said, was its moral tone. Unlike most modern histories, and more like the ancients, it stressed the lessons of common morality. History should present the natural rewards of virtue and the punishment of vice, as it is the special duty of the historian to celebrate and inspire public spirit. Fox was therefore far superior to Hume, even to Robertson (who admired the ambition of Charles V, a cold-blooded and selfish destroyer) and well above Voltaire (who made a hero of Louis XIV). In every part of his work, Fox had dutifully made it clear to his readers whether they ought to admire or detest the characters he described. It was impossible to read him without becoming more ready than before to sacrifice oneself for one's country, to fight for freedom and to risk one's all against oppressors. In sum, the admiring reviewer pointed out, Fox

stigmatises those time-serving and bigoted historians who have endeavoured to disguise the enormities of that period, to write the apology of venality and despotism, to repress the virtuous emotions of hatred and indignation which the scenes in question are calculated to excite, and who have contributed so largely to corrupt the moral sentiments of our people, and extinguish among us the love of country, independence of spirit, disinterestedness, and courage in public affairs.[3]

But, unlike his son, who was to enlarge on his judgement against Hume, James Mill granted that Hume had superior subtlety and penetration.

It seems clear that James Mill never reacted against his early moral attitudes. He remained typical of the Kirk, the sort of man Hume disliked and feared. He strongly opposed political oppression, but that he should have shared Bentham's concern for tolerance of widely varied, even eccentric tastes, seems inconceivable. He remained after all a puritan, who, in his Commonplace Book, described the actor as 'a slave of the most irregular appetites and passions of his species', a man whose 'profession it is to assume false appearances', who had not a 'direct, true, undisguised, simple, and

---

[1] *Ibid.* pp. 89–90.
[2] George Spencer Bower, *Hartley and James Mill* (London, 1881), p. 15 .
[3] Bain, *op. cit.* p. 94.

sincere mind'.[1] Bentham's own awareness of the difference between them has been recorded in his remarks on Mill's positiveness, on his domineering and oppressive tone. He is supposed also to have accused Mill of being a reformer not because he loved the many, but because he hated the few. Taken literally, this charge wrongs Mill, and was probably never meant quite as Bowring took it, but it is a fair indication of his ruling passions.

One can only surmise the course of Mill's change from a critic of the government to an arch enemy of the whole political machinery, and a disciple of Bentham. His biographer and admirer, Alexander Bain, who would have preferred to believe that Mill was a radical almost from birth, searched in vain through his articles in the *Literary Journal* and the *St. James Chronicle* to discover some clear expression of radical views. Though he attributed any article implying such sympathies to Mill, he was forced to conclude merely that nothing Mill said in those years was inconsistent with his radical views, and that it was at worst lacking conviction, 'milk and water'.[2] It seems more likely that Mill did not develop his radical views until later, and was therefore in no danger of withholding his true opinions.

The change in tone from the optimism of the first years in London to the bleakness of 1807, when he was willing to leave London and return to the Church, suggests that personal disappointment may have encouraged Mill to reconsider his political views. Upon arriving in England, he had been struck by the inferiority of most of the men who were ruling the country to his own superior talent and industry. And yet, despite some early success, he remained outside, with no invitation from the great to do the work for which he felt, with some reason, so much better qualified than they. These feelings may have been exacerbated by the austere Scotsman's disgust with the un-inhibited manners and morals of London's upper classes. The amusements of Holland House, Carlton House, and Devonshire House, in any case closed to him but probably not unheard of, were not likely to arouse his admiration. Nor would they have encouraged him to consider the visitors there fit for high office. By the time he met Bentham, Mill's sentiments may easily have been akin to Carlyle's when he came to London (in 1824) and declared that the literary men there were devoid of heart, indolent, opium eaters, fre-quenters of gin-shops and pawnbrokers, and that most Scotsmen lived there 'like a shrub disrooted and stuck into a bottle of water'.[3]

The change in James Mill's religious views is equally obscure, but seems also to have been connected with feelings about the injustice that prevailed on earth. He never became an atheist, but by 1810 he had begun to say that

[1] *Ibid.* pp. 461–3.
[2] *Ibid.* p. 54.
[3] James Anthony Froude, *Thomas Carlyle—A History of the First Forty Years* (New York, 1910), vol. I, pp. 263–4.

nothing could be known about the origin of things. If Mill developed a moral objection to religion, as his son claimed, it was not the same kind as Hume's. He supposedly became an agnostic because he could not believe that a benevolent Deity was the maker of a universe so full of evil. He felt that Christianity set up creeds, devotions, and ceremonies unconnected with the good of mankind, and caused these to be accepted in place of genuine virtues, praising exorbitantly a Deity who could create men with the foreknowledge, and therefore the intention, that most of them would be sentenced to everlasting torment. Although Christians were not in fact as demoralized as they should be by such a creed, the inconsistencies of the creed were too grave to be endured. A Manichean theory of a good and evil principle struggling for dominion would have been more to his taste, and Mill is said to have expressed surprise that no one revived it in his time. But Christianity as it stood encouraged a morality that was a matter of 'blind tradition, with no consistent principle, nor even any consistent feeling to guide it'.[1]

What he proposed to put in place of this insufficient morality, however, was not essentially different from what he had practised all along. John Mill later gave a complicated description of his father's views of life, as partaking

of the character of the Stoic, the Epicurean, and the Cynic, not in the modern but the ancient sense of the word. In his personal qualities the Stoic predominated. His standard of morals was Epicurean, inasmuch as it was utilitarian, taking as the exclusive test of right and wrong, the tendency of actions to produce pleasure or pain. But he had (and this was the Cynic element) scarcely any belief in pleasure ... he deemed very few of them worth the price which, at least in the present state of society must be paid for them. . . . He thought human life a poor thing at best. . . .[2]

It was true that Mill described man's final obligation in un-Christian terms—to be a source of happiness to himself and others—but what he prescribed to this end might have been characterized more succinctly as the morality of the Kirk. Not the Kirk's severity, but the laxity and logical impurity of its moral system offended him and the amendments he proposed, though stated in another vocabulary, tended towards greater strictness.

James Mill was not, as he seemed to some, a man without passions, or, as his son charged, without any knowledge of poetry and allied arts. The reading he prescribed for John Mill, apart from what is known of his own reading, suggests a man of wide culture. Neither can one reconcile the popular picture of him as a hard, narrow man, possessed only of a gift for logical analysis, with the accounts of his forceful personality, the admiration he aroused in friends of distinction and discernment. His agnosticism has confused the picture. He is best characterized as a secular puritan, who was well acquainted

---

[1] John Stuart Mill, *Autobiography* (New York, 1924), pp. 29–30.
[2] *Ibid.* pp. 33–4.

with man and his best works but judged everything by the same harsh standdard, and observed it himself with impeccable faithfulness.

For all his addiction to the language and theory of Benthamism, Mill often spoke in terms not so different from what he once might have preached. In the Kirk he probably would not have said, as in the essay on education, that man's distinction lay in his being the most progressive creature on earth —'When he is the most rapidly progressive, then he most completely fulfils his destiny upon the globe'.[1] Even so, he was not condoning anything frivolous. But his denunciation of Nature as the enemy to be guarded against might have satisfied the orthodox. Nature meant to him all those appetites and desires that led men away from a clearly set course. Nature seduced men into thinking they need not overcome their base appetites. The good man, however, never relaxed his vigilance over his natural tendencies, or departed from perfect self-control and purposefulness. Judgement must be fortified 'against the illusions of the passions', so that a man may 'pursue constantly what he deliberately approves'.[2]

The strength to overcome natural propensities was what Mill believed the ancient philosophers meant by 'temperance'. For he liked to think that he had drawn his new creed from pagan philosophy, above all, from Plato. Mill's definitions cannot, however, easily be identified as Platonic: Justice—'to abstain from doing harm', and generosity—'to do positive good' were included, but subordinated to intelligence and self-discipline; and intelligence was described as a combination of knowledge and sagacity, a capacity for always choosing the best means. The resemblance to Plato's philosophy is faint; it rests only on Plato's exaltation of reason, which was probably the source of Plato's attraction for Mill. But the relation between reason and human nature, the character of reason itself, was simplified beyond recognition. Mill went so far as to say, in dead earnest, that the whole of Plato's *Republic* may be regarded as a development of the principle that identity of interests between governors and governed provides the only guarantee of good government.[3]

His other philosophical mentor, Locke, fared not much better in Mill's hands. In his most ambitious work, the *Analysis of the Phenomena of the Human Mind*, Mill outlined the metaphysics and the practical consequences of association psychology which he supposed himself to have learned from Locke and Hartley. It was to be the philosophical basis of Benthamism, a completion of the creed, and it occupied Mill continuously between 1822 and 1829. In some of its assumptions, the *Analysis* did not depart significantly from Locke—it described the mind as a blank page on which experience was

[1] *James Mill and John Stuart Mill on Education*, ed. F. A. Cavenagh (Cambridge, 1931), p. 67.
[2] James Mill, *Education*, p. 22.
[3] James Mill, *Fragment on Mackintosh* (London, 1870), p. 285.

recorded. To this Mill added some of the elaborations worked out by Hartley. But the rigour of Mill's treatise made it very different. Nothing was permitted to interfere with clarity—all the complexities that might have qualified his doctrine were ruthlessly eliminated so that human beings became strictly nothing but blanks to be written upon by circumstances. His chief object was to find one comprehensive law to explain all; what could not be explained was discarded. He reduced everything to association far more radically than even Hartley had dared. The problem of accounting for the will, consciousness, conscience, and imagination, which Locke recognized by obscurities and inconsistencies even if he could offer no solution, was simply obliterated by Mill. While Locke's language is often so indeterminate that some readers have been able to find in him tendencies opposed to pure empiricism and sensationalism, no one could do as much for James Mill.

Besides, the moral of the story was quite different. James Mill seemed to be following Locke when he urged men to 'break the shackles of authority and trust to their native strength'.[1] But whereas Locke emphasized that men should not try to go beyond knowledge of practical matters, Mill emphasized how much men could know about practical questions if only they proceeded correctly. Locke was attacking a frame of mind that led men to unwarranted certainty; Mill was destroying the foundation for current false beliefs which he proposed to replace with true ones. Locke said at the beginning of his *Thoughts Concerning Education*: 'of all the men we meet with, nine parts of ten are what they are, good or evil, useful or not, by their education'. Mill said: 'This much, at any rate, is ascertained, that all the difference which exists or can ever be made to exist, between one class of men, and another is wholly owing to education'.[2] The difference is in a way slight, but it is all important. In the one case, the author tries to emphasize that education is more important than it is frequently thought to be. In the other, the author asserts, as a self-evident truth, that education determines wholly what a man is. The one is modifying an extreme position; the other is asserting one. The difference runs all through Mill's writing.

The theory of association showed, according to Mill, that his philosophy started from facts, and he was therefore justified in making the highest claims for its conclusions and denying the pretensions of all other theories. Moreover, by showing that the ultimate constituents of the human mind could be connected with one another in any conceivable way, that nothing established or believed by men could not easily be otherwise, Mill could argue that education was omnipotent and that social arrangements could be modified at will. But as the ultimate constituents of the mind were perfectly constant, some absolute statements were nevertheless possible. So the laws that Mill discovered

[1] *Ibid.* p. 31.
[2] James Mill, *Education*, p. 29.

were absolutely true because they had been deduced from one or two formulae describing essential and invariable facts. He could reduce human desire to some definite, measurable thing, such as utility in ethics, value in political economy, self-interest in politics, and argue confidently to an eternal conclusion. In short, James Mill used Locke's philosophy to encourage the sort of ambition it had been designed to dampen.

Nor did Mill's doctrine resemble Bentham's unphilosophical, mundane view of human nature any more closely than it did Locke's or Hartley's. Despite Mill's emphasis on teaching the virtues in accordance with the theory of association (pleasure was to be connected with desirable objects), and his conviction that his temperance was quite different from Christian temperance, which aimed only at pleasing God or at securing happiness in a future life, his notion of virtue remained altogether foreign to Bentham. Whereas Bentham praised reason only insofar as he saw in reasoning of a certain sort the best way of preventing any man's opinions from tyrannizing over others, James Mill identified the dominion of reason with a particular, austere way of life that all men must follow. His main purpose was to lay down a rule of duty, almost mathematically certain, which no one could deny. The principle of utility, he declared, 'marshals the duties in their proper order, and will not permit mankind to be deluded, as so long they have been, sottishly to prefer the lower to the higher good, and to hug the greater evil from fear of the less'.[1]

Agnostic and Benthamite though he was, James Mill thought and lived entirely in the spirit of the Kirk. Nothing suggests that he could ever have approved a lapse from a life of labour for a distant purpose, from unrelenting discipline and suppression of momentary impulses or desires, or indeed any attempt to savour life as a pleasure rather than endure it as a duty. Bentham's utilitarianism lacked moral content, and each of its advocates might fill that in as he chose. James Mill, who had a much more detailed moral code than Bentham and felt strongly about it, succeeded in impressing it upon utilitarianism which, now that it resembled their old creed, attracted renegade dissenters.

The only mark of a transformation in James Mill, due to his conversion from Presbyterianism to utilitarianism, was a declared antipathy to mysticism of any kind expressed in a determination to reduce everything to logical argument. But whereas Bentham confined his logical exercises to an ethics without content, to constitutions and codes, and made only fragmentary excursions into psychology, James Mill preferred metaphysics and philosophy. He put the influence of association, of early training and circumstances in place of original sin and reasoned from there with unsparing logic.

---

[1] James Mill, *Fragment*, p. 270.

In a series of articles for the *Encyclopedia Britannica*, he reduced a number of subjects such as government, education, and jurisprudence to a set of axioms and syllogisms. The essay on government became notorious after Macaulay's attack in the *Edinburgh Review*. Its central point was no different from Bentham's—that the only way to prevent those who have power from misusing it is to enable the victims to displace their rulers. But Mill stripped away the cumbrous definitions, all the irritating but softening eccentricities of Bentham's style and produced a series of bald syllogisms. 'As the surface of history affords no certain principle of decision', Mill declares, 'we must go beyond the surface and penetrate to the springs within.'[1] The only reasonable procedure is to deduce the principles of government from the laws of human nature, and this means from the self-preference principle, which tells us that 'one man if stronger than another, will take from him whatever that other possesses and he desires'.[2] As the desire for the power to do so is infinitely great, it follows that there is no 'point of saturation' with the objects of desire either for king or aristocracy. Mill examines and rejects the mixed government of Britain, because two branches of the government will always agree to swallow up the third, an unfortunate argument that he borrowed from Bentham. The only solution left is the 'grand discovery of modern times', the representative system. The logic is simple and undeniable: it would be a 'contradiction in terms'[3] to suppose that the community at large can have an interest opposed to itself. Though the community cannot act as a whole, it can act through representatives who can be prevented from misusing their power. This can be done by making them subject to election frequently and by a broad franchise.

It is the style, rather than the conclusion, that is significant. Bentham's search for exactness involved him in ludicrously elaborate definitions, but they testified to a feeling for the difficulty of being precise. James Mill indulges in neither qualifications nor complexities. He speaks as if he is laying down a universal law that the strong will always plunder the weak, that rulers will necessarily reduce their subjects to abject slavery, that the representative system is literally a machine which will inevitably remove these evils. Moreover, it was a machine with pretensions, for it would mould the people into a condition suitable to the new political order. As Mill explained in his essay on education, if the 'political machine' is constituted so as to make the grand objects of desire 'the natural prizes of just and virtuous conduct, of high services to mankind, and of the generous and amiable sentiments from which great endeavours in the service of mankind naturally proceed', it would become natural 'to see diffused among mankind a generous ardour in the acquisition of those admirable qualities which prepare a man for admirable

---

[1] James Mill, *Essay on Government* (Cambridge, 1937), p. 16.

[2] *Ibid.* p. 12.

[3] *Ibid.* p. 10.

action, great intelligence, perfect self-command, and over-ruling benevo-lence'.[1]

To Macaulay's accusation that he wrote like a fifteenth century Aristo-telian who had inherited the spirit and style of the Schoolmen and was una-ware that any actual government had ever existed, Mill replied, in his *Frag-ment on Mackintosh*, that he was discussing only general tendencies, and therefore need not have considered the exceptions which he nowhere denied. He explained that he was not giving an exhaustive description of a good state but merely pointing out the one essential of good government that was radically lacking in England—a strong sense in the governors of their responsibility to the governed. That in his own mind James Mill was not as simple-minded or dogmatic as his essay suggests is very likely. When he gave evidence on India, he showed that he was aware that qualifications were necessary before principles could be applied. Yet the fact remains that he wrote what looks very much like a scientific treatise on politics, rather than a proposal for parliamentary reform. For all the similarities to Bentham's writing, the curt logic, the completeness, and undistracted march from assump-tion to conclusion is vastly different.

It reflects Mill's interest in reducing all knowledge to a few basic principles and containing the world in one all-embracing system. Against Mackintosh who argued that this ought not to be done in moral and social matters, Mill replied: 'the man who subjects the largest province of human knowledge to the fewest principles is universally esteemed the most successful philosopher'. This, he believed, was the essence of philosophy according to Plato. It is, he says, what Plato called 'seeing the one in the many, and the many in the one'.[2] For the same reason, Mill was attracted to Hobbes' certainty and simplicity and he quoted approvingly the opening of his *Treatise of Human Nature:* 'The true and perspicuous explication of the elements of law natural and politic . . . dependeth upon the knowledge of what is human nature, what is a body politic, and what it is we call a law . . . and seeing that true knowledge begeteth not doubt nor controversy . . .'.[3] It was just this view of politics as a simple extension of undeniable principles about human nature that made Hobbes most offensive to Locke. But James Mill, having lost his faith in the theological doctrine that had enabled him to see the one in the many, and the many in the one, set himself to restoring such a vision on a secular foundation.

The system-making that obsessed him was of a peculiarly simple sort. He was intent on producing a philosophy that could serve as a catechism. For he insisted that there was no break between sound theory and good practice. Theory was not sound unless it could be applied to practice at once; and good

[1] James Mill, *Education*, pp. 72–3.
[2] James Mill, *Fragment*, p. 25.
[3] *Ibid.* p. 28.

practical rules were nothing but sound theory: 'What is theory? The whole of the knowledge which we possess upon any subject, put into that order and form in which it is most easy to draw from it good practical results'.[1] Arguments against the 'overwhelming presumption' of the 'practical' man filled his commonplace book, and one of his last articles in the London Review was a dialogue on the question of theory versus practice. The villains, as James Mill saw it, were all those light-hearted rulers of the world who indulged their appetites and governed on the strength of tradition, or some other indefinable substitute for clear reason set forth in a succession of syllogisms, for which they hoped to excuse themselves by arguing that practice was opposed to theory.

There was not, to his mind, any intrinsic difficulty about grasping and holding the truth. He knew that it took labour, as well as honesty and talent to find the truth, but he suffered none of the doubts that had made Hume turn first against the certainty of the Kirk, and finally against any man's assurance that he could know the truth. The dragon that Mill chose to engage was not dogmatism, but falsehood. Truth for him was not complicated or slippery, or in any way baffling, but simply the opposite of falsehood. With all his learning, his admiration for Plato and the spirit of Socrates, he never discovered anything from them to weaken his conviction that truth could be caught by anyone who hunted diligently and fairly.

What made truth seem difficult to other men was frivolity. Anything that was embellished or fanciful was frivolous, for embellishment weakened the force of pure reason. The good and true was plain and unadorned, and anything plain could not be dangerous or evil, for it was pure reason. Mill even believed it was sensible to argue that religious readers ought not to consider writers like Helvetius dangerous enemies to religion, because whatever Helvetius said against religion was always put straightforwardly, and therefore without any seduction. As he appealed only to the judgement, he could never lead men astray by deluding the fancy.[2] James Mill was firm, and according to his theory, absolutely correct in avoiding any hint of fancy. He was equally meticulous about giving the opposition a full hearing, and bore no grudge against his own critics (he supported Macaulay even after the latter's attack on him). But once these conditions were satisfied, he saw no reason to feel doubtful about the line between truth and error, good and evil, to put a 'perhaps' before one's sentences as he upbraided Mackintosh for doing,[3] nor to hesitate before putting one's knowledge to work.

It was through the efforts of this severe puritan that an amiable champion

---

[1] James Mill, *Education*, p. 4.
[2] *Ibid.* p. 26.
[3] James Mill, *Fragment*, p. 27.

of tolerance became a great influence in philosophy and politics. But James Mill converted Bentham's eccentric 'gadgeteering' into a rigorous creed that gave no leave for dissent.

CHAPTER XVII

THE YOUNG DISCIPLE

ONCE he was enrolled in the new faith, it was only natural for James Mill to hope that his gifted eldest son would become a revered leader of the congregation. The story of how he educated John Stuart for this task is well known. The rigours of the education and the early age at which it began were certainly as formidable as the son felt them to be, but the versatility is often overlooked. Though not unusual among the generation of James Mill, it was the sort of liberal education that became more rare among John Mill's contemporaries. The young Mill read not only Aristotle and Plato, but Homer, the Greek tragedians, Herodotus and Thucydides, as well as Xenophon, the orators, Cicero's letters, and Virgil, along with mathematics and science. To the ancient classics were added a very large selection of modern poets and dramatists, and in fact the only striking omission that John Mill could point to later was Wordsworth, who was not, as he seemed to forget, esteemed by all who loved poetry.

But whether the way in which he was taught or his natural inclinations were to blame, the music, the imagery, the drama in what he read made little impression on him. He was carried away only by the 'truths' he found. Analysis, note-taking, arguments for and against, not dreamy enjoyment were the results of his labour. While his acquaintance with the classics probably told in his life in ways that Mill himself never recognized, the effects were not to become obvious for some years.

Until he was fourteen his father had a monopoly of intellectual and moral influence over him. Everything he read and thought was overseen by James Mill, either while studying beside him or on long walks, when John Mill discoursed on his reading and was corrected on basic principles as well as on matters of detail. The result was, understandably enough, that the son became a caricature of the father. A visitor to Ford Abbey, Anne Romilly, who met him at the age of seven or eight wrote: 'Little Mill makes more observations than almost any child I ever saw who was crammed, but they are always in slow measured tones, and deliver'd with the air of a person who is conscious of his superiority, and if you hazard an observation in return, you are perhaps assured that the "*authorities* will not bear you out in what you have asserted" '.[1] At eleven he impressed Francis Place with his accomplishments, but still not as a lovable character: 'John is truly a prodigy, a most

[1] Anne Romilly to Maria Edgeworth, *Romilly Edgeworth Letters*, p. 178, in Anna Jean Mill, *John Mill's Boyhood Visit to France* 1820–21 (Toronto, 1960), p. xii.

wonderful fellow', Place wrote to his wife after a meeting at Ford Abbey, 'and when his Logic, his Languages, his Mathematics, his Philosophy, shall be combined with a general knowledge of mankind and the affairs of the world, he will be a truly astonishing man; but he will probably be morose and selfish'.[1] His other leading characteristic as a child appears in Bentham's letter to his brother, after Samuel Bentham had invited John Mill to visit him in France: 'J. M. to whom the sheet for him had been sent grinned pleasure and twice declared himself "much gratified": "gratified" is a conjugate to grateful and gratitude: but nearer to "gratitude" than this he never comes, for he is, and always was proud as Lucifer'.[2]

The most complete picture of John Mill as a boy comes from his visit to France at the age of fourteen, when he lived for a year with Bentham's brother, as a member of the family. His careful record of all that happened to him began at once. What he noticed along the way was mostly of a completely impersonal nature, and given in exact detail. The diligence to Paris was much more than twice as long, and considerably broader than an English stage coach, yet it was supported on two wheels only. The country was flat, then hilly at Boulogne, which consisted of two towns; there they dined table d'hôte, which was the cheapest. In Paris, he visited the Palais Royal and remarked that it was 'an immense building that belonged to the profligate Duc d'Orleans (in the time of Louis XVI) who, having ruined himself by debauchery, resolved to let the arcades of his palace to various tradesmen: whose shops make a beautiful appearance. The upper rooms are appropriated to gaming and all species of vice'.[3] Notre Dame had a finer organ than Westminster Abbey, with which it was in other respects much on a par; the Jardin des Tuileries was nothing compared to Kensington Gardens, but the palace was much finer than anything in London; in the Louvre, he liked best the statue of the Fighting Gladiator. On the way from Paris to the Benthams at Pompignan there were a number of annoyances: 'A marchand de boeuf with the largest belly I ever saw in my life, who was continually smoking tobacco got here into the cabriolet: you may imagine how I was annoyed'.[4] When on the fourth day, a vacancy occurred in the interior of the carriage, Mill claimed it as the passenger of longest standing. A lady contested it, but he persisted and the case was referred to the mayor. The retiring passenger, a young lawyer, pleaded his case and won, and Mill triumphantly took his seat with the more tidy passengers.

Once he arrived at the Benthams', he lost no time in beginning his programme of reading, despite the fact that Sir Samuel's books were packed for

[1] Graham Wallas, *The Life of Francis Place* (London, 1898), pp. 74–5.
[2] Anna Jean Mill, *John Mill's Boyhood Visit to France*, p. xiii.
[3] *Ibid.* p. 5.
[4] *Ibid.* p. 9.

the move to Montpelier. Everything was reported meticulously. While the amount of work with which he filled his day is impressive enough, even more striking is the precision with which he noted down how he spent literally every minute of his day, and his business-like efficiency in turning from one task to another. Even if he exaggerated somewhat for his father's sake, though his rectitude about small sins makes this unlikely, it is remarkable that he should have been able to keep in his head, or bother to write down, so many details of his life. He doled out his time like a clerk in a counting house, who dared not let the smallest expenditure escape his book. One feels moreover that he behaved in this way as much for his own peace of mind as for the satisfaction of his master. The journal for any day will do as an example:

Rose at 5 o'clock, went to the river at half after five; found the water much clearer than yesterday. Borrowed Voltaire['s] Essai sur les Moeurs etc. of Dr Russell; returned home at ½ after 7. Finished my letter dated this day; sent it off: at 8 o'clock M. Layrieu the dancing master came as usual to give a lesson to the young ladies but as Miss Clara had not yet risen, I took a lesson in her stead. Breakfasted at ¼ before 9: at half past nine began to read Voltaire from the place where I had left off in England. Read six chapters which occupied me two hours. Read 47 lines of Virgil's Georgics; at a quarter after twelve began to read a treatise on the Use of various Adverbs, in the French grammar I have already mentioned. At half after one, began the second book of Legendre; read the definitions and five propositions. Miscellaneous employments till 3 o'clock; then took my second lesson of Principes de Musique.—Dined; Sir S. B., Mr George, and the young ladies went again to see Franconi, but I did not on account of my dancing lesson. Wrote French exercises, etc., practised Music; went to M. Layrieu's but he was gone to Franconi's, and as, after I had waited about an hour, I was told he would not return before half an hour more was elapsed, I came away.—Found two of the Messrs Courtois, great bankers of Toulouse, at the house; they did not stay long.— P.S. to this day's journal—My new waistcoat came home last night.[1]

When he spoke to the French people, he was mainly interested in gathering useful information. A conversation with four workmen illustrated for him the evil effects of the French law that obliged every father to divide the property equally among children—'but for this law, two, or one at least, might have been placed in a situation to gain his living without cultivating the ground'.[2] His political opinions were in other respects all they should have been. He reported with great satisfaction news of revolutions in Italy—'a constitution is establishing in the kingdom of Naples, and all Italy, Rome inclusive, is revolutionized—the Pope's temporal power is done away with: (a most fortunate circumstance;) and all Europe seems to be following the example so successfully set by Spain'.[3] He hoped, too, that his father had kept his letters as they might be of use on his return.

[1] Ibid. p. 34.
[2] Ibid. p. 24.
[3] Ibid. p. 57.

It is no wonder that the worldly and unconventional Benthams decided after meeting John Mill that their job was to make him better acquainted with the amenities of life. They made a great effort to distract him from his books, to teach him dancing and singing, to love beautiful scenery and enjoy parties. They were so far successful that he left them very reluctantly and kept for ever after a warm affection for France, as well as for his first year there. But while he was more polished and somewhat softened, a striking change in him did not come until later.

At sixteen, John Mill took his place in the adult world, when his father arranged for him to get the post of junior clerk in the Examiner's Office of India House. From this time on he became a young Benthamite in his own right. He became acquainted with a number of young men, among them, Arthur Roebuck, a vehement young barrister from Canada, later a colourful and influential political figure, who relentlessly opposed the Whigs. The friendship with Roebuck, which became close and lasted for some years, was an act of independence since James Mill disapproved. Roebuck said later that James Mill looked down on him because he was poor and not well connected, that Mill was rude and curt to him although gracious to young men of wealth and position.[1] It is at least as likely that James Mill was offended by Roebuck's hearty, boisterous, and aggressive nature, which may easily have impressed him as sinful as well as crude.

In all other ways, John Mill was a faithful disciple. To bring down Tory misrule and build society anew on Bentham's principles, he cultivated a small group of fellow officers. These he called the Utilitarian Society, taking the name from a novel (*Annals of the Parish*, by John Galt) in which a Scots clergyman warns his parishioners not to leave the Gospel and become utilitarians.[2] The troops and their staunch and tireless colonel met regularly, first in Bentham's dining room, then twice a week before their office hours, from eight-thirty to ten, at Grote's place in the city. They endeavoured to improve themselves and to map out their campaign. Though their spirit was militant, the texts were sober and judicious—Ricardo and Bailey on political economy, Aldrich, Whately and Hobbes on logic, Hartley and James Mill on analytical psychology. The discussions were utterly earnest and no problem, however trivial, was dismissed before all had agreed on a solution.

When Roebuck discovered the Owenites preaching the brotherhood of man in a hall in Chancery Lane, he easily persuaded Mill to join in their debates and demonstrate to the Owenites that according to the laws of political economy their schemes were but utopian delusions. Out of these encounters

---

[1] John Arthur Roebuck, *Life and Letters*, ed. by Robert E. Leader, (London, 1897), p. 29.
[2] Cf. Michael St John Packe, *John Stuart Mill* (London, 1954), p. 53 n. According to Packe, Bentham had used the name in 1802.

there grew up the London Debating Society modelled on the Speculative Society of Edinburgh. It included along with Mill and Roebuck some of the brightest stars from the universities—Hyde and Charles Villiers, brothers of the Earl of Clarendon, who both entered politics; Romilly, the son of Bentham's friend and later a liberal Member of Parliament; Charles Austin, younger brother of John, known as Bentham's most eloquent disciple; Macaulay, the historian; Wilberforce, the son of the anti-slavery reformer; even the wealthy and elegant Richard Monckton Milnes. They met in Freemason's Tavern in Chancery Lane, and by August, 1825 counted over a hundred names, among them all the young men likely to lead the country's affairs during the next fifty years. The success promised by the brilliant beginning did not, however, come so easily.

But throughout, John Mill remained the most impressive, as well as indefatigable, enemy of aristocracy. Whoever heard him felt he was somehow singular: 'He is an animated, determined-looking youth', Henry Taylor wrote to his mother, 'and speaks, I am told, without hesitation, digression, ornament, or emphasis, in a tone to me in the little I heard almost ridiculously simple and with very odd, but very considerable effect'.[1] At the same time, Mill was editing, which meant in effect almost writing, five large volumes of a treatise on the *Rationale of Judicial Evidence* from Bentham's papers. And he was, of course, a regular contributor to the *Westminster Review*.

What his intellectual temper was like at that time appears clearly in an article he wrote for the fourth issue of the *Westminster*, a review of Brodie's history of the seventeenth century,[2] written to criticize Hume's history. The review perfectly summarizes the differences between Hume's outlook and the creed John Mill had learned from his father.

One of Britain's greatest minds, Mill declared, had lent his talents to a vicious cause. He had violated truth and justice, made a tyrant masquerade as a noble hero, slandered honest patriots struggling for the improvement of mankind. For all his powers, Hume was no better than a shallow, hypocritical dilettante. Instead of concerning himself with the proper object of history—the effects of events 'on the great interests of mankind'—Hume was prey to, and propagator of, 'one of the most pernicious of all habits.' He sympathized more with the misfortunes of heroes, who are only men in exalted station, than with the anonymous multitudes—'whenever the interests of mankind and his hero are at variance, he must endeavour to make the reader take part with the hero against mankind. Such was the object of Hume and the object to which he deliberately sacrificed truth, honesty, and candour'.[3]

[1] *Ibid.* p. 71.
[2] George Brodie, *A History of the British Empire from the Accession of Charles I to the Restoration*, 4 vols. (Edinburgh, 1822).
[3] *Westminster Review*, October, 1824, pp. 347–8.

Mill called upon Englishmen not to be led astray by such pied pipers who play on the emotions and thus gain large audiences by foul means.

Hume's moderate tone, his attempts to present the other side, did not in the least mollify John Mill. They were but further proof of his wickedness. With great knowingness, Mill explained that Hume 'avoids the appearance of violence, and yields some points, in order to make a show of moderation, knowing well that a writer, if he acknowledges only a tenth part of what is true, obtains a reputation for candour which frequently causes people to over-look the mis-statement of the other nine-tenths'.[1] But even if Mill had thought Hume's concessions sincere, he still would not have approved. For then Hume would simply have been one of those trimmers whom Mill condemned quite as energetically for their lack of courage and conviction.

There was, however, no question in Mill's mind that Hume's history was simply a defence of Charles I, and an attack on his opponents in parliament. Mill was equally certain that Charles and his party were in fact engaged in a deliberate and subtle plot to institute an absolute monarchy and to establish Catholicism. Hume's insistence that Charles claimed nothing new in the way of absolute power, but aroused opposition because the circumstances and sentiments had changed, struck Mill as not only untrue but petty. Even if there had been a precedent for Charles's claims, there was not, according to Mill, any good reason for considering the question. He attacked Brodie for trying to establish that the English constitution had never sanctioned the powers Charles claimed. Whether or not 'misgovernment' was of an ancient date in Great Britain, Mill declared,

resistance to it was equally a duty; . . . and it is a strange doctrine, that we are not entitled to good government, unless we can prove that our ancestors enjoyed it: although, as mankind, educated as they have hitherto been, are governed by custom and precedent much more than by reason, it was perfectly natural that each party at the time should endeavour to throw the reproach of innovation upon its opponents.[2]

What outraged Mill even more than the regard for tradition and custom was Hume's levity about religious grievances. Mill was convinced that the religious grievances were not, as Hume said, mere tinder for an explosive constitutional condition, but a serious and important cause of the conflict. He refused to dismiss the controversies over robes, ceremonies, and ritual, for nothing, he felt, could be more Popish, and Laud was certainly an agent of Rome. Because of its addiction to such frivolities, the English Church differed from the Roman only by its failure to use torture and burning: 'The assertion, therefore, that there was no danger of popery . . . is in substance one of the grossest falsehoods ever palmed off upon the credulity of the world'.[3] Some-

[1] *Ibid.* p. 351.   [2] *Ibid.* p. 352.
[3] *Ibid.* p. 364.

thing more was also involved in the struggle between an enlightened religion and a base superstition. Catholicism inevitably supported tyranny because it lent itself so well to the uses of absolute power; that was why James and Charles wished to embrace it. Mill refused to concede even a sincere religious faith to such villains.

Nor would he allow explanations in terms of personal friendship. The personal feelings that mattered so much to Hume were from Mill's standpoint irrelevant: 'Such a thing as friendship between a king and his subject, cannot be said to exist'.[1] In truth there were only saints and villains and the tools of villains. Pym and Hampden were saints of the highest order, mercilessly pursued by the forces of evil. Hume's condemnation of the Puritans' enthusiasm was but an attempt to slander the defenders of justice and freedom. His effort to show that a more moderate and prudent stand by the opposition might have prevented the differences between king and parliament from bursting into a revolution meant only that he believed a king might be as cruel as he liked as long as he persecuted only those who resisted him. That Hume might have been objecting more to the manner of the opposition than to its existence, that he might have been emphasizing the dangers of revolution and violence did not occur to Mill, who saw only a choice between supine acquiescence and valiant opposition: 'The only question which deserves the slightest consideration is, which party was substantially in the right'.[2]

Yet Mill's ardour for the saints did not lead him to deviate from orthodox utilitarianism. He remembered his father's teaching that all men may abuse power—'If the popular leaders had possessed undue power, they would probably, like other men have abused it'.[3] He showed no undue regard for the wisdom of the people—that the people when they got power should have misused it was only to be expected, since the people can be relied on to destroy, but not to construct. He welcomed law reform, whatever the auspices: the Long Parliament were despots, he granted but still they did more to reform the law then any English parliament before or since. 'Had their authority continued, landed property would have been made liable for simple contract debts; the absurd fictions of fine and recovery would have been abolished; a system of universal registration would have been established for contracts in land, and the whole body of law would have been digested into a code . . .'.[4] But Mill took no notice of the Long Parliament's regulations of private behaviour. He says nothing to dispute Brodie's insinuation that only his having imbibed too much of French courtliness could explain Hume's opposition to the Commonwealth's highly beneficial laws against adultery and fornication.[5]

[1] *Ibid.* p. 379.
[2] *Ibid.* p. 373.
[3] *Ibid.* p. 372.
[4] *Ibid.* pp. 400–1.
[5] George A. Brodie, *History of the British Empire*, vol. IV, pp. 324–5 and fn.

In fact Hume offended Mill not so much by his prejudices on the wrong side (he would have been found more sympathetic had he been a militant royalist), as by his conviction, which Mill did not comprehend but rightly sensed throughout the history, that human powers were best employed in showing that the truth cannot easily be known. 'Regard for truth formed no part of his character. He reasoned with surprising acuteness; but the object of his reasoning was, not to attain truth, but to show that it is unattainable'.[1] This was at the heart of all Mill's objections. Because decisions about right and wrong were not for him matters of judgement where good men might differ, he could not see how an event might honestly, and even reasonably, be interpreted in different ways. Neither could he understand that Hume's unwillingness to assign the responsibility for events came from thinking that circumstances combine in unintended ways, compelling men to do what they might otherwise have avoided. Since Mill believed that the motives of men were not only impossible to discover but irrelevant to judging their actions, he was irritated by digressions on any one's character. When Hume says that Cromwell lacked the refinement that a knowledge of the classics can give, Mill is so far from understanding such a concern with the style of a man's character, that he declares the statement nonsense because Cromwell had read much. When Hume praises men who opposed the king, Mill either ignores it or accuses Hume of pandering to popularity. The historian's only proper concern, Mill insisted, is how actions affected the advancement of mankind. He is obliged either to condemn or praise only on this basis.

All of life seemed to Mill at this time quite simply a struggle between good and evil. Virtuous men enrolled themselves as champions for the right side. To sit back and watch the show pass, as Hume seemed to be doing, to concern oneself with how men think and behave without trying to aid the triumph of right was indecent, and most likely, hypocritical. James Mill had taken great trouble to save his son from conceit by explaining to him that his accomplishments were due only to a remarkably careful education. But he had not tried to give him any detachment about what he believed, or any doubts about the possibility of knowing the truth. John Mill grew up not so sure of his own powers as he appeared to be, but certain in an impersonal way that there was only one right answer, and that it was sinful not to speak out with assurance against the villains and for the saints.

After entering India House, Mill was for a few years content. He was proving himself a worthy disciple. He was part of an army working for the greatest happiness of the greatest number, and felt assured of a good and happy life because he had placed his happiness 'in something durable and distant, in which some progress might be always making, while it could never be exhausted by complete attainment'.[2]

[1] *Westminster Review*, October, 1824, p. 346. [2] J. S. Mill, *Autobiography*, p. 93.

And then, in his twentieth year, the glory departed; it was, he said, as if he had been awakened from a dream. He continued his activities but his assurance and energy gave way to depression. He no longer felt certain that what he was doing would accomplish what he hoped; even worse, he lost his assurance that if what he hoped for came to pass, the world would be greatly improved by it. Outwardly he remained much the same, and most of his friends were unaware of his distress, but he was so markedly unhappy that he called this period 'a crisis in my mental history'. The worst symptoms disappeared as quietly as they had come, five months later when he was reading the memoirs of Marmontel, a minor French playwright of the eighteenth century, and found himself weeping over the account of the father's death and the son's resolution to take upon himself the responsibilities of the family. That he could weep convinced Mill all feeling was not, as his apathy made him fear, completely dead in him. He began to take heart again and search for the causes and cure of his misery, to examine critically all he had believed.

In some ways, Mill's crisis was as peculiar to himself as he fancied. He had been indoctrinated by his father with unusual thoroughness and deliberation, so that his first doubts, though about a secular dogma, were as painful as a mature Christian's loss of faith. His uninterrupted labour since the age of three may easily have brought on extreme physical and mental exhaustion. His father's stern and domineering character, despite all his solicitude, must have taken its toll, while his mother seems to have been only a source of embarrassment because of her shortcomings and his father's public discourtesies to her. Indeed his relations with his family were strained enough to make it likely that his crisis was connected with a repressed hostility to his father, especially as his release came through reading Marmontel's story of his father's death.[1]

But in other ways, Mill's 'crisis', at least insofar as it was a reaction against utilitarianism, was only to be expected. He had reached his time to question what he had until then received on faith, to decide which part of the intellectual and moral baggage thrust upon him he wished to carry along. Besides, a changing world had deprived utilitarianism of the capacity to satisfy an ardent champion of truth.

[1] A. W. Levi, 'The Mental Crisis of J. S. Mill,' *Psychoanalytic Review*, vol. xxxii, 1945. At the time of James Mill's last illness and death, Mill had another and more severe breakdown that left him with permanent physical ailments.

CHAPTER XVIII

THE FAILURE OF UTILITARIANISM

By the 1820's, Bentham's principles, even if they had been transmitted in the master's true spirit, had become, if not irrelevant, somewhat out of place. The world that had inspired Bentham, and that even James Mill knew best, the world in which personal relations were all and it was a struggle to make men attend in the least to organization and impersonal techniques, was gone. Melbourne and his like were still about, but they were beginning to look like relics. The men who were replacing them in power and eminence were very well aware of the importance of administrative efficiency, and often aware of and capable of loving little else.

There was a greater stir and more rapid development in every sphere of public activity. The change was not revolutionary, but the process that had been transforming England into an industrial society since the seventeenth century had by now become marked enough to attract and deserve more notice. Inventions worked cumulatively to speed up the rate of change and any statistics about industrial output in the first few decades of the century give a striking picture of rapid growth. But much more was involved than a remarkable increase in numbers of power looms and factories. The whole character of industry and commerce was being altered. New methods of administration and selling became popular. Better roads and larger towns made it possible to replace the pedlar and the fair by small shops supplied through a commercial traveller. Production of all sorts, even of food, came increasingly to be financed and run like factories. Large-scale impersonal organization was taking over everywhere. The business man developed more deliberate and routine methods of measuring, counting, and observing. He was indifferent to, if not ignorant of, old traditions and customs, many of which were no longer applicable to his work. Tradition belonged with the old regime of outmoded techniques. The businessman now preferred to weigh every act as it arose for the profit it would yield, and his success depended on his ability to calculate quickly, boldly, and correctly.

The spirit that dominated in business and industry was spread throughout the society. Technical knowledge in all spheres became a special domain, with a status of its own, and occupations formerly open to anyone were transformed into professions. The development of the apothecaries was not unusual: a bill in 1815 gave the Society of Apothecaries the right to examine all apothecaries in England and Wales; to secure their professional prestige, they required an apprenticeship of five years; and soon hospitals organized schools of their own which sent out the first general practitioners. By a similar process, the engineer acquired an unprecedented importance. The mechanical engineer, as we now know him, became common in London and Lancashire, and civil engineering was recognized as a profession based upon applied science. Roads, bridges, canals, docks, harbours, drainage, indeed all the technical foundations of modern industrial society, came under the aegis of the new profession.

To provide training for the growing numbers of those wishing to rise in the industrial society, new institutions sprang up continuously, and England no longer lagged so far behind the Continent in technical education. The Mechanics Institute movement began in London in 1823. In 1827, the Society for the Diffusion of Useful Knowledge was founded to educate the artisan class. Many schools were established to use the methods of Lancaster and Bell, 'a mechanical system of education', whereby a master taught only the elder children, who taught the younger ones, so that, as Andrew Bell claimed, twenty-four pupils today could overnight be made into twenty-five teachers. The system was, its admirers felt, a cheap way of instilling a number of facts into children's minds, and this seemed to them what education was meant to be. That even men who might have been expected to think differently about education were dazzled by such mechanisms is evident from an article by Brougham, where, in the course of urging education for the poor, he wrote:

It is manifest that any rule in algebra may be communicated by the same process [i.e. by one ignorant boy reading the rules to another and making him work examples mechanically] from the simplest to the most intricate and refined. . . . Every part of geometrical science may be taught by similar means—from the first proposition in Euclid, to the sublime theories of Newton and Laplace. . . . In like manner, whatever branches of natural philosophy admit of a symbolical notation . . . are all capable of being communicated by a person ignorant of them, but able to read, to as many others as can hear the sound of his voice at once. . . . This method may, therefore, most truly be pronounced a capital discovery, in every point of view; and we have little doubt that it will speedily be extended from the sciences to the arts, which seem all to admit of being taught upon similar principles.[1]

Education was spreading, but it was education devoted to furthering an industrial civilization, to giving short order vocational learning and bringing deliverance through more efficient organization.

Impersonal organization was taking over even the leisure time of Englishmen. Members of the working class as well as the middle class, women along with the men, rushed to join some society or movement, whether democratic, Irish Nationalist, or 'romantic'. There was something for everyone.

Government also became more attentive to techniques and organization.

---

[1] *Edinburgh Review*, November, 1810, p. 74. Cf. *Athenaeum*, No. 11, 1828, pp. 162 ff., for criticism of Brougham.

The House of Commons regularly appointed Select Committees to investigate and recommend new lines of policy. Well before parliamentary reform, there were committees on reform of various aspects of the criminal law, on the handling of mendicity and vagrancy, on the Poor Laws, on education, on national income and expenditure. The committees did not always search very far or very deeply, but the principle of making methodical investigation a prelude to legislation was established, and prepared the way for the many royal commissions of the 1830's which used not only members of parliament, but outside experts on political economy and administration. The spirit of the government that Liverpool formed in 1821 was all for administrative reform and efficiency. Peel introduced consolidated legislation regarding three-quarters of all criminal offences on the statute books, abolished capital punishment for a very large number of crimes, revised the scale of lesser punishments, improved legal procedure and conditions of imprisonment, and in 1829 created a new Metropolitan Police Force. At the Board of Trade, Huskisson had only to follow the policies of his predecessor, Wallace, who had already recognized the need for a 'full and complete revision of our commercial system'. And in foreign policy, Canning supported Spanish and Portuguese constitutionalism, scorned the principle of legitimacy, and gave a hearty welcome to the new independent South American States.

To urge the importance of organization, administrative efficiency, rational reform was no longer radical but conventional. The forces for more and larger organization clearly had the upper hand. The radical was now he who criticized them, and tried to remind England that after all persons were more important. Carlyle was opposing what he regarded, with reason, as an orthodoxy when in 1829 he wrote his bombastic article, 'Signs of the Times'. The new age was above all others a 'Mechanical Age'—'It is the Age of Machinery. . . . On every hand, the living artisan is being driven from his workshop to make room for a speedier, inanimate one'.[1] Machinery had come to rule the internal and spiritual, as well as everything else, Carlyle wailed. Everywhere one looked there were machines—

Instruction, that mysterious communing of Wisdom with Ignorance is no longer an indefinable process . . . but a secure, universal, straightforward business to be conducted in the gross, by proper mechanism, with such intellect as comes to hand. . . . Has any man or any society of men, a truth to speak, a piece of spiritual work to do, they can nowise proceed at once, and with the mere natural organs, but must first call a public meeting, appoint committees, issue prospectuses, eat a public dinner; in a word, construct or borrow machinery. . . . [2]

Even the artist was being hustled into an academy and literary men could not succeed without becoming enmeshed in

[1] *Edinburgh Review*, June, 1829, p. 442.
[2] *Ibid.* p. 443.

Trade dinners, its Editorial conclaves, and huge subterranean, puffing bellows. . . . Men are grown mechanical in head and in heart as well as in hand. . . . Not for internal perfection, but for external combinations and arrangements, for institutions, constitutions—for Mechanism of one sort or another, do they hope and struggle. Their whole efforts, attachments, opinions, turn on mechanism, and are of a mechanical character.[1]

The individual working alone, without help from other men or mechanical aids or elaborate organizations, Carlyle reminded his contemporaries, was becoming an unknown phenomenon.

When set against such conditions, Bentham's proposals were bound to look very different than they had to an earlier generation. The change is especially obvious in education. Bentham's *Chrestomathia* was designed for the society he had known as a young man, where opinion was largely indifferent to the educational needs of the poor or indeed of anyone other than clergy and gentlemen of independent means. Under such circumstances, the *Chrestomathia*, for all its weirdness, was likely to seem well-intentioned and worthy to anyone seriously concerned about educating the lower classes. For when the poor are left illiterate and untrained for practical work, there is some point in emphasizing instruction that will give them the rudiments and fit them for an occupation, and in forwarding ways of making such instruction cheap and easily available. Where it is impossible for those who cannot or will not devote themselves to philosophy, art, or religion to get training in science or some skill for which they have talent, it is useful to stress, as Bentham did, the importance of preparing people for something other than cultivated leisure, literature, or the church. Although the defects against which his proposals were directed still existed when Bentham was writing the *Chrestomathia*, in the years following 1813, the love of apparatus was rapidly engulfing all other interests. As education was being more and more oriented to what Peacock called the 'Steam Intellect' society, proposals like Bentham's became part of the devil's work. Thus to critics of the new age, to men like F. D. Maurice, education that taught arithmetic not as an instrument for cultivating the faculties and 'rescuing them from the delusions of the senses', but as a means to worldly success, seemed but an attempt to make every child 'in its cradle a selfish calculator' fit only for the most sordid pursuits. Under the threat of an imminent danger that the gentleman of culture would be trampled to death by the march of greedy philistines, it was easy to forget that Benthamism had spoken out for the needs of ordinary men and against indifference to inefficiency and corruption, and to see only that Benthamism confirmed the mechanical spirit, indeed the worst tendencies of the age.

But apart from the special conditions of the 1820's, utilitarianism, as it came to be called, was a far more vulnerable doctrine than Benthamism. It

[1] *Ibid.* p. 444.

was no longer a set of principles for legal and constitutional reform, but had been elevated by James Mill to a philosophy. As a philosophy, it was incomplete and arid. This was partly because of Mill's method and purpose, but partly also because he had unconsciously grafted it onto an inherited religion and morality. Utilitarianism left unsaid a great deal that was still part of James Mill. He had in his mind a definite picture of a good man, and however much it might displease some, it gave a substantial ethical foundation to his arguments. He did not, however, make this evident in his writing. Yet when he converted utilitarianism into a complete philosophy, every principle he stated was taken to be not merely a guide to social action or legal reform, but a moral principle. It is doubtful whether anyone who knew Bentham, other than the undiscerning Bowring, would have taken literally his remark that pushpin is as good as poetry. It is unlikely that anyone connected with James Mill would have dared not to take a remark of his literally. Not only his own pronouncements were affected. Whatever Bentham had said was now interpreted as if it had come from James Mill. Besides, many dicta came from James Mill that Bentham would have vigorously denied, if he could have been brought to believe that Mill had really meant them.

Inherited by young men brought up, as John Mill was, to nothing else, the philosophy of utilitarianism was reduced to its most doctrinaire possibilities. Whatever qualifications James Mill may have been aware of in his own mind were not communicated to his younger disciples. As masters often do, he taught them more than he knew. Utilitarianism ceased to be, as it had remained somehow even with James Mill, mainly an opposition theory, designed above all to destroy existing evils; it became a dogma that summed up all a man need believe or know. If the younger disciples did not always agree with their master (as on the question of women's suffrage, which James Mill opposed), generally their disagreements exaggerated rather than softened the dogmatic temper.

When James Mill declared himself against those who argued from or for feeling, he was thinking mainly of aristocrats who governed without information or care for administrative details, or of moral sense philosophers, or perhaps of sinners in the puritanical sense. As John Mill once remarked to Carlyle about the older Benthamites, 'their rationative and nicely concatenated reasons were at some point or other . . . corrected and limited by their experience of actual realities . . .'.[1] But the young disciples learned only that whatever could be defended by logic was good, and all else sentimental

---

[1] John Stuart Mill, *Letters*, 2 vols., ed. by S. R. Hugh Elliot (London, 1910) vol. I, p. 88 (Jan. 12, 1834). Mill might, however, have been pardoned for having been less generous to some of the older men—Ricardo, Place, Joseph Hume—who, for all their talents and self-lessness, were narrow men not because, like James Mill, they made themselves seem so by discipline, but because of a genuine lack of liberal culture.

nonsense. They were sometimes tempted also to improve on their own dogmatism for the pleasure of shocking an audience. John Mill said later that many of the caricatures of a Benthamite may have originated in paradoxes thrown out by Charles Austin during Cambridge debates.[1]

But however much the young utilitarians exaggerated their dogmatism, there was good reason for identifying them with the 'mechanical spirit'. Their official journal, the *Westminster Review*, more than confirmed John Mill's opinion that they seized on his father's views with 'youthful fanaticism' and infected them with 'a sectarian spirit, from which, in intention at least, my father was wholly free'.[2] The *Westminster* reviewers showed no sign of having suspected Bentham's interest in preserving freedom of taste. They were righteous and indifferent to the pain imposed on those who violated conventional standards and opinions. In questions like education and literature, they bore out all too well the worst accusations against utilitarianism.

An article entitled 'The Present System of Education' announces that although Englishmen have converted the distaff, the horse-mill and the coracle into the cotton-engine, the steam engine and the three-decker, and although they continue to improve these machines along with the political machine, parliament, they neglect that 'fundamental engine, that very machine of all machines with which we must work out these results'.[3] Education is defined as 'the process by which the mind of man, possessed with powers but unfurnished with ideas, is stored with knowledge, and enabled to apply this to the business of life',[4] although elsewhere it is allowed that education should 'cultivate and enlarge the human faculty to its utmost verge'.[5] A reviewer of the *Chrestomathia* pleads for an education suited to those engaged in the 'active business of life', who are 'to think only in order to act'. Although he declares himself 'by no means unfriendly to the cultivation of classical literature', it does nothing, he pointed out, 'to enable those who are actually to conduct the affairs of the world, to carry them on in a manner worthy of the age and country in which they live, by communicating to them the knowledge and the spirit of their age and country . . .'.[6] He then outlines in detail Bentham's *Chrestomathia*, and speaks most enthusiastically about the last stage in the system, where students receive a sort of trades orientation course; this would enable such different artisans as the cabinet-maker, the ship-builder, the black-smith, the tailor, the sugar-maker to 'receive from one another instruction in points of practice at present peculiar to each' and to

---

[1] J. S. Mill, *Autobiography*, p. 55.
[2] *Ibid.* p. 76.
[3] *Westminster Review*, vol. IV, July, 1825, pp. 148–9.
[4] *Ibid.* p. 150.
[5] *Ibid.* p. 154.
[6] *Westminster Review*, vol. I, Jan. 1824, pp. 45, 69, 45.

gain a 'comparative and comprehensive view' of the points of resemblance and difference. The *Chrestomathia* system would, moreover, lead to great moral improvement, because thanks to self-government, there would be no idle boys, only competitive boys seriously engaged in the business of life— 'If the temptation to bodily listlessness and mental dissipation occur, they are immediately roused to exertion by the active spirits around them, and compelled to put forth their strength, in order to keep pace with companions, by whom they would feel it an intolerable disgrace to be outstripped'.[1] And they would be certain to have a true standard of social values because they would study intensively political economy.

Of the enjoyment of learning for its own sake there is no mention, and literature is hardly respectable. Man has risen to his present excellence, a reviewer declares, not with the aid of literature or extinct languages, but

by the sciences of politics, of law, of public economy, of commerce, of mathematics; by astronomy, by mechanics, by natural history. It is by these that we are destined to rise yet higher. These constitute the business of society, and in these we ought to seek for the objects of education. . . . Literature is a seducer; we had almost said a harlot. She may do to trifle with; but woe be to the state whose statesmen write verses, and whose lawyers read more in Tom Moore than in Bracton.[2]

Indeed literature and the fine arts, 'in other words, the cultivation of the powers of imagination, at the expense and almost to the destruction of the powers of judgement', had become fashionable only because the aristocracy are both indolent themselves and wish to prevent a 'spirit of examination and intellectual exertion' from spreading among the lower classes. They therefore assiduously inflate the value of literature, and encourage only that sort of literature that upholds the prevailing errors in morals and legislation and does nothing to excite controversy or arouse dissatisfaction.[3]

Literature was accused of being not only useless, but also untrue and positively harmful. An article on Moore's *Fables for the Holy Alliance*, in the first number, declares that as the poet's business is to select facts for their ability to stimulate the imagination, which he tries to do as forcefully as possible, it follows that 'an habitual process such as this cannot but tend to disqualify any man for the severer exercise of his reason'. Poets cannot reason, because they cannot laboriously consider all the details:

They are the mere creatures of sympathy and antipathy; their heart tells them this, and their heart tells them that; . . . Their fine feelings supply them instinctively with all the rules of morality. In their view, logic has indeed a closed fist and a scowling aspect, and the tune of 'triste raison' is always foremost in their ears.[4]

[1] *Ibid.* p. 74.
[2] *Westminster Review*, vol. IV, July, 1825, pp. 151, 166.
[3] *Westminster Review*, vol. II, Oct., 1824, pp. 334 ff.
[4] *Westminster Review*, vol. I, Jan., 1824, pp. 18–19.

Not good men, but the licentious, bold, and lawless interest poets, who dress evil things in gay attire so as to mislead and pervert the people.[1] Yet they bring no cheer into the lives of men—'Instead of pointing our hopes to the future, they are eternally damping our few enjoyments with unavailing regrets for the past, and conjuring up every image which shall constantly remind us of the brevity of life and the transient nature of human enjoyment'.[2] Thus the *Westminster* reviewers disposed of poets.

Nor did they ever discover literary quality among writers who had the wrong political opinions. Walter Scott was a favourite butt. His novels were attacked not only for any weaknesses as novels, but for false historical portrayals. *Woodstock* was a failure, its reviewer declared, because it portrayed Cromwell as ferocious and cruel, when in fact he was famous for his gentleness. The author was clearly nothing but a base Tory admirer of men of good family, spreading Tory propaganda under the cover of fiction.[3] On the other hand, for Byron, the only poet it could claim politically, even though he was really not much to taste of good utilitarians, the *Westminster* did what it could. It paid handsome tribute to his work in Greece in the course of reviewing 'The Deformed Transformed', which is mentioned, however, only in the first sentence.[4]

Even when it was not directly advocating utilitarianism, the *Westminster's* attitude toward literature was what Arnold later denounced as philistine. Simple-minded realism was the only quality *Westminster* reviewers were prepared to admire. They wished the story-teller to concentrate on character, 'on tracing the conduct of individuals as modified by their respective dispositions',[5] and to make the story or narrative much less important. Boccaccio erred, a reviewer discovered, because he concentrated so much on the story. Realism meant also that poetic drama must be condemned, because the business of drama is 'to call up our sympathies, to raise our hopes and fears, by a representation of the hopes and fears, of the joys and miseries of other men'. This could be achieved only by drama that correctly imitated 'the actions and language of mankind in the drama of life', and renounced the use of poetry which is 'not the language of real life'. For poetry prevents the dramatist from expressing the thoughts that men actually have in the situations portrayed in the language men ordinarily use at such times. Readers of the *Westminster* were given to understand, that, in real life, a man faced with death is not likely to indulge in a trope, 'nor a thief or a murderer to pause in the perpetration of his villainy, to enunciate a well-turned and elegant simile'.[6]

[1] *Ibid.* pp. 21 ff.
[2] *Ibid.* pp. 134–5.
[3] *Westminster Review*, vol. v, April, 1826, pp. 399 ff.
[4] *Westminster Review*, vol. II, July, 1824, pp. 225 ff.
[5] *Westminster Review*, vol. VII, Jan., 1827, p. 117.
[6] *Westminster Review*, vol. VI, July, 1826, p. 104.

Despite these prejudices, some of the reviews included astute insights into the literature of the day. A few, like those written by Peacock, were distinguished essays. Now and then, a review departed altogether from utilitarian doctrine. In an article on the poem, 'Men and Things in 1823', W. J. Fox deplores the growth of philistinism and of the commercial spirit, and accuses England generally of being heartless.[1] But the prevailing tone was set by young men who seemed to have taken over the pronouncements of James Mill in the crudest fashion. They took the last step in the conversion of Utilitarianism from a gadget against political dogmatism into a way of life. To them should go the credit for inspiring the portrait of a Benthamite that appeared in the *Athenaeum*, only one variation of many on the picture that the history books have since taken for true:

A pair of compasses and a quadrant are means, not only of intellectual progress, but of moral regeneration. . . . He weighs the happiness of mankind as a usurer his ingots, and numbers it as a farmer his sheaves; . . . but those faculties of our nature, which cannot employ themselves by reading bills of exchange and reckoning oxen,—are a sound,—a fancy,—nothing. . . . He sees in political economy, not merely the exercise of the laws which regulate wealth, but the science which alone must govern the welfare of the species.[2]

Although they regarded Bentham as their spiritual father, how far the young utilitarians had strayed from his teaching even in economics can be seen in their attacks on advertising. The argument they make is, as always, clear and simple and has by now a familiar ring: competition forces business houses to sell as many books as possible, regardless of their merits. To sell more books, they advertise. They encourage two-volume novels, because they can charge more for two volumes than for one, and yet need advertise only one. It does not pay for them to advertise a book which does not promise to sell, and 'it is needless to say that books of readiest sale are not likely to be the best'.[3] Good books are therefore discouraged. Criticism is likewise corrupted, because the 'newspapers are in the hands of men, generally speaking, whose sole object is mercantile'. Newspapers look to advertising for profits, and much of the advertising comes from booksellers, whom the newspapers are anxious not to offend. 'Here is the secret of laudatory critiques, of favourable quotations, of sly allusions and grossly eulogistic paragraphs.[4] What is most un-Benthamite here is not so much the suggestion of conspiracy and corruption by advertising, which Bentham would never have taken to be so

---

[1] *Westminster Review*, vol. I, Jan., 1824, pp. 1 ff.

[2] A. K. Tuell, *John Sterling* (New York, 1941), p. 92—a most useful account.

[3] *Westminster Review*, vol. IX, April, 1828, p. 443.

[4] *Ibid.* p. 445. For a complete discussion of the Westminster reviewers see G. A. Nesbitt, *Benthamite Reviewing* (New York, 1934).

obvious or unmitigated, as the assumption that what most people like is bound to be bad, that it is the duty of the righteous to improve their tastes, even against their will. The disposition to discover immorality or low tastes and to link them with undesirable politics and economics came from James Mill.

But in this, as in their political opinions generally, the young utilitarians were in step with the most advanced fashion. They no longer had the advantage of being a glamorous unorthodoxy. Maurice may have exaggerated when he said that among the more distinguished undergraduates at the universities utilitarianism was the prevailing faith,[1] although James Mill also claimed that his books had become texts for the students. But certainly radical political opinions were by no means rare or even unconventional among the clever and forward looking. Such opinions were declared openly enough to cause embarrassment to the dons, and students were forbidden to debate any question nearer to the day than about twenty years back. This was hardly a confining restriction, as it was easy to debate on whether Catholic Emancipation should have been carried twenty years before the current year. Merrivale tells how Kemble was called to order by the president of the Union for thus dodging the regulation, and how he elicited 'thunders of applause by vociferating, "I stand in the year 6"'. Milnes remembered that on his first evening with the Union he heard the voice of 'a Mr. Sterling who said they were soon going to have a revolution, and he didn't care if his hand should be the first to lead the way'.[2]

The universities were expressing in more definite terms a feeling fairly widespread in England in the 'twenties, that some fundamental change, or collapse, was imminent. The schisms in the Church and in politics seemed a sure sign. Even men who were not democrats had come to believe that there was very little chance that the old institutions and traditions would survive. Although there was little direct evidence of the radical forces at work, the panic was great—every shabby and hungry-looking man on the road was suspected of being a radical, country gentlemen scoured the fields and lanes and met on heaths to fight an enemy who never came, and ladies stood ready to barricade the windows against the siege from rebels expected every night.

Clever young men joined the excitement by denouncing everything. Political abuses were declared only one aspect of the general rottenness in a society certainly doomed. The universities did nothing but perpetuate pieties under the tutelage of the Church, which was allied with the state monopoly, with the agricultural interests, the rotten boroughs, the East India Company, and the Bank of England. Some more optimistic souls thought that immediate

[1] *Life of Frederick Denison Maurice* (New York, 1884), vol. I, p. 176.
[2] J.A. Merrivale, ed., *Dean Merrivale* (London, 1889), p. 65; T. W. Reid, *Monckton Milnes* (London, 1891), vol. I, p. 50.

action might save England from revolution, but the time was certainly short. Young idealists agreed that the cause of England was the cause of free trade, the cause of prosperity, and of democracy. They urged England to put herself at the head of revolutionary parties in oppressed states and create the strong alliance for free trade on which everything England valued depended.

Good causes abounded and societies flourished. The Colonization Society was committed to scientific colonization, that is, to selling land to healthy young colonists instead of distributing it to paupers and convicts. The Anti-Charter Society fought the charter of the East India Company. The Spanish Constitutionalists who had fled to London easily gathered ardent support among these young radicals, who worked untiringly to find money and equipment for General Torrijos' venture against the Spanish government. A number joined Torrijos' party when they left England to restore justice and freedom in Spain, and one lost his life when the attack failed and the men were summarily executed.

Utilitarianism could no longer claim the distinction of being either unpopular or the only outlet for political protest. It had become but part of a broad radical stream. The fact that it was older and more thoroughgoing than other forms of radicalism only added to its disadvantages. New conditions had made some of the utilitarian principles look reactionary rather than radical. Its pretensions to being more than a programme for political reform made it vulnerable to attack on other grounds. As a philosophy, especially in the hands of James Mill's young disciples, it was superficial, coarse, indeed vulgar. It was certainly not fit to satisfy sensitive restless souls.

CHAPTER XIX

INTIMATIONS OF A NEW CREED

JOHN MILL was echoing the popular charges against utilitarianism when he declared that it had led him to neglect the feelings in favour of speculation and action. His training, he said, had been all on the side of developing analytic habits, so that he inevitably analysed whatever he felt until he wore away his feelings. Analytic habits, he had discovered, were

favourable to prudence and clear-sightedness, but a perpetual worm at the root both of the passions and of the virtues; and above all, fearfully undermine all desires, and all pleasures, which are the effects of association. . . . All those to whom I looked up, were of the opinion that the pleasure of sympathy with human beings, and the feelings which made the good of others, and especially of mankind on a large scale, the object of existence, were the greatest and surest sources of happiness. Of the truth of this I was convinced, but to know that a feeling would make me happy if I had it, did not give me the feeling. My education, I thought, had failed to create these feelings in sufficient strength to resist the dissolving influence of analysis. . . .[1]

His former companions no longer satisfied him. He had to admit that his closest utilitarian friend, Roebuck, enjoyed poetry, loved and understood music, drama, and painting, even demonstrated considerable talent in practising the arts. Nor was he inclined to repress his emotions, being generally accused of showing too much vehemence and passion. Yet even he would not do. The trouble was, Mill explained, that Roebuck was not really interested in cultivating the feelings, and tended to regard imagination merely as a source of illusions. Moreover, his shortcomings were typical of Englishmen:

But like most Englishmen who have feelings, he found his feelings stand very much in his way. He was much more susceptible to the painful sympathies than to the pleasurable, and looking for his happiness elsewhere, he wished that his feelings should be deadened rather than quickened. And, in truth, the English character, and English social circumstances, make it so seldom possible to derive happiness from the exercise of the sympathies, that it is not wonderful if they count for little in an Englishman's scheme of life. In most other countries the paramount import-ance of the sympathies as a constituent of individual happiness is an axiom, taken for granted rather than needing any formal statement; but most English thinkers almost seem to regard them as necessary evils, required for keeping men's actions benevolent and compassionate.[2]

Taken literally, it was a strange criticism coming from one who had seen James Mill and Bentham labouring to teach Englishmen the importance of

[1] J. S. Mill, *Autobiography*, p. 97.
[2] *Ibid.* p. 106.

following their reason or logic rather than their feelings. John Mill had good cause to know that all Englishmen had not always been indifferent to the importance of feeling. In fact, his discontent was more profound. He was looking for something else, something that England in truth could not provide.

The direction for the first stage of Mill's search came from new friends. In 1828, the Debating Society, which had been sadly deficient in worthy opponents for the utilitarians, acquired, along with some good Tory speakers, two Coleridgeans, John Sterling and Frederick Denison Maurice. Mill had met Maurice earlier through a friend who had known him at Cambridge, and they became and remained friendly. But to the unusually charming and sensitive Sterling, Mill became more attached than to any other man. They were exactly of an age and completely different. Sterling was Irish, the son of a journalist who, until he settled down as the 'Thunderer' of *The Times*, had led a rather unorthodox existence, and Sterling's childhood had been spent partly in Wales, partly in Paris. When he went up to Cambridge, he was a flaming radical and remained so, but was led by his tutor, Julius Hare, to abandon his utilitarian leanings. Brilliant, ardent, and romantic, he stood out even among the Apostles. His hopes were fastened on literary distinction. Yet when General Torrijos organized his unfortunate party against the Spanish government, Sterling worked hard to find support for it, and stayed back only at the last moment upon the insistence of the girl he married. For Mill in his new mood, he presented an irresistible combination of virtues.

Sterling and Maurice were enthusiastic disciples of Coleridge, and eager to enrol new converts. Mill's reading had already made him familiar with their interests. A few years before, in 1825, his programme for self-cultivation had assigned a course of German lessons with Sarah Austin. Languages always came easily to him and he soon began reading German authors. It was only natural that he should also have come to know Coleridge. His new friends offered an opportunity to discuss his reading, and he went with them to hear the sage himself in Highgate. He even became as interested as they were in the work of Thomas Carlyle, although he did not meet Carlyle until a few years later.

The Coleridgeans (who soon managed to become 'Carlyleans' as well) felt that in England the soul was starved. And they placed the blame on the philosophic tradition that had for so long dominated there. The tradition of Descartes and Locke, Coleridge declared, had 'untenanted creation of its God' and substituted a 'universe of death'.[1] Only the unlearned had retained an interest in what was important:

---

[1] Basil Willey, *Nineteenth Century Studies* (Columbia, 1950), p. 27.

Whoever is acquainted with the history of philosophy during the two or three last centuries cannot but admit that there appears to have existed a sort of secret and tacit compact among the learned not to pass beyond a certain limit in speculative science. . . . The few men of genius among the learned class who actually did overstep this boundary anxiously avoided the appearance of having so done. Therefore the true depth of science, and the penetration to the inmost centre, from which all the lines of knowledge diverge to their ever distant circumference, was abandoned to the illiterate and the simple, whom unstilled yearning and an original ebulliency of spirit had urged to the investigation of the indwelling and living ground of all things.[1]

Coleridge's charge was echoed by Carlyle, despite his disdain of metaphysics and his very English insistence on keeping clear the distinction between the ideal and the actual. He went so far as to describe Coleridge 'as a kind of Magus, girt in mystery and enigma',[2] who gathered round himself 'logical swim-bladders, transcendental life preserves', but never emerged from 'the high seas of theosophic philosophy. . . .'[3] Nevertheless, Carlyle agreed that British philosophy was no philosophy of the mind, but rather 'a mere discussion concerning the origins of consciousness of ideas, revealing nothing about the secret of our Freedom, of our mysterious relations to Time and Space, to God and the Universe.'

A more concrete popular statement of these sentiments, which probably expressed more exactly what Mill felt, was given by Sterling. There was no vision of eternal truth in England, Sterling complained. Her 'coarse, mechanical strength' was mixed with conscience, humanity, and hope, but 'all tortured into maimed shapes and wrapped in thick gloom'.[4] In England (and also in France) philosophers tried rather to explain away whatever is 'awful and divine', and reduced man to something 'small and frivolous'.[5] They laboured under the evil of 'fatally partial or superficial' schemes: 'Someone breaks off a corner of our nature—calls it suggestion, or association, or self-interest, or sympathy, or pleasure and pain, or profit and loss, or the nervous system; and, lifting up the fragment, says, "Behold! this is the essence of man" '.[6] All literature was for household use, mainly a domestic convenience, and Englishmen had become so accustomed to nothing better than moral truisms flavoured with 'a few immoral refinements and paradoxes' which constituted ethics and religion for them, that they could not even conceive of a 'genuine, coherent view'.[7] Consequently, England had discovered much

---

[1] Samuel Taylor Coleridge, *Biographia Literaria*, ch. IX, para. 4.
[2] Thomas Carlyle, *Life of John Sterling* (Boston, 1851), p. 70.
[3] *Ibid.* p. 73.
[4] John Sterling, *Essays and Tales*, 2 vols. (London, 1848), vol. I, p. 411.
[5] *Ibid.* p. 420.
[6] *Ibid.* p. 253.
[7] *Ibid.* p. 256.

clear but shallow knowledge, which had enabled Englishmen to live with less dirt, better food, more machinery, but provided no nourishment for their souls. The eighteenth century in England had been a 'flat and meagre' century, 'which produced the houses, the furniture, the thoughts, the people, that we are most accustomed to consider decayed and out of date. . . .'[1]

Behind these charges against the whole British tradition lay the dilemma of puritans bereft of a creed. For they were all troubled by a puritanical sense of sin. Coleridge's terror of duty was so great and so morbid, that it became almost impossible for him to do anything that appeared to be a duty. Although Carlyle and others accused him of lacking will, it seems more likely that his will was paralysed by an exaggerated effort to rely on it, and an overwhelming sense of guilt. In all his thinking, the questions of original sin and free will were central. Carlyle, who, like James Mill, was originally a poor, pious Presbyterian, remained always painfully conscious of his fundamental puritanism. When his reading at the University of Edinburgh stripped him of his faith and drove him into 'the howling deserts of infidelity', he found himself in a universe 'void of life, of Purpose, of Volition, even of Hostility . . . one huge, dead, immeasurable Steam-Engine, rolling on, in its dread indifference, to grind me limb from limb'.[2] From any acceptance of ease, he withdrew in terror—'the horrible feeling is when I cease my own struggle . . . and become positively quite worldly and wicked'.[3] But he no longer knew how to direct the struggle, and in his agony he expressed better than anyone else 'the indistinct wailings of men in search of a personal centre.'[4] His life was devoted to finding a new basis, more acceptable to a modern mind, for the Calvinist relation between God and man.[5]

Sterling was gentler and more controlled, but his conscience was made of the same stuff. It is perhaps a tribute to the 'spirit of the age', that although he grew up in a worldly, easygoing atmosphere, he too was forever and deeply conscious of his sinful nature,[6] and yearned not merely to improve the circumstances of men's lives, but to emancipate their consciences—'to call forth their sense of responsibility, to make them feel their own sinfulness, their need of redemption'.[7] Sterling seems to be speaking of a malady that he knows well when he describes Johnson as one of those 'fervid and meditative spirits who cannot be sufficiently consoled by rules of duty'. They

---

[1] *Ibid.* p. 318.

[2] Thomas Carlyle, *Sartor Resartus* (New York, Burt), Bk. II, chap. 7, p. 165.

[3] J. A. Froude, *Thomas Carlyle* (New York, 1910), vol. II, p. 76.

[4] Frederick Denison Maurice, *Life*, vol. I, pp. 348–9.

[5] Cf. Maurice, *op cit.* vol. I, pp. 404–5.

[6] Julius Hare, 'Life of Sterling', in Sterling, *Essays and Tales* (London, 1848), vol. I, pp. lxx f.

[7] *Ibid.* vol. I, p. xlviii.

are driven, Sterling says, by conscience; they carry conscience with them 'as a divine curse'; they are tortured by an 'absence of peace', by a 'sad unrest'.[1] Although at one point he entered the Church and served as a curate to his former tutor, Julius Hare, although he never denied his faith in God, Sterling could not find a satisfying support for his conscience in religion. Carlyle was probably right in thinking that

here was ardent recognition of the worth of Christianity for one thing; but no belief in it at all, in my sense of the word belief—no belief but one definable as mere theoretic moonshine. . . . Nay it struck me farther that Sterling's was not intrinsically, nor had ever been in the highest or chief degree a devotional mind . . .. Fear, with its corollaries, on the religious side, he appeared to have none, nor ever to have had any.[2]

But this made Sterling an ideal friend for Mill, with whom he could spend long hours discussing 'Reason, self-government, and subjects collateral'.[3]

Thus Mill had found in this circle others like himself who had somehow acquired the puritan conviction that man could escape sin only by perpetually exercising his will. Driven by a sense of duty and determined never to lapse into mere comfort and decency, they were pledged perpetually to struggle for something. But the justification and direction for the struggle had disappeared. The old Christian creed could no longer be believed; the new utilitarian dogma could not fill its place.

Besides, these latter-day puritans had acquired new tastes. They had learned to value art, and could not believe that any genuine product of human exertion, such as art seemed to be, could be worthless. They wanted a creed that could reconcile their devotion to duty with their appreciation of art. Nor was it any easier for them to justify their interest in solving social problems. For the old puritan denial of free will condemned men to irremediable misery. This had not troubled James Mill, who had lost his old faith while in the thick of the battle—he had had no time to wonder about the justification for his new activities, or to consider how the moral convictions he retained could be separated from the puritan indifference to suffering. But for those who had lost their creed because they could find no battle to join, there was ample time to reflect on the difficulty of reconciling their sense of human unworthiness with their anxiety to relieve suffering.

Certainly no British philosophy could satisfy these needs. The British philosophies had been designed to supplement, at most to deny, but never to substitute for theology. They were meant for people who took the connections of things and the purpose of life for granted; and on the position and

---

[1] *Ibid.* p. 319.

[2] Carlyle, *John Sterling*, pp. 163-4.

[3] Caroline Fox, *Memories of Old Friends*, ed. by Horace N. Pym, 2 vols. (London, 1882), vol. I, p. 140.

calling of man they could offer no distinct doctine which might support the will and bring it into harmony with the social state of the world. They were bound to seem arid to latter-day puritans who could neither lose themselves in merely enjoying being alive and refining that enjoyment, nor believe in hell-fire and election.

For those seeking a new creed, Germany had much more to offer. At the time of Mill's 'crisis', the German vogue was well on the way. Whereas in 1816, an article in the *Edinburgh Review* on Goethe was so unappreciative that it was widely circulated in Germany as evidence of British stupidity, by 1827 the *Edinburgh* printed so laudatory an article on German literature that Goethe remarked to Eckerman on the striking improvement in English taste. German literature and philosophy was very much a preoccupation of advanced young intellectuals. At Cambridge, several young dons were spreading the light —Whewell and Connop Thirlwall, as well as Julius Hare, whose splendid German library initiated many undergraduates. German names—Niebuhr, Richter, Goethe, Kant, Fichte, Schiller, Tieck, Novalis—were repeated as if they were a spell for opening the gates of heaven.

There were some, like Walter Scott, who were impressed simply by the great burst of literary genius in Germany, by the discovery of a new 'race of poets' ready to discard the old pedantries.[1] But the main group in the German party, led by Coleridge and Carlyle, ignored and even denied the qualities Scott praised. Carlyle, for all his admiration of genius and passion, hardly mentioned the glorification of primitive uncorrupted nature, instinct, and passion by the 'Sturm and Drang' writers. And Sterling vehemently denied that German writers advocated unusual freedom. 'They used their fine and robust faculties', he affirmed, 'not to escape from duty but to fulfil it more abundantly. . .'.[2] One could not guess from either Sterling's or Carlyle's discussions of German literature that Novalis was in a sense an apostle of aimlessness, who reduced life to a chaotic dream, or that Schlegel's *Lucinde* might be considered an open glorification of the flesh and an attack on the notion of spiritual progress. Nor were the writers they admired most so highly regarded in Germany. Carlyle's enthusiasm for Goethe was not easily shared by many English votaries of German literature, who found it as difficult as Sterling and Mill did to learn to appreciate him. But they all readily joined in praising the historian of Rome, Niebuhr, who sold more in England than in Germany, and was required for examination in Oxford. Even good Christians like Julius Hare, and not only those who might enjoy his willingness to raise questions about the Gospel, were devoted to Niebuhr.

But generally the English hierophants of German philosophy and literature

---

[1] G. M. Young, *Today and Yesterday* (London, 1948), pp. 263–4.
[2] Sterling, *Essays and Tales*, vol. I, p. 412.

drew no distinctions among German writers. Coleridge was the only one who stressed the contrast between what he called 'Kant's Aristotelianism' and the 'Platonism' of others like Schlegel. Sarah Austin's anthology of excerpts from German literature included and mixed every sort of writer from Lessing to Tieck, without noticing the great variety of styles, objectives, and moral standards. Even Carlyle, who was probably the most sensitive and knowledgeable reader of German literature, seems to have attached little importance to the differences. He could name Tieck, Richter, Herder, Schiller, and Goethe in one breath without remarking much on disagreements. He described Kant, Fichte, and Schelling as propagators of a new, more precise way of speaking about the highest questions, as if no revolution in metaphysics had taken place between Kant and Fichte, as if in Kant's plan for universal peace there was nothing very different from Fichte's sense of national mission. What impressed the English admirers was simply the contrast between all German writers and the British tradition they lamented.

Sterling described the unique quality of the Germans as 'earnestness', a term first used by Sarah Austin to indicate that German writers were not distinguished for wit and humour. But Sterling gave 'earnestness' a much profounder meaning. The earnestness that made the Germans the 'wisest, most melodious, most creative' people[1] came of seeing, he said, that human life was not merely a matter of toil, broken joys, and sorrows, but 'full of a divine meaning and capable of immortal good'.[2] Philosophy in Germany was properly 'constructive'; it sought to 'ascertain and consecrate the laws around and above us from which we and all things spring and become intelligible; and not merely to use the tools of the workshop within us in taking those tools to pieces'.[3] Because the Germans recognized, as no other people had, the worth of man, everything produced in Germany exhibited the meaningfulness of human life. What made Niebuhr so appealing was not only his heroic 'feeling for the Noble and True', nor his ingenuity in combining scattered facts, but above all his demonstration of how worthwhile it was to trace out man's faintest footprints.[4] Thus German writers had elevated, not dwarfed, the soul of man and shown that there is 'godlike within us'. They had made evident 'a greatness of human nature, which rebukes the littleness of each'.[5]

How different it was in England, where Sterling found merely a modest, fragmentary view, which assumed that man was a prisoner shut up in a dark room. Nothing but a thin gleam of light, coming through a chink in the shutters, informed the poor prisoner of what lay outside. Locke's statement

[1] *Ibid.* p. 410.
[2] *Ibid.* p. 411.
[3] *Ibid.* pp. 420–1.
[4] *Ibid.* p. 419.
[5] *Ibid.* pp. 420–1.

that, 'Our minds are not made as large as truth, nor suited to the whole extent of things . . .' expressed perfectly the English outlook that so depressed Sterling. But German writers endowed him with a vision of man as the centre of the universe, intimately connected to and revealed by everything in the universe, a vision in which man could see all around him and comprehend the whole. He was a microcosm who found himself again in the macrocosm. To read a German book was therefore, Sterling declared, 'like knocking one's head through the blue sky and getting a view the other side of the stars— not, I think, the wrong side'.[1]

This was the vision that enabled Coleridge to diagnose and prescribe for the ills of English philosophy, literature, and morals. It taught him to distinguish the faculty of understanding, which judges according to sense and merely generalizes and arranges the objects of perception, from the faculty of reason, the organ of the supersensuous, that can reduce the many to one and reveal the whole as one. True philosophy, he then saw, depended on reason, on an intuition of things by which we become one with the whole, and no longer think of ourselves as separated beings, and opposed to nature. British philosophers had forgotten that the final object of philosophy is to 'reduce the aggregate of human knowledge to a system', comprehending all.[2]

In poetry, neglect of the 'one-making power' meant that fancy, the power that merely made new patterns with materials provided by memory, had taken the place of imagination, the power to see all things as one and the one in all things. Although the fine arts depended on the images of sight and sound and other sensible impressions,[3] the true artist did not merely reproduce the outward world. Through his imagination he created a new world; he revealed the deepest reality, because his imagination repeated in his finite mind the eternal act of creation in the infinite mind of God. Thus Coleridge was able to establish that the artist was not a purveyor of sensual pleasures, serving casual appetites, but a seeker after the highest truth. He could reassure the puritans of his day that the artist's creations were not the work of the devil since the feeling essential to art was spiritual feeling, not for a world in which the self in any personal sense mattered, but for an ideal world created by an earnest contemplation of the universe.

In morals, too, Coleridge discovered how to justify a puritan morality and find a way to redemption. Sin or evil, he now understood, inevitably attended the finite when it was separated from the infinite. Sin was the propensity in every man, not only Adam, to let his will follow the natural inclination to remain finite. Redemption could come by subjecting the individual will to the universal light of conscience, which could restore the particular will to com-

---

[1] Hare, 'Life of Sterling', in Sterling, *Essays and Tales*, vol. I, p. ccxi.

[2] Coleridge, *The Friend* in *Works* (New York, 1884), vol. II, p. 420.

[3] John H. Muirhead, *Coleridge as Philosopher* (London, 1936), p. 197.

munion with the Divine Spirit. All the false notions of morality, Coleridge explained, came from letting the wrong faculty decide morals. By means of the understanding, the mind could not go beyond the finite and could not frame its own laws. Only reason, which includes conscience or moral sense, could discover the necessary laws of moral life. For morals were a matter of insight into the whole, not of analysis and classification. Reliance on the understanding, on reasoning rather than on reason, led men to suppose that morality was unstable or variable, for reasoning necessarily varied with each individual. But through 'the organ of the supersensuous', men could discover an absolute ground for their actions.

Even Maurice who remained conscious and secure of his faith in God, and shared Carlyle's suspicion of attempts to enclose the universe in a single rational system, felt a need that German writers satisfied. He was seeking a new insight into God's relation to man because he could no longer believe in the character that orthodox theology assigned to it. German thought reassured him that there was in man a divine root, a spiritual centre answering to a higher spiritual centre. It showed him that man was a fragment of an enduring whole, and helped him to realize that 'the pursuit of unity' was the end set before him, 'from his cradle upwards, by God'. It helped him to grasp 'the vision of unity as infinite, embracing, sustaining the confession which I made in the creed'.[1] He could now say confidently that 'through sacrifice —through the giving up of a man's self' comes escape from the danger of succumbing to brutishness. The opposition between passion and reason in the old-fashioned puritan sense that emphasized the wickedness of the body was transformed by Maurice into an opposition between the self-centered self, mainly indifferent to others, and the self driven by 'hunger of the Infinite', willing to get lost in humanity.

To those who were less metaphysically minded, the message of Germany was brought home by Carlyle. He showed them, as Sterling said, that 'the Universe, including Man as its Chief Object, is all a region of Wonder and mysterious Truth, demanding before all other feelings, Reverence . . .,'[2] that the Divine Substance may be found in the smallest as well as in the grandest thing, that man is made chiefly to be himself a 'Maker'. In his 'visionary furnace,' Carlyle obliterated the distinctions between God and man, supernatural and natural, spirit and matter, sacred and profane, and fused it all into a holiness accessible to everyone. Thus he 'cast a spell over his listeners, and gave them a sense of deepened insight'.[3] What counted, Carlyle insisted, was not contemplating the idea of the universe, or analysing it, but working

---

[1] C. F. G. Masterman, *Frederick Denison Maurice* in *Leaders of the Church 1800–1900*, ed. by G. W. E. Russell (London, 1907), p. 227.

[2] Sterling, *Essays and Tales*, p. 257.

[3] Willey, *Nineteenth Century Studies*, p. 105.

upon it. Those who understood this truth would see that the minutest fact and lowest confusion were connected with the all-pervading purpose of the universe. This purpose was longing for expression, and the proper object of life was to toil conscientiously, in whatever realm one chose, to reveal it.

Carlyle had discovered again the meaning of duty, and felt reassured that it was a 'divine Messenger and Guide,' not a 'false earthly Fantasm, made up of Desire and Fear.'[1] It once more became clear to him that man was full of a divine strength that was bound to be cramped and tortured, not ripened, by a worldly life. From his new knowledge, he developed his Gospel of Work:

First, I would have you know this; that 'doubt of any sort can only be removed by *action*'. But what to act on?—you cry. I answer again in the words of Goethe, 'Do the duty which lies nearest!' do it (not merely pretend to have done it); the next duty will already have become clear to thee . . . he who (by whatever means) has ever seen into the infinite nature of duty has seen all that costs difficulty. The universe has then become a temple for him and the divinity and all the divine things thereof will infallibly become revealed . . . study to clear your heart from all selfish *desire*, that *free will* may arise and reign absolute in you. True vision lies in thy heart; it is by this the eye sees, or forever only fancies that it sees. Do the duty that there lies clear at hand. . . . For health of mind, I have the clearest belief that there is no help . . . but action—religious action.[2]

To speculate, to dwell on oneself and try to know oneself was vain and harmful. The only good knowledge for man was to know what he could work at. That meant he must never tolerate any evil or falsehood he recognized as such—'What is bad is a thing to be the sooner the better abolished. . . . Not toleration, therefore, but the quickest possible abolition, that were our rule'.[3] Above all, the man of virtue must cultivate self-denial, for 'life goes all to ravels and tatters where that enters not'.[4]

The war between holy reason and evil passion could go on with vigour. The puritan conscience could again rely on a taskmaster, now become 'a sort of amalgam of Jehovah, Odin, Calvin's predestinating God, and the Soul of the World',[5] who would punish transgressions or sloth and reward devotion to duty. There need be no danger of withdrawing from the battle, of being reduced to a life of comfort, contemplation, or pleasure. No wonder that young puritans in search of their duty were grateful to Carlyle. As one of them, Caird, explained some years later:

The new ideal Carlyle seemed to teach was after all nothing new or strange. It was in new words, words suited to the new time, the expression of those religious and moral principles which all in this country—and especially we Scotsmen—had

---

[1] Carlyle, *Sartor Resartus*, Bk. II, chap. 7, p. 161.
[2] Froude, *Carlyle*, vol. II, p. 210.
[3] *Ibid.* p. 248.
[4] *Ibid.* p. 249.
[5] Willey, *Nineteenth Century Studies*, p. 113.

received into ourselves almost with our mother's milk. It was Puritanism idealised, made cosmopolitan, freed from the narrowness which clung to its first expression or with which time had encrusted it. . . . Carlyle seemed to change the old banner of the Covenant into a standard for the forward march of mankind toward a better ideal of human life.[1]

This revelation, of a world he had never before suspected, entranced Mill. Soon after his first encounter with the Coleridgeans, he found himself at one with his old friend John Austin, who had gone to Germany to prepare his lectures on jurisprudence, and had come back a confirmed admirer of German achievements. Mill now shared with Austin a strong distaste for 'the general meanness of English life, the absence of enlarged thoughts and unselfish desires, the low objects on which the faculties of all classes of the English are intent'.[2] Even the kinds of public interests which concerned Englishmen seemed to them unworthy of esteem. Instead they cultivated what Mill described as 'a kind of German religion, a religion of poetry and feeling with little, if anything of positive dogma. . . .'[3]

Mill did not adopt anything particular from his exposure to Germany. But he did become permanently addicted to a new style of thinking. He learned consciously to seek a complete view of man and the universe, not a partial hesitant sketch of a corner. He now saw a possibility of discovering a creed far more satisfying than the old, a creed that would draw the connections between his sins and virtues and some cosmic plan or purpose, and make his activities more than mere, trivial incidents in the universe. The influence of German thought on him was fundamental but not obvious, and he himself was never conscious of its nature. It was lost in the structure that he built according to its specifications. But it determined the shape of what he constructed, and it was a shape that Bentham could never have looked upon with favour. It led to a break with Benthamism far more radical than Mill's talk of feelings might suggest.

Mill was convinced that he had never borrowed anything substantial from Germany because he never lost his antipathy to the 'innate principle metaphysics'. His early training remained forceful enough to prevent him from abandoning altogether the British philosophical tradition. Instead he adapted the style of German thought to the English cast of mind. In the end, his provincialism, which kept him from assimilating a foreign outlook, made him great. For he succeeded in putting an alien way of seeing man and the universe into a familiar form. And he was able, as the others were not, to convert some thoroughly home-bred Englishmen to some very strange ideas. That is why,

---

[1] Edward Caird, *Essays on Literature and Philosophy*, 2 vols. (Glasgow, 1892), vol. I, pp. 234–5.

[2] J. S. Mill, *Autobiography*, p. 124.

[3] *Ibid.* p. 125.

whereas Coleridge is known best to students of literature and aesthetics, Maurice to the religious minded, Carlyle to lovers of eccentric English prose, Sterling, hardly at all, Mill became a popular hero of philosophers and politicians, economists, sociologists, poets, critics, and working men, the intellect of both Victorian individualism and Victorian socialism.

Mill did not, however, find it easy to blend two incompatible views of man and the universe. He tried a number of methods and mixtures, and the search for a way of making them into a single stable creed occupied the rest of his life.

CHAPTER XX

MANY-SIDEDNESS

THE first effect of Mill's new experience was a yearning for something less severe, more gentle and graceful than he had known before, and he allowed himself to rest a moment from the struggle for improvement. It was almost as if he were trying to reach back, beyond his father, even beyond Bentham, to a less censorious, more easy-going outlook. But before long, he had to define his new faith, to state its essence. His letters of the late twenties and thirties, the decade following his crisis, especially those to Sterling and Carlyle, are filled with discussions of his new views on poetry and art.

Mill's earliest translation of the vision of unity held by his new acquaintances was the importance of balance. The opposite of comprehensiveness, which characterized the admirable German thought, he reasoned, was one-sidedness; and the cure for one-sidedness was many-sidedness or balance. Reason had to be balanced by emotion, logic by art, science by poetry, criticism by appreciation, universal suffrage by an aristocracy of learning.

Now that he was a convert to many-sidedness, Mill believed himself to disagree with his former colleagues not only in temperament, but also in principle:

Wordsworth seems always to know the pros and the cons of every question; and when you think he strikes the balance wrong, it is only because you think he estimates erroneously some matter of fact. Hence all my differences with him, or with any other philosophic Tory, would be differences of matter of fact, or detail, while my differences with the Radicals and Utilitarians are differences of principle . . ..[1]

Utilitarianism was fundamentally wrong because it did not recognize the need to balance logic with poetry or art, or, as Mill sometimes put it, the importance of balancing the literal with the symbolic, reasoning with intuition. Whereas reasoning proceeded by a series of steps or links, art discovered truth by a direct, mysterious intuition. The highest truths indeed could be discovered only by persons who perceived intuitively; these truths needed neither explanation nor proof, but were assented to as soon as stated. The function of the poet or artist was 'to declare *them* and make them *impressive*'.[2] The *Westminster* reviewers and their sermons against the wicked poets were left far behind as Mill declared poetry to be higher than logic, and the union of the two, philosophy.[3] Nevertheless, the truths stated by the poet could be translated into terms

[1] J. S. Mill, *Letters*, vol. I, p. II (Oct. 21, 1831).
[2] *Ibid.* p. 54 (July 5, 1833).   [3] *Ibid.* p. 55 (July 5, 1833).

that the logician could understand. Was not the mysticism of truth distinguished from 'mere dreamery, or the institution of imagination for realities', precisely by the fact that mysticism could be 'translated into logic'?[1] All things had two aspects, an artistic and a scientific one. The former could be expressed best by the language of poetry; the latter by logic. But for those who found the language of poetry unintelligible, what the poet said had to be translated. He himself, Mill confessed, much as he venerated mysticism and refrained from trying to justify it logically, always liked to see how a truth looked in 'the logical dialect before I feel sure of it'.[2] Many years later, in his *Autobiography*, he explained that, 'instead of my having been taught anything, in the first instance, by Carlyle, it was only in proportion as I came to see the same truths through media more suited to my mental constitution, that I recognized them in his writings'.[3]

Most ordinary people were even more incapable than he of receiving intuitive truths, which they regarded as a species of dreaming or madness, the more so perhaps in proportion to the power of the artist. But even a man of this sort could be won over, if he were shown that such truths 'are not inconsistent with anything he *does* know, that they are even very probable, and that he may have faith in them, when higher natures than his own affirm that they are truths. . . .'[4] This, Mill believed, was his own humble function: 'I am not in the least a poet in any sense, but I can do homage to poetry. I can to a very considerable extent feel it and understand it, and can make others who are my inferiors understand it in proportion to the measure of their capacity. I believe that such a person is more wanted than even the poet himself . . .'.[5] In the hands of the artist, truth became 'impressive and a living principle of action'. But in an age when the understanding was more highly cultivated than the intuition, it was essential to show most men the logical side of truth first—'ostensibly with little besides mere logical apparatus'; only then could it be turned around, so 'that they may see it to be the same Truth in its poetic that it is in its metaphysical aspect'.[6] Whereas Carlyle had learned from German philosophy that it was every man's duty to show the connection between some part of the universe and the Divine Purpose that pervaded all, Mill discovered that it was his function to show how different forms of expression hid the same truth. In a more mundane way he would also help to reveal the all-pervading purpose. A public declaration of his many-sidedness was made in essays on Bentham and Coleridge, which told far more about Mill than about either of the subjects and are among his least distinguished work.

[1] *Ibid.* p. 96 (March 2, 1834).
[2] *Ibid.* p. 96 (March 2, 1834).
[3] J. S. Mill, *Autobiography*, p. 123.
[4] J. S. Mill, *Letters*, vol. I, p. 55 (July 5, 1833).
[5] *Ibid.* p. 55 (July 5, 1833).
[6] *Ibid.* p. 35 (July 17, 1832).

So Mill explained to his satisfaction the differences between his own country and that other, mysterious, glorious land which enchanted, but eluded him. The rest of his life was dedicated to trying to make his way into it. All the things he could not be, and somehow yearned for, were bound up with it. But whatever doubts he had about his poetic capacities, he would never resign himself to failure; he was too firmly convinced that if only one worked long and hard enough, nothing was beyond conquest. Perhaps, he would never be a native in that other world, but he could at least draw very good maps of it, even better possibly than those born to it.

For a time, the doctrine of balance and many-sidedness so possessed him, he later confessed to Carlyle when attempting to withdraw from him, that he became extremely confused. 'I tried', Mill said, 'to go round every object which I surveyed, and to place myself at all points of view, so as to have the best chance of seeing all sides . . . I became catholic and tolerant in an extreme degree, and thought one-sidedness almost the one great evil in human affairs . . . I saw, or seemed to see, so much of good and of truth in the most positive part of the most opposite opinions and practices, could they but be divested of their exclusive pretensions, that I scarcely felt myself called upon to deny anything but denial itself.'[1] It was no wonder that his old colleagues were outraged and offended.

Yet the change in Mill's opinions was less revolutionary than it seemed. He had acquired a tolerance unknown to, or at least never preached by, his father, but his basic emotions and assumptions remained very much the same. Like all his new departures, it reflected his great talent for remaining true to his early convictions while adopting new ways of thought. What he arrived at was unlike anything seen before either abroad or in England.

His 'many-sidedness' was in fact almost the contrary of Goethe's 'Vielseitigkeit', which he believed himself merely to have translated. For Goethe truth was a living ocean in which the spirit of man dwelled, and the infinite aspects of truth were revealed in every single phenomenon. They could be understood only by the man who approached each phenomenon from innumerable different angles, not so that he could see all the sides, but in order to penetrate to its essence. Knowing, to Goethe, meant perceiving what inner experience comes into play when a man confronts an object; its ultimate purpose was to establish a living relationship with an ever-moving reality. All distinctions and abstract formulations of laws were therefore destructive. The flowering of a personality, the growth of perception depended on obliterating distinctions between spirit and matter, experience and knowledge, knower and known, and above all, science and art.

[1] *Ibid.* p. 88 (Jan. 12, 1834).

Out of this vision of communion between the inner being of man and the inner being of the universe, Mill distilled a simple practical lesson, that truth had two aspects, and that some men understood one better than the other. His interest in the laws governing phenomena was not in the least diminished, but under the influence of his search for many-sidedness grew even greater and more positive. It was only necessary, he told himself, to balance his interest in natural laws with reading Wordsworth. It did not occur to Mill when he said that Goethe 'could never succeed in putting symmetry into any of his own writings, except very short ones', that men like Goethe, or Coleridge and Carlyle, were not only incapable of 'putting symmetry into the universe', but would not wish to do so. Mill seemed never to have suspected that for them life and the universe were rather 'a lightsome chaos on which the Spirit of God is moving'.[1]

In his conversion to 'many-sidedness', Mill reminds one of the lady who informed Carlyle that she 'accepted the universe' (on which Carlyle commented, 'Gad, she'd better'). After all, Mill could not refrain from distinguishing sharply between men and their ideas, between ideas and feelings. It was civilized to complement thought with feeling, science with art, but one would not expect to be taken literally if one said, as Goethe did, that when a man knows, he feels that a living harmony of ideas and perception resounds within him. Despite all his humility before poetry, his assertions about the superiority of intuitive truth, his awe, reverence, and wistfulness before art, in his heart Mill never really believed that the poet said something so irrevocably different and untranslatable that a perceptive mind could not summarize it in reasonable language.

From time to time he would let something slip that betrayed a feeling, though he tried at first to repress it, that art teaches us how to express truth more effectively or beautifully, while science tells us how to arrive at it. Many years later (in 1854), when he was no longer anyone's disciple, he wrote in his diary for his wife a frank avowal of his feeling:

The Germans and Carlyle have perverted both thought and phraseology when they made the artist the term for expressing the highest order of moral and intellectual greatness. The older idea is the truer—that art, in relation to truth is but a language. Philosophy is the proper name for that exercise of the intellect which enunciates the truth to be expressed. The Artist is not the Seer; not he who can detect truth, but he who can clothe a given truth in the most expressive and impressive symbols.[2]

There was indeed a special beauty that poetry alone could give, and it was essential to a well-balanced life, but beauty was after all secondary to the

---

[1] R. J. White, 'John Stuart Mill', in *Cambridge Journal* (November, 1951), p. 92.
[2] J. S. Mill, *Letters*, vol. II, pp. 385–6 (April 11, 1854).

truth conveyed. At heart, Mill loved beauty as a religious soldier adored his patron saint—for her aid and countenance to him in battle.

Although Mill hoped to escape from the intolerance of the young Utilitarians, his 'many-sidedness', remote as it was from Goethe's 'Vielseitigkeit', was not any closer to what had been understood as tolerance in England by men like Hume or Bentham. The essence of Hume's tolerance—the mood of reserve, of ironic detachment that plays lightly among opposites and is in no great haste to take sides, a mood guided by the suspicion that what matters is not decision but serenity—seemed no more virtuous to Mill at thirty than it had at sixteen. Bentham's conviction that every man had a right to his own tastes he did not begin to understand until much later, and even then, he did not really grasp Bentham's meaning. His tolerance was more priggish, a disciplined determination to hear the other side before deciding. It was only a slight extension of James Mill's belief in the importance of letting the opposition have its say. One day, John Mill was still certain, men would know the truth. But he was less interested than his father was in the quarrelsome present, more easily upset by controversy, and inclined more to dream of the beautiful future.

His tolerance meant collecting as many boxes as possible, and then arranging them in perfectly symmetrical groups. It was the number and the symmetry of his boxes, not a disdain of boxes, that distinguished John Mill from the utilitarians. He never gave up trying to find a way of balancing every box in his possession, a habit that has led some to dismiss him as a thinker who could only find compromises between other men's ideas. His was the 'geometric tolerance' of a man who is in fact certain that there is a right way and a true answer; it was not the haphazard fuzzy willingness to hear all, characteristic of the man who expects always to find contradiction, irrelevancies, uncertainty, and rather enjoys the mess.

In sum, as a result of his crisis and disenchantment with utilitarianism, Mill added a few more categories to his thought, more questions that he felt bound to answer, more tags that he could attach to what he saw or experienced. But he still classified everything into one category or another; he still had to see sharp outlines and neat shapes to be comfortable: 'I never in the course of my transition was content to remain, for ever so short a time, confused and unsettled. When I had taken in any new idea, I could not rest till I had adjusted its relation to my old opinions, and ascertained exactly how far its effect ought to extend in modifying or superseding them'.[1] He had not in the least dropped, but had strengthened his mental habit of thinking of social and even personal problems as puzzles to be solved, and 'never abandoning a puzzle but again and again returning to it until I understood the whole'.[2]

[1] J. S. Mill, *Autobiography*, p. 110.   [2] *Ibid.* p. 86.

The main effect of his crisis was that instead of restricting his powers to the problem of reforming the machinery of government, he now felt obliged to concern himself also with the souls of men. But the greater size of his new task did not in the least shake his conviction that truth and falsehood should and could be clear and distinct, that truth could be besieged and won, and that he was gradually conquering more of the citadel. As Roebuck said ruefully: 'during all this time [Mill] never doubted as to his own infallibility. Whatever he thought at the time was right; but whatever might be the change in him, he was never wrong. . .'.[1]

Although the conviction that there ought to be a great variety of boxes, and that they should be balanced, was but a modification of the old views, acquiring it was an important departure in Mill's life. It gave him the first clue to the substance of a new outlook on life, radically different from the old one.

But it was not only in his intellectual life that Mill broke somewhat with his past. Late in 1830 he met Harriet Taylor, and, though she was married to an admirable man, when three years later he finally spoke openly of his love for her, it had long been an established fact among their friends. Whatever else he may have seen in her, she was undoubtedly wonderfully suited to give him the footing he wanted in the alien world of beauty and emotion. The very impropriety of their alliance, troublesome as it was, had its advantages. That he could be so overcome by passion as to fall into a difficult triangular relationship with a wife and mother, a 'friendship' that his family and right-minded utilitarian friends, as well as others, regarded as outrageously irregular, must certainly have been proof that he was no longer a calculating utilitarian.

Mrs Taylor introduced Mill to something like a Bohemian circle, bound to satisfy his longing to separate himself from the utilitarians. To Harriet's friends, Fox, the passionate Unitarian minister and his illicit love, Eliza Flower, rational calculation as a rule of life was hardly comprehensible. Harriet herself, everyone agreed, was made to be a romantic heroine. Her large deeply set eyes and her fragility, emphasized by daintily elaborate dress, betokened a lady who sighed over Shelley and lived by feeling and intuition. She was the first truly feminine woman Mill came to know; his mother, though she had once had such aspirations and had been a pretty girl, had been reduced by poverty and an unappreciative husband to a sombre state. And his sisters seem not to have attempted rebelling against their austerity. Roebuck was partly right in thinking that Mill, who knew nothing whatever about women, was bound to be captured by the first one who showed him some attention. But even if Harriet was not the paragon Mill made her out to be, she possessed a combination of sensitivity, beauty, delicacy, and intellect that would in any case have called to

[1] John Arthur Roebuck, *Life and Letters*, ed. by R. E. Leader (London, 1897), p. 37.

Mill. Harriet came to mean beauty as a value in its own right, and all women appeared to him as creatures appointed by their qualities of mind, soul, and body to envelop those associated with them in grace and elegance.

Harriet served Mill in another way as well. He was unable to rest in uncertainty. His crisis had muddled his convictions. Even when he found some clear ones, he found it difficult to feel secure about them, because unlike James Mill, he could not feel strong alone. He was haunted by a fear of loneliness, unknown to his predecessors. Even Bentham, despite his love of disciples and his complaints about the panopticon episode, was both certain enough of his victory in the end, and detached enough to take doubts in his stride, to need no confirmation from others. His task was a personal one at which he had to toil alone. If he did it well, others would carry on. He was content to play the role of law-giver and could go on playing even when the theatre was empty. John Mill, however, had to feel himself part of an army, or at least a band of fellow crusaders. He is the first notable example of a character so familiar now, an intellectual with great powers of independent thought, who nevertheless needs the warmth of membership in a group, organization, or cause.

Mill soon learned to do with less, but when he was first deprived of his utilitarian certainties and colleagues, he was desolate. For he lost, as he told Sterling,

that feeling which has accompanied me through the greater part of my life, that which one fellow-traveller, or one fellow soldier has towards another—the feeling of being engaged in the pursuit of a common object, and of mutually cheering one another on, and helping one another in an arduous undertaking. . . . There is now no human being (with whom I can associate on terms of equality) who acknowledges a common object with me, or with whom I can cooperate even in any practical undertaking, without the feeling that I am only using a man, whose purposes are different, as an instrument for the furtherance of my own.[1]

His earnestness made it impossible to reconcile himself to any partial relationship; anything short of total oneness between himself and some other being meant imperfection and loneliness. It was not, in Mill's eyes, properly part of human destiny and tragedy to feel alone; only those afflicted by some special misfortune were thus doomed. With Harriet, he regained a fellow crusader.

He was even more anxious than she to make theirs an all-encompassing union in which every activity and every moment were completely shared. She lent herself to this role admirably, especially as she had that very feminine capacity of repeating back to him, in her own words, his opinions. In this way, she restored to him the assurance he could feel only when his beliefs seemed to have come from a higher source.

Also in another way, his relationship with Harriet conformed to the old

[1] J. S. Mill, *Letters*, vol. i, p. 2 (April 15, 1829).

patterns. It was not a love that demanded from him much capacity for living in the moment, for purposeless joy; like all other relationships he had known, his love for Harriet required of him the utmost self-discipline and gave him many opportunities for torment and confession. Harriet was anything but a yielding mistress. Before very long, she openly reprimanded her lover. If he worried over her being compromised in the eyes of society, she accused him of being but an indifferent lover and seeking shallow worldly fame; if he urged her to leave everything and go off with him, he was scolded for cowardice, for wishing to desert his post and his duties to humanity. His letters or his behaviour were either too cold or too importunate, and if he ever showed signs of withdrawing, she promptly summoned all her arts and arguments to draw his bonds closer. Soon she moved from being his disciple to being his critic and mentor; his phrasing, his sentiments, and his doctrines all were subjected to the closest scrutiny in which she made it clear that not his, but her purposes (even if learned first from him) were to dominate, and that if he demurred, he was at fault. He never wrote to her without an ample store of apologies, difficulties, and doubts, all requiring her direction and solace.

At the same time, the obstacles that remained in their way for many years, obstacles that Harriet wisely cherished, left Mill's vision of love unimpaired by everyday experience. The habit once acquired, it could never again be lost, either through marriage or death. Not joy in the present, but some distant glory remained the source of Mill's happiness even in love; and if ever a few moments of careless pleasure were granted him, there was enough self-denial and suffering before and after to satisfy his conscience.

By 1834, eight years after his crisis had begun, three years after meeting Mrs Taylor, Mill felt certain enough of his bearings to risk even a rupture with Carlyle. They had met in 1831, when Carlyle came to London and inquired after 'the new Mystic' who had written a series of articles called *The Spirit of the Age*. Somewhat to the surprise of their mutual friends, they took to one another at once; Mill was invited to visit the Carlyles, and was welcomed as a most promising disciple. When Carlyle went off to live in Craigenputtock, they carried on an uninterrupted and intimate correspondence, in which Mill discussed everything close to his heart, but not Harriet Taylor. Thanks to her, however, he no longer stood in need of a paternal mentor such as Carlyle meant to be. It had been a great help in his time of uncertainty to have the firm and colourful counsel of Carlyle. But now he felt readier to rely on himself, or at least to be dependent on no one but Mrs Taylor. As Carlyle was coming to London, he felt constrained to declare his independence. Carlyle, however, refused to understand and continued for some time to deny any differences. When they finally broke off some years later, it was over Carlyle's attitude to Mrs Taylor, on whom Carlyle blamed what he regarded as Mill's aberrations.

But Mill had never really been a 'mystic'. He had merely, for a brief period, been uncertain of what he believed. Now the worst difficulties were over. He felt himself to be 'more *knowing*, more *seeing*, having a far greater experience of *realities*, not abstractions, than ever before; nor do I doubt that this superior knowledge and insight will one day make itself available in the form of greater power, for accomplishing whatever work I may be called to. . .'.[1] He still had moments of spiritual illness, 'almost of skepticism', when he had no 'theory of human Life at all, or conflicting theories, or nothing amounting to a belief'. But he could bear such moments because he now felt confident they were a passing state. When doubts afflicted him he felt it was best to shut himself away and meditate, until he could get a 'firm footing on some solid basis of conviction, and could turn what comes into me from others into wholesome nutriment'. Then he could emerge with firmer convictions,[2] with his 'edifice of Thought' higher than ever, so that from its towers he would look around and 'see more Truth than I could see before'.[3]

[1] *Ibid.* p. 98 (April 28, 1834).
[2] *Ibid.* p. 48 (May 18, 1833).
[3] *Ibid.* p. 53 (July 5, 1833).

CHAPTER XXI

THE CREED OF PROGRESS

IT was Comte who helped Mill to see precisely how he could express his revelation in works. A St Simonist whom he met at the Debating Society introduced him to Comte's work, but Mill never became the centre of English St Simonism as d'Eichthal had hoped. He was admiring, encouraging, friendly, but never wholly committed himself. Even before the St Simonists developed their most extravagant tendencies, Mill was well beyond being tempted by them. For Comte, however, he developed a lasting admiration, and declared him to be 'by far the first speculative thinker of the age'.[1] He read Comte's earliest work, and later, the *Cours de Philosophie Positive* impressed him as 'one of the most profound books ever written on the philosophy of science',[2] and despite some mistakes, 'very near the grandest work of this age'.[3]

Comte served Mill in the same way as German philosophy had his Coleridgean friends. Although, on the surface, the two systems of thought seemed to be worlds apart, they were of the same style and could satisfy the same needs. Comte fully recognized the reality of those wants that only metaphysics and theology had hitherto tried to fill, and insisted only that positivism could more completely fulfil them. Metaphysics had satisfied intellectual cravings by systematizing knowledge in relation to one grand principle. Theology had provided that harmony between the self and the universe essential to man by offering belief in some 'Grand Être' who transcended all. But positivism could do both at once, and without going beyond experience.

All this was made possible by recognizing the subjective unity of the human race that had grown out of the conscious or unconscious cooperation of all past generations, and was evident, Comte said, in the love and reverence of men for each other. The existence of this 'Great Being', which Comte called 'Humanity', unlike the God of theology, could be empirically verified; and though man could not know absolute causes, he could discover the laws of the development of humanity. Because Comte never claimed that humanity was in itself the ultimate end of all thought and all action, but only the ultimate end for human beings, he appeared not to speak of any mysterious unseen realities, but only of what men could themselves observe and feel. Yet his humanity was a whole that could inspire moralists and idealists and provide a basis for social science, as a notion like James Mill's 'Mankind'

---

[1] *Ibid.* vol. I, p. 124 (March 27, 1843).

[2] *Fortnightly Review*, May, 1897, p. 674 (to Prof. George Nichol, Dec. 21, 1837).

[3] Alexander Bain, *J. S. Mill, A Criticism* (London, 1882), p. 63.

could not. For James Mill never went beyond saying, 'our complex Idea of Mankind is made up of the aggregate of the Ideas of Individuals, including the interesting trains called Love of their Pleasures, Hatred of their Pains, Love of their Kindness, Aversion to their Unkindness'.[1] 'Mankind' was, after all, but a collection of individuals; 'Humanity' transcended them.

Yet positivism never had recourse to the metaphysical categories of German idealism.[2] Whereas metaphysical philosophy spoke about innate properties, essences and forms, and contrasted potentiality to reality, positivism defined human nature as unchanging, with certain latent characteristics that were brought out by evolution, and translated potentiality and actuality into order and progress. Whereas metaphysics related all the phenomena of the universe to a single principle, positivism made the idea of humanity central, and showed how the laws of human organization were related not only to the conditions under which human societies existed, but also to all the physical and chemical laws of the earth and indeed of the entire solar system. In metaphysics the order of the universe was the abstract basis of the moral order; in positivism the conduct of man was regulated externally by the conditions of the world he inhabited. For metaphysics, the history of humanity was directed by a providential wisdom or a final cause; for positivism, the evolution of humanity was accomplished according to empirical laws. The object of metaphysics was to find *a priori* causes; positivist science consisted in a rational prevision of facts.

To Mill, positivism meant the exaltation of two ideas—humanity and social progress. That was why he continued to commend Comte's earlier work, which had taught him to appreciate these ideas, even while he roundly condemned Comte's later work, all his political conclusions, and his 'inordinate demand for unity and systematization.'[3] Others had seen that the idea of the general interest of the human race had great power over the mind, 'both as a source of emotion and as a motive to conduct', but no one before Comte had realized

all the majesty of which that idea is susceptible. It descends into the unknown recesses of the past, embraces the manifold present, and ascends into the indefinite and unforeseeable future. Forming a collective Existence without assignable beginning or end, it appeals to that feeling of the Infinite, which is deeply rooted in human nature, and which seems necessary to the imposingness of all our highest conceptions.[4]

[1] James Mill, *Analysis of the Phenomena of the Human Mind*, 2 vols. (London, 1869), p. 230.
[2] Cf. F. A. Hayek, *The Counter-Revolution in Science*, for relations between Comtists and Hegelians; also L. Lévy-Bruhl, *Philosophy of Auguste Comte*, on positivism and idealism.
[3] J. S. Mill, *The Positive Philosophy of Auguste Comte* (Boston, 1866), p. 127.
[4] *Ibid.* p. 122.

Throughout his life, Mill acknowledged himself a convert to the Religion of Humanity, in the sense that humanity played the same role in his thoughts and emotions as God or the Principle of the Universe did for others.

Comte's other leading idea—social progress—pointed out the course of Mill's future work. It suggested the possibility of an empirically based social theory that was wonderfully many-sided, for social progress embraced every sort of activity. Comte did not teach, Mill declared enthusiastically,

a cramped and contracted notion of human excellence, which cares only for certain forms of development. He not only personally appreciates, but rates high in moral value, the creations of poets and artists in all departments; deeming them, by their mixed appeal to the sentimental and the understanding admirably fitted to educate the feelings of abstract thinkers, and enlarge the intellectual horizon of the people of the world. He regards the law of progress as applicable in spite of appearances, to poetry and art as much as to science and politics.[1]

At the same time, Comte's theory took into account differences between historical periods and countries. It did not merely set the present against a single static plan for perfecting the machinery of government as soon as possible with no eye to the requirements of the moment when, or the place where, the transformation was to take place. Instead, it encouraged the social philosopher to contemplate stages of human development, each one better than the last, each requiring different arrangements to harmonize with different conditions, stretching far out to some distant glory.

The version of progress that Comte's philosophy of history provided was especially reassuring. The progress that had inspired men in the eighteenth century promised merely the indefinite perfectibility of man and society, hardly a basis for foresight. But progress, as Comte saw it, meant development subject to fixed conditions and operating according to necessary laws, advancing towards a definite, though never attained goal. Mill therefore felt that Comte was speaking of something admirably concrete. For the succession of states of the human species, moving according to determined laws, was just like the development of the organisms that the physiologist studied. Whereas the old notion of progress, of indefinite perfectibility, had no basis in observation and was no more than a faith, the laws of positive progress required nothing but observation, that is, analysis of history. To the end of his life, Mill was certain that Comte's analysis of history would never be superseded.

The theory of social progress introduced him, Mill believed, to a sort of induction quite different from that of English historians (such as Macaulay), 'the Plausibles who in our own land of shallowness and charlatanry babble about induction without even having considered what it is, relying on that

[1] *Ibid.* p. 106.

rhetoric which is defined by Plato as the art of appearing profoundly versed in a subject to those who know nothing about it'.[1] How much superior were the continental historians who had a theory of progress. Unlike the English who simply recounted events without benefit of an overall theory, they never degenerated into mere story-tellers; they were profound and scientific.

Given a belief in social progress, Mill could contemplate a steadily improving succession of stages stretching out to the ideal state of things, when truth will have been captured, and the confusions of the present dispensed with. Perhaps the end was unattainable, but the St Simonians had proposed a system for approximating it by gradual steps, all of which were good in themselves, so that almost all attainable goods lay on the way.[2] In the meantime, Mill was rescued from utilitarian narrowness by seeing that although the institutions of the Middle ages were bad for England in the nineteenth century, in their day they had been as good as conditions then permitted. With his new perspective, he could be more tolerant of present evils while acquiring an even heightened zest for reform, which would be guided by scientific knowledge of where to go. He could see that the present was an age of transition, that while destruction and controversy were essential to further improvement, at some future time the noise would subside. So he was able to send Sterling the comforting thought: 'In the present age of transition, everything must be subordinated to freedom of inquiry; if your opinions, or mine, are right, they will in time be unanimously adopted by the instructed classes, and then it will be time to found the national creed upon the assumption of their truth'.[3] Social progress provided a useful and safe dream that could serve as a refuge from life, without interfering with the conviction, which Mill never would abandon, that freedom of inquiry must be preserved.

His new elaborate theory of progress was doubly welcome, because it represented a many-sided, novel variation on a familiar theme. Mill had after all inherited a faith in progress from his father, for James Mill never doubted that there was a truth and that one day it would be known. But he did not like to put that conviction into so many words, and probably never in his own mind dwelled much on the distant future. For him, progress was an end, not a creed. Comtist progress, however, with all its distinctions and categories alien to orthodox utilitarianism, could serve John Mill as a creed.

The first practical lesson that Mill drew from his new creed was that societies were organizations of classes, each of which had a complementary function in keeping the whole organism fit. Politics was not simply a mech-

---

[1] J. S. Mill, *The Spirit of the Age* (Chicago, 1942), p. 46.
[2] J. S. Mill, *Letters*, vol. I, p. 20 (Nov. 31, 1831).
[3] *Ibid.* p. 6 (Oct. 20, 1831).

anical matter of insuring that no man possessed unchecked power. One had to consider much broader spiritual needs, which would differ with time and place. And in each case, one class would be more fit to rule than any other.

Nothing of this sort had ever occurred to the utilitarians, for all their attacks on the aristocrats. They were anxious to see government entrusted to more devoted servants of the public good, but they thought always in terms of individuals. Even if they described government as a machine, it was a machine moved by individuals, and any man, whatever his origins or qualifications, was as dangerous when possessed of power as any other. The middle class was no more to be trusted with power than any other.[1] The crucial social distinction for the utilitarians remained always that between those who did and those who did not possess power. They were certain that mischief was bound to result from not making men's duties accord with their interests.

But John Mill thought of some classes as inherently qualified to rule, and made so by the inevitable course of history. He had discovered, as a matter of historical science, that there were more lasting and higher duties for him than the reform of parliament. For moral and intellectual ascendancy, which the priests had exercised in the middle ages, would pass into the hands of philosophers 'when they become sufficiently unanimous and in other respects worthy to possess it'.[2] In the normal condition of society, he explained in his articles on *The Spirit of the Age*, the 'opinions and feelings of the people are, with their voluntary acquiescence, formed for them, by the most cultivated minds which the intelligence and morality of the times call into existence'. It is 'natural' to pick out the most qualified men, and give them that power 'which, if it were in any other hands, would divide or eclipse their moral influence: but which placed in theirs, and acting partly as a *certificate* of authority, and partly as a *cause*, tends naturally to render their power over the minds of their fellow-citizens paramount and irresistible'. It was only in a time of transition, such as his own, that the 'mass of uninstructed' did not habitually defer to some superior class of person whom they trusted 'for finding the right and pointing it out . . .'.[3] England's confusion arose from a governing class that did not include many of those truly qualified to direct men's minds, for while the people had advanced in intelligence and in the capacity for self-government, the ruling class had become 'enervated by lazy

---

[1] For a definitive discussion of the utilitarian attitude to the middle class, see Joseph Hamburger, 'James Mill on Universal Suffrage and the Middle Class', *The Journal of Politics*, vol. 24, 1962. A complete authoritative account of the orthodox utilitarian view of politics is to be found in Joseph Hamburger, *James Mill and the Art of Revolution* (Yale, 1963).

[2] J. S. Mill, *Autobiography*, p. 148.

[3] J. S. Mill, *Spirit of the Age*, p. 76.

enjoyment'.[1] Those who possessed power must be divested of it so that the 'most virtuous and best-instructed' of the nation might 'acquire that ascendancy over the opinions and feelings of the rest, by which alone England can emerge from the crisis of transition, and enter once again into a natural state of society'.[2]

The Spirit of the Age was followed by a steady flow of attacks, both public and private, on Benthamite individualism. Mill professed himself not only sympathetic with 'speculative Toryism', but an antagonist of liberalism, which he found lacking in all reverence for government in the abstract, or in any understanding that 'it is good for man to be ruled; to submit both his body and mind to the guidance of a higher intelligence and virtue'. There was little moderation in Mill's indignation about liberalism, 'which is for making every man his own guide and sovereign-master, and letting him think for himself, and do exactly as he judges best for himself; giving other men leave to persuade him if they can by evidence, but forbidding him to give way to authority. . .'.[3] He even reread the New Testament carefully, declared that it 'completed my hatred of the Gig'; in his readiness to admire strong leaders, he was especially struck by the contrast between the vigorous Christ of the Gospels and the 'namby-pamby Christ of poor modern Christians'—'How clearly one can trace in all of them [the Gospels] the gradual rise of his conviction that he was the messiah; and how much loftier and more self-devoted a tone his whole language and conduct assumed as soon as he felt convinced of that'.[4]

From 1831 on, when he published *The Spirit of the Age*, the theme of almost all Mill's articles, whatever the subject, was the importance of distinguishing in politics between those who really knew and those who did not. The lines of his future work were there laid down. In a review of a book by the physicist, Herschel, on *The Study of Natural Philosophy*, he declared that the uncertainty that still dogged moral and social philosophy made it clear that mankind should everywhere adopt the methods that had brought so much success to natural science. It was unfortunate that natural scientists had been reluctant to reflect on their methods, but Herschel had now made such an attempt, and Mill quoted with particular approval and enthusiasm Herschel's statement that:

The successful results of our experiments and reasonings in natural philosophy, and the incalculable advantages which experience, systematically consulted and dispassionately reasoned on, has conferred in matters purely physical, tend of necessity to impress something of the well weighed and progressive character of

---

[1] *Ibid.* p. 91.
[2] *Ibid.* p. 93.
[3] J. S. Mill, *Letters*, vol. I, pp. 14 f. (Oct. 21, 1831).
[4] *Ibid.* pp. 68–9 (Oct. 5, 1833).

science on the more complicated conduct of our social and moral relations. It is thus that legislation and politics become gradually regarded as experimental sciences; and history, not as formerly, the mere record of tyrannies and slaughters . . . but as the archive of experiments, successful and unsuccessful, gradually accumulating towards the solution of the grand problem—how the advantages of government are to be secured with the least possible inconvenience to the governed . . . why should we despair that the reason which has enabled us to subdue all nature to our purposes should . . . achieve a far more difficult conquest. . . .[1]

The political implications were made clear by Mill in a variety of contexts. When he wrote on the peerage question in France, he said that 'the opinions and feelings of the nation are entitled to consideration, not for their own sake, but as one of the circumstances of the times . . .'.[2] After the Reform Bill was passed, he declared at once, 'It is most important for the success of the great experiment upon which we are about to enter, not to forget what a popular government really means'.[3] It means, he explained, not that the people govern but that they choose their governors. Public questions in a good government should be decided by the 'most judicious persons whom the people can find', rather than by the people themselves. The many must have security for good government by being able to elect and dismiss, but the actual business of government must be conducted 'by the few for the many'. Therefore, it is quite improper, indeed illogical, to exact pledges of representatives and reduce them to mere delegates. Pledges are useful as long as members of parliament remain inept, but pledges are essentially a reflection on the capacities of the representative. Once he becomes what he ought to be, it would be foolish 'to set the smaller wisdom to instruct the greater'. Instead of thinking about controlling unqualified representatives, it was time to realize that legislation was a 'profession,' and that talented young men should be encouraged by good pay to enter it.[4] Public affairs could no longer be handled by men who did not devote themselves to the science of politics, and such men could not be mere delegates for public opinion. Only one sort of pledge might be required of the new sort of representative—that he vote for shortening the duration of parliaments, for that was how Mill meant to retain control over representatives given full autonomy while in power. But on all other questions, the public must come to regard the member of parliament in the same light as a physician. No one would dream of telling his physician what to prescribe; why then, 'should we have one rule for the body politic, another and an opposite one for the body natural'? The science of

---

[1] 'Review of "A Preliminary Discourse on the Study of Natural Philosophy" by J. F. W. Herschel,' in *Examiner*, March 20, 1831, p. 179.

[2] 'The Peerage Question in France', *Examiner*, Sept. 4, 1831, p. 563.

[3] *Examiner*, July 1, 1832, p. 417.

[4] *Ibid.* Sept. 4, 1831, p. 563.

politics is no more uncertain than medicine; the physician may as easily be a quack or ignoramus as the politician. But if either is chosen wisely, he is far more likely to know the right answers than the layman. When, however, Mill went on to say how one could judge the fitness of a candidate for parliament, he suggested questions only about his probity and his devotion to the public good, but none that could reveal any special, professional knowledge.

Mill ceased to confine the task of political philosophy to supplying a set of model institutions, and urged the Philosophical Radicals 'no longer to rely upon the infallibility of Constitution mongering'.[1] Yet it was not until he reviewed Tocqueville's first volume on America that Mill succeeded in drawing a public reprimand from his democratic utilitarian colleagues. He did not say that the great political defects Tocqueville had discovered in America meant that democracy should be discarded; rather, Tocqueville's findings emphasized that there was a true and a false idea of representative democracy, and a way of insuring a 'rational democracy'. Without some such provision, there would be no escape from the direct sovereignty of the bigoted and ignorant people, who would, as in America, try to reduce the representative to a mere delegate. But this, 'the one and only danger of democracy', was not a necessary danger. It accompanied only that 'false idea of democracy propagated by its enemies, and by some of its injudicious friends . . .'.[2] Roebuck was moved to protest ardently in *Pamphlets for the People:* The reviewer 'believes, if I mistake not, in the advantages to be derived from an Aristocracy of Intellect'. As a loyal utilitarian, Roebuck had 'no faith in such an Aristocracy'. 'I am not terrified', he said, 'by the so much dreaded fickleness and vagaries of the people; nor are my suspicions to be lulled asleep by ingenious plans for giving intellect her dominance'. And he argued, much as Bentham might have, that 'Wisdom is a good thing when directed by probity; but it is robbed of that worthy counsellor when it is given irresponsible power'. By inducing the people to have faith in an aristocracy of intellect, 'you pursue the most efficient means to this mischievous end'.[3]

Being attacked by his former friend did not in the least shake Mill; he was rather pleased that he had made his differences with the Radicals so plain. The exact method of insuring the right relation between the instructed and the uninstructed remained to be worked out. As always, true to his purposes, Mill did so some years later in *Representative Government.* For the moment, he contented himself with pointing out at every opportunity that only uncultured, narrow men, who had no notion of the grandeur of the human spirit, could remain Benthamite individualists and allow the man who loved

[1] J. S. Mill, *Letters*, vol. I, p. 39 (March 9, 1833).
[2] 'Review of Tocqueville's *Democracy in America*,' *London Review*, Oct., 1835, pp. 112 and 116.
[3] Roebuck, 'Democracy in America,' in *Pamphlets for the People*, pp. 3–4.

only pushpin to have as much say about what society needed as the man who knew the glories of poetry.

Comte was partly but not wholly responsible for Mill's aberration. Mill's new theory was in a way only an extension of the moral convictions he had received as a child; the interest he had acquired in a more comprehensive view of all things led him to draw his early principles to conclusions unforeseen by his father. When, under the stimulus of Comte, he began to see society as an organism and to think in terms of governing and subject classes, it was almost an inevitable step to seeing in this, as in all other human things, a dichotomy between reason and passion, which in society meant a division between those qualified to rule and the untutored masses straining to rush ahead, unseeing and unguided. All his life he had thought in terms of a governing principle and an obeying one; within himself, he thought of reason governing his passions; all the people he had known had been either teachers or disciples. Any subtler, less easily identified relationship was hardly within his power to understand. A political system based on fine distinctions like those assumed in Burke's 'virtual representation' or in Bagehot's 'deference' would not have satisfied him as sufficiently real or precise.

James Mill had also believed that those who know should be followed reverently by the people; almost everything he wrote on politics suggests that something like a faith in the Elect was left over from the Kirk. But the dangers of power overrode all else for him. In any case, government as he thought of it had only to insure to every man the greatest possible quantity of the produce of his labour. Its highest duty was to make certain that no one interfered with the liberty of each man to do what he judged best for himself. This much could perhaps be done by a fairly broad group of men, if only their power were properly controlled. But John Mill was concerned with the human soul. He now felt that personal cultivation mattered most, and that it was the first duty of those who knew what men should be like to guide and, if necessary, gently compel all other men to live better, fuller lives. James Mill's energies had been entirely absorbed by the importance of making power responsible and making the ladder more accessible to men of talent. John Mill, coming later, when it was already a truism that all power was dangerous and that able young men should be allowed to rise, seeking besides a non-mechanical, more spiritual and comprehensive view of politics, began to think more of the distance between the workman and the educated gentleman. He became interested in a more elevated and inspiring problem than the dangers of power—how to provide leaders for the mass of people who otherwise wandered in darkness.

CHAPTER XXII

RADICALS IN POLITICS

FOR a few years, between 1829 and 1832, John Mill went so far as to speak of the Radical programme—universal suffrage, the shorter parliament, the ballot—as 'mere conditions of election'. He told himself and his friends that he would do best to stay away from politics and work out principles 'which are of use for all times, though to be applied cautiously and circumspectly to any: principles of morals, government, law, education, above all, self-education'. If he could throw some light on the 'science of investigation', he could do most to forward 'that alliance among the most advanced intellects and characters of the age, which is the only definite object I ever have in literature or philosophy, so far as I have any *general* object at all'.[1] All the same, he could not help feeling that political activity was the most important, if not the highest of all. He was probably not being unduly modest but merely expressing his veneration for politics when he told Sterling that apart from logic, political economy, and metaphysics, he could boast of no distinction. To a soldier in the army of progress, which John Mill still was, having and using power to improve society was bound to seem a better way of getting closer to the front lines.

When the Radicals were very successful in the elections of late 1832, Mill could not resist using the influence that under the circumstances could be his. 'My friends have buckled to that work; I must not desert them but give them such help as lies in me', he explained to Carlyle.[2] In spite of very poor health and personal agitation, he displayed boundless energy and enthusiasm during his years of political activity. When at the end of the 'thirties, his efforts and expectations in active politics failed, politics seemed no less, rather more important to him. Only then the emphasis shifted to working out the new creed, because the failure of his political activity confirmed his belief that politics must be based on a more inclusive and profound theory.

While Mill was engaged in politics, the main effect of his new broader outlook was to make him anxious to found a less sectarian radicalism. It did nothing, however, to soften his extremism in the practice of politics, which remained for him, as for the other young Philosophical Radicals, a matter of clear-cut alternatives. He longed for the whole constitutional framework to topple, for then it would be easier to put it together again correctly. As reform had been so long delayed, the people had lost all attachment to the old

---

[1] J. S. Mill, *Letters*, vol. I, pp. 6–7 (Oct. 21, 1831).
[2] J. S. Mill, to Carlyle, Dec. 27, 1932, National Library of Scotland, MS vol. 618.

institution and distrusted anything which 'looks like patching up the old edifice', he wrote to Sterling before the Reform Act. Destruction would certainly have to precede renovation:

If it goes all at once, let us wait till it is gone; if it goes piece by piece, why, let the blockheads who will compose the first Parliament after the Bill passes do what a blockhead can do, viz. overthrow, and the ground will be cleared, and the passion of destruction sated, and a coalition prepared between the wisest Radicals and the wisest anti-Radicals, between all the wiser men who agree in their general views and differ only in their estimate of the present condition of this country.[1]

All would be well, if only he and Sterling could select a few dozen persons 'to be missionaries of the great truths in which alone there is any well-being for mankind, individually or collectively'.[2]

Once the Reform Bill was passed, Mill confidently expected the millennium to arrive. 'The Tory party, at least the present Tory party', he announced triumphantly, 'is now utterly annihilated. . . . There is nothing definite and determinate in politics except Radicalism, and we shall have nothing but Radicals and Whigs for a long time to come, until society shall have worked itself into some new shape not to be exactly foreseen and described now'.[3] He regretted somewhat that his position in India House made it impossible for him to be in parliament. The time really was one when 'the doer of deeds' could do more than 'the sayer of words', he wrote to Carlyle.[4] It was much better in France where 'there are editors of daily journals, any one of whom, may be considered individually the head, or at lowest the right hand of a political party',[5] and he looked forward to a moral revolution in England which would 'exalt public writers to a station and consequence proportioned to their real power'.[6] Still, he felt that even in England he was wielding important influence through journalism. He meant to use it for two objects: to modify the principles of Radicalism so that they became less distasteful and could include more of the men whom he admired, and to form a third party, a Radical party, that would free Radicalism from the ignominious position of being a tail trying to wag the Whig party.

The means of supporting a higher Radicalism appeared ready at hand when in 1834 Molesworth, who always obeyed Mill, founded the *London Review*; in 1836, he bought out the old *Westminster*, by now thoroughly undercut, and the two merged. The death of James Mill in 1836 made it easier for John Mill to pursue his ends more openly, and he set himself most

[1] J. S. Mill, *Letters*, vol. I, p. 6 (Oct. 20–22, 1831).
[2] *Ibid.* p. 15 (Oct. 20–22, 1831).
[3] *Ibid.* p. 31 (May 29, 1832).
[4] *Ibid.* p. 50 (May 18, 1833).
[5] 'Letters from an Englishman', *Monthly Repository*, VIII, June, 1834, p. 393.
[6] *Ibid.* p. 391.

determinedly to 'draw together a body of writers resembling the old school of Radicals only in being on the movement side, in philosophy, morality, and art as well as in politics and socialities, and keep the remnant of the old school (if it is dying out) in their proper place. . .'. Neo-Radicalism would not urge a 'bigoted adherence' to any form of government or institution but would take into account the whole of human nature, the emotions, as well as the 'rationative faculty'. It would neither 'palter nor compromise with evils'. It would 'cut at the roots'.[1] Much to the horror of the old Radicals, especially Mrs Grote, he even invited Carlyle to write for him; when, during his absence, one of Carlyle's articles was refused, he asked for it again and had it printed. He was sure of his purpose and eager to work for it; when Molesworth could no longer carry the financial burden, Mill took it upon himself. Though it never became a financial success, *The London and Westminster Review* exerted a remarkably great influence.

For a while, Mill's hopes continued high. After the election of 1834, the Radicals seemed well on the way to power, with about twenty out and out Radicals, including all the leading ones, in parliament. Given the support of a number of independents and odd Whigs, their party could count on seventy or eighty votes, even without the Irish members, who might at times go with them. The Whig majority was only twenty-three, and it seemed reasonable to hope that the Radicals could dictate to the Whigs. But the ways of politics were not quite so simple as the Radicals supposed. They had little notion of how to work as an effective group in parliament; there were some real differences among them and anyway each went his own way, and blamed all the others for the confusion. Mill felt that the old group lacked energy, except for Roebuck, who had no judgement, and Buller, who would not persevere. The most 'considered', and most nearly a leader was Grote, not a man whom Mill admired much—hard and narrow, 'with much logical but little aesthetic culture', lacking the 'readiness, decision, and presence of mind' parliamentary success required.[2] Old political hands, like Lord John Russell or Melbourne, easily found ways to divide the Radicals or employ them in harmless tasks.

For the people whom they were to lead, the Radicals had little real feeling and Mill no more than the rest. There was nothing in his experience either to temper his idealized picture of an uneducated but reverent multitude following a messiah their instinct had rightly chosen, nor to acquaint him with what real capacities for self-government even illiterate and unsophisticated people might have. He never advocated lying to the people for their own good, nor engaging in any sort of esoteric leadership; speaking the truth at all times to

[1] J. S. Mill, *Letters*, vol. I, p. 103–4 (Nov. 23, 1836).
[2] *Ibid.* pp. 58–9 (Aug. 2, 1833).

all people was a sacred article of faith. Yet, seen by less pure eyes, much of what the Philosophic Radicals did to speed the good of the people suggests a great willingness to use, in any way, whatever influence was available. As they were eager to prove to the ministry that the country was on the verge of revolution, they first prepared the people to show what they felt. And then, by means of the press (with which they had a great number of contacts), and of spontaneously organized threats, deputations, personal talks with ministers, they communicated the feelings of the people to the ministry.

The Radicals acted very much along lines Mill had described in the year before the Reform Bill to the editor of the *Examiner:*

The people, to be in the best state, should appear to be ready and impatient to break out in outrage, *without actually breaking out.* The Press, which is our only instrument, has at this moment the most delicate and the most exalted functions to discharge that any power has yet had to perform in this country. It has at once to raise the waves and to calm them; to say, like the Lord, 'Hitherto shalt thou go and no further'. With such words ringing in their ears, Ministers cannot waver (even) if they would. . . .[1]

In his *Autobiography*, Mill confessed that he hoped at this time for the spread of anti-property doctrines among the poorer classes, 'not that I thought those doctrines true, or desired that they should be acted on, but in order that the higher classes might be made to see that they had more to fear from the poor when uneducated than when educated'.[2] When Roebuck, in later years, described the efforts of his party, he strongly confirmed the picture of Radicals manipulating popular sentiments with regard only for political purposes:

to attain our end much was said that no one really believed; much was done, that no one would like to own . . . often, when there was no danger, the cry of alarm was raised to keep the House of Lords and the aristocracy generally in what was termed a state of wholesome terror. When the Bill proceeded with ease . . . a grave calm was preserved in our demeanour and writings . . . when its provisions were threatened either with destruction or even mutilation, black clouds rose obedient to our call . . . our language grew violent, we stormed, we threatened and prophesied and, like some other prophets, we were determined to accomplish our own predictions.[3]

Nevertheless, for all their manipulating, the Radicals failed to rally the people behind them. In the elections of July, 1837, the young queen had greater appeal than the Radicals, and there was a Tory gain. The Whigs lost heavily, and few Radicals were returned; Grote scraped in by just six votes.

---

[1] Albany Fonblanque, *Life and Labours*, ed. by Barrington de Fonblanque (London, 1874), p. 29.

[2] J. S. Mill, *Autobiography*, p. 121.

[3] 'Some Chapters in the Life of an Old Politician', *Bentley's Miscellany*, XXIII, 1848, pp. 520–1.

Roebuck, along with Hume, was defeated; and though two years earlier he had been outraged by Mill's review of Tocqueville, he now declared: 'Take the masses separately and talk to them, what do you find? Why, profound ignorance and, especially, inveterate prejudice. . . . There is no chemical fusion to make a hundred ignorant individuals one instructed body'.[1] He decided, as he told his wife in words more reminiscent of Coriolanus than of an ardent democrat, 'If they desire to be well governed, let them, but I am not going to crawl to them in order to persuade them to their own good'.[2]

Francis Place was at first inclined to find solace in the growth of the Working Men's Association during the trade depression of 1836–37:

> The most active and well-informed among the people, seeing themselves utterly abandoned by those who had promised at the hustings to be their friends, began to stir for themselves, at first with very small numbers for a reform of Parliament on the broadest possible plan. . . . This is a 'new' feature in society produced by the increased intelligence of the working people.[3]

He thought that Chartism had little chance of an immediate success, but expected that a properly conducted agitation for the Charter, at first part of the Working Men's Association movement, would in the end produce a strong democratic party, led by the newly risen, educated workmen.[4] Here Place hoped to find more positive results than parliamentary politics had achieved, and he curtly refused to stir himself for the Radical cause in parliament when Mill asked him not to retire. He believed he could persuade the working men to 'steady, patient, liberal conduct . . . making no absurd pretensions to anything, and especially not to superior wisdom and honesty, but acting with becoming modesty. . .'.[5] When Chartist agitation gathered its own momentum, and became just the sort of agitation Place most disliked, he, too, became disillusioned with the people and spoke of the 'misled, ill-judging multitude', who 'look upon their best friends as their worst enemies . . .'.[6]

The failure of July, 1837 had a somewhat different effect on Mill, who had never had any great faith in the people, although he was willing to use their agitation. He put all his efforts into getting the Radicals to act. He blamed the Radicals, even more than the Whigs, for being indecisive and ineffective. In the leading article in the *Westminster* for October, he summed up the causes of failure and his own views of correct political behaviour. He showed himself

---

[1] Roebuck to Place, Sept. 18, 1837 in Roebuck, *Life and Letters*, p. 104.
[2] Roebuck, *Life and Letters*, p. 119, June 24, 1838.
[3] Place to Hume, Sept. 13, 1838 in Wallas, *Francis Place*, p. 368.
[4] *Ibid.* p. 369.
[5] *Ibid.* p. 370.
[6] *Ibid.* p. 384.

to be more than ever eager for action and movement, in fact, a fairly ruthless Radical. The only way to succeed in politics, at any time, he urged, was to 'attempt much', to engage in many and bold enterprises. This was the only insurance against blunders, the only way a politician could 'draw upon the surplus popularity accumulated by successes', and be indemnified for failures. Radicals and Whigs alike were afflicted by 'conscience', which prevented them from taking action unless they were certain it was right and popular. They did not realize that the more measures they proposed, the better. They were obliged to propose more than they could expect to get passed, because when new legislation is continually being offered, 'in the first place, the enthusiasm will be greater', and, secondly, 'one measure will explain the motives and correct the misrepresentations of another'. The important thing was to build up a stock of activity: 'If a conscience altogether has been described as an expensive article, a conscience like theirs—a purely negative conscience, which never bids them to anything, but only not to do—is the most expensive of all; for, while it is making continual drafts upon their popularity, it never brings anything in'.[1]

Mill also advised the Radicals to be more assiduous in courting popularity. While a politician was bound to resist his supporters when they urged unjust measures upon him, he ought not to 'neglect any honest means by which he may retain the confidence of his supporters even while he opposes their wishes'.[2] The Radicals could succeed only by making themselves the leaders of the working classes, by making themselves known as the defenders of the poor, just as the Whigs were the party of liberty, and the Tories of authority: 'To serve the people is not the same thing as to please the people; but those who neglect the services which please, will find themselves disqualified from rendering those which displease'. Only Roebuck and Colonel Thompson had made any efforts to gain the confidence of the poor; the rest did not seem to realize that it was their job to be the 'tribunes of the poor. . . . Those who will not flatter the people must make it doubly obvious that they are willing to serve them. . .'.[3]

If the Radicals did not do more than 'bear witness passively for the truth',[4] Mill prophesied, the poorer classes would find others to lead them. There was already growing up a new class from which radical leaders might be drawn, a class just 'below the rank in society which would of itself entitle them to associate with gentlemen'. These were people of energy and ambition, who were rapidly educating themselves, and were deeply radical. They would rise in the world, and as they did so, some would forget their radicalism, but

[1] *Westminster Review*, Oct., 1837, pp. 15–16.
[2] *Ibid.* p. 16.
[3] *Ibid.* p. 17.
[4] *Ibid.* p. 18.

others would not. And these would be the new leaders of the poor, if the Radicals failed. 'These are the men who will know how to speak to the people. They are above them in knowledge, in calmness, and in freedom from prejudice, and not so far above them in rank, as to be incapable of understanding them and of being understood by them'.[1] Unlike Place, Mill, who also saw the new democratic possibilities, was never optimistic about them and hoped rather to keep them from becoming actual.

For the moment, Mill was against what Roebuck seemed to favour: forming an independent Radical party and going into Opposition against the Whigs. There were advantages in this policy, to be sure, but as the Radicals had shown themselves to have no leaders while they were allied with the Whigs, what reason was there to think they would do better on their own? Before they could be successful, either with or without the Whigs, they had better concentrate on developing qualities of leadership, on demonstrating their capacity for practical affairs. That was the great attraction of Robert Peel: 'If Radicalism had its Robert Peel, he would be at the head of an administration within two years'.[2] And yet Peel had no gifts; he did not 'know his age'; he knew only the House of Commons, all 'that the mere routine of office experience can give, to a man who brought to it no principles drawn from a higher philosophy. . .'. This was enough to give him enormous influence—he seemed to have a talent for business simply because of his steady activity.[3] The Radicals must learn to propose measures not only on one subject, but on several; they must become versed in all the questions that a ministry and parliament had to decide. The Radicals had 'talents inferior to no party in the house' and 'acquirements superior to any'; it was now their job to make use of their superiority and acquire the influence that rightly belonged to them.

At the same time, Mill urged 'the people' to hold themselves ready for anything. For anything might happen at any time. Ireland was already organized. 'Let England and Scotland be prepared at the first summons to start into Political Unions. Let the House of Commons be inundated with petitions on every subject on which Reformers are able to agree. Let Reformers meet, combine, and above all, register. . .'. All other subjects would wait, but there was no postponing the Ballot. Securing the vote was the paramount political issue. 'This let the Reformers do; and let them stand at their arms and wait their opportunity'.[4]

But in November, Lord John Russell acquired the nickname, 'Finality Jack', by declaring that reform was over, that the Reform Bill of 1832 was

[1] *Ibid.* p. 24.
[2] *Ibid.* p. 25.
[3] *Ibid.* p. 25.
[4] *Ibid.* p. 26.

sufficient, and the Whigs would do no more. This convinced Mill that there was nothing more to hope for from an alliance with the Whigs, and without a backward glance, or apology, he forgot his doubts about the Radicals' capacity for political leadership, and began at once to advocate that they assume the same position towards Lord Melbourne as they had taken against Lord Grey in the first reformed parliament. They must separate from the ministry and go into declared opposition. As the ministry needed a majority, and the Tories could not command one, there would follow a coalition either of Whigs and Tories, or of Whigs and Radicals. Even if such tactics brought in the Tories, there would be sufficient compensation in the creation of a compact and vigorous radical opposition. 'If the Whigs did not choose a coalition with the Tories . . . the Radicals might, and in common honesty, must, join them'. By ordinary good management on the part of the Radicals, the Whigs would have to form a ministry in which the Radicals would have an equal voice. The Radicals would then have ceased to be a mere tail, and the Radical–Whig ministry would at the very least prepare the way for a ministry of moderate Radicals.[1] At first John Mill urged this policy on his friends, publicly and privately, with little effect; he 'raved and stormed' but was only thought an impractical enthusiast. But by the end of the year, he reported that the Radicals had at last 'resolved to form a party', to quit the ministerial benches, and take up a separate position in the House.[2]

His main hopes now came to rest on finding a Radical leader. He himself could propose daring, even effective policies, but he had not the personal qualities needed to weld the Radicals into a party. His choice was Lord Durham, who had sat in Lord Grey's cabinet but was no Whig, who had resigned office in the reformed parliament, and remained on the outside, brilliant, dissident, independent, and very attractive to the people. Mill was so far right that Melbourne also thought Durham was dangerous. To get him out of the way, Melbourne sent him off to Canada, which had become very disaffected, in the hope that Durham would fail there and be permanently discredited. Mill counted on Durham's success, and the probability that he would then be strong enough to become Prime Minister. He urged the Radicals to put all their efforts into establishing a Durham ministry within a year, or, at the least, modifying the Whig ministry enough to push the Whigs into further reform. He himself prepared to forget his own differences with the Radicals and worked with them wholeheartedly. Again, he counted without the political dexterity of Melbourne, or indeed without considering either Canada or the forces against Durham. Durham was recalled, under attack from Tories, Whigs, and Roebuck Radicals, with Canada in revolt. Still Mill

---

[1] *Westminster Review*, Jan. 1838, pp. 508–9. Cf. also J. S. Mill, *Letters*, vol. I, pp. 107–9 (March, 1838) to Bulwer.

[2] *Fortnightly Review*, May, 1897, p. 675. John Mill to Prof. John Nichol, Dec. 21, 1837.

managed, rather remarkably, to silence the charges against him, and to gather support for his views on Canada. Mill carried authority as a political journalist, but he could not make Durham into a Radical leader. Durham was too ill, and anyway unwilling; the Radicals agreed with Roebuck that he would not do. Durham died not long after, and with him the hopes for a Radical party. For Mill the period came to be summed up in the letter he received from Place after the failure of the 1837 elections, declaring that he was withdrawing from parliamentary politics. This letter Mill kept 'as a memorial of the spiritless heartless imbecility of the English Radicals'.[1]

Instead of the Radicals, the people chose to follow the Chartists, those 'pretended leaders of the working classes', as Molesworth called them.[2] The Radicals were all outraged. Place had no good names for any of the Chartists:—Stephens was 'a malignant crazy man who never seemed exhausted with bawling atrocious matter', Bronterre O'Brien, a 'three parts insane and savage man', and collectively they were 'the misleaders of the people', who were 'ill-informed', 'credulous', easily led into folly by the delusions of their leaders. Chartism was at bottom a selfish 'bread and cheese question', with erroneous economic ideas, as it was made clear in the Chartist opposition to property and to the anti-Corn Law agitation.[3]

Mill came to think, along similar but more general lines, that reason could do little in other than very exceptional individuals to make men act on anything higher than material interests and class feelings. The only hope perhaps was to make a large Reform Party of those who were 'out':

We have a strong faith, stronger than either politicians or philosophers generally have in the influence of reason and virtue over men's minds, but it is of the reason and virtue of their own side of the question; in the ascendancy which may be exercised over them for their own good, by the best and wisest persons of their creed. ... Men's intellects and hearts have a large share in determining what sort of Conservatives or Liberals they will be; but it is their position (saving individual exceptions) which makes them Conservatives or Liberals. ... We must find out who are the Privileged classes, and who are disqualified. The former are the natural Conservatives of the country; the latter are the natural Radicals.[4]

By the time Tocqueville's second volume appeared in 1840, Mill was even more disenchanted with democracy than he had been before. But he blamed the evils not on egalitarianism, but on commercialism and industrialism, as his Coleridgian friends had always done. He therefore proposed a partial undoing of 1832. The agricultural population should be stimulated

[1] Wallas, *Place*, p. 352.

[2] Sir William Molesworth, *State of Nation. Condition of the People* (London, 1840).

[3] Henry Jephson, *The Platform—Its Rise and Progress* (London, 1892) vol. ii, pp. 195, 197, 201, 203.

[4] *London and Westminster Review*, vol. 32, p. 478.

by a system of national education to exert more influence, and complement the middle class energy with agrarian calm and reflection. The middle class majority in Commons should be restrained by a Commission of Legislation and by an Upper House modelled after the French Senate, with members appointed for life after having held important government positions. It was this sort of organization that accounted for the excellence of Roman government, for its remarkable consistency of purpose, its skill and talent.[1] He had already written his criticism of Bentham balanced by praise of Coleridge. Having thus made himself inimical to all parties, Mill retired from politics. 'I am out of heart about public affairs, as much as I ever suffer myself to be', he wrote to D'Eichthal in 1840.[2] No one, he told Caroline Fox, 'should attempt anything intended to benefit his age, without at first making a stern resolution to take up his cross and bear it; for if he did not begin by counting the cost', all his schemes must end in disappointment.[3]

He was now entering, he felt, on an era when 'the progress of liberal opinions will again, as formerly, depend upon what is said and written, and no longer upon what is done . . .'.[4] And he mellowed toward the Whigs, telling Fonblanque[5] that he was as warm a Whig supporter as he, agreeing to contribute to the *Edinburgh Review*, and pronouncing the Whig speeches in the great debates to be 'really the speeches of philosophers'.[6] He now classified political opinion into Conservative, Whig, Radical, and Chartist, declaring that if he was to do any good, it would be only 'by merging in one of the existing great bodies of opinion; by attempting to gain the ear of the liberal party generally, instead of addressing a mere section of it'.[7] Mainly, however, he would concern himself with moulding philosophical truths into practical shapes. To this end, he set himself to work wholeheartedly on his *Logic*, which had been in the making for the past decade.

---

[1] *Edinburgh Review*, Oct., 1840. Cf. Also J.S. Mill, *Dissertations and Discussions* (London, 1867), vol. II, p. 81.

[2] *Cosmopolis*, IX, Dec. 25, 1840, pp. 373–4.

[3] Fox, *Memories*, vol. I, p. 138.

[4] Mill to Napier, July 30, 1841, Ad. MSS. 34622 F. 85.

[5] Fonblanque, *Life and Labours*, p. 82.

[6] Fox, *Memories*, vol. II, p. 328.

[7] Macvey Napier, *Correspondence*, ed. by H. Napier (London, 1879), pp. 325–6.

CHAPTER XXIII

SOCIOLOGY

THE reason for the Radicals' failure, for the generally sad state of politics, had been clear to Mill even before it had been revealed in practice. Had he not said before that without scientific knowledge, nothing much could be accomplished either in politics or in morals? Now that he was no longer absorbed by political activity, his thoughts began to dwell again on the urgency of perfecting a science of morals and politics.

As things stood, moral principles were derived by simply turning current prejudices into holy shibboleths because men persisted in believing that truth could be known intuitively.[1] Or else, all ideas of right and wrong were wrenched 'into accordance either with the notions of a tribe of barbarians in a corner of Syria three thousand years ago, or with what is called the order of Providence. . .'.[2] The many unsuccessful attempts to find a rational basis for morals had only increased the confusion and left the human race torn between a number of competing principles. As long as several principles of conduct continued to be recognized, what was condemned by one could be pardoned by another. Until one standard prevailed, there could be nothing but moral chaos. In this, John Mill followed his father closely. He remained convinced that without sound theory, sound practice was impossible. Until a satisfactory systematic treatise on morals was available, 'we cannot expect much improvement in the common standard of moral judgements and sentiments'.[3]

The state of politics was even worse than that of morals. The only question men thought to ask was whether a law or a form of government was good for a country, or possibly, for all countries, but there was never any more general and profound inquiry into how the laws of human nature operated, or how they determined the effects of governments. The vulgar had consequently concluded that nothing else was possible, that anyone who urged searching for something more was a fraud, 'that no universality and no certainty are attainable in such matters'.[4]

When Mill was thinking about these problems, the movement toward a scientific analysis of human conduct was in its earliest stage. The eternal enemy, history, was still very much alive and popular, so that almost of necessity the first challenger to the humanistic attitude was philosophy of

---

[1] J. S. Mill, *Autobiography*, p. 158.
[2] J. S. Mill, *Letters*, vol. I, p. 156 (Nov. 22, 1850).
[3] *Ibid.* p. 129 (April, 1847).
[4] J. S. Mill, *Logic*, 2 vols. (London, 1851), vol. II, p. 450.

history, which generalized about the agencies at work and endeavoured to present the leading ideas that shaped the whole. Mill was to take the process one step further, to build a social science independent of both history and philosophy, and hence much more appealing to the empirically minded. But the source of his early inspiration, the philosophy of history learned from Comte, marked him enough to make him feel that the primary task of social science was to predict the future stages of social progress. This seemed to him to be a reasonable and modest hope; for he did not expect to predict the future, in detail that is, to write history in advance, but merely to discover a general view of what was to come by which men could guide themselves. It was proper for all really scientific thinkers to try 'to connect by theories the facts of universal history'.[1] Mill generously acknowledged the service rendered both to history and social science by the continental studies of the 'law of progress'. But this was not enough; the 'law of progress' was merely an empirical law, and the ultimate aim of science was to discover more, the laws of human nature, and to connect empirical generalizations with their fundamental causes.[2]

To ask more fundamental questions, to inquire into the laws that govern the general conditions of society, was the only way out of the narrow, Benthamite view of politics. The alternative suggested by critics like Macaulay was of no use, for Macaulay advocated an empirical, common sense mode of treating political phenomena, a method that might, Mill said, have recognized Kepler, but would have excluded Newton and Laplace. The method of common sense, in any form, was opposed to science and not in the least acceptable to Mill; he saw in it a return to the foggy old days when the mercantilists argued that national wealth would grow if foreign commodities were excluded, simply because England happened to have flourished while there were such restrictions. Macaulay's method could work only if it were possible to try endless social experiments, and even then the experiments could never be conclusive.

On the other hand, the more rigorous 'geometric' method, adopted by James Mill and Bentham, overlooked the fact that in human affairs, unlike geometry, no single cause accounted for any effect; they had constructed a science on the basis of only a few of the agencies that determined social phenomena and left the rest to be discovered in practice or surmised by wisdom. Mill hoped for a science that could do more. He was convinced that by starting from fundamental laws governing social phenomena, one could understand how a society had become what it was, how it was changing, what forms present features would take in the future, and how any of these effects might b prevented, encouraged, modified, or replaced. This was the proper

[1] *Ibid.* p. 515.
[2] *Ibid.* p. 498.

object of social science. No doubt, social science could also be of some help on more specific questions like predicting the effect of imposing or repealing the corn laws, of abolishing monarchy, or introducing universal suffrage under known conditions, but these were not the main business of social science.[1]

The proper method for social science would combine the deduction that James Mill had used with 'induction'. Yet even Comte had ignored induction; he had denied the possibility of constructing a theory of induction and had therefore contributed nothing to sociology.[2] Mill set himself to remedying this oversight. Whereas deduction operated only on those tendencies in human nature that were the same in all ages and countries, he explained, 'induction' meant paying attention to people as they actually were, taking into account differences of time and circumstances, rather than arguing from some formal concept. By combining the wisdom of induction with the Benthamite deductive, geometric method, Mill hoped to systematize not only what was common to human beings but also what differentiated them. From the time he read Macaulay's attack on James Mill, the logic of induction became Mill's most persistent interest.

Although he readily granted that Bentham and James Mill had tried to form a science of society, he guided himself very largely by opposition to their methods. He would not isolate any aspect of human nature from the rest. His basic scheme would be large enough to include everything, and any separate study he made would be clearly subordinated and related to the whole. For as he now believed that no action was without consequence for everything else, that the more we come to know, the more we tend to connect every event with a wider range of causes and effects, he refused to consider any action by itself. Many valuable suggestions could be drawn from what had been done in the past, most of all from Bentham's work in ethics. But the systematic treatise that would treat ethics properly, as a branch of social science, could not be written until psychology, especially the laws governing the formation of human character, was well advanced.

Whereas Bentham and James Mill had been satisfied to construct a scheme that served well for specific practical purposes, John Mill wanted to explain human nature as it really was, with all its joys, sorrows, hopes, aspirations, loves and hates. He wanted the key to the whole living man, not to any small part of him. Nothing partial, however precise and detailed, would do because it savoured of that narrowness he had learned to dislike. To speak of political reform without building it on mental regeneration was therefore worthless. He was no longer interested in any particular political measure. 'It is becom-

[1] *Ibid.* p. 494.
[2] J. S. Mill, *Auguste Comte and Positivism* (London, 1882), p. 55.

ing more and more clearly evident to me', he wrote to Barclay Fox, 'that the mental regeneration of Europe must precede its social regeneration, and, also, that none of the ways in which that mental regeneration is sought,—Bible Societies, Tract Societies, Puseyism, Socialism, Chartism, Benthamism, etc.— will *do*, though doubtless they have all some elements of truth and good in them.'[1] Impressed by Mill's new interests, Sterling reported that Mill had turned away from politics to the reform of individual character.[2]

It would have been more precise, although quite foreign to Sterling's vocabulary, to say that Mill had come to think of politics as sociology. He had redefined sociology. It was no longer 'a particular class of subjects included within politics'. but

a vast field including it—the whole field of inquiry and speculation respecting human society and its arrangements, of which the forms of government and the principles of the conduct of governments are but a part. And it seems to me impossible that even the politics of the day can be discussed on principles, or with a view to anything but the exigencies of the moment, unless by setting out from definite opinions respecting social questions more fundamental than what is commonly called politics.[3]

From this it followed that either one included all the agencies that affected human behaviour within the science of human behaviour, or one had to give up any pretence of studying scientifically any part of it.[4] There was, however, an impediment to Mill's love of social science. He could not see how it was to be made compatible with free will and the variety of human conditions and character, which he was so anxious not to deny. Or, in other words, it seemed as if one could not believe both in free will and in the possibility of reducing human behaviour to scientific laws. The problem of liberty and necessity had long disturbed him. Ever since his crisis, free will had become for him, as it had for Coleridge, an essential part of his new view of man. Yet free will seemed to be denied by the one inherited doctrine Mill still wished to believe, and had to believe, as an improver of men's souls. He had been taught that character was moulded by circumstances, and that by changing the circumstances, much could be done to improve mankind. James Mill and Bentham had rested there, satisfied that thus they had explained the salutary effects their reforms might have. But John Mill had begun to turn the problem round: if circumstances moulded character, how could any man claim to be master of himself? 'I felt as if I was scientifically proved to be the helpless slave of antecedent circum-

[1] Fox, *Memories*, vol. II, p. 338 (Dec., 1842).
[2] *Ibid.* pp. 8–9.
[3] J. S. Mill, *Letters*, vol. I, p. 163 (June 9, 1851).
[4] J. S. Mill, *Logic*, vol. II, p. 472.

stances; as if my character and that of all others had been formed for us by agencies beyond our control'.[1]

In the end, Mill found a solution that required no fundamental change in his beliefs. It consisted of explaining that when one said that circumstances shaped character, one meant only that character, like everything else, was an effect caused by circumstances. But this did not rule out the possibility that the circumstances could themselves be shaped—'our will, by influencing some circumstances, can modify our future habits or capabilities of willing'.[2] Although the will could not operate directly to shape men's destinies, it could influence what happened by controlling circumstances. Mill had, in fact, only driven the problem one step further. But as long as he could attribute some importance to the will, he was not bothered by the circularity of saying, as he now did, that the will could modify circumstances, but was itself shaped by circumstances.

Mill denied that any metaphysical question was involved in his statement that, 'A volition is a moral effect, which follows the corresponding moral causes as certainly and invariably as physical effects follow their physical causes'.[3] This sequence was simply a fact that any man could observe for himself. As any facts that follow one another according to constant laws may be scientifically known, he concluded complacently that a science of human behaviour was possible. His doctrine was not 'Necessitarian'. Only 'free-will philosophers', like Mansel and Sir William Hamilton, who tried to deny causality in human affairs, would accuse a philosopher of rejecting free will because he affirmed that there was a constant sequence of motive, mental disposition, and action. 'Necessitarian', used properly, Mill explained, meant believing that the sequence was a 'necessary' one, whereas he maintained only that it was 'unconditional'. Just how an 'unconditional' sequence differed from a completely determined 'necessary' one, Mill did not dwell on. By ignoring such questions, he protected his assurance that believing in free will was compatible with a belief in social science.

Once he had explained to his satisfaction that liberty of the will could be reconciled with his other beliefs, and felt reassured that he could be both a reformer and a scientist, he was ready to think that all psychological phenomena could be traced to physiological causes. He did not in the least qualify Hartley's attempt to explain all experience by the association of ideas. And he accepted Hartley's proposition that ideas were the result of vibrations set up by sensation.[4]

[1] J. S. Mill, *Autobiography*, pp. 118–19.

[2] *Ibid.* p. 119.

[3] J. S. Mill, *An Examination of Sir William Hamilton's Philosophy* (London, 1867), p. 562.

[4] David Hartley, *Observations on Man*, Part I, ch. I, Prop. IV.

The unbroken chain of causality from natural to mental effects became an article of faith with Mill. He mapped out in some detail the process Comte had just vaguely assumed. Yet, as always, Mill had a reservation that prevented him from agreeing entirely with Comte; in practice, he hesitated to make mental science nothing but a branch of physiology. And he managed to hold off by arguing that at least for the present, while our knowledge of physiology was not yet great enough to deduce mental states from nervous processes, it would be better to study mental phenomena directly, as a distinct and separate science of the mind. Differences in education and outward circumstances could, after all, account for a great portion of individual peculiarities. There was no need to deny that ultimately one could make the connection with physiology or to reject physiological explanation when the psychological one failed. But for the moment one need not insist on making the connection a basis for living.

At least for many years, a completely accurate prediction of all phenomena would not be possible because the circumstances influencing human character were so very complex. This was where the old Benthamites had made such grave errors. They had discredited all social science by insisting on one form of government, or system of laws, to fit all cases.[1] They had laid down universal precepts, instead of distinguishing, as Mill had learned to do from Comte, between 'laws' of human behaviour and the application of those laws under varying circumstances. By emphasizing the difference between explaining the general character of phenomena and making perfectly accurate prediction of details, and concentrating on the former, Mill felt that he had set himself apart from his first tutors.

Still, he would not refrain altogether from applying social science even before it was complete and perfect:

we must remember that a degree of knowledge far short of the power of actual prediction is often of much practical value. There may be great power of influencing phenomena, with a very imperfect knowledge of the causes by which they are in any given instance determined. It is enough that we know that certain means have a tendency to produce a given effect, and that others have a tendency to frustrate it.[2]

Predictions made from the general laws about tides, for instance, often lacked complete accuracy yet they corresponded well enough to the results observed to prove useful. Similarly, 'the phenomena of society might not only be completely dependent on known causes, but the mode of action of those causes might be reducible to laws of considerable simplicity, and yet no two cases might admit of being treated in precisely the same manner'.[3]

[1] J. S. Mill, *Logic*, vol. II, p. 450.
[2] *Ibid.* p. 442.
[3] *Ibid.* p. 451.

While it would be splendid to foretell exactly the thoughts, feelings, and actions of any individual, we can never expect to know all the circumstances affecting an individual. But the alternative is not hopelessness. The circumstances and qualities common to mankind determine important effects much more than individual idiosyncrasies do. It is therefore possible to make some general statements that are valid and significant. For the purposes of social science and politics, such general propositions may be considered equivalent to universal ones.

In sum, one had only to beware of making social science too simple. The way to avoid such over-simplification was to recognize that all knowledge about human behaviour must be derived from the laws of human character. John Mill set himself therefore to outlining the components of social science in greater detail than had ever before been attempted.

The foundation of social science had to be psychology, or the general laws of the mind, which describe how mental events follow one another. Psychology, like other basic sciences, is an experimental science, and its laws are simple enough to be reached by induction. But the step after psychology is more complicated. It is ethology, or the science of human character, which depends on too many concurrent causes and effects to be reached by induction alone. The laws of ethology have to be deduced from psychology, that is, by 'supposing any given set of circumstances, and then considering what, according to the laws of mind, will be the influence of those circumstances on the formation of character'.[1] Ethological laws can only be hypothetical, affirming that an effect will follow a certain cause if it is not counteracted, not that something will always, or certainly, happen. The final step in completing social science consists in what Mill called verification—making predictions on the basis of ethology, and then seeing whether they accord with empirical laws, that is, with generalized observations of human behaviour. There were already available enough such observations, Mill felt, to make verification possible. Thus social science could be freed of the defects that discredited James Mill's *Essay on Government*, where the author had just brashly singled out one or two ill-founded principles as the basis for deductions about government, which he did nothing to verify, Mill's social science was far more complicated, and therefore more true.

Once ethology was created, the rest, Mill felt certain, would come easily. For the subject of ethology was nothing less than

the origin and source of all those qualities in human beings which are interesting to us, either as facts to be produced, to be avoided, or merely to be understood; and the object is, to determine, from the general laws of the mind, combined with the general position of our species in the universe, what actual or possible combina-

---

[1] *Ibid.* p. 441.

tions of circumstances are capable of promoting or of preventing the production of those qualities. . . And when ethology shall be thus prepared, practical education will be the mere transformation of those principles into a parallel system of precepts and the adaptation of these to the sum total of the individual circumstances which exist in each particular case.[1]

It was hardly a modest hope. It was indeed vastly more ambitious than anything Bentham or James Mill could have imagined.

Sometimes Mill remembered the difficulties in the way of reaching the millennium. He agreed when Austin expressed some doubts about a science of government:

I suspect there are none [governments] which do not vary with time, place and circumstance. I doubt if much more can be done in a scientific treatment of the question than to point out a certain number of pros and a certain number of cons of a more or less general application, and with some attempt at an estimation of the comparative importance of each, leaving the balance to be struck in each particular case as it arises.[2]

Yet with all this common sense sort of qualification in his heart, and sometimes in his scientific treatises, Mill clung to the vision of something far grander and more certain than he could strictly defend, reassured by his readiness to take account of everything, to treat nothing abstractly, to keep always before him nothing less than the whole universe.

In another way, however, the *Logic* showed John Mill to be altogether loyal to his early preceptors, although his loyalty in the end led him farther afield than his opposition. He considered the *Logic* to be his own contribution to that great war against mysticism that Bentham and James Mill had both waged. The particular form of mysticism, most insidious in his day, he believed, was the doctrine of innate ideas. For all his foreign entanglements, Mill was still too matter-of-fact to accept, or even really to understand, any way of thinking that put more stock in intuition and imagination than in logic and observation. The doctrine that truth could be known by 'intuition or consciousness, independently of observation and experience', was to Mill nothing less than

the great intellectual support of false doctrines and bad institutions. By the aid of this theory, every inveterate belief and every intense feeling, of which the origin is not remembered, is enabled to dispense with the obligation of justifying itself by reason, and is erected into its own all-sufficient voucher and justification. There never was such an instrument devised for consecrating all deep-seated prejudices.[3]

Mill was most outraged when the intuitionists insisted, somewhat as Hume

[1] *Ibid.* p. 447.
[2] J. S. Mill, *Letters*, vol. I, p. 129 (April, 1847).
[3] J. S. Mill, *Autobiography*, p. 158.

had, that when the mind was faced with a problem that reason could not settle, it had to, and should, depend on faith. It was this sort of argument that inspired his fierce attack on Sir William Hamilton, who tempered Kant with Reid's common sense philosophy, but still did not endear himself to Mill. When Hamilton's follower, Mansel, laid it down that as the nature of God could not be known by man, His goodness, His omnipotence, along with the existence of evil must all be taken on faith, that men must simply believe that somehow God could by a moral miracle bring good out of evil, Mill lost all patience. Such a suspension of reasoning was intensely distasteful to him. He could never say calmly, as Hume did, 'even after the observation of the frequent constant conjunction of objects, we have no reason to draw any inference concerning any object beyond those of which we have had experience'. Mill had either to deny that such a question should be asked, or to establish precisely how the inference could be supported. This disposition in Mill led Carlyle to say once to Caroline Fox, 'If John Mill were to get up to heaven, he would hardly be content till he had made out how it all was . . . whether there was an operative set of angels or an industrial class'.[1]

Any attempt to found philosophy on metaphysical truths impressed Mill as an invitation to confusion, that would only leave men 'revolving in the eternal round of Descartes and Spinoza'.[2] There were moments, Mill confessed to Sterling, when he was tempted to 'postulate, like Kant, a different ultimate foundation, a "subjectiver bedurfnisses willen" if I could'.[3] But when such moods passed, his antipathy to 'supernatural philosophy' was thoroughly restored. He could no more tolerate anything akin to metaphysics than Bentham could, and, as a result, despite his honesty, he tried to deny, whenever possible, the relevance of metaphysical issues.

He liked to think that questions about the nature and discovery of knowledge were simply questions of logic. He would 'keep clear, as far as possible', he declared, 'of the controversy respecting the perception of the highest realities by direct intuition, confining Logic to the laws of the investigation of truth by means of extrinsic evidence, whether ratiocinative or inductive'. But as he himself could see, he failed to keep the demarcation neat—'I could not avoid conflict with some of the subordinate parts of the supernatural philosophy, which for aught I know, may be as necessary to it as what may appear to me its fundamental premises and its only important results'.[4] This was, of course, only to be expected, since, whether or not he liked it, Mill's antagonism to the intuitionist metaphysics was not free of metaphysics, but based on opposed metaphysical assumptions.

[1] Fox, *Memories*, vol. I, p. 309.
[2] J. S. Mill, *Letters*, vol I, p. 185, Dec. 5, 1854.
[3] *Ibid.* p. 114, Sept. 28, 1839.
[4] *Ibid.* pp. 113–114, Sept. 28, 1839.

In writing the *Logic*, Mill saw himself as the saviour of all those who had been thrust into the German supernatural camp simply for lack of any alternative that would be 'a clearly formulated philosophic system'. The progress of German philosophy in England had been useful up to a point because it had encouraged what England sorely needed and could have found nowhere else, 'a real tendency to scientific generalization and to the systematization of all human knowledge'. But while German philosophy had helped to destroy unfortunate prejudices, it had promoted 'a vague and arbitrary philosophy'. Once the 'negative metaphysics' was defeated, there was left no source for a 'systematic coordination of thought', other than German metaphysics which had become dangerously popular. His *Logic*, Mill hoped, would provide a rallying point for scientifically minded young Englishmen in search of a philosophy.[1] His success more than matched his hopes.

The first edition was sold out at once, and the author's fame was established. By the time Mill died, the *Logic* had become a standard examination book at Oxford; it was the text also at Cambridge, and though the Moral Science Tripos still had relatively few students, many read Mill's works just out of interest. One of the reasons for the impact of the *Logic* was explained some years later by John Grote, in a review of Mill's extended footnote to the *Logic*, his book on Sir William Hamilton:

For ourselves we still recall the mist which was cleared from our minds when we first read the *System of Logic* very soon after it was published. We were familiar with the Syllogistic Logic in Burgersdicius and Dutrieu; we were also familiar with examples of the best procedure in modern inductive science; but the two streams flowed altogether apart in our minds like two parallel lines never moving nor approaching. The irreconcilability of the two was at once removed, when we had read and mastered the second and third chapters of the Second Book of the *System of Logic*; in which Mr Mill explains the functions and value of the syllogism, and the real import of its major premise.[2]

Although his *Logic* came to have the reputation of the first substantial treatise on the methods of experimental science, Mill had been preceded by Whewell and Herschel, to both of whom he acknowledged his debt. Herschel's *Preliminary Discourse on the Study of Natural Phenomena*, published in 1830 and reviewed by Mill, probably helped to stimulate his interest in a work on logic, which he began to plan at about that time. A decade later, a more complete discussion of the methods of science appeared in Whewell's *Philosophy of the Inductive Sciences*. When Mill's *Logic* came out, Whewell congratulated Herschel and himself on having aroused interest in their problems, and

---

[1] L. Lévy-Bruhl, *Lettres Inédites de J. S. Mill à Comte*, (Paris, 1899), March, 1843, pp. 167-8.

[2] 'Review of J. S. Mill's *Hamilton*', *Westminster Review*, Jan. 1, 1866, p. 6.

having made acceptable, as uncontested truths, notions that had seemed new and strange.

Whewell also had some telling criticisms of Mill. He had not a very high opinion of Mill's general knowledge of science:

... when he comes to Induction, he appears to me to write like a man whose know-ledge is new (indeed he confesses that he had much of it from Herschel and me),— and not very well appropriated. For instance, a great number of his examples of scientific investigation are taken from Lubig's researches on physiological chemistry—*just published*. The most profound and sagacious physiologists and chemists cannot yet tell which of these will stand as real discoveries; still less can they put these new views into the true relation to the old without long thought and study. How then should Mill do it, to whom the whole subject is new?[1]

As Whewell foretold, Mill's examples were rejected, but that aroused no doubts about the theory they were meant to support. Neither did Whewell's pamphlet, 'Of Induction with special reference to J. S. Mill's *System of Logic*, 1849', make any impression. Even in Cambridge, Whewell's own university, which owed its growth in scientific eminence very much to his efforts, Mill was the accepted authority. Once the *Logic* was published, Herschel and Whewell were reduced to the rank of Mill's predecessors.

Yet both had greater claims to be heard as authorities on science. Although Herschel was an eminent physicist, his case is less striking as he was more nearly in agreement with Mill, and anyway more concerned with experi-mental work than with methodology. Whewell, however, who presented a very different theory, wrote a number of very substantial studies on both the history and philosophy of science, and was at the same time a scientist of some distinction in more than one field. He wrote several treatises on mathe-matics and mechanics; he collected and ordered most painstakingly a great deal of data on tides which contributed much to the development of the theory; he did significant work in chemistry and mineralogy; all of which his scientific contemporaries readily recognized. He was, in fact, well acquainted with the new developments in all the physical sciences as he counted among his closest friends the leading scientists of the day.

Although Whewell was accused by Mill of denying the relevance of observa-tion and experiment in science, he regarded himself as a defender of experi-mental science against deduction. He declared emphatically that deduction could never arrive at new truths, but could only make clear the consequences of accepted principles; deduction was 'mere reasoning', whereas science was a process through which man persisted in his efforts to understand the con-nections of natural events until he found an explanation that brought him conviction and repose. In fact, Whewell always stressed the importance of

---

[1] Isaac Todhunter, *William Whewell* (London, 1876), vol. II, p. 313.

observation and experiment, and his own work bears impressive testimony to his sincerity.

He was understandably irritated when Mill not only misinterpreted him, but in taking over much of what he had said, treated his original observations as if they were fairly obvious truths. Mill's only contribution was not to a general defence of the experimental method but on the point where he differed markedly from Whewell, his logic of induction, setting forth the 'Four Methods of Experimental Inquiry'. It was this part of the *Logic* that interested him most, and that won him fame.

As Mill described it, induction consisted simply of imitating something that is in the facts observed: 'If the facts are rightly classed under the conceptions, it is because there is in the facts themselves, something of which the conception is itself a copy; and which if we cannot directly perceive, it is because of the limited powers of our organs and not because the thing itself is not there'.[1] He granted that explanatory principles were not merely general descriptions and did involve a conception of the mind, but that conception, he believed, corresponded to something in the facts, which could be evident to our senses if they could perceive it. When Kepler asserted that the planets moved in an ellipse, he had not, Mill insisted, added anything new, but merely recognized what an observer in the right position with suitable visual organs could have seen directly. The ellipse was a fact that Kepler 'found in the motions of the planet'.[2] The process that involved a hypothesis, and that Whewell described as induction, was really only a preparatory stage that provided the data for induction according to the Method of Agreement:

The Colligation of Facts, therefore, by means of hypothesis, or as Dr Whewell prefers to say, by means of Conceptions, instead of being, as he supposes, Induction itself, takes its proper place among the operations subsidiary to Induction. All Induction supposes that we have previously compared the requisite number of individual instances, and ascertained in what circumstances they agree. The Colligation of Facts is no other than this preliminary operation.[3]

Thus Mill reduced the process of scientific discovery to the perfectly ordinary operation of comparison. The conception, he affirmed, 'is not furnished *by* the mind until it has been furnished *to* the mind'.

Whewell denied that there were any facts independent of theory or insight on the part of the observer: 'the ideas are applied so readily and familiarly, and incorporated with the sensations so entirely, that we do not see *them*, we see *through* them. . . . The most recondite theories, when firmly established

[1] J. S. Mill, *Logic*, vol. I, p. 304.
[2] *Ibid.* p. 306.
[3] *Ibid.* vol. II, pp. 184–5.

are Fact; and the simplest Facts involve something of the nature of Theory'.[1] The scientist, as Whewell understood him, did not merely contemplate; he created an intelligible relation; he supplied a conception to bind the facts together. Each step of an investigation therefore required 'Invention, Sagacity, Genius', not merely observation. In Whewell's version, Kepler 'bound together the facts by super-inducing upon them the conception of an ellipse and this was an essential element in his Induction'. Similarly, Whewell explained that when Newton attributed his discoveries to 'keeping his thoughts steadily occupied upon the subject which was to be thus penetrated', he meant only that he kept the phenomena clearly in view while he tried 'one after another, all the plausible hypotheses which seem likely to connect them, till at last the true law is discovered'.[2] The induction was made not when Newton was observing, but when he applied a *new* word, when he said that the planets *gravitate* toward the sun. Scientific discovery depended on a 'leap' made by the mind beyond, and essentially different from, anything learned by observation or logic. The characteristic feature of induction was the new idea added by the mind.

Herschel agreed that the mind played an active part in forming scientific laws, and he occasionally used phrases that might have been Whewell's, although he limited the mind's activity to organizing the data and did not grant that the mind added anything not previously there. Nevertheless, Herschel recognized Whewell's genuine respect for empirical experiment and observation, and was inclined to play down his differences with him. But Mill insisted that the relations described by science were to be discovered in nature, just as sensory data were, that they were objectively determined items of experience, and that Whewell was denigrating observation and experiment, and destroying the essence of science. Mill's interest lay in finding the right method for making the comparisons that were for him the heart of science. Although he tried to reply to Whewell, he would have preferred to persevere 'in the same abstinence I have hitherto observed from ideological discussions; considering the mechanism of our thoughts to be a topic distinct from and irrelevant to the rules by which the trustworthiness of the results of thinking is to be estimated'. He had been forced into a digression because Whewell's work 'rested the whole theory of Induction upon such ideological considerations'.[3]

What Mill called 'ideological considerations' were nevertheless at the heart of his opposition to Whewell. They had wholly opposed attitudes to science and to the nature of human knowledge, and were consequently

---

[1] William Whewell, *History of Scientific Ideas* (London, 1858), vol. I, p. 44.

[2] Whewell, *Philosophy of Discovery* (London, 1860), p. 183.

[3] J. S. Mill, *Logic*, vol. II, p. 185.

interested in different problems. Their disagreement was as far-reaching as that between Hume's emphasis on custom and Bentham's faith in logic. For one there was no certainty or escape from human fallibility, while the other promised to reach perfect truth.

Whewell, like Herschel, was really concerned with the way in which scientific generalizations were discovered, with explaining the mysterious process by which men arrived at generalizations based on a limited experience, which were nevertheless valid beyond that experience. As scientists, Whewell and Herschel were too aware of the difficulties involved in the actual work of discovery to feel that any formal scheme, even if defensible, would be of much help. Whewell did prepare some tables which he called the 'Criterion of Inductive Truth', but they were no more than genealogical tables of scientific theories.[1] When the logician, de Morgan, criticized the tables for providing nothing like a logic of induction, Whewell replied, in effect, that he did not really believe there was a logical operation such as induction. He was, he explained, trying only to analyse how scientific discoveries had come about, and called this 'induction' merely because 'all the world seemed to have agreed to call it so'.[2]

Whewell offered no logical tests for the validity of a scientific theory. That it truly described all the facts, he said, could be proven only by examining all the cases, and this was obviously impossible. The final test of a scientific theory must be rather whether it could successfully predict future events.[3] The development of a true theory was marked by progressive simplification and by successful explanation of new facts, whereas a false theory gradually became encumbered with complications, added to explain new facts; these modifications were really partial rejections which accumulated until the theory was altogether abandoned. Against the established opinion of his time, Whewell maintained that when Newton had condemned hypotheses, he meant only to denounce the 'rash and illicit general assumptions of Descartes'; Newton's supposed induction, Whewell insisted, was really a process of formulating and testing hypotheses.

The 'Four Methods' outlined by Mill, and praised for being a more systematic and precise way of proving scientific theories, seemed to Whewell irrelevant to the real problem of science. Mill's theory suffered, he believed, from the same defects that he had found in Aristotle. When Aristotle argued that from the observation that 'several animals who are deficient in bile are long-lived', it could be inferred that 'all animals deficient in bile were long-lived', he not only made mistakes in fact, Whewell pointed out, but assumed

[1] Whewell, *Novum Organum Renovatum* (London, 1855), p. 115.

[2] Todhunter, *Whewell*, vol II, p. 416.

[3] Whewell, *Novum Organum Renovatum*, pp. 85 ff.

the very proposition he should have been examining. For Aristotle was interested only in collecting evidence for his conclusion; similarly, Mill believed that the difficulties of science centred on collecting evidence. Contrary to both, Whewell insisted that the really difficult and important scientific problem was to discover what evidence was relevant, that is, to decide which of the similarities among long-lived animals mattered. For they shared not one, but a great number of common characteristics, and the scientist's primary task was to discover which one of these affected longevity. He had to form a theory about why one of the common characteristics was more important than any of the others. And at this point, he had to do more than collect observations; he had to make a 'leap' beyond anything he had observed.

Mill managed to avoid this issue by restricting inductive logic to the problem of proof, that is, the problem of devising canons for testing the value of evidence. Indeed Mill's philosophical disposition obliged him to ignore the question raised by Whewell, for it is at this stage that the 'mystery' of induction enters, a mystery to which Mill had no answer, and to which he wanted no answer as he preferred to deny its existence. There was to Mill something savouring of magic about Whewell's theory. There was none of that certainty that only 'hard' facts can give. Whewell's talk of contending conceptions, of more or less familiar theories, of facts assuming a different aspect when summed up by a new conception struck Mill as a story about phantoms with which he would rather not meddle.

In a sense, there were some genuine phantoms behind Whewell's theory of science. In analysing the character of scientific principles, Whewell argued somewhat along Kantian lines, that there was an *a priori* necessity to scientific truths, and that the laws of physical science were necessary in the same sense as the laws of mathematics and logic. He meant that when scientific generalizations were truly laws of nature, they involved a Fundamental Idea. When a scientific generalization did not involve such an idea, it was not properly a scientific law. Whewell never said that scientific truths could be known *a priori*, but that in discovering them, men were in fact making explicit the conditions of experience. He sometimes spoke as if the ideas were selected to fit the data, and at other times, as if they were imposed by the understanding. Mainly, especially when he discussed the Fundamental Ideas in connection with particular sciences, the ideas were for him points of view from which natural phenomena could be understood and ordered, but points of view that reflected something true about nature: 'Men cannot help believing that the laws laid down by discoverers must be in a great measure identical with the real laws of nature. . .'.[1] He never attempted a transcendental deduction of categories like Kant's, preferring a more nearly inductive approach,

[1] *Ibid.* p. 87.

that is, he derived his list of fundamental ideas by studying the history of science which he regarded as an account of how scientists had discovered the ideas fundamental to the various sciences. Major advances in the established sciences came about, he believed, when someone found the new idea that was necessary for the further development of the science.

But this probably did not worry Mill nearly as much as Whewell's insistence that discovery depended ultimately on personal genius:

> Scientific discovery must ever depend upon some happy thought, of which we cannot trace the origin;—some fortunate cast of intellect, rising above all rules. No maxims can be given which inevitably lead to discovery. No precepts will elevate a man of ordinary endowments to the level of a man of genius: nor will an inquirer of truly inventive mind need to come to the teacher of inductive philosophy to learn how to exercise the faculties which nature has given him.[1]

The happy thought that led to a discovery was not, Whewell pointed out, pure chance, because the training, gifts, interests, and knowledge, of the observer had to prepare him for his insight. But however it was formed, it was Newton's intellect, not the falling of the apple, that accounted for his theory. One could not then hope for a method that would 'enable all men to construct Scientific Truths as a pair of compasses enables all men to construct exact circles'.[2]

Whewell's theory of science implied that there was no escape from a personal, or at least a human element in science, since 'all Facts involved Ideas'. Worse still, it meant that the sciences could never be completed because scientific development consisted of 'a series of changes, a repeated progress from one principle to another, different and often contradictory'.[3] The fundamental ideas could be expressed in different ways, and more or less precisely; progress consisted in finding the best way of making them explicit. Although Whewell assured his readers that earlier truths are not so much expelled as absorbed, that each science is built on a series of developments rather than a succession of revolutions, he could not promise any simple progress. There was not, according to his view, any definite end to science:

> This successive and various progress from fact to theory constitutes the history of science; and this progress, though always leading us nearer to that central unity of which both the idea and the fact are emanations, can never lead us to that point, nor to any measurable proximity to it, or definite comprehension of its place and nature.[4]

Mill's theory promised much more. At the time he was writing the *Logic*, Mill was too preoccupied with the superiority of men of genius to draw all

---

[1] *Ibid.* p. 44.
[2] *Ibid.* p. v.
[3] Whewell, *History of Inductive Science* (New York, 1875), vol. I, pp. 9–10.
[4] Whewell, *Philosophy of Discovery*, p. 307.

the conclusions implied in his discussion of scientific method. Still, it followed from his theory, as his contemporaries may have sensed, and as many who came after him were to insist, that scientific method could be taught and used by anyone, that once scientific method was truly and widely recognized, the progress of humanity need no longer depend on persons. Method would do all. In this respect, Mill had carried to its logical conclusion Bentham's preoccupation with method, with providing impersonal mechanisms to replace fallible human beings. Since human fallibility could be circumvented, truth would steadily accumulate until ultimately science could reveal all.

Nevertheless, Mill appeared to be far more tentative about science than Whewell. Their opposition was generally supposed to be between an experimental spirit and an unscientific *a priorism*. But in fact the issue between Mill and Whewell was a metaphysical one, and the same that had been so crucial for Galileo—whether a scientific law really described the external order of things, or was only man's way of dealing with the universe, that is, useful but not true. For all Galileo's addiction to the experimentation that the Church opposed, he had insisted, much as Whewell did, that his theory described something real. Mill, however, declared that the universality and necessity that Whewell attributed to the laws of nature were illusions, to be explained by man's preceding experience and mental habits. He preferred not to discuss the nature of scientific knowledge, but if pressed to do so, he denied its reality. In this way, Mill seemed to retain the scepticism considered appropriate to empiricism. Yet in practice he was far less sceptical than Whewell. For he refused to accept Whewell's notion of science as incapable of ever being complete and perfect, destined always to need revision.

Both in his sceptical metaphysics and in his faith in absolute progress, Mill was much more congenial than Whewell to the English temper. Few hard-headed Englishmen of his time were inclined to doubt the facts of experience, or to approve of any theory tinged with *a priorism*. At the same time, the 'spirit of the age' seemed to bid them to build grandly and confidently on facts. What they wanted, therefore, was a warrant guaranteeing the general inferences they made from any given set of facts. Otherwise there could be no way of reaching certain, universal truths based purely on observation. If induction were not a process such as Mill described, of eliciting generalizations from experience alone and verifying them by experience, if the modes of classifying or describing facts were always conditioned by the insight, intent, or preference of the inquirer, there could be no accumulation of truths. Instead of progress, there would be endless controversy, or, at the least, a conversation that could never be concluded. Whereas Whewell only confirmed this gloomy prospect, Mill brought assurance of better things. He provided, or seemed to have provided, detailed and precise directions for discovering certain, thoroughly empirical knowledge about the Whole Universe. Whewell therefore attracted no following in England, and Mill became the apostle of scientific method.[1]

But despite the success of his logic of induction, and his primary interest in developing sociology, Mill has been passed over in the history of social science. For his theory was in other respects still too closely tied to the old framework. As psychology was its basis, the individual remained central. Not many sociologists could manage to keep their attention fastened on existing, unique human individuals while, at the same time, looking towards a science of society and the disappearance of important differences among men. Mill himself had difficulty in keeping the balance. While he let his hopes for the future rest on the assumption that differences of character, individual and national, were due to accidents and circumstances that might in part be controlled, he continued to think always in terms of individuals. But the sociologists who followed Mill preferred an easier, more obviously consistent approach. They would rather follow Comte and begin with society or with institutions as the basic realities, and derive individuals from them. Even a liberal, as congenial to Mill as Bagehot, advocated (in *Physics and Politics*) the organic sociology. Mill was moving with the 'spirit of the age' both in his addiction to sociology and in his theory of induction, but he could not go so far as to accept a sociology that did not start from individuals.

Yet partly because of this, Mill helped to encourage social science and a sociological view of politics. Because he stayed within an individualist framework, he could more easily build on established English prejudices a sympathy for the new. Without frightening away converts to social science by presenting a totally alien view, he did much to prepare the way for more radical notions than his by insisting on a comprehensive theory that left nothing outside. Benthamite theory, however hard and narrow, applied only to a small, very clearly circumscribed aspect of human life. All the rest was and, according to the theory, should be left to common sense, to prudence. But John Mill, made confident by the greater inclusiveness and flexibility of his theory, by his qualifications on how it was to be applied, made everything subject to science. The implications were readily drawn by many of his readers, but he saw only that he had, without betraying what was best in utilitarianism, made it grander and nobler.

He could not agree with Carlyle that 'logic gave a semblance of wisdom to a soulless reason—dry and dull, and dead argumentation'.[2] Not, after all, a poet

---

[1] For further discussion of the relation between Mill and Whewell, along somewhat similar lines but from different standpoints, see R. P. Anschutz, *The Philosophy of J. S. Mill*, and Marion Rush Stall, *Whewell's Philosophy of Induction*. A contemporary theory of science opposed to Mill's for reasons similar to Whewell's is presented by Prof. Karl Popper in *The Logic of Scientific Discovery*.

[2] Fox, *Memories*, vol. I, p. 184.

but a crusader, Mill could not be content with merely extolling poetry or art. He had to make everything part of the whole and include it somehow in a scientific analysis of man. Having done so, he was satisfied that he was not a narrow reformer like Bentham indifferent to perfecting the human soul. It was left for others to discover how much the all-encompassing sociologists would do to make men more feeling, imaginative, and sensitive to beauty.

CHAPTER XXIV

SOCIOLOGY APPLIED

For some time after completing the *Logic*, Mill toyed with ethology, upon which everything else depended; but nothing came of it. In the end, he had recourse to the qualification he had made in the *Logic* when he explained that although every part of society influences every other, some social facts have causes that can be studied separately.[1] For example, in economics one could single out phenomena which were very largely dependent on the desire for wealth and were determined by the psychological law that a great gain is preferred to a smaller one. Thus Mill cleared the way for a work on political economy prior to ethology, contenting himself with emphasizing that political economy is a hypothetical science. Because its premises do not exhaust all the causes affecting the result, it can speak only about tendencies, not matters of fact.

He had learned economics four times over: from his father's lectures to him as a boy, from reading Ricardo, then directly from Adam Smith (whom he had scrutinized for errors in the light of Ricardo), and for the fourth time from James Mill's own *Elements of Political Economy*, which the Utilitarians had used as a text for discussion. He saw no need for radical innovations in the principles. But he did want to show how those principles looked when put in a proper setting, to instruct both those who rejected the principles on account of their context, and those who saw no reason for supplementing the abstract science. In short, Mill felt that political economy needed to be made less rigid and inhuman, and set himself to make it so. By adding other truths to which economists were strangers, Mill hoped 'to deduce conclusions capable of being of some use to the progress of mankind'.[2] He would write a book to replace Adam Smith, that would give the abstract science in its most complete form, incorporate all important improvements, and at the same time, by concentrating on applications, show the concrete consequences of the principles.

The right method was still, as he had explained in an earlier essay,[3] deductive for the most part, since the influences on economic phenomena were so various and complex that induction could produce nothing more than doubt-

[1] J. S. Mill, *Logic*, vol. II, p. 480.
[2] J. S. Mill, *Letters*, vol. I, p. 149 (Sept. 26, 1849).
[3] 'Political Economy—Nature and Method of Political Philosophy,' *Westminster Review*, Oct., 1836 reprinted in *Essays on Some Unsettled Questions of Political Economy* (London, 1944).

ful empirical generalizations. The principle of competition would also remain central, as economic laws prevailed only insofar as rents, profits, wages were determined by competition: 'Assume competition to be their exclusive regulator, and principles of broad generality and scientific precision may be laid down according to which they will be regulated'. But it was 'a great misconception' to think that competition actually had unlimited sway. In applying political economy to real life, one had to consider 'not only what will happen supposing the maximum of competition, but how far the result will be affected if competition falls short of the maximum'. Mill, himself, made no such detailed attempt, simply offering his observations as 'a general correction to be applied whenever relevant'.[1]

Nevertheless, the flavour of John Mill's political economy was very different from that of its predecessors. Even when the substantive changes seemed minor, they showed the effects of his new style of thinking. The first part, on the laws and condition of production, had nothing novel in it because there he believed himself to be dealing with something like physical truth. Whether or not men liked it so, their production was necessarily limited by 'the amount of their previous accumulation, and that being given, it will be proportional to their energy, their skill, the perfection of their machinery, and their judicious use of the advantages of combined labour'.[2] But the distribution of income and wealth was another matter.

Distribution depended on the opinions and feelings of mankind. Although, like everything else, opinions and feelings were governed by fundamental laws, they could vary, and therefore each age and country distributed its wealth differently. By calling the laws of both production and distribution economic laws, political economists had made it seem that nothing could change the manner in which goods were divided among labourers, capitalists, and landowners. Unlike his tutors, Mill felt that the way in which England distributed wealth was not the only or the best way. He had learned to think of the present state of economic organization as a stage on the road to better things. This constituted for him 'the properly human element' in his *Political Economy*,[3] the element of vision and sympathy missing in other economic treatises. It also helped to reconcile his enterprise with his ultimate interest in sociology. It was not 'anti-scientific', Mill explained, to treat political economy apart from sociology, as long as one carefully established 'the purely provisional character of any doctrine on industrial phenomena which leaves out of sight any general movement of humanity'.[4]

His new perspective led Mill also to include topics never before considered

[1] J. S. Mill, *Principles of Political Economy*, ed. by W. J. Ashley (London, 1909), pp. 242–3
[2] *Ibid.* p. 199.
[3] J. S. Mill, *Autobiography*, p. 175.
[4] Lévy-Bruhl, *Lettres Inédites de J. S. Mill á Comte*, p. 322.

part of scientific economics. They concerned the relation between economic arrangements and the character, taste, and abilities of a society. Mill refused to accept his predecessors' assumption that only the pursuit of wealth, isolated and abstracted from the whole, was relevant to economics as a science. He chose rather to dwell on the possibility that men might, indeed should, prefer other goods. Before discussing, for instance, the economic effects of peasant properties, he examined their moral and social influence, their value as an instrument of popular education, their effect on prudence, temperance, and self-control. And he concluded that the sorts of cares and anxieties besetting a peasant owner made him a superior being to the English day-labourer:

The mental faculties will be most developed where they are most exercised; and what gives more exercise to them than the having a multitude of interests, none of which can be neglected, and which can be provided for only by varied efforts of will and intelligence? . . . From the anxiety which chills and paralyses . . . few persons are more exempt. . . . His anxieties are the ordinary vicissitudes of more and less; his cares are that he takes his fair share of the business of life; that he is a free human being, and not perpetually a child. . . . He is no longer a being of a different order from the middle classes. . . .[1]

In addition, Mill felt obliged to point out that competition did not actually prevail in distribution. Economists neglected influences other than competition: 'They are apt to express themselves as if they thought that competition actually does, in all cases, whatever it can be shown to be the tendency of competition to do'.[2] The fact was, Mill found, that competition was so modern a phenomenon that until recently rents had been set by custom; and, still, there was often not only one price in a given market, as there ought to be under perfect competition, but several. As in so many other instances, Mill attributed to his tutors what they had never intended. With all his new human interests, he could not take for granted anything that had not been said explicitly. He confounded, as they had not, an abstract theory with a description of actual conditions. He did not consider, as they did, that as each was a separate and complicated task, it was less dangerous to treat them separately, and perhaps overlook some interactions, than to lose sight of the distinctions. But then it was painful for Mill, especially now with his emphasis on the whole truth, to recognize two equally valid, but different levels of discourse, a scientific and a historical, to admit one for some purposes but not for others. Such distinctions detracted more than Mill could bear from the indivisibility and perfection of the truth.

What was genuinely new in his outlook was summed up in his remarks on the stationary state. Whereas other economists had been worried by its economic effects, Mill was interested in another aspect:

[1] J. S. Mill, *Political Economy*, p. 286.
[2] *Ibid.* p. 242.

I am not charmed with the ideal of life held out by those who think that the normal state of human beings is that of struggling to get on; that the trampling, crushing, elbowing, and treading on each other's heels, which form the existing type of social life, are the most desirable lot of human kind, or anything but the disagreeable symptoms of one of the phases of industrial progress.[1]

The stationary state appeared to be the Nirvana Mill had always, though not openly, dreamt of: 'There would be as much scope as ever for all kinds of mental culture, and moral and social progress; as much room for improving the Art of Living, and much more likelihood of its being improved, when minds cease to be engrossed by the art of getting on.'[2]

These questions led to others about the new kinds of economic organization that the future might bring. That was the most important question of all. Mill had come to believe that no reasonable man could speculate on society without having a complete picture of an ideal society. Ever since he had begun to think about progress along Comte's lines, he had felt that the ideal society would consist of something better than a race divided into families ruled by a patriarchal despot. 'The aim of improvement should be not solely to place human beings in a condition in which they will be able to do without one another, but enable them to work with or for one another, in relations not involving dependence'.[3] Precisely what this implied Mill was not sure, although he tried to present his ideas on the subject in a chapter on 'The Probable Futurity of the Working Classes'. This chapter, along with the earlier one on property, made his book on political economy notorious, and with the benefit of Harriet's most minute attention, was revised in almost every edition.

With part of him, Mill dearly wished to believe that socialism in some form was possible. That seemed to fit in so well with his new style of thinking. But left to himself, his old training could not let him overlook the difficulties in the way of its realization. In the first edition, Mill argued that, 'In an age like the present, when a general reconsideration of all first principles is felt to be inevitable', the notion of making all land and instruments of production 'the joint property of the community' was bound to spread. He concluded, however, that while a small community might work on this principle, it was difficult to conceive of a large country as a single cooperative society. The aim then should be not to subvert the system of individual property, but to improve it by letting every member of the community share more of its benefits. This was, Mill hoped, a balanced statement on socialism that showed clearly his openness to alternative kinds of organization, even his dreams for the future, without proposing anything unworkable for the present.[4]

---

[1] *Ibid.* p. 748.
[3] *Ibid.* p. 763.
[2] *Ibid.* p. 751.
[4] *Ibid.* p. 217.

Many of his readers nevertheless misunderstood. From America, from Germany, he received letters or reviews praising him for his condemnation of socialism. His attempt to express 'temperately and argumentatively' his objections to socialism had blinded them, he discovered, to his respect and admiration for it, to his feeling that socialists were 'the greatest element of improvement in the present state of mankind'.[1] He was far from intending his objections to the best-known socialist extremes to mean, he explained patiently to his correspondents, that he condemned socialism 'as an ultimate result of human improvement'. He had emphasized the defects only to point out the 'unprepared state of the labouring classes, and their extreme moral unfitness at present for the rights which Socialism would confer and the duties it would impose'.[2] Partly to refute these misinterpretations, partly urged on by Harriet, who, as always, could see no point in his hesitations and qualifications, the third edition was significantly revised. The emphasis fell rather on making mankind fit to live in a 'state of society combining the greatest personal freedom with that just distribution which the present laws of property do not profess to aim at'.[3] He whittled away the argument that under socialism productivity would be low; he put more stock in the value of public spirit as an incentive; he withdrew the Malthusian argument. The chapter on 'Property' became more clearly an argument against private enterprise, if not unequivocally for socialism, and the only obstacle left was 'the backward state of morals and education'.

What precisely Mill meant by socialism, whether a centralized organization run by an all-powerful state, or more nearly a form of syndicalism, was not quite clear. The chapter on the 'Future of the Labouring Classes', almost dictated by Mrs Taylor, suggested the latter. But many state socialists adopted Mill as one of their party. Certainly Mill had not, with his usual thoroughness, thought through the details of the socialist state. It was rather a shadowy vision that he liked to contemplate from time to time without committing himself too firmly. When his first statement was repeated too vociferously by one party, he tried to redress the balance by pointing out the benefits of socialism. He reluctantly accepted the positive statements insisted on by Harriet. Although he never gainsaid her opinion, after her death, when less harassed, he restated his opinions with the fuzziness nicely restored. To some, the discussion of incentive in the posthumous chapters on socialism, the remarks on the dangers to liberty seemed to tip the scales once more against socialism. Perhaps, even if that was a misapprehension, in the end that satisfied Mill better than the other sort of misunderstanding. For despite

[1] J. S. Mill, *Letters*, vol. I, p. 138 (Nov., 1848).
[2] *Ibid.* p. 168 (March 18, 1852).
[3] Preface to 3rd edition.

his revolutionary ardour, his enthusiasm over 1848 in France, though he occasionally enjoyed saying extreme things, he did not really want to see England's social system overturned at once. He liked to think of himself as ready to accept such a change, but there were many reasons why it had best be delayed a while.

He had nevertheless made a revolution, not by what he said about economics or economic organization, but by what he implied about the role of the social scientist in politics. What he had said in the *Logic* suggested that the economist should only sparingly, if at all, abstract from the complex realities of actual life, that he should deal with men as they really are, moved by diverse motives and influenced by the actual conditions of their society. In the *Political Economy*, Mill did draw a clear line between the scientific and practical part of economics, in order to dissociate economics from some of the policies his former colleagues had advocated. But at the same time, he encouraged the notion, developed on the Continent more than in England, that the economist *qua* economist must not merely analyse the motives and effects of economic activity, but must also weigh and compare the moral merits of different economic policies. The economist was not only given leave but obliged to discuss the effects on justice and morality as well as the economic aspects of the production and distribution of wealth. He had to set forth an idea of economic development, keeping in view the intellectual and moral, as well as the material ends of life, and to discuss the ways and means—such as strengthening right motives, spreading sound customs and habits in industrial life, direct intervention by the State—of achieving that ideal.

By requiring the economist as such to speak on political and moral issues, Mill suggested that there was a connection between his competence as an economist and as a moralist and politician. Unlike Adam Smith, Mill never distinguished between 'What is properly called political economy', a science that 'treats of the nature and causes of the wealth of nations', and the tasks of civil government.[1] Mill was an economist more nearly like the Physiocrats whom Smith had rebuked for failing to make this distinction. What was even more radical for Bentham's heir was the implication that as moral and political questions were within the province of the economist, they were not properly in the realm of common sense or political wisdom to decide. They became instead the business of the expert and beyond the ordinary man, matters of science, not prudence.

In this way, John Mill carried a faith in the unity of theory and practice much further than James Mill had. The verdicts of a theoretician of James Mill's sort, who concerned himself with limited, well-defined subjects, were easy to disqualify on the grounds that they took so little into account. Or,

---

[1] Adam Smith, *Wealth of Nations* (Modern Library ed.), p. 643.

such a theoretician, himself, might have said, as early classical economists were wont to do, 'I shall show you the consequences of this sort of behaviour. I leave you to decide how far the behaviour of the men you are considering corresponds to it'. But a theoretician such as John Mill described, who is obliged to consider the whole, ethical as well as scientific questions, must either be allowed to decide all, or be completely repudiated. He does not merely complement, he absorbs the role of the ordinary politician.

This view of the social scientist had more radical implications for politics than anything Mill had believed in his early enthusiasm. What these were, Mill explained some years later in his *Considerations on Representative Government* (1861). Ever since his disillusion with utilitarianism, he had been thinking about the difficulties of combining popular government with rule by those who knew best. In his first article on Tocqueville, three years after the first Reform Bill, he had predicted that

the grand difficulty in politics will for a long time be, how best to conciliate the two greatest elements on which good government depends; to combine the greatest amount of the advantage derived from the independent judgement of the specially instructed few, with the greatest degree of the security for rectitude of purpose derived from rendering those few responsible to the many.[1]

Then he had felt that there was a simple solution: The people need not be wise themselves if only they were 'duly sensible of the value of superior wisdom'. They had only to understand that they must exercise their judgement not upon issues but upon the people they chose to decide for them: 'They would then select as their representatives those whom the general voice of the instructed pointed out as the *most* instructed'.[2]

It had since become clear, however, that the legislators chosen by the people were not likely to be all that wise or knowledgeable. With talk of further reform to widen the suffrage, the problem became more pressing. Moreover, now that Mill saw clearly how far social science might go, the distinction between those who knew — the scientifically trained experts — and the public had grown sharper.

The solution he eventually adopted was first suggested publicly by Edwin Chadwick, a friend of Mill's and Bentham's last secretary. In a speech before the Society for the Amendment of the Law in 1859, Chadwick declared that since the House of Commons often mutilated whatever good legislation came before it, its power ought to be limited to approving or rejecting measures presented for its consideration. These should be prepared by standing committees, one for each type of legislative inquiry, supplemented by subordinate

---

[1] J. S. Mill, *Dissertations and Discussions* (London, 1867), vol I, p. 469.
[2] *Ibid.* p. 470.

commissions of scholars and eminent men who would investigate the facts without reference to public feelings, and reach impartial conclusions.[1] This was very like what Chadwick had already told Prince Albert when he had advised him that the sole function of cabinet ministers should be to supervise and defend 'the specialists, the chief permanent officers'.[2] When Chadwick's paper was published, Mill added a commendatory preface; two years later he incorporated and extended Chadwick's argument in his own book on representative government.

It was common to taunt representative assemblies, he observed there, with being places of mere 'talk and bavardage'. He himself had thought so once. But now he realized that representative assemblies should talk, indeed that they should only talk. They went wrong only when they refused to recognize that 'talking and discussing' was their proper business, since 'doing, as the result of discussion is the task not of a miscellaneous body, but of individuals especially trained to it'. Doing should be left to 'those high public officers who really conduct the public business'; parliament must choose them carefully, but having chosen, it must not interfere with them except by unlimited latitude of suggestion and criticism and by applying or withholding the final seal of national assent.[3] Mill meant not simply that parliament should refrain from interfering with the administration of laws, or that it should call in outside advisers, but that it should not even try to write the laws. This he felt was the main contribution of his scheme for representative government. His hope was to see a legislative commission become a permanent part of the constitution; when parliament decided a law was needed it would turn the work over to this commission. Once the bill was drawn up, parliament might reject or accept it, but would never tamper with it directly; at most it might send the amendments proposed as suggestions for the commission to consider.

Mill's scheme for a legislative commission was far more radical than anything tried before. Expert advice on laws was an old recourse: advisory commissions had become common since the twenties; a parliamentary counsel helped to write Pitt's financial bills; and in 1837, the Home Office, which was responsible for initiating most legislation, appointed an official counsel to aid in drawing up bills. In 1869, there was established an Office of Parliamentary Counsel to the Treasury, with Thring as Parliamentary Counsel, and an assistant and office staff to aid him. But even this was not what Mill had in mind. It was, for one thing, too informal, and too vague. Besides, the use of such advisors could not accomplish what he was most interested in securing —preventing parliament from interfering in law making. It would not help

---

[1] B. W. Richardson, *The Health of Nations* (London, 1877), vol. I, pp. 133 f.

[2] Letter on the Civil Service to the Prince Consort, in Samuel Edward Finer, *Chadwick* (London, 1952), p. 479.

[3] J. S. Mill, *Representative Government* (Oxford, 1947), pp. 173-4.

much to call on experts if afterwards their work could be mauled about by uninformed members of parliament.

In his *Autobiography*, Mill tried to make it clear that what he proposed in *Representative Government* was as yet untried.[1] He emphasized that he wished quite literally to separate the task of legislation from the task of approval 'by disjoining the office of control and criticism from the actual conduct of affairs, and devolving the former on the representatives of the Many, while securing for the latter, under strict responsibility to the nation, the acquired knowledge and practiced intelligence of a specially trained and experienced Few'.[2] Mill's scheme was very different also from what Bagehot proposed later, under the name of 'deferential democracy', where 'certain persons are by common consent agreed to be wiser than others and their opinion is, by common consent, to rank for much more than its numerical value'.[3] Those men to whom Mill wished the rest to defer were not aristocrats, or men merely of education and sense, but scientists who understood the laws governing human character and how to apply them under various circumstances. Their counsel would not be merely superior opinion; it would carry more than the weight of experience and wisdom. It would be proven scientific knowledge that none but the ignorant would presume to question.

[1] J. S. Mill, *Autobiography*, pp. 185-6.
[2] J. S. Mill, *Representative Government*, p. 174.
[3] Walter Bagehot, *The English Constitution* (London, 1900), pp. 159-60.

CHAPTER XXV

LIBERTY AND THE IDEAL INDIVIDUAL

THE MID-VICTORIAN CALM

WHILE Mill was meditating on the possibility of discovering and applying scientific truth about men and society, the agitated England he had known as a young Radical was growing more sedate. By the time the *Political Economy* was published in 1848, England was well on the way to the 'age of Bagehot and Trollope', the time when England seemed to have emerged permanently from dreams and nightmares into a mature, confident serenity. The country was permeated by a sense of satisfaction, Bagehot declared, 'because most of the country feels it has got the precise thing which suits it'.

The calm was founded on considerable prosperity. Trade flourished, and the superiority of English manufacturers was for the moment without challenge. Although agriculture was still troubled, by the end of 1851, after a good harvest, there was reason to hope for that agricultural revival that, encouraged by the growth of industry and the opening of the railroads, persisted during the next decade. The interests of landlords and captains of industry, of masters and men were for the moment in harmony; the 'condition of England' question that had so plagued the 'forties no longer seemed so important. The Oxford, Chartist, and Free Trade movements, the agitation for the repeal of the Corn Laws, all belonged to the past. The last Chartist demonstration in England, in 1848, turned out to be mainly a festival in celebration of England's escape from continental revolutions, and old Chartists took to lecturing on Christian evidences. For the moment, both the ambitions of the poor and the conscience of the rich were more or less at rest, and improvements were urged in gentle, apologetic, almost supplicating terms. Instead of struggles over constitutional and social changes, there were mainly political manoeuvres and skirmishes between pressure groups— between the vested interests of private water companies and the General Board of Health, or between those who favoured the new tax on houses and those who clung to the old window tax. All this peace and self-satisfaction were suitably proclaimed to the world in the Great Exhibition of '51 with the Crystal Palace displaying England's wares to dazzled crowds and declaring, by its very architecture and all the objects produced by 'mechanical ingenuity', the ascendancy of the middle classes and the rising of the artisans.

The whole country was becoming middle class and comfortable. The upper classes were taking their cue from the Queen and the Prince Consort, who were the model of a respectable middle class family, thoroughly at home in South Kensington. The working class, too, admired moderation and propriety—the Amalgamated Society of Engineers declared that its object was to do nothing 'illegally or indiscreetly . . . but on all occasions to perform the greatest amount of benefit for ourselves, without injury to others'. Everyone was finding life richer and easier. The middle class family could boast of carpets and hangings, plate and linen, luxuries that had been rare in earlier decades even among squires. Merchants and manufacturers became country gentlemen, married into the older aristocracy, and sent their sons to a public school.

The spirit of mid-Victorian England was summed up in the public schools, where the nation's gentlemen were being moulded into an obvious uniformity. The model became Rugby, where Arnold very successfully put into practice his belief, shared by many decent Englishmen, that the school was a training ground for character, 'a temple of industrious peace'. Not that Arnold wished to denigrate intellectual ability. But for the moment intellect seemed more plentiful than the character demanded by the times, and the fear of Mephistopheles had the upper hand. Later in the century there was to be a reaction against Arnold's 'well-groomed, well-mannered rational manly boys, all taking the same view of things, all doing the same things', but for the moment, Arnold's pupils were becoming masters and housemasters of schools where boys of all sorts were being transformed into 'Christian gentlemen'.

Even in religion, ardour seemed to have vanished. Evangelicalism was no longer at war with indifference or brutality. It had grown 'complacent, fashionable, and superior'. The only religious crises were over a supposed threat from Rome, but this was as nothing to the old soul-saving enthusiasm of the 'money-making witness-bearers'. Piety was now expressed in a scholarly manner, by worldly men like Peel and Gladstone.[1] What was lacking in ardour was made up for by respectability: 'Milman is ostracized for calling Abraham a sheik; Miss Mitford is publicly reproved for calling a pudding a rolypoly; old lords have to guard their words for fear of shocking young lords, and a Member of Parliament wishing to say contracted pelvis must put it in the decent obscurity of learned language . . .'.[2] Everyone was being exceedingly respectable.

In politics this meant that most reasonable men of the time felt that the politician was seeing things in their just proportions when he was entirely absorbed in providing sound leadership and decent administration. The best statesman was not one who tried to make England great by grand improve-

---

[1] G. M. Young, *Portrait of an Age* (London, 1949), pp. 4–5.

[2] *Ibid.* pp. 17–18. Cf. also Asa Briggs, *The Age of Improvement* for the 'age of Trollope and Bagehot'.

ments, but who believed, as we are told in the *Prime Minister*, in 'men rather than in measures', and worried mainly about holding his own in any personal conflict—'Your man with a thin skin, a vehement ambition, a scrupulous conscience, and a sanguine desire for rapid improvement, is never a happy and seldom a fortunate Politician'.[1] Parliament's first duty was thought to be, as Bagehot said, the executive management of the state; secondly came the importance of its debates for political education; and last, its legislative work.

By these standards, Palmerston was an ideal politician. He survived the Radical attacks and the loss of his own majority, and from 1859 to 65 ruled as Prime Minister over a powerful coalition of Whigs, ex-Peelites, and Radicals, the forerunner of Gladstone's Liberal Party. He was graceful, aristocratic, and sage, but not a brilliant statesman. If earlier in his career he had been admired for his bold policies, now it was his reasonableness and good temper that impressed the public. Trollope and Bagehot approved of him precisely because he was not too extraordinary. He was 'by no means a man of genius, and was possessed of not more than ordinary gifts of talent',[2] Trollope pointed out. He had only the business capacity of a first-rate man, but the creed of a second-rate man.[3] Just because of this he appealed to the 'common, sensible, uncommitted' mass of the nation, who 'have something to lose, who have no intention of losing it, who hate change, who love improvement, who will be ruled in a manner they understand'.[4] Palmerston concentrated on what was wanted and was practicable at the moment, and was never tempted by grand, comprehensive principles. As a foreign minister he was less effective than he might have been, for although he listened carefully to everything, he never really understood anything new. Yet this very lack of imagination that led him to pursue only common objects made him fitting for his age. For the country was ready to let things go their way, with but a slight urging in one direction or another, as the moment might seem to require.

That the mid-Victorians were stodgy, even their admirers recognized. But they were thankful for the benefits of dullness. Bagehot explained that what was called stupidity, though admittedly not a boon in common society, was Nature's favourite device for preserving steady conduct and stable opinion. The dullness meant that the country was too quiet to accept sweeping innovations, and yet too reasonable to eschew all changes. It meant that opportunity for advancement was balanced by social order, that every class accepted its lot, while each individual tried constantly, by the virtuous use of his faculties, to better himself. It was because of this that instead of the harsh police laws

---

[1] Anthony Trollope, *The Prime Minister*, vol. I, ch. XI.
[2] Anthony Trollope, *Lord Palmerston* (English Men of Letters Series), p. 9.
[3] Bagehot, *Works*, vol. II, p. 183.
[4] *Ibid.* vol. X, pp. 388–9.

and interference with private order prevailing on the continent, in England a mild social discipline sufficed to maintain the necessary rules, while deference to social superiors and respect for established institutions safeguarded parliamentary democracy.

To John Stuart Mill, who could still remember the excitement of the old days, when he and his friends coolly awaited the downfall of aristocracy, Church, and state, the calm looked like stagnation and dead conformity. He could find nothing interesting in a man like Palmerston, who certainly bore no resemblance to 'the fancied portrait of an ideal statesman laying down in his closet plans to be worked out twenty years hence'; as he was nothing but 'a statesman for the moment',[1] in Mill's eyes, Palmerston was hardly a thinking man. The reasonable tone of Palmerstonian politics made it boring to Mill. Even the events of the 'forties had not tempted him into renewing his interest in England's affairs. The Corn Law agitation, Peel and his shifts took up no space in his letters, and he emerged only at the time of the French Revolution of 1848, to defend it to his old friends, the Austins, who had by then grown so conservative that they could see nothing but the horrors of the revolution.

Indeed all the Radicals had in one way or another retired. Grote was writing his history, Roebuck had become so patriotic that he was all for bombarding Naples, while Bowring actually did bombard Canton. Nowhere could Mill find any sign of the exuberance and excitement of those glorious days when Utilitarians clashed with Coleridgeans, when friendships were threatened by a preference for Byron or for Wordsworth, when disciples of Carlyle crept furtively to Highgate to be thrilled by Coleridge. Nothing seemed to be left but respectability, Sabbath observance, discipline in the home, regularity in business. There were no schools or sects, no great men and devoted followers.

The creative energies of the time flowed in more private channels. Darwin was working quietly at home, mostly alone and not generally recognized until he burst upon the world; Dickens, soon to be followed by the great Victorian novelists, was turning out novels that were read by high and low, and had no small influence, but not in the name of any doctrine; the pre-Raphaelites were a small heterogeneous band with no single aim, just common aspirations; Ruskin lectured at his Working Men's College, but his closest approach to becoming a leader with disciples was his group of students building a road in Oxford to prove their love and capacity for work. There were originals, even eccentrics, but they were artists, like Swinburne, who were unknown to the public at large, and also to Mill. So in the year that saw the publication of the *Origin of Species, Adam Bede*, and *A Tale of Two Cities*, Mill declared that genius in England was dead.

---

[1] *Ibid.* vol. IV, p. 330.

Even if John Mill had been more aware of what was going on in out of the way houses and chambers, he would not have found it very exciting. He had grown up to associate vigour and genius with leading, or at least enrolling in, some great crusade for the advancement of mankind. Lone critics who poked here and there but proposed no universal programme, scientists who tried to deny or soften any social implications of their theories, artists who did not inspire great controversies or infatuations were no substitute. He had not lost his veneration for practical action in the cause of progress. Even later in his life he could not agree with John Morley's enthusiasm for Victor Hugo because the novelist had 'not brought forward one single practical proposal for the improvement of the society against which he is incessantly thundering'.[1]

The ideals of the age seemed to Mill negative and passive—too sicklied over by a Christian veneration of 'innocence rather than nobleness, abstinence from evil, rather than energetic pursuit of good'. He believed, perhaps more than ever before, that England needed a violent revolution 'in order to give that general shake-up to the torpid mind of the nation which the French Revolution gave to Continental Europe'. Unfortunately, England had never had 'any general break-up of old associations, and hence the extreme difficulty of getting any ideas into its stupid head'.[2] When in 1851, he was asked his opinion on a prospectus of a revived *Westminster Review*, he took issue with the statement that 'strength and durability are the result only of a slow and peaceful development'. Quite the contrary, Mill said, he believed that 'changes effected rapidly and by force are often the only ones which in given circumstances would be permanent'. Neither would he agree that the government ought merely to reflect the average intellect and virtue of the people; on that doctrine, he said, there would never have been a Reformation, a Commonwealth, or the Revolution of 1688—'the stupidity and habitual indifference of the mass of mankind would bear down by its dead weight all the efforts of the more intelligent and active-minded few.'[3]

While on the one hand, England seemed by Mill's standards to have settled into a stupid torpor, on the other hand he saw a new, and not altogether salutary, spirit of philanthropy breaking down the old respect for the individual's freedom. Protective legislation appeared at an ever accelerating rate. It was cumbrous and not very effective legislation, but it marked the beginning of controls unknown before in the modern world. It was supplemented by innumerable philanthropic organizations, often doing good to someone without asking for that someone's leave. The cant still belonged to an earlier period. Members of parliament agreed that 'legislative interference

---

[1] *Fortnightly Review*, xv, Jan., 1874, p. 9.
[2] J. S. Mill, *Letters*, vol. I, p. 131 (April 13, 1847).
[3] *Ibid.* pp. 162–3 (June 9, 1851).

is an evil'. But having said so, they voted for the factory acts. It was clear to anyone who looked that the old suspicion of government and the traditional insistence on self-reliance were retreating. Although Mill favoured most of the legislation and philanthropy, he saw in them a tendency that would soon need to be checked: 'opinion tends to encroach more and more on liberty', he wrote to Harriet, 'and almost all the projects of social reformers of these days are really liberticide'.[1]

For something like two decades, he had been reacting against his father's narrow theories of government; he had enlarged politics to sociology and attacked the simple-minded Benthamite notion that each man knew his own interest best. The time had come to turn back. He himself had perhaps gone too far in his new enthusiasms. His habit, by now firmly established, of balancing the boxes, and maintaining symmetry in his opinions and writings, bade him look to the other side. More than ever, he believed that truth was a matter of reconciling and combining opposites, that one had always to foster that side which was at the moment less popular, and so protect those interests likely to be neglected. In any case, he had nowhere fully explained one aspect of his new creed, his enthusiasm for the pagan ideal of self-development, which he had discovered through his German reading. Besides, his notions of virtue and conformity had been affected by his unconventional friendship with Harriet, and the disapproval he had felt among his friends and family. The morality of the age was too ascetic, fostering a 'pinched and hidebound type of character'. He had come to see, and wanted to tell others, that 'pagan self-assertion' must complement Christian self-denial, that the Greek ideal of self-development must be blended with the Platonic and Christian ideal of self-government, that if God created man, he gave him faculties to be cultivated and unfolded, not rooted out. It was time, as well, to recall those utilitarian ideals that had after all stayed with him, to declare his opposition to Comtist politics which had by now shown all its colours, and to reconcile and integrate with all this his persisting horror of the coarse-booted multitude trampling down genius.

What looked to Bagehot and Trollope like admirable serenity, deference, and social discipline meant to Mill 'living under a hostile censorship',[2] a supine dependence on what other people thought, an eagerness to do nothing but what was socially acceptable. Men no longer thought, he lamented, about what they preferred, or what would develop the highest in them, but only about what was suitable to their position. Mill saw those Englishmen praised by others for their common sense as benighted creatures using nothing but the lowest, ape-like faculties of imitation. Their moderation suggested to him

[1] F. A. Hayek, *John Stuart Mill and Harriet Taylor* (London, 1951), p. 216 (Jan. 15, 1855).
[2] J. S. Mill, *On Liberty* (Oxford, 1947), p. 54.

only that England no longer had men of vigorous reason and strong feelings who could lead her to noble things. Both his new views, that made him long for big and grand visions, and his old Benthamite belief in the value of individual liberty prevented him from finding anything very laudable in the restrained paternalism of his day. There was even something ominous in it.

ON LIBERTY

While in Rome in 1855, he began to plan a volume on liberty. Harriet had, some years before, written an essay on tolerance; he himself had written a number of short papers on related subjects—on *Genius*, on *Civilization*, on *The Spirit of the Age*, as well as an unpublished one on liberty; it now seemed fitting that he and Harriet should cram 'as much as possible of what we wish not to leave unsaid' into a complete statement on the subject.[1] The result was an essay which is the most famous of Mill's works, but above all, a perfect expression of his new creed, that was to guide the mainstream of English thought after him. It is carefully reasoned, and in some ways admirably lucid, yet its central message is by no means perfectly clear. So subtly is it woven, that the pattern almost escapes detection. Not that Mill meant to write an esoteric essay, for what he made most evident was, as he expected, most offensive to his contemporaries. The intricacies of *On Liberty* simply reflect the complexity of Mill's own thought, which had by then taken in, altered, and created more than he himself realized.

But on the surface, *On Liberty* is simply an ardent and persuasive argument for the most unhindered individualism. While the problem of political liberty, that is, freedom from the tyranny of government, was no longer an issue in England, Mill declared, the yoke of opinion was even heavier than in other countries. This might in time lead again to political tyranny as well, when the majority learned to think of government as its own. But for the moment the pressing problem was the tyranny of public opinion, imposed through custom, enforcing the ideas and practices of the majority on all. The purpose of the essay was therefore to assert that, 'There is a limit to the legitimate interference of collective opinion with individual independence . . .'.[2] and to help stem the tide that was inclined to 'stretch unduly the powers of society over the individual'.[3]

Mill's arguments for liberty of thought were already familiar to his readers. They are mainly those of James Mill, emphasizing that free competition among various ideas of truth is the only means of discovering truth. Mill

---

[1] Hayek, *Mill and Taylor*, pp. 216, 223.
[2] J. S. Mill, *On Liberty*, p. 4.
[3] *Ibid.* p. 12.

probably felt he was contributing something original by saying that conflicting doctrines might share the truth, which expressed his new many-sidedness —'Truth in the great practical concerns of life, is so much a question of the reconciling and combining of opposites that very few have minds sufficiently capacious and impartial to make the adjustment with an approach to correctness, and it has to be made by the rough process of a struggle between combatants fighting under hostile banners'.[1] He also emphasized, as his father had not, the beneficent effects on character and conduct of having truth contested.

When he went on to discuss the nature of individuality, to plead for pagan self-assertion, to defend eccentricity, Mill exposed himself most to public disapproval. Here he reverted more than once to pure Benthamite language— 'neither one person, nor any number of persons is warranted in saying to another human creature of ripe years, that he shall not do with his life for his own benefit what he chooses to do with it. He is the person most interested in his own wellbeing . . .'.[2] It is impossible for custom to determine what is right for all, Mill argued in orthodox fashion, either because it may be built on too narrow an experience to include this particular area, or because its established interpretation may not fit him—'Customs are made for customary circumstances and customary characters; and his circumstances or his character may be uncustomary'.[3] His father's puritan morality seemed to be renounced, for Mill declared himself against asceticism, against an exaggerated horror of sensuality, of passion, impulse, and feeling, against all attempts to impose a puritanical code of morals such as prohibition of alcohol, or Sabbatarianism, and he roundly condemned 'the fanatical moral intolerance of the Puritans'.[4]

Some of the implications Mill drew for the practical management of society were far from the 'socialism' of his *Political Economy*. He declared himself strongly against a monopoly of education by the state: universal state education was bound to become a contrivance for moulding people into uniformity, and 'as the mould in which it casts them is that which pleases the predominant power in the government whether this be a monarch, priesthood, an aristocracy, or the majority of the existing generation; in proportion as it is efficient and successful, it establishes a despotism over the mind, leading by natural tendency, to one over the body'.[5] The government should leave parents to choose the means of education, contenting itself with giving them financial help where needed and possibly establishing a few institu-

[1] *Ibid.* p. 42.
[2] *Ibid.* p. 68.
[3] *Ibid.* p. 51.
[4] *Ibid.* p. 74.
[5] *Ibid.* p. 95.

tions of education to act as a stimulus and competition for private ones, which should, however, remain predominant. In other spheres, too, Mill denied the value of government interference, mainly along Bentham's lines, and often with the same vigour. He urged 'the greatest dissemination of power consistent with efficiency; but the greatest possible centralisation of information and diffusion of it from the centre',[1] a rule that Bentham would have approved.

But above all, Mill wanted to make clear 'two maxims which together form the entire doctrine of this essay, and to assist the judgement in holding the balance between them in the cases where it appears doubtful which of them is applicable to the case'. These maxims were, first,

that the individual is not accountable to society for his actions in so far as these concern the interests of no person but himself. Advice, instruction, persuasion, and avoidance by other people, if thought necessary by them for their own good, are the only measures by which society can justifiably express its dislike or disapprobation of his conduct.

Secondly, to balance the first, 'for such actions as are prejudicial to the interests of others, the individual is accountable and may be subjected either to social or to legal punishment if society is of opinion that the one or the other is requisite for its protection'.[2] The point was the notorious distinction between self-regarding actions and actions affecting others.

On Liberty was read by everyone, and though admired by many, was also widely attacked as a defence of libertarianism. The opposition he aroused confirmed Mill's feelings that his contemporaries had little love for liberty. The vulgar declared that Mr Mill was advocating drunkenness and fornication, certainly attacking Christianity, and generally urging depravity in the name of idealism. More sophisticated critics like James Fitzjames Stephen found that Mill had no understanding of either the requirements of social order or the resilience of genius. Most men, Stephen argued, were incapable of deciding their way of life for themselves, and needed the aid of custom. Those who wished to go their own way, if they were indeed men of genius, would only be strengthened by the need to weather opposition from public opinion. Without coercion of some sort, there could be neither education nor morality; parents must decide for their children, legislators and founders of great institutions must do the same for the world at large.

Stephen also pointed out the weakness that has since exposed Mill's essay to the most damaging criticism—the difficulty of distinguishing between acts that affect only the doer and those that affect society as well. All acts are social in some way, Stephen maintained, and are therefore subject to coercion

[1] *Ibid.* pp. 102–3.
[2] *Ibid.* p. 84.

by society. The only question is whether and in what form coercion is expedient. Since Stephen, it has been made abundantly clear, perhaps mostly by those who claimed to be following Mill, that his principle designed to protect individuality could easily justify very liberal invasions of privacy.

Nevertheless, Mill gave his readers good reason to conclude that he had made his way back to the easy-going tolerance of Hume and Bentham. However odd the route he had taken, he might seem to have come to rest in a house much more gracious than his father's, and yet very different from any of the foreign establishments he had visited on the way. But in fact *On Liberty* included much more. It was not the classic defence of individualism it was taken to be. It did not signify either a return to Benthamism or a rejection of the sentiments declared in *The Spirit of the Age*. It defended an individualism very different from Bentham's.

The difference appears in the theme of *On Liberty*. It is progress at least as much as liberty. As one of Mill's more perceptive disciples, John Morley, pointed out: 'the idea of perfectibility . . . is the key alike of the *Liberty*, the *Utilitarianism* and some of the most original chapters on the *Political Economy*'.[1] Mill's interest in liberty did not reflect a view of civilization as an unending conversation, as permanent as men because each will inevitably discover different aspects of the truth, indeed different truths. Instead he saw in the distance the light of perfection—'as mankind improve, the number of doctrines which are no longer disputed or doubted will be constantly on the increase: and the wellbeing of mankind may almost be measured by the number and gravity of the truths which have reached the point of being uncontested'.[2] The advent of the great day seemed so likely that he worried about how one could arrange for truth to be contested, so as to provide mental exercise when controversy would no longer be needed to establish truth. It was in order to speed the ultimate capture of truth that Mill was so anxious to secure liberty. He granted that perhaps liberty and progress were not always identical, because improvement may be achieved under coercion and liberty may temporarily ally itself with reaction, but 'the only unfailing and permanent source of improvement is liberty'. The real problem was to break the sway of custom so as to make room for progress; it was liberty as the antagonist of custom that he wished to defend: 'the progressive principle . . . whether as the love of liberty or of improvement, is antagonistic to the sway of Custom'.[3]

Mill was aware of the fact emphasized by Stephen that most men found custom indispensable. But when he declared that, 'where not the person's own

[1] *Fortnightly Review*, vol. xvi, 1874, p. 648.
[2] J. S. Mill, *On Liberty*, p. 38.
[3] *Ibid.* p. 50.

character but the traditions or customs of other people are the rule of conduct there is wanting one of the principal ingredients of human happiness, and quite the chief ingredient of individual and social progress',[1] he was not thinking of the mass of ordinary human beings. *On Liberty* was not a defence of the common man's right to live as he liked; it was more nearly an attack on him. In a fairly harsh passage Mill made his antagonism clear:

'In sober truth, whatever homage may be professed, or even paid, to real or supposed mental superiority, the general tendency of things throughout the world is to render mediocrity the ascendant power among mankind. In ancient history, in the Middle Ages, and in a diminishing degree through the long transition from feudality to the present time, the individual was a power in himself; and if he had either great talents or a high social position, he was a considerable power. At present individuals are lost in the crowd. In politics, it is almost a triviality to say that public opinion now rules the world. The only power deserving the name is that of masses, and of governments while they make themselves the organ of the tendencies and instincts of masses. This is as true in the moral and social relations of private life as in public transactions. Those whose opinions go by the name of public opinion are not always the same sort of public: in America they are the whole white population; in England, chiefly the middle class. But they are always a mass, that is to say, a collective mediocrity. And what is a still greater novelty, the mass do not now take their opinions from dignitaries in Church or State, from ostensible leaders, or from books. Their thinking is done for them by men much like themselves, addressing them or speaking in their name, on the spur of the moment, through the newspapers. I am not complaining of all this. I do not assert that anything better is compatible, as a general rule, with the present low state of the human mind. But that does not hinder the government of mediocrity from being mediocre government. No government by a democracy or a numerous aristocracy, either in its political acts, or in the opinions, qualities, and tone of mind which it fosters, ever did or could rise above mediocrity except in so far as the sovereign Many have let themselves be guided (which in their best times they always have done) by the counsels and influence of a more highly gifted and instructed *one* or *few*. . . . I am not countenancing the sort of 'hero-worship' which applauds the strong man of genius for forcibly seizing on the government of the world and making it do his bidding in spite of itself. All he can claim is freedom to point out the way.[2]

Mill was not concerned about the merely odd man, who might be without great gifts, or an opium-eater, a sot, a poet in a trance; he was indifferent to the ordinary eccentric whom Bentham wanted to save from his righteous neighbours. Only an eccentric in the most literal sense, that is, someone who moved in circles much larger than those travelled by punier souls, interested Mill. It was the man of genius whom the many threatened. For they are not only conventional, but also inferior and jealous of their betters: 'Persons of genius are, *ex vi termini*, more individual than other people—less capable

[1] *Ibid.* pp. 62–3.
[2] *Ibid.* pp. 58–9.

consequently, of fitting themselves, without hurtful compression, into any one of these moulds, which society provides in order to save its members the trouble of forming their own character'.[1]

More than great gifts distinguishes the man of genius under Mill's protection. He is not merely superior. He is an ideal individual, better able than others to discover the true ideal and to pursue it. He can lead ordinary men to better things:

If from timidity they [persons of genius] consent to be forced into one of these moulds, and to let all that part of themselves which cannot expand under the pressure remain unexpanded, society will be little the better for their genius. If they are of a strong character and break their fetters, they become a mark for the society which has not succeeded in reducing them to commonplace, to point out with solemn warning as 'wild', 'erratic', and the like—much as if one should complain of the Niagara river for not flowing smoothly between its banks like a Dutch canal.[2]

The freedom of the man of genius to be himself is essential to progress because he sets the ideal that all men ought to emulate. And precisely what this ideal meant was made perfectly plain by Mill in a number of contexts. Indeed the image of the ideal individual haunts everything he wrote.

First of all, Mill's ideal individual self-consciously chooses for himself how he will live. He does not let his actions or his character be influenced by others, whether through custom or otherwise. Nor is he led by his tastes. He surveys all the alternatives before him and chooses with a clear perception of the reasons for his choice. He can explain his aspirations, the ends of his conduct and their relation to one another, clearly and unambiguously. He is a man who makes full use of all his powers, especially the highest, reason: 'He who lets the world, or his own portion of it, choose his plan of life for him has no need of any other faculty than the ape-like one of imitation. He who chooses his plan for himself employs all his faculties'.[3]

Secondly, the ideal individual relies on his will to make certain of his faculties dominant over the rest. The pinched ascetic of low energy and mild feelings and no unruly urges was not in the least to Mill's taste. His old notion of human nature as divided between reason and passions that had to be subdued seemed as true as ever. He had only modified it to mean that whereas in better men the passions were stronger than in ordinary persons, they were also more firmly controlled by a heroic will. Thus Mill could argue that the same

[1] *Ibid.* pp. 58–9.
[2] *Ibid.* pp. 58–9.
[3] *Ibid.* p. 52.

energy which produces strong susceptibilities also generates 'the most passionate love of virtue and the sternest self-control. . .'.[1] Strong passions under the governance of a strong will are the mark of a superior individual.

Nature was still the enemy, just as it had been for James Mill. 'Follow with earnestness the path into which it [your individuality] impels you', John Mill wrote to Sterling, but 'taking Reason for your Safety Lamp, and perpetually warring with Inclination, then you will attain to that Freedom which results only from obedience to Right and Reason . . .'.[2] In his essay on *Nature*, written between the *Political Economy* and *On Liberty*, he declared that natural men are inevitably liars, unclean and cowardly, and that hardly 'a single point of excellence in human character' is not 'decidedly repugnant to the untutored feelings of human nature'. The natural instincts of the race, though useful for perpetuating it, must be most firmly controlled if they are not 'to fill the world with misery, making human life an exaggerated likeness of the odious scene of violence and tyranny which is exhibited by the rest of the animal kingdom except insofar as tamed and disciplined by man'. If man was put on earth for any good reason, it was to struggle 'with vigour and progressively increasing success'[3] against the natural evil powers.

For anything like Rousseau's morality,[4] or worse still, Fourier's, even for Proudhon, Mill had nothing but profound aversion.[5] They all disregarded the importance of cultivating a sense of duty and suggested that the passions, if left to themselves, could spontaneously move men to act well. Nor was Mill any more sympathetic to an ideal like Goethe's that looked to a harmonious development of all human potentialities:

To me it seems that nothing can be so alien and (to coin a word) antipathetic to the modern mind as Goethe's ideal of life. He wished life itself, and the nature of every cultivated individual in it, to be rounded off and made symmetrical like a Greek temple or a Greek drama. It is only small things, or at least things uncomplex and composed of few parts, that admit of being brought into that harmonious proportion. . . . Nay, at bottom, are your well-balanced minds ever much wanted for any purpose but to hold and occasionally turn the balance between the others? Even the Greeks did not and could not make their practical lives symmetrical as they made their art; and the ideal of their philosophers, so far from being an ideal of equal and harmonious development, was generally one of severe compression and repression of the larger portion of human nature. In the greater huddle of multifarious elements which compose modern life, symmetry and mental grace are still less possible, and a strong hand to draw one thing towards us and push another away from us is the one thing mainly needful. . . .[6]

[1] *Ibid.* p. 52.
[2] Fox, *Memories*, vol. I, p. 141.
[3] J. S. Mill, *Nature* (London, 1874), pp. 46; 57–8; 38–9.
[4] *Ibid.* p. 51.
[5] J. S. Mill, *Letters*, vol. II, p. 205; Hayek, *Mill and Taylor*, p. 148.
[6] J. S. Mill, *Letters*, vol. II, p. 368 (Feb. 12, 1854).

Goethe's ideal was fit only for art. In life repression was more valuable than harmony.

Thirdly, John Mill was certain that the best sort of man is much more than harmless, that he exerts himself energetically for all humanity and not only for the good of a few beings dear to him. Many activities admired by others were accordingly deplored by Mill. So much talent had been wasted, he felt, on 'useless' pursuits such as German metaphysics or Christian theology. He could muster no sympathy for the obsessed scholar, the hermit, the isolated artist or saint, indeed for anyone who merely lives from day to day or does nothing but contemplate his own vision of truth and beauty.

Mill admired only the active character who struggles against evils and 'endeavours to make circumstances bend to itself,' unlike the passive character who merely 'endures' evils, and 'bends to circumstances'.[1] Moralists, and mankind generally, he knew, favoured the latter, because 'the passiveness of our neighbours increases our sense of security, and plays into the hands of our wilfulness'.[2] But in fact, the person who never stirs and therefore lacks many advantages possessed by others is more of a menace because he regards his successful neighbours with hatred and malice. Thus Orientals, who are passive, are also the most envious of people; so are the Spaniards and even the French, because they have been made passive by Catholicism and despotism. What appears to be contentment is really discontent, 'combined with indolence or self-indulgence . . .'.[3] But even genuine contentment is laudable only when 'the indifference is solely to improvement in outward circumstances, and there is a striving for perpetual advancement in spiritual worth, or at least a disinterested zeal to benefit others'. Those who have no ambition to advance themselves, their neighbours, their country, or mankind at large exhibit nothing but 'unmanliness and want of spirit'.[4]

Even in the speculative realm, the active character produces more. It is easier for him to learn patience than for the passive character to become energetic. Nothing more than a 'feeble and vague culture' is acquired by the passive type, who most often stops at amusement or 'simple contemplation.' But anyone capable of 'real and vigorous' thinking would not rest in contemplation—he would seek to ascertain truths 'instead of dreaming dreams'. He would want his thoughts put to use: 'Where that purpose does not exist to give definiteness, precision, and an intelligible meaning to thought, it generates nothing better than the mystical metaphysics of the Pythagoreans or the Vedas'. Human life will, therefore, be improved only by the sort of character

[1] J. S. Mill, *Representative Government*, p. 144.
[2] *Ibid.* p. 145.
[3] *Ibid.* p. 147.
[4] *Ibid.* p. 147.

III   JOHN STUART MILL

that 'struggles with natural powers and tendencies, not that which gives way to them'.[1]

The striving, go-ahead temper of the United States and what was left of it in England seemed to Mill admirable. He criticized it only insofar as the energy was spent on secondary objects, such as physical comfort and a show of riches. Yet even this was preferable to the French habit of meeting a crisis with: *Il faut de la patience*. The misdirection of energy hindered improvement less than inactivity and lack of aspiration.[2]

Thus Mill remained loyal to his father's most fundamental convictions, and indeed to those of most Englishmen with whom he believed himself to be disagreeing. However much solace he had found in poetry, Mill never, any more than Carlyle, found it easy to admire Coleridge. He came nearest to forgetting his middle-class ideals in his love for Sterling, who, he felt, had gladdened the world just by being what he was. But then Sterling shared Mill's preference for an active life, and was prevented from engaging in it by circumstances beyond his control. In a sense, Mill genuinely favoured variety in human character and believed that human existence must not be constructed on 'some one or some small number of patterns'.[3] But the variations he approved of were all on one ideal. His individualist is someone who always has before him a vision of perfection. He is not an undecided, restless searcher, but the bearer and instrument of a clearly defined truth. He knows where he is going and how he means to get there.

Whatever confusion *On Liberty* may have created about Mill's allegiance to an ideal individual should have been removed by his essay on *Utilitarianism*. The ethical theory he formulated to replace Bentham's was far from adequate, but he made clear his intent to distinguish between higher and lower in pleasures as well as characters:

Human beings have faculties more elevated than the animal appetites, and when once made conscious of them, do not regard anything as happiness which does not include their gratification . . . there is no known Epicurean theory of life which does not assign to the pleasures of the intellect, of the feelings, and imagination, and of the moral sentiments, a much higher value as pleasures than to those of mere sensation.

His hierarchical morality was still entirely empirical, Mill felt, because it rested on an appeal to those who knew best, that is, those who knew both 'higher' and 'lower' pleasures. Even though a superior character might require more to make him happy and might suffer more than his inferiors, he would never 'wish to sink into what he feels to be a lower grade of existence'. Whenever a question arises about the relative worth of two pleasures, or two modes

---

[1] *Ibid.* p. 145.
[2] *Ibid.* p. 148.
[3] J. S. Mill, *On Liberty*, p. 60.

of existence, one has only to ask those who know both—'What is there to decide whether a particular pleasure is worth purchasing at the cost of a particular pain, except the feelings and judgement of the experienced?'[1] Thus John Mill carelessly knocked down the barricades piled up by Bentham against the tyranny of those who claimed to know how their neighbour should live.

But then Mill's purpose, not only in *Utilitarianism*, but also in *On Liberty* as well as in everything else written after his crisis, was exactly contrary to Bentham's. He meant to secure the leadership of those who knew better. Otherwise the human race could not progress to its ultimate perfection. His reason for fostering individuality was not any simple objection to letting one man impose his will on another, but what he considered utility in the largest sense, 'grounded on the permanent interests of man as a progressive being'.[2] It was fitting that *On Liberty* should have been a joint effort with Harriet, for its moral was that people like she and Mill did not need rules and conventions. Certainly the purity of their relationship over many years was proof enough. Ordinary mortals, who could not do as well, whose liberty easily degenerated into licentiousness, needed external controls. But in higher natures, who are moved by a genuine desire to do that which is best for the happiness of all, general rules are merely aids to prudence, not obligations. The problem then was to make the ordinary many see that the few unusual souls, whose natural inclinations were supremely disciplined, and who could lead society to better things, must be exempted from the rules properly binding on the majority.

The purpose of *On Liberty* was not to insist on the priority of liberty over morality, but on the priority of the higher over the lower morality: 'All the difficulties of morality in any of its brands, grow out of the conflict which continually arises between the highest morality and even the best popular morality which the degree of development yet achieved by average human nature will allow to exist'.[3] The best popular morality is that which pacifies as many natures as possible, and so it must be much inferior to what higher natures want and require. As popular morality is essentially a compromise between the lowest and the highest, the best people lose most; they are

the greatest, indeed the only real, sufferers by the compromise; for *they* are called upon to give up what would really make them happy; while others are commonly required only to restrain desires, the gratification of which would bring no real happiness. In the adjustment, moreover, of the compromise, the higher natures count only in proportion to their number, how small! while the conditions of the compromise weigh heavily upon them in the states of their greater capacity of happiness. . . .[4]

[1] J. S. Mill, *Utilitarianism* (Chicago, 1906), pp. 11, 12, 13, 16.
[2] J. S. Mill, *On Liberty*, p. 9.
[3] Hayek, *Mill and Taylor*, p. 60.
[4] *Ibid.* pp. 58–9.

If the leadership of the superior few were permitted, all human beings would ultimately become noble, more given to high thoughts and elevated feelings. Then there would be no objection to being bound closely to the race, because the race would be more worth belonging to. In the meantime, however, one had to free the superior few from the vulgar many. But Mill so thoroughly merged his plea for liberating the minority of ideal individuals from the common herd with his vision of progress toward a race of ideal individuals, that his chief purpose was easily overlooked. Had it been recognized, his rule for distinguishing public from private interests would not have seemed so ambiguous and inadequate. For if there is a clear notion of what 'good' private interests are and a definite goal ahead for society, if there are men who can judge where happiness lies, which pleasure or life should be preferred, then it is not so difficult to decide in most cases whether public or private interests should prevail. It is only when individuality can take widely different forms, when there is no one goal to be reached, that Mill's rule is useless in those cases where the conflict is most serious. For then the 'public' interest is just one among many interests and there is no scale on which to measure any.

The ambiguity in *On Liberty* did not arise from careless or faulty reasoning. If reflected a profound division within Mill. He had after all been educated as Bentham's heir, and with part of him believed ardently that human dignity required the freedom of each man to go his own way. But he had also inherited from his Calvinist father a conviction, reinforced by his later experiences, that there were superior beings who should guide the rest. Of course, neither Hume nor Bentham would have denied that some men were in some ways superior to others, or that the average man would do best to look for a superior model to follow. But they did not believe there was a clearly defined class of superior beings. And they did not think it was easy to put everything into words. Besides, they were not trying to formulate a complete creed. Hume was content to let customary ways regulate deference without harping on the subject. Bentham, who believed the deference had gone too far in some areas, set out to destroy it there. Neither tried to include all good things in their political recommendations. But Mill could leave nothing unsaid—he even felt obliged to write a contract guaranteeing his recognition of Harriet's equality. He could not allow himself or society to achieve any good thing without deliberately aiming at it. As he insisted on including everything within one system, neither could he, as Hume and Bentham did, give priority to one object for the purposes of social policy alone. He would have liked society self-consciously to pursue two incompatible ends. The dilemma was not made obvious because Mill's plea for freeing the superior few from the inferior mass was so sweetly enclosed in general arguments for liberty and individuality that it could be accepted somehow by all sorts of individualists.

On Liberty is consequently a classic statement of late Victorian and twentieth century liberalism. For it enables the liberal to feel assured of his tolerance, and at the same time to feel it is right, even obligatory, to impose his own views on the less fortunate mass of people in want of uplifting. Thus he can pay homage to both liberty and progress without having to acknowledge any conflict between them. Mill had poured his new learning—that there was perfection ahead—into the old mould—that it was indecent to prevent any adult from choosing his way of life. He himself managed to remain devoted to both aspects of his creed at once. But he made it easy for his successors to discard the mould. He provided a justification for withholding personal liberty from any claimant unable to demonstrate that he was pursuing the 'right' ideal and was possessed of sufficient will power to pursue it steadily and energetically.

THE IDEAL INDIVIDUAL AND POLITICS

His interest in perfectibility led Mill to adopt a new ground for preferring popular government. If the object were only to insure good government, he pointed out, it might sometimes be true that where a good despot could be found, a despotic monarchy would be preferable. (Mill was, however, still enough of a Benthamite to indicate that the monarch would have to be all-seeing as well as benevolent.) The real argument against even a perfect monarchy was that it would damage the character of the people.

Caretaking, in the Benthamite sense, removing impediments to the safety and industry of men, was only a small, and in a sense, the least important part of a government's duties. To emphasise it was tantamount to believing that a parent's duties were fulfilled by feeding and housing his children. John Mill had learned to ask for more: 'The most important point of excellence which any form of government can possess is to promote the virtue and intelligence of the people themselves'.[1] The other, utilitarian view, which lacked any vision of progress, looked only to static excellence. Once one came to think in terms of progress, it became obvious that society must try to move onward, and that government must do its part to encourage this movement. He had therefore to think of what its goals were. The problem of deciding between forms of government, Mill pointed out in *Representative Government*, had less to do with power than with determining whether the good of humanity required that the active or the passive character should predominate. For the ultimate test of good government was its effect on the moral and spiritual development of the people.

From his vision of these grander political objectives, Mill moved to the

---

[1] J. S. Mill, *Representative Government*, pp. 126–7.

conclusion that political responsibility was the highest expression of human dignity. For, in the first place, even if the rulers did not impose perfect acquiescence, subjects who had no voice in the government inevitably acquired a feeling of impotency. To submit to the will of others was to lose one's self-reliance. Moreover, if improvement rather than enjoyment or contemplation is the end of life, nothing affords so much scope for improving activity as politics. Since Mill was committed to improvement on a large scale, he was bound to place political activity first.

He had never doubted that assuming responsibility for improving oneself and others brought out the best in a man. In the *Political Economy*, he had stressed the salutary effects of peasant proprietorship on just those grounds. In *Representative Government*, he argued for the benefits of extending such responsibility further: 'The maximum of the invigorating effect of freedom upon the character is only obtained when the person acted on either is, or is looking forward to becoming, a citizen as fully privileged as any other'.[1] Even more important was the 'largeness' that political activity added to men's conceptions and sentiments. Having something to do for the public was the best stimulus, Mill believed, to developing grand thoughts and feelings, which now meant, 'thoughts and feelings extending beyond individuals'. When called upon to participate in a public function, a man is forced to weigh interests not his own, to forego private partialities, to think of the common good. Where there is no political participation, all thoughts and feelings, either of interest or of duty, are absorbed by the individual himself or by his family. In private life, men are not forced unselfishly to identify themselves with the public, nor to think of the collective interest, or of objects to be pursued jointly with others. They are left to tend their roses. 'Were this the universal and only possible state of things, the utmost aspiration of the lawyer or the moralist could only stretch to make the bulk of the community a flock of sheep innocently nibbling the grass side by side'.[2] Bentham would not have been much troubled by this prospect, just so each of the sheep could get his own. But John Mill, who was reaching out for something beyond the slope before him, hoped to see men climbing together, their ranks ever tightening as they moved upward to the topmost peak, where each and everyone, by perfecting himself and working for the perfection of all the others, could bask in perfect unity, knowledge and goodness.

This was the final and true justification of representative government. There was no longer any way, in the large communities of modern times, for each man to participate directly in public life. But he could do so, effectively enough, Mill thought, through representative government:

[1] *Ibid.* p. 149.
[2] *Ibid.* p. 151.

It is evident that the only government which can fully satisfy all the exigencies of the social state is one in which the whole people participate; that any participation, even in the smallest public function, is useful; that the participation should everywhere be as great as the general degree of improvement of the community will allow; and that nothing less can ultimately be desirable than the admission of all to a share in the sovereign power of the State. But since all cannot in a community exceeding a single small town, participate personally in any but some very minor portions of the public business, it follows that the ideal type of a perfect government must be representative.[1]

Mill thought carefully about how to reconcile such broad political participation with leadership by those who knew best, and his suggestions in *Representative Government* for redefining the functions of parliament and adding a staff of legislative experts were his answer. He did not, however, consider whether impersonal secondhand discussion of matters decided by others would have the effects he looked for. Letting everyone feel a sense of public responsibility was his only concern.

But not all communities were ready for representative government. It was an ideal for which some nations would have to be prepared. One had therefore 'to judge, in cases in which it had better not be introduced, what inferior forms of polity will best carry those communities through the intermediate stages which they must traverse before they can become fit for the best form of government'.[2] The best government at an inferior stage is the one that will do most for progress to a higher stage, that will promote 'the general mental advancement of the community, including under that phrase advancement in intellect, in virtue, and in practical activity' while at the same time making the most of what qualities exist already. For such purposes, the government might in many cases[3] have to be 'in a considerable degree despotic', a government over which the subject people 'do not themselves exercise control, and which imposes a great amount of forcible restraint on their actions'.[4] Despotism is therefore a mode of government as legitimate as any other

if it is the one which in the existing state of civilisation of the subject people most facilitates their transition to a higher stage of improvement. There are . . . conditions of society in which a vigorous despotism is in itself the best mode of government for training the people in what is specifically wanting to render them capable of a higher civilisation. There are others, in which the mere fact of despotism has indeed no beneficial effect, the lessons which it teaches having already been only too completely learnt; but in which, there being no spring of spontaneous improvement in the people themselves, their almost only hope of making any steps in advance depends on the chances of a good despot.[5]

[1] *Ibid.* p. 151.
[2] *Ibid.* p. 135.
[3] *Ibid.* p. 129.
[4] *Ibid.* p. 112.
[5] *Ibid.* p. 313.

The responsibility of England to India was of this sort. To permit native despotisms would not do for they could not provide the advantages of a superior civilization. That his father's portrayal of Indian civilization betrayed no respect for it, that the civilization in India was perhaps more alien than inferior and not subject to the same sort of judgements, did not occur to Mill.[1] His benevolent zeal for progress made it difficult for him to recognize any differences without grading them on his scale. But he was very sensitive to the problems of organizing a government by foreigners, and helping the Indians to advance without allowing their foreign rulers to take advantage of them or to impose new ways tactlessly. He was inclined to think that the system set up under the East India Company was in many ways superior to what had succeeded it. But he had no doubt that ultimately the Indians, like the rest of the world, would do best under a representative government such as he outlined, and that England's duty was to prepare them for it. For otherwise they would be left out of the progress of the human race.

[1] Cf. criticism of James Mill on India in *Athenaeum*, No. 34, 1828, pp. 527 ff.

CHAPTER XXVI

THE LIBERAL GENTLEMAN

ONCE *Utilitarianism* and *Representative Government* were out of the way, there remained only one more pressing subject to cover—the *Subjection of Women*, which Mill wrote at about the same time as *Representative Government*, but did not publish until a few years later. For the most part, his duties had been fulfilled. He had had his say on all the vital subjects, and was ready to enjoy being the oracle he had become abroad as well as in England. The old narrowness, he felt confident, was gone; Harriet was no longer by his side to prick him on to new discontents; his step-daughter confined her tutoring more to details.

But before he could settle down to a life of ease, Mill spent three years engaging directly, at last, in politics. The old excitement about parliament that he had felt so strongly in the 'thirties, when his job in India House had closed a political career to him, no longer stirred him; he was in a way reluctant to leave his books for debates. When he consented, he did so entirely on his own terms, which were anything but those of a politician. His notion of proper political behaviour was even more unyielding than before. He stood as a Liberal, but he refused flatly to pay any election expenses or even to campaign; he appeared before his constituents only ten days before the election and insisted on making all his opinions perfectly clear without mincing any words. Somehow, contrary to what his supporters feared, his candour was attractive; the workers declared that they did not mind his saying that they were liars; they preferred truth to flattery. There was a certain appeal in his severe figure, and he gave the impression of authority difficult to resist. His sharp, taut features, the hair curling around in a monk's cap, the high forehead emphasised the intelligence and discipline evident in his face. One might fear his disapproval, or wish he would laugh more easily, or not take it all in such deadly earnestness, but it was impossible not to feel his sincerity, thoughtfulness, and selflessness.

To tell his constituents what he believed, Mill drew up a declaration of political opinions in ten points, affirming, among other things, that he favoured universal suffrage, that he did not wish any class, even if the most numerous, to swamp all the others. He gave notice that he no longer favoured a secret ballot—voting was a public act, and each voter should be made to take full responsibility for his opinions before the whole public. As voters could now resist being coerced by landlords, employers, or customers, there was no longer any justification for the secret ballot. He advocated greater

312

economy in government, but no disarmament; wished that succession duties on land might be assessed on its full value, not merely on the life interest; and he saw no way in which legislation could help to resolve differences between workers and employers, except by insuring equal liberty to both to combine or not, as they wished. It was not a very startling programme, but a good indication of how he would behave in parliament.

There he was neither quite the philosopher many of his admirers expected nor a consummate politician, but a little of both, as he had been all his life. As he was more certain than ever about what was true and false, right and wrong, and no less earnest about pushing his views, his rectitude, which combined oddly with his delicacy and elegance, gave him an air of what Disraeli described unkindly as that of a finishing governess. Yet he was not altogether unsuccessful, even if his success was rather different from what he had dreamt of in his early Radical days. He started off badly, speaking on an unimportant question—whether landowners should be indemnified for losses suffered from a cattle disease. Mill declared himself against this on the orthodox economic ground that they had already been indemnified by the high meat prices, an argument that those less sophisticated in economics found it irritatingly difficult to answer. He spoke in a similar vein on a number of other subjects, pleased no one, and finally, noticing his unpopularity, retired. But he managed to regain the attention of the House with a speech on Mr Gladstone's Reform Bill, which was probably urged on him by Chadwick at Roebuck's suggestion. Then he spoke more nearly as a man of large perspective, who could see farther and higher than the workaday politician. Perhaps he had also learned, as Roebuck hoped he would, not to roll from side to side, or join his hands behind him, and look 'like a schoolboy saying his lessons'.[1]

Mainly, his role in the House was that of a gadfly. He spent most of his energies on particular, unpopular causes, where he often acted, at least in the beginning, as a party of one. When the governor of Jamaica instituted over five hundred highly suspicious wholesale court-martials to repress an incident that took a toll of twenty-two, all Mill's moral fervour was aroused. Nothing less than trying the governor for murder would do. Although a number of philanthropists, scientists, liberals, and old Radicals supported his indignation, he was commonly thought to be going too far. He formed an organization, wrote a pamphlet, made himself very unpopular with everyone and failed. On other occasions, he used his authority to moderate mob violence. When the Reform League threatened a meeting in the park, which had been forbidden by the Home Secretary and seemed likely to inspire another Peterloo, it was Mill who dissuaded the working men with the argument that

---

[1] Packe, *John Stuart Mill*, p. 453.

they ought not to go ahead unless they felt a revolution was necessary and could succeed. Often he made bad mistakes. He did much to ruin his own in re-election by supporting the candidacy of Bradlaugh, an avowed atheist. In the course of defending himself against Bradlaugh's enemies, he fell into declaring himself against atheism, which greatly disturbed his step-daughter and some of his friends who thought he was betraying his principles. But his campaign for women's suffrage, dearest of all to him, was far more successful than he had hoped. Thanks to his highly provocative book and some of his moves in parliament, the subject became a common matter for discussion and made the idea of women's suffrage familiar to the public, thus preparing the way for its acceptance. To other smaller matters, like the Contagious Diseases Act, Mill devoted quite as much effort. On all issues he was firm, in fact quite immovable, and many of his opinions were unconventional. He confined himself to modest, immediate questions. The grander ones would be attended to by others, and, in any case, he felt he had done all he could by his books.

When after three years he was defeated for re-election, he was relieved. He insisted that it was because the Tory machine was so much better organized and primed with money, although his friends believed it was because of his opinions and political awkwardness. In any case, he retired happily to Avignon where his step-daughter had prepared many new comforts for him, and he performed his worldly duties by a conscientious correspondence, answering all letters in a most forthright and precise manner. He was generous with praise and approval whenever possible, but begged off joining anything. His correspondence covered every sort of question, from the nature of intuition to new university examinations. And his advice was generally in the direction of caution and moderation.

When the secretary of the International Working Men's Association sent him a pamphlet called, *The Law of the Revolution*, Mill took exception to the phrase, 'the Revolution'. In English, Mill told him, 'revolution' designates a change of government, and 'the Revolution' refers to some particular revolution. It is not an English name for any sort of principles or opinions. Only in French does 'principles of the Revolution' mean the

political ideal of any person of democratic opinions who happens to be using it. I cannot think that it is good to adopt this mode of speech from the French. It proceeds from an infirmity of the French mind, which has been one main cause of the miscarriages of the French nation in its pursuit of liberty and progress; that of being led away by phrases, and treating abstractions as if they were realities which have a will and exert active power.

English thought, Mill pointed out sternly, has insisted on propositions rather than vague words. The Association rightly considered certain maxims to be essential to just government, and 'there is a tendency increasing as mankind advance in intelligence and education towards the adoption of the doctrines of just government'. Those were the facts of the case, and the only facts; if these were stated clearly and unambiguously, it would be easier for people to see what they were about. 'When instead of this men range themselves under banners as friends and enemies of the "Revolution", the only important question which is just and useful is kept out of sight, and measures are judged not by their real worth but by the analogy they seem to have to an irrelevant abstraction'.[1]

Now that Mill felt free to be somewhat less harsh with himself, his life acquired much of the gentleness he had yearned for. In Avignon, he spent many hours collecting plants; a neighbouring naturalist became a good friend and accompanied him on long walks, hunting for varieties of mushrooms, while Mill went on collecting one of each kind of plant. The specimens were sorted and kept in good condition in the Herbarium that Helen Taylor had constructed. Apart from this, Mill concerned himself with preserving beautiful surroundings wherever he could. The anxiety of workingmen to put all waste land under cultivation led him to protest strongly—to preserve natural beauty was quite as important as increasing the country's agricultural efficiency. The good life required beauty as well as cheap food.

Once again, Mill was the centre of a circle, mostly younger men, disciples, who more nearly resembled his earliest friends than the later ones like Carlyle and Sterling: Fawcett, intensely practical, with little interest in abstract subjects of any kind; Spencer, opinionated, knowing scarcely anything of history or literature, a man who was never puzzled; Thornton, who had shown Mill the fallacy of the wage fund theory; Bain, knowledgeable and very helpful in questions about recent scientific advances, a more ardent advocate of the association psychology than ever Mill was; his old friends, the Grotes, who in this company represented perhaps a broader culture than they had by comparison with his poetic friends; Morley, very much under Mill's influence, of a temper more to his taste than the others; and the Amberleys, the only sparkling personalities, who if not great intellects, were handsome, fairly rich, noble in birth and sentiment. It was not a brilliant or artistic group, but they were all congenial companions for Mill. The entertainment Mill gave them when he was back at Blackheath was far more graceful and elegant than anything Bentham had ever managed. And Mill had none of the old man's eccentricities. But the serenity of his life in these last years resembled Bentham's.

Mill's opinions too were softened, and in some ways, became perhaps too 'reactionary' for a liberal gentleman. In his inaugural address as Rector of

[1] J. S. Mill, *Letters*, vol. II, pp. 347–8.

St Andrew's, he came out against the new scientific trend. He made a grand, if not wholly practical plea, for keeping classics just as important as they had ever been, and by more efficient teaching merely adding the new science subjects. He spoke as a man of culture arguing for an education that would form gentlemen. His address was indeed very different from his father's article on education for the Encyclopedia Britannica, with its syllogisms about man and progress. John Mill spoke in detail on what a liberal education ought to teach; he justified it ultimately, it is true, in terms of usefulness to the race, but mainly he described and defended an education that would produce a person of taste and character, as well as knowledge. Once more he let the emphasis fall on art, tying it as usual somewhat to improvement:

If I were to define Art, I should be inclined to call it, the endeavour after perfection in execution. If we meet with even a piece of mechanical work which bears the marks of being done in this spirit—which is done as if the workman loved it, and tried to make it as good as possible, though something less good would have answered the purpose for which it was ostensibly made—we say that he has worked like an artist. Art, when really cultivated, and not merely practiced empirically, maintains, what it first gave the conception of, an ideal Beauty, to be eternally aimed at, though surpassing what can be actually attained; and by this idea it trains us never to be completely satisfied with imperfection in what we ourselves do and are: to idealize, as much as possible, every work we do, and most of all, our own characters and lives.[1]

In politics, he was ready to expect somewhat less. In the beginning chapters that he completed for a book on socialism, he declared:

It must be acknowledged that those who would play this game [of social revolution] on the strength of their own private opinion, unconfirmed as yet by any experimental verification—who would forcibly deprive all who have now a comfortable physical existence of their only present means of preserving it, and would brave the frightful bloodshed and misery that would ensue if the attempt was resisted—must have a serene confidence in their own wisdom on the one hand and a recklessness of other people's sufferings on the other, which Robespierre and St Just, hitherto the typical instances of those united attributes, scarcely came up to.[2]

He advised a 'calm comparison' between socialism and a competitive economy to discover which offered the best resources for overcoming the 'inevitable difficulties of life'. He suggested that perhaps the question was more difficult and depended more on intellectual and moral conditions than had been supposed, but there was consolation in the thought that there was time to work out the answer by actual trial. The only way to tell whether socialist arrangements were practicable or beneficial, he believed, was to try

[1] *James and John Stuart Mill on Education*, ed. by Cavenagh (Cambridge, 1931), pp. 195–6.
[2] J. S. Mill, 'Chapters on Socialism', *Fortnightly Review* (February, March, April, 1879), April, 1879, pp. 513–14.

them, bit by bit. Most of all, it was the intellectual and moral grounds of socialism that deserved consideration, perhaps more than the practical proposals; the present economic system, if only it were modified somewhat along socialist principles, might yet prove its worth.[1]

Mill became willing even to indulge a hope for immortality, although there was no rational ground for more than a hope. In this one instance, perhaps, one need not regulate all feelings and opinions entirely by reason. Human life was so small and was so likely to remain that way even after much moral and material progress, that men needed some 'wider range and greater height of aspiration' than fact could support. It was therefore wise to 'make the most of any, even small, probabilities on this subject, which furnish imagination with any footing to support itself on'.[2] To cultivate such a tendency in the imagination would not, he thought, pervert the judgement; one could soberly estimate the evidence on both sides of the question and yet 'let the imagination dwell by preference on those possibilities, which are at once the most comforting and the most improving'. On this practice, after all, much of our happiness depended. It was the basis for a cheerful disposition, which comes of a tendency to emphasise agreeable prospects whether or not the facts warrant it. Of course, he pointed out also that this outlook had real, practical advantages, for 'a hopeful disposition gives a spur to the faculties and keeps all the active energies in good working order'.[3] The province of reason was truth. But where the faculty of reason was strong, it was safe to let the imagination have its own way somewhat, to let it 'do its best to make life pleasant and lovely inside the castle, in reliance on the fortifications raised and maintained by Reason, round the outward bounds'.[4] Mill's willingness to let his imagination and feelings roam more freely was tentative and not effortless, but still he had come a long way from the boy who would not yield his right to a seat in the carriage.

What sustained him, however, more than anything else, was a belief that he felt reason could support. In the past, men had been fortified and inspired by the conception of God as a morally perfect being. That was no longer possible for anyone who took a rational view of nature. One could, however, still be guided by Christ. It did not matter that the Christ of the Gospels was not perfectly historical, or that some of his admirable qualities were added by followers.

But about the life and sayings of Jesus there is a stamp of personal originality combined with profundity of insight, which if we abandon the idle expectation of finding

---

[1] *Fortnightly Review,* March, 1879, p. 382.
[2] J. S. Mill, *Three Essays on Religion* (London, 1874), p. 245.
[3] *Ibid.* p. 247.
[4] *Ibid.* p. 249.

scientific precision where something very different was aimed at, we must place the Prophet of Nazareth, even in the estimation of those who have no belief in his inspiration, in the very first rank of the men of sublime genius of whom our species can boast.[1]

The chief use of the impression made by the life of Jesus was to aid, not Christianity, but 'that real, though purely human religion, which sometimes calls itself the Religion of Humanity, and sometimes that of Duty'.[2] The conditions of human life were all extremely favourable to the growth of this new religion, for even the humblest man could take part in the constant battle between good and evil, 'in which every, even the smallest, help to the right side has its value in promoting the very slow and often almost insensible progress by which good is gradually gaining ground from evil, yet gaining it so visibly at considerable intervals as to promise the very distant but not uncertain final victory of Good'.[3] The humblest contribution towards bringing 'this consummation' even a very little nearer was the most 'animating and invigorating thought which can inspire a human creature. . .'. Therefore, this Religion of Humanity, or of Duty, with or without supernatural sanctions, was certain to be the religion of the future.[4]

John Mill's faith in the ultimate triumph of good was much greater, more far-reaching, and more demanding than his father's. It had led him to rather strange places. But it remained for him a faith, distant and somewhat blurred. He had no wish to transform it into anything more immediate or clear or real. For the present, he was content to do his modest bit and to dream of other things while he pottered about in his Herbarium. Others would translate his dreams into realities; and it was just as well that he would not be there to see it.

[1] *Ibid.* p. 254.
[2] *Ibid.* p. 255.
[3] *Ibid.* p. 256.
[4] *Ibid.* pp. 256–7.

PART IV
BEATRICE WEBB: SCIENCE AND THE APOTHEOSIS OF POLITICS

G. Bernard Shaw phot   Emery Walker Ph. sc

Beatrice Webb

IV

CHAPTER XXVII

A NEW CLIMATE OF OPINION

THE NEW SCIENCE

WHEN Mill pleaded at St Andrews for the liberally educated gentleman, he was defending a losing cause. Faith in science had triumphed to a degree he had not dreamt of even in *The Spirit of the Age*. Public school masters agreed with scientists that the school curriculum must be revised to make room for science, even at the expense of classics.[1] Mere men of letters who moved easily between history, philosophy, science and poetry could no longer count on public esteem. The universities came under attack not only for indolence but for their failure to live up to the continental pattern that had already formed the Scottish universities, for concentrating on a few, unconnected and out-moded branches of learning and turning out nothing but gentlemen and public officials. Faculties were consequently reorganized, a number of pro-fessorships added, and vaguely defined subjects divided up into independent disciplines. Mid-Victorian culture was separating into distinct strands. It was no longer enough to be cultivated and original; the specialized professional and, above all, the scientist were coming into their own.

Religion, once the great source of opposition to science, had lost its force. The age of the great doubters—Froude, Tennyson, Francis Newman, Hale White, George Eliot—who had been so tormented by their first suspicions of their faith, was well over. The storm raised by the *Origin of Species* marked the climax of several decades of religious controversy and soul-searching, which, for all its severity, died quickly. Even before the *Origin of Species* was published, the work of Hutton and Lyell had led students in University College, London to discuss 'the manner in which the innumerable races of animals have been produced', and the seventeen-year-old Stanley Jevons noted in his journal that he firmly believed 'all animals have been transformed out of one primitive form by the continued influence for thousands, perhaps millions of years of climate, geography, etc. . . .'[2] Mark Pattison was not exaggerating very much when he declared that Oxford had been altogether converted as early as 1850: 'Theology was totally banished from the Common Room, and even from private conversation', and replaced by 'very free opinions on all subjects'.[3] In 1862, when the British Association of Science

---

[1] Cf. F. W. Farrar, (ed.), *Essays on Liberal Education*; T. H. Huxley, *A Liberal Education and Where to Find It*.

[2] Stanley Jevons, *Letters and Journals* (London, 1886), p. 23.

[3] Mark Pattison, *Memoirs* (London, 1885), pp. 244–5.

accepted a eulogy of Darwin without a murmur, Huxley, who was leading the battle for evolution, began to complain that 'Darwinismus' was creeping up everywhere, insinuating itself even into a lecture on Buddhist temples. The works of Darwin, Lyell, and Huxley, the *Daily Telegraph* reported in 1863, were being torn from the hands of Mudie's shopmen as if they were novels.[1]

By the 'seventies, Darwin was beginning to fear that his theory had become so orthodox it would inspire a reaction. The Athenaeum felt it could withdraw its opposition 'without doing violence to anyone's antipathies'; the Metaphysical Society brought together scientists and churchmen for discussions of the current scientific theories; and the question began to be not whether such opinions were wicked, but whether from the point of view of scientific method they were undeniably true. When in 1874, the British Association of Scientists heard its new president almost directly deny creation, the *Spectator* commented that 'Professor Tyndall will be much less persecuted for denying the existence of God than he would be for denying the value of Monarchy'. One could no longer be radical by opposing an entrenched religious orthodoxy.

Having made its peace with religion, science had to contend only with art or 'culture'; and the problem of the relation between science and art, that had so absorbed John Mill in his early years, became a general social concern. There were still those like Matthew Arnold who insisted that science was not culture. The study of nature, he said, although it should be included in education, was the study of 'the operation of non-human force, of human limitation and passivity'. The study of letters, however, was 'the study of human force, of human freedom and activity. . .'. In order to use science well, men had to know what the human spirit was capable of; they had to know the best in poetry, philosophy, and history. The classics were essential because they made modern men able to share in the character and beauty of antiquity, to acquire that 'love of the things of the mind, the flexibility, the spiritual moderation' that distinguished the ancients.[2] A study of 'belles lettres' was not, Arnold insisted, a slight and ineffectual study, good for nothing but ornamental purposes, as so many advocates of scientific education implied. It was as disciplined as science and as indispensable to those who would know human nature—

The more that the results of science are frankly accepted, the more that poetry and eloquence come to be received and studied as what in truth they really are,—the criticism of life by gifted men, alive and active with extraordinary power at an unusual number of points;—so much the more will the value of humane letters,

---

[1] T. H. Huxley, *Life and Letters* (London, 1900), vol. I, p. 202.
[2] Matthew Arnold, 'Higher Schools and Universities in Germany', pp. 167–170, in *Thoughts on Education*, ed. by Leonard Huxley (New York, 1912), pp. 180; 184.

and of art also, which is an utterance having a like kind of power with theirs, be felt and acknowledged, and their place in education be secured.[1]

But Arnold had not the appeal of his more forward looking opponent, T. H. Huxley, who called him a 'Levite of culture'. Huxley maintained that he did not in any way deny the value of humane learning, but simply wanted science to be made as important as 'literary or aesthetic' culture.[2] Certainly, he did not go as far as Herbert Spencer who saw in art mainly an expression of sexual interests, and considered the classics humbug, indeed nothing but false information surrounded by superstitious awe. Nevertheless, more than a difference in emphasis divided Huxley from Arnold. Although Huxley was the most colourful and cultivated of the scientists, rather more given than the others to metaphysical and religious speculation, his view of man and of culture was altogether opposed to Arnold's. Whereas Arnold spoke of the whole man, of training character, to Huxley man was more nearly a thinking apparatus, associated with a body and a spiritual capacity.[3] Civilization to him, as to John Mill, was a growing accumulation of truths, and he ruthlessly drew the conclusion somehow qualified by Mill that the thinking apparatus need only acquire more and more knowledge and be purified of falsehood. Reaching the right answer counted most with him:

I protest that if some great Power would agree to make me always think what is true and do what is right, on condition of being turned into a sort of clock and wound up every morning before I got out of bed, I should instantly close with the offer. The only freedom I care about is the freedom to do right; the freedom to do wrong I am ready to part with on the cheapest terms to any one who will take it of me.[4]

Although, unlike Darwin, Huxley was sensitive to the arts and avidly read literature, philosophy, and history, he did not approach them in the spirit of a man of letters. He never loitered in a book, but read it through as quickly as possible to extract just those points that interested him, remembering only how the substance of the book fitted into his own categories.[5] He liked Keats for his simple beauty, Tennyson for his understanding of science, and Browning for his strength and feeling. He agreed with Bentham's view of Plato as the 'founder of all vague and unsound thinking', who deserted 'facts for possibilities, and then, after long and beautiful stories of what might be, telling you he doesn't quite believe them himself'.[6] And when Huxley tried to wade through Wordsworth, time and patience utterly failed him.[7]

---

[1] Matthew Arnold, 'Discourse in America', pp. 124–6, in *Thoughts on Education*, p. 265.
[2] T. H. Huxley, 'Scientific Education', in *Essays* (New York, 1896), vol. III.
[3] T. H. Huxley, *Life and Letters*, vol. I, p. 298.
[4] *Ibid.* p. 328.   [5] *Ibid.* vol. II, p. 418.
[6] *Ibid.* p. 426.   [7] *Ibid.* p. 419.

All knowledge, Huxley explained, was divided between matters of science and matters of art. Under science, he included those things 'with which the reasoning faculty alone is occupied', and to art he left 'all things feelable, all things which stir our emotions'. But unlike Mill, he did not leave it at that.

Against Arnold, he insisted that it was the chief business of mankind to learn what the natural order is and to govern themselves accordingly. And he suggested, perhaps unwittingly, that humane learning was not only less essential, but also inferior morally to science. 'The great truth which is embodied in the Christian conception of entire surrender to the will of God', he said, was taught by science—'Sit down before fact as a little child, be prepared to give up every preconceived notion, follow humbly wherever and to whatever abysses nature leads, or you shall learn nothing'.[1] Indeed Huxley seemed to reduce everything legitimate to a part of science when he described science as 'trained and organised common sense'.[2] Since the man of science, as he explained, 'simply uses with scrupulous exactness the methods which we all habitually and at every moment, use carelessly',[3] there seemed to be no rational ground for denying the superiority of science.

Even those who were not directly debating the question of what to teach in the schools also suggested that science was somehow morally superior to all other activities. In a widely read article, the popular journalist and Comtist, Frederick Harrison, attacked culture as the enemy of method, logic, and system. Culture, he said, implies the amenities of education, the training of the taste—belles-lettres and aesthetics—and it blithely confounds truth and falsehood:

There is harmony, but no system; instinct, but no logic; eternal growth and no maturity . . . perpetual opening of all questions and answering of none. . . . It tells us the beauty of picturesque untruth, the indelicacy of mere raw fact, the gracefulness of well-bred fervour, the grotesqueness of unmannerly conviction; truth and error have kissed each other in a sweet serener sphere; this becomes that, and that is something else.[4]

Echoes of this view appeared as far away as in Disraeli's statement that the frontier of India 'is a haphazard not a scientific frontier'.[5] Nor was the moral status of culture improved by those who wished to defend it. The aesthetic movement of the 'eighties, seemed to justify the accusation that the 'fleshly' poets—Morris, Swinburne, and Rossetti—glorified the body at the expense of soul. Earlier, Pater's *Studies in the Renaissance* was taken as a shocking

[1] *Ibid.* vol. I, p. 219.
[2] T. H. Huxley, 'The Educational Value of Natural History Sciences,' *Essays*, vol. III, p. 45.
[3] *Ibid.* p. 46.
[4] Frederick Harrison, 'Culture: A Dialogue', *Fortnightly*, Nov. 1, 1867, pp. 609–11.
[5] *The Times*, Nov. 10, 1878.

glorification of aesthetic pleasure, of passion, as against the Christian doctrine of self-denial and renunciation. Arnold himself encouraged a prejudice against culture by his distinction between Hellenism and Hebraism, which suggested to some that those who loved the arts disdained discipline and conscience. 'The governing idea of Hellenism is *spontaneity of conscience*, that of Hebraism, *strictness of conscience*. . . . Self-conquest, self-devotion, the following not our own individual will but the will of God, *obedience* is the fundamental idea. . .'.[1] Sidgwick accordingly accused Arnold of refusing to admit the basic antagonism between culture, which emphasized self-development, and religion: 'Culture . . . inevitably takes one course. . . . Religion of which the essence is self-sacrifice, inevitably takes the other course. . . . It is because he ignores this antagonism . . . that I have called Mr Arnold perverse'.[2] But between science and religion there was no conflict on this score. Although Arnold had said that Hellenism had given rise to science, no one seemed to take any notice. To its votaries, science promised a secular and rational road to virtue.

The halo around science was but a reflection of the hold it had acquired over the public imagination. This it had achieved partly because the great number of new theories that had so rapidly been proposed and accepted in the course of the nineteenth century had immediate practical consequences and were therefore especially impressive. To the public, science seemed to be nothing less than a growing collection of certain truths. But perhaps even more important, science now seemed able to provide what Huxley described as 'a complete theory of life, based upon a clear knowledge alike of its possibilities, and of its limitations'.[3] It was a peculiarly English theory that grew directly out of experimental science and was free of the metaphysical foundations that had made continental theories suspect in England. While John Mill had been unsuccessfully searching abroad for ways of justifying his faith in an unbroken chain of causality from natural to mental phenomena, the scientists at home had been making his faith into a scientific truth.

On the Continent, where the sciences had very early become rigidly marked off from other fields of knowledge and from one another, philosophy had been totally divorced from science. There were few efforts, like that of Alexander von Humboldt, to make a grand theory explaining the universe. But in England, Humboldt's view was the common one. For the older conception of science as natural philosophy was still alive and speculation about general forces had not been abandoned to the philosophers. Even early Victorian scientists reflected on broad theories, and later, such reflection was greatly

---

[1] Matthew Arnold, *Culture and Anarchy* (Cambridge, 1948), p. 132.
[2] Henry Sidgwick, 'The Prophet of Culture', *Macmillan's*, Aug., 1867, p. 274.
[3] T. H. Huxley, 'Science and Culture', *Essays*, vol. III, p. 143.

stimulated by discoveries that suggested drastically simplified ways of accounting for natural phenomena.

Scientists working on very different problems contributed, for instance, to the notion that all of nature could be understood in terms of matter and energy. Faraday proposed that electric and magnetic phenomena depended on a property that belonged to all matter and pervaded all space. Clerk Maxwell developed this idea, and in his great work, *Electricity and Magnetism*, urged that these phenomena, as well as light, could be looked upon as mechanical systems and analysed in terms of the distribution of energy. The way to making energy central in scientific thought had already been prepared by Mayer and Joule when they found how to make mechanical work and heat convertible. Not much later Thomson and Rankin conceived of a general science called 'Energetics'. When in 1863 Thomson and Tait published their *Natural Philosophy*, in which energy was a key concept, it quickly became a popular text in schools and universities.

At the same time, distinctions between different forms of matter began to seem trivial. Almost simultaneously with Tait and Thomson, Tyndall published his theory that heat was produced by the motion of particles. This led Lord Kelvin (Thomson) to the thesis that there were no rigid barriers between solids, liquids, and gases, and that apparently static properties could be explained by different sorts of motion. Research that showed how brittle substances like pitch could under some conditions flow like liquids, that gases and liquids could behave like solids, revolutionized not only science but popular notions and vocabulary. Working men flocked to hear difficult lectures explaining the new physical theories, showing how energy could exist as motion either of electricity or of masses, how it could be lost in the form of heat or stored up, how it could transform a solid into a liquid. There were disagreements among the scientists, and some continued, for instance, to see electricity as a substance rather than as a state of motion in the electromagnetic field, but not many escaped the general interest in reducing physical phenomena to a few basic ones, to finding a common denominator for all of nature.

Made bold by discoveries, the most meticulous scientists indulged in grand leaps beyond their immediate work. Lord Kelvin envisaged the universe as an all-pervading boundless fluid, in which the various phenomena existed as whirling rings, which possessed the properties of matter and identity, permanent quantity, stability, rigidity and elasticity. Tyndall was the most radical and, in his presidential address to the British Association in 1874, declared his faith in the evolution of life from matter. After all, once one accepted the hypothesis that energies were all convertible and that heat was a form of motion, it was but one step further to say that all of life, indeed the human mind itself, was 'once latent in a fiery cloud'. It was a favourite problem of

Tyndall's, Huxley said, 'Given the molecular forces in a mutton chop, deduce Hamlet or Faust therefrom. He is confident that the Physics of the Future will solve this easily'.[1]

Huxley himself, though he vehemently repudiated materialism as well as Comtism, and invented the name of agnostic for himself, anxiously awaited someone who would 'think out into a connected system the loose notions that are floating about more or less distinctly in all the best minds'. But he preferred a synthesis inspired by biology rather than physics. Unhappily, Darwin made no such effort and claimed nothing of the kind for his theory of evolution, although Wallace had commended him as the 'Newton of Natural Philosophy', creator of 'such a grand view and a simple philosophy'. Huxley nevertheless set himself to indicating the general lines such a synthesis might follow. He explained, precisely and colourfully, that the difference between the lowest plant and the highest animal was one of degree not kind, and dependent solely on the degree of division of labour. Since all of life consisted of corpuscles with nuclei, protoplasm was but the clay of the potter, 'which, bake it and paint it as he will, remains clay, separated by artifice, and not by nature, from the commonest brick or sun-dried clod'. Living protoplasm must die and be resolved into its living constituents, but renewal takes place because the protoplasm of one living thing is easily converted into the protoplasm of another. And in conclusion, Huxley declared that the very thoughts he was uttering were the expression of molecular changes within his body. These views were presented by Huxley in a series of Sunday evening addresses in Edinburgh, in 1868. When they were published the following year in the *Fortnightly*, they had to be printed in five editions to satisfy the demand for them.[2]

John Mill's early complaint against English indifference to connecting special truths with general views was no longer justified. When Henry Adams came to England in the 'sixties, he found 'the British mind . . . doing a great deal of work in a very un-English way, building up so many and such vast theories on such narrow foundations as to shock the conservative and delight the frivolous'.[3] The scientists were convinced that a sound empirical theory explaining all was possible. Among the public, a growing interest in covering the whole circle of knowledge encouraged a search for principles and ideas that could be extended to a variety of phenomena and would make it easy to know everything by knowing one thing. It was no wonder that Herbert Spencer, who offered what seemed to be a complete synthesis integrating

[1] T. H. Huxley, *Life and Letters*, vol. I, p. 231.
[2] T. H. Huxley, 'On the Physical Basis of Life', in *Half Hours with Modern Scientists* (New York, 1871), pp. 13, 16–17.
[3] Henry Adams, *The Education of Henry Adams* (Modern Library), p. 224.

biology with physics, stranger though he was to personal and literary charm, became a popular hero and was crowned 'The Philosopher'.

Spencer was an engineer who had become convinced that 'the astronomic, geologic, biologic, psychologic and sociologic groups of phenomena form a connected aggregate of phenomena', which nothing but the caprice of human convention had separated. To conceptions borrowed from natural history and biology, he joined sociological notions, and later incorporated with these the idea of purely mechanical processes, until he came to see the various scientific laws as expressions of a single fundamental law: that the universe and every-thing in it, inorganic as well as organic, was moving toward a state of equilib-rium, when all forces in the world would be perfectly balanced. In the biological world, this meant that an organism would, under the pressure of external and internal forces, evolve until it became perfectly adapted to its environment. Biological change was nothing but the redistribution of matter in regular patterns, that is, a continuous and rhythmic motion that continued until equilibrium was reached. Spencer subsequently added refinements, which showed, for instance, that organisms became more perfectly adapted by becoming less homogeneous and developing more specialized parts, but the basic theory remained unchanged.

Although Spencer had a great gift, very much valued by scientists, for recognizing far-reaching analogies and for discovering data with which to verify his general scheme, he did not altogether satisfy the contemporary scientists. They not only found him 'far too opinionated for candid argu-ment', inclined, when worsted in an argument, to finger his pulse and say abruptly, 'I must talk no more',[1] but also incorrect. The going theories about energy had discredited his central notion of force, and Huxley liked to tell how Spencer's idea of a tragedy was a beautiful theory slain by a brutal little fact. Nevertheless, for all their criticisms and doubts, even the scientists applauded Spencer's attempt to weld all scientific knowledge into a system.

His philosophical admirers could not praise him enough. On the Continent as well, he was celebrated as the first Englishman to understand that philosophy ought to unify all knowledge. There were, it is true, a few dis-senters like Canon Barnett, who found him 'strangely ignorant of history and literature'. But most commentators agreed with G. H. Lewes, who had intro-duced Spinoza and popularized Comte in England, that for the first time in her history, England had produced philosophy:

Science she has had, Poetry and Literature, rivalling when not surpassing those of other nations. But a Philosophy she has not had, in spite of philosophic thinkers of epoch-making power: Hobbes, Locke, Berkeley, Hume have produced essays, not systems. There has been no noteworthy attempt to give a conception of the World,

[1] Karl Pearson, *The Life, Letters, and Labours of Francis Galton* (1930), vol. III, pp. 626 ff.

of Man, and of Society, wrought out with systematic harmonising of principles. There has not been an effort to systematize the scattered labour of isolated thinkers. Mr Herbert Spencer is now for the first time deliberately making an attempt to found a philosophy.[1]

Spencer had actually done what others had hinted at. He had shown that the 'science of Mind must be a branch of the general science of Life'.[2] He had made morality essentially one with physical truth, indeed, a kind of transcendental physiology. If he had not unified psychology and physiology as completely as Lewes would have liked, still he had successfully destroyed the old dualism that divided matter and force from feeling and thought.

Although Spencer had no qualms about pursuing his leading ideas to their ultimate conclusion, even though it meant that the end of universal processes was an equilibrium difficult to distinguish from death, his system was not really a thorough-going synthesis. Spencer not only made no attempt to construct a theory of knowledge, but he dealt neither with the origin nor the end of things as a whole. He nowhere discussed the meaning and significance of life, and indeed declined altogether to consider whether there was an underlying spirit, or anything of ultimate spiritual value. His job, as he saw it, was simply to show how all changes and all phenomena were cast in the same mould. Everything else he relegated to the Unknown.

This incompleteness, however, constituted one of Spencer's great attractions. He seemed to be relying only on 'scientific evidence', and therefore did not offend scientific prejudice or inspire any questions about his theory of knowledge. Yet by his willingness to acknowledge an Unknowable, he soothed the anxiety of those who liked to think that they had kept some sort of religious sense. Homage to 'the Great Unknowable' became the stock in trade of many scientists and rationalists, and even orthodox believers like Canon Barnett were apt to use the phrase. Tyndall, after declaring that life had undoubtedly evolved from matter, went on to say that religion was an instinct, indestructible and admirable: 'it will be wise to recognise [religions] as forms of a force, mischievous if permitted to intrude upon the region of *knowledge*, over which it holds no command, but capable of being guided to noble issues in the region of *emotion*. . .'.[3] A number of popular writers enthusiastically acclaimed Tyndall as a friend of true religion. George Eliot's friend, the philosopher, Charles Bray—who had renounced Christianity but was not an agnostic, because 'to me God is not an unknown God. . . . He is known to me as everything else is by what he does'[4] —explained that: 'Prof. Tyndall's address . . . does not land us in Atheism, but just the reverse; it

---

[1] G. H. Lewes, *Problems of Life and Mind, First Series* (Boston, 1874), vol. I, p. 77.
[2] G. H. Lewes, *Problems of Life and Mind, Third Series* (London, 1879), vol. I, pp. 59–60.
[3] Tyndall, Presidential Address to British Association, Belfast, 1874.
[4] Charles Bray, *Phases of Opinion and Experience* (London, 1885), p. 199.

leads thru Nature up to Nature's God, or rather, to the fact that God and Nature are One. . .'.[1] A reviewer, in the *Inquirer*, of Tyndall's address echoed Bray's sentiments, declaring that while science had broken down the old notion of God the Artificer, it had made possible a deeper devotional life on a new basis. It allowed man to see God 'in a form which is immeasurably grander. . . . To Tyndall as to Herbert Spencer, matter is but the manifestation of a great Entity, in itself unknown and unknowable. . . . What is this Great Entity, what is this Great Cosmical Life, but the Eternal God himself. . .'.[2] The old god was a battered idol, that had set science and religion at odds. But now the scientists had let in the light.

Thus the belief in the possibility of summing up the universe in a single scientific theory acquired both an aura of humility and the sanction of religion. It did not deny that there were other ways of seeing the universe, but relegated them all to the sphere of emotions. Modestly, it claimed supremacy only in the sphere of reason.

SCIENCE AND POLITICS

It was only natural that the new theories should be expected to work wonders in politics as well. The apparently easy progress of science encouraged impatience with all human problems, and the feeling that they were avoidable made them seem all the more grave. At the same time, England was facing a number of new problems, or old problems in new forms, which were not easily disposed of in the old ways.

Disraeli's phrase, 'the two nations', aptly summed up what many Englishmen felt about the dangers of the division between rich and poor. The increasingly rapid growth of huge industrial enterprises, the willingness of more and more Englishmen to go in quest of 'the land where the gates of night and morning stand so close together that a good man can earn two days' wages in one'[3] meant a greater crowding into cities that endowed the evils of city life with a new urgency. Intensified efforts to aid the poor gave rise to incidents like the Mansion House Fund scandals which fostered a sense of helplessness. In each case, in 1867 and again in 1885, an advertisement appeared saying that a large sum of money was to be given away. But applications came not only from the needy with specific wants. Ne'er-do-wells from all parts of the country flocked to London to get something for nothing, as much as possible; and the settlement house workers at Toynbee Hall found themselves besieged by long lines of ragged, gaunt, and dirty men filled with antagonism to those who were giving away money, but not generously enough. With the best

---

[1] Charles Bray, 'Toleration', p. 12, in *Scott's Tracts*, 1875, vol. IX.

[2] *Inquirer*, Sept. 5, 1874, p. 7, in *Scott's Tracts*, 1875, vol. IX.

[3] G. M. Young, *Victorian England* (Oxford, 1949), p. 101.

intentions in the world, the workers of Toynbee Hall were not only unable to satisfy all the demands on them; they could not decide to their own satisfaction what they should have done. The Mansion House scandals made the inadequacy of an unaided social conscience a public issue. Would-be philanthropists came to feel that knowing how to help the poor was perhaps even more pressing a need than mustering help for them.

What was happening abroad was no less disquieting. The Prussian campaign against Austria in 1866 seemed to have imposed on the world a new conception of efficiency. Those who had scoffed that Prussia was not to be taken seriously were the more severely shocked when, on September 2, 1870, after a short summer's war, the armies of France surrendered to Bismarck. When, in the Hall of Mirrors at Versailles, the king of Prussia became emperor of Germany, Englishmen felt that they had lost their place in the world. Less than a year after the German victory, Matthew Arnold told his countrymen: 'Hardly a German newspaper can discuss territorial changes in Europe but it will add, after its remarks on the probable policy of France in this or that event: "England will probably make a fuss, but what England thinks is of no importance".'[1]

Where there was no new threat, there was disturbing confusion. The traditional enemy, autocratic Russia, remained, and while Disraeli propped up Turkey as England's best defence against Russia, Gladstone, inflamed about the Bulgarian atrocities, showered England with high-minded pamphlets proclaiming the national rights of Serbs, Greeks, and Bulgars. The country was torn as well between Disraeli's championship of colonies and empire, and Gladstone's demand that Britain's policy of imperial expansion be reversed, and during the struggle over Irish Home Rule, the government wavered uneasily between coercion and conciliation. Problems elsewhere in the Empire, dramatically underscored by Gordon's martyrdom at Khartoum, further weakened confidence. Even England's leadership in industry was being challenged, by both the United States and Germany, and periodicals discussed ways and means of meeting the commercial threat. The complacency of the age of Palmerston had given way to self-criticism and restlessness bordering on fear.

Amidst all the uneasiness and confusion, Huxley was reflecting a widespread feeling when he declared that there was one thing he knew for certain, that there was misery in the world, that one could help, and that the way to help effectively was to know more about society. The way to such knowledge, he insisted, lay through a science of social life, that 'higher division of science' which deals not merely with isolated beings as biology does, but 'considers living beings as aggregates'.[2] Huxley had no use for sociology in Comte's sense,

[1] Matthew Arnold, 'Friendship's Garland', *Works* (London, 1903), vol. VI, p. 356.
[2] T. H. Huxley, *Essays*, vol. III, p. 58.

which he found 'honey-combed with the *a priori* method'. But he did not doubt that another, valid sort of sociology was possible: 'Men are beings of a certain constitution, who under certain conditions, will as surely tend to act in certain ways as stones will tend to fall if you leave them unsupported',[1] and 'social phenomena are as much the expression of natural law as any others'. There could be no real improvement in social arrangements that did not harmonize with the requirements of what Spencer described as 'social statics and dynamics', and this knowledge could be had only by applying 'the methods of investigation adopted in physical researches to the investigation of the phenomena of society'.[2] To further this end, Huxley campaigned for the teaching of sociology in the universities.

What made the new science seem especially easy to achieve was the acceptance of a new image in thinking about society—'the social organism'. It had not, of course, been unknown before. It had been popular among medieval writers; Hobbes had in a way drawn on it for the *Leviathan*; and more recently it had appeared in England under the auspices of Comtism. Although these were not acceptable auspices they gave the 'social organism' the added advantages of familiarity when, thanks to the new biology, it appeared again in a more congenial context. In its late Victorian form, the 'social organism' had none of the metaphysical complexities with which medieval writers had endowed it. It was not composed of individual immortal souls, nor had its good to be balanced against an eternal order. It did not merely illustrate one aspect of society, but described its nature in a forthright simple fashion.

Although the vogue for the 'social organism' has been frequently credited to Darwin, he at most suggested an analogy between society and a biological organism and that only unwittingly. His description of the struggle for survival between 'races', that is, between varieties or species, implied to some a struggle between social as well as individual organisms.[3] But it was Herbert Spencer, more than anyone else, who gave the image of the social organism currency. He not only showed that 'the phenomena of both individual life and social life conform to law'. He compared 'the aggregation of citizens forming a nation' to the 'aggregation of cells forming a body'; he analysed society into organs just as a biologist would anatomize an animal—the labourers were the alimentary organs, the merchants and communication workers were its vascular system, the doctors, lawyers, engineers, governors and priests were the nervous system and brain; and he explained that progress in society, like progress in all organisms, moved from a whole made up of

---

[1] T. H. Huxley, *Life and Letters*, vol. II, p. 384.

[2] T. H. Huxley, *Essays*, vol. III, p. 158.

[3] For a full discussion of the relation between Darwin's views and those of his contemporaries, see Gertrude Himmelfarb, *Darwin and the Darwinian Revolution* (New York, 1959).

like parts to a whole made up of unlike parts dependent on one another.[1] He emphasized, moreover, that his notion of the social organism was 'entirely without kinship . . . to the fanciful notions of Plato and of Hobbes'.[2] The moral of Spencer's story about the social organism was that the highest society is organized by voluntary cooperation, rather than by coercion, by competition between individuals and groups rather than by centralized planning from above. Often, too, he altogether abandoned the biological analogy to argue in fairly traditional terms that a small, tight group of officials with definite aims can too easily impose its views on an unorganized public; that under socialism the 'regulators' would still be pursuing their own interests with no less selfishness than before, but could no longer be checked 'by the combined resistance of free workers';[3] that in a competitive system, although every man tries to get as much as he can, each is restrained by the interests of others. In fact, the social organism was not for Spencer an already existing fact, but rather a description of a final state of affairs. It represented the achievement of perfect equilibrium, the evolution of 'the ultimate man' whose private requirements would coincide perfectly with public ones. It promised a time when uncertainty in politics would disappear.

Despite Spencer's many denials and protests, he was accused of believing that a natural harmony already existed, of arguing that government was unnecessary, and that an unregulated struggle for survival would produce the best possible ethical results.[4] His critics did not, however, quarrel with his using the image of the social organism or with his vision of a time when politics would be easy and simple. They accused him rather of not pressing the analogy far enough. However much Spencer's contemporaries disagreed with his particular conclusions, they readily learned from him that the answers to social questions ought to be as certain as the answers to biological and physical problems seemed.

Every sort of man was drawn into the game of trying to reduce politics to science. Even Walter Bagehot, whose political views belonged more nearly to the tradition of Hume, wrote a book entitled *Physics and Politics, or Thoughts on the Application of the Principle of 'Natural Selection' and 'Inheritance' to Political Society*. In early times, he said, man adapted to his environment by the survival of those who had useful qualities and the extinction of those with less suitable characteristics. But with the advent of reason, men with inferior natural tendencies became able to adapt by imitating the behaviour of their more favoured colleagues. Reason thus made possible an

---

[1] Herbert Spencer, *An Autobiography* (New York, 1904), vol. II, pp. 7–8.

[2] Herbert Spencer, *Life and Letters* (New York, 1908), vol. II, p. 333.

[3] Herbert Spencer, *Man Versus the State* (Idaho, 1946), p. 78.

[4] Cf. Herbert Spencer, *Various Fragments* (New York, 1898), p. 117; *Life and Letters*, vol. II, pp. 26–45; *Man Versus the State*, pp. 206 ff.

'age of discussion', where the primitive struggle for survival could be replaced by the 'conflict of ideas'. And Bagehot concluded that 'government by discussion' was the prerequisite of man's continued progress, that is, the 'increase of adaptation of his internal powers and wishes to his external lot and life'.[1] In fact, Bagehot's book was nothing like a rigorous application of Darwinism to politics, but the author and even Darwin himself believed it to be a statement of social Darwinism.[2]

The fact that a man was actively engaged in the arts was no protection against the new enthusiasm. Probably Spencer's greatest friend and admirer was George Lewes, not only a philosopher, but also a novelist, dramatist, drama critic and actor, and personally utterly unlike Spencer. Yet before he was twenty, he planned a physiological interpretation of Scottish philosophy, and finally devoted the latter part of his life almost exclusively to science. In his philosophical and scientific essays, he emphasized the 'twofold root' of the human mind, man being 'not only an animal organism, but a unit in the social organism'.[3]

One of the most radical uses of the new theories was made by an even more powerful figure in the literary world, Leslie Stephen,[4] who after Matthew Arnold's death was considered the first man of English letters. Yet he believed that his greatest achievement was a book on *The Science of Ethics*, which is hardly remembered, or else dismissed as his most uninteresting work. It was the result of twenty years of speculation on 'an ethical doctrine in harmony with the doctrine of evolution'. The organic conception of society on which *The Science of Ethics* is based seemed to Stephen the most fruitful and characteristic postulate of modern speculation, for 'a statement which seemed only to describe the average mode of behaviour of independent beings has really a vast significance when considered as describing a quality of a persistent organism'.[5]

He argued that since, according to the theory of evolution, all organisms strive for maximum efficiency and society is an organism, society strives for maximum efficiency. Moral rules are the outcome of the social organism's search for efficiency, or, in other words, they state the conditions required by efficiency. The history of the human race had shown that societies whose members excelled in courage, temperance, truthfulness, justice, and benevolence were stronger; these then were the qualities morality required of individuals. Thus Stephen reduced morality to the perfect performance of

---

[1] Bagehot, *Physics and Politics* (New York, 1909), p. 209.

[2] Cf. Himmelfarb, *Darwin and the Darwinian Revolution*, pp. 403 ff.

[3] G. H. Lewes, 'Preface', *Physical Basis of Mind, 2nd Series of Problems of Life and Mind* (Scribner, 1877).

[4] For a vivid portrait of Stephen, see Noel Annan, *Leslie Stephen.* (London, 1951).

[5] Leslie Stephen, *The Science of Ethics* (London, 1907), pp. vi and 32.

one's social function—'A man is virtuous or the reverse so far as he does or does not conform to the type defined by the healthy condition of the social organism'.[1] If ever the requirements of society conflicted with the welfare of individual members, the latter had to give way: 'It is at least conceivable that the sacrifice of some of its members may be essential to the welfare of society itself', and more generally, 'The virtuous men may be the very salt of the earth, and yet the discharge of a function socially necessary may involve their own misery'.[2] In accordance with this theory, Stephen opposed the classical ideal of the contemplative life and condemned it as immoral. He idealized instead the active, efficient man.

Stephen recognized that he could offer no argument to show every man why he should want to be moral since morality implied 'the development of certain instincts which are essential to the race, but which may, in an indefinite number of cases, be injurious to the individual'.[3] But he was not inclined therefore to question his theory. Nothing could shake his confidence in the fruitfulness of the image of social organism. The moral of his study of utilitarianism was that it was impossible to understand the conditions of human welfare without understanding the laws of growth and equilibrium of society. It was essential, therefore, to acquire a conception of society as a complex organism, regulated and developed by processes that cannot be discovered through inspecting the constituent atoms. It could then be shown that such and such rules tend to the permanent vitality of the race. Sociology would supply a single and decisive test for social welfare instead of the vague and complicated criteria suggested by the crude individualistic forms of utilitarianism. Thus Stephen hoped to adapt utilitarianism to the scientific age.

The most literal and shocking attempt to move from biology to politics appeared in Benjamin Kidd's *Social Evolution*. Inspired by Weissman's embryological theory, which suggested to him that progess and retrogression were the only alternatives, Kidd declared that man must either progress or become extinct. He defined progress entirely in biological terms, only substituting 'social organism' for 'species' in the Darwinian picture. Science then demonstrated, according to Kidd, that all progress depended on physical struggle and where there was no struggle, retrogression followed. By equating the progress of man with the progress of the 'social organism', Kidd converted the utilitarian end, the greatest happiness of the greatest number, into the greatest happiness of 'the members of generations yet unborn or unthought of'. His conclusion was just what Bentham opposed most, that the

---

[1] *Ibid.* pp. 381 f.

[2] *Ibid.* p. 382. Inadvertently, Stephen uses 'virtuous' as if it were defined by something other than social function.

[3] Leslie Stephen, *Social Rights and Duties* (London, 1896), vol. I, p. 242.

present generations must suffer in the interests of the future. Physical conflict, with its attendant suffering and violent death, had to go on, for it was the condition of progress. The social equivalent of the physical struggle in nature meant to Kidd the economic struggle, and he accordingly argued that economic hardship must in no way be softened, that poverty, with all its trials, must be allowed to take its course unhindered because that way lay man's only hope for progress.

Kidd added a novel and most discouraging twist to biological politics when he declared the teaching of science to be opposed to the teaching of reason. Reason, he argued, told the individual that he wished above all to survive, and that therefore he did not wish to perpetuate the natural struggle among men. But science showed that if men made their lives easy and safe, if they restricted or ended the natural struggle, the social organism would degenerate. The interests of individuals, taught by reason, were irrevocably opposed to the interests of the social organism, revealed by science. That is why, Kidd explained, all attempts to find a rational basis for the progressive society must be ultimately fruitless. Since the real interest of mankind was to insure the progress of the social organism, since progress was incompatible with peace and comfort for all, every attempt to improve the conditions of individuals must be abandoned.

Kidd's dire thesis created a great flurry. Oddly enough, though it could hardly have been more contrary to what eighteenth century economic theory taught, it came to be considered the model of all arguments against socialism. It seemed to confirm the criticisms of Benthamism already made current by John Mill, and any defence of a competitive economic system was from then on invariably taken to mean advocating a merciless struggle for existence such as Kidd favoured.

Those who looked to science in one form or another for the solution of all social problems included men of very diverse characters and opinions. Yet there was a common standpoint—a pre-eminent interest in the welfare of human society as a whole, in the progress of the human race. However much they kept their distance from thoroughgoing materialism, they were all inclined to agree with Charles Bray that: 'Individuals are only individuals to our forms of thought. . . . The pains, of which individually so much is made, are as much swallowed up in the happiness of the whole as the pain or "sacrifice" we are all called upon to make of our lower nature to the highest purpose of existence'.[1]

Quite another view was being suggested at Oxford by the idealist philosopher, T. H. Green. Although today his reputation is far above Spencer's, he was spoken of in his time as the other leading philosopher of the age, who

---

[1] Charles Bray, 'Toleration', p. 14.

also displayed great systematizing power. For Green, the idea of consciousness or personality was central both in ethics and politics, as well as in metaphysics, and the personal progress of the individual was his leading concern. He began his thinking from the image of a man trying to realize some moral ideal, and defined society as the consciousness among men that they were all pursuing this end and could only reach it by working together. Yet he considered it a cardinal error in philosophers like Hobbes and Spinoza to admit a right in the individual apart from life in society. Political life meant to him the moral regeneration of character through citizenship, and he objected to paternal government because it narrowed the possibilities for moral development which could come only by imposing duties on oneself. The self-imposition of duties, rather than self-sacrifice, was the moral centre of his doctrine. The business of the state, he insisted, was not to promote moral goodness directly but to remove obstacles, to maintain conditions in which human faculties could be freely exercised.

It was not only, or even primarily, his purely philosophical teaching that gave him such great influence—he presented his students with 'ideals to live for and principles to live by'.[1] His own life reconciled philosophy with religion and politics. And he led students not only to think more of philosophy and poverty than of poetry and the arts, but also to start missions in the wildest tracts of London. The political programme Green's followers subscribed to did not aim at a total reformation of society, but included a variety of worthy objects, such as national education, temperance legislation, land reform at home and in Ireland, pacific foreign policy, abolition of dissenters' disabilities, opening of careers to talent regardless of birth. They believed generally in capitalism and the Liberal Party with the addition of a gospel of 'social duty'.

Green's views found their most striking practical expression in Toynbee Hall, which set out to renovate society in the name of religious and social rather than purely materialistic ideals. The Settlement House work there attracted numbers of independent volunteers, young men and women like Beatrice Webb's sister, Kate Potter, like Arnold Toynbee, or Mrs Ward's hero, Robert Elsmere, who left their comfortable homes and went to live among the poor in East London. They tried to influence the poor through personal friendship, and to help them to live better not only by relieving their physical distress, but by bringing a better kind of life within their experience. It was in the midst of a lecture on 'Progress and Poverty' to the poor of East London that Toynbee collapsed. He had been telling them:

We—the middle classes, I mean, not merely the very rich—we have neglected you; instead of justice, we have offered charity, and instead of sympathy, we have

[1] R. G. Collingwood, *An Autobiography* (Oxford, 1939), p. 48.

offered you hard and unreal advice; but I think we are changing. If you would only believe it and trust us, I think that many of us would spend our lives in your service. . . . We are willing to give up the life we care for, the life with books and those we love. . . .

But this attitude was not in step with the 'spirit of the age'. For all his emphasis on social duty, Green's teaching insisted too much on the importance and reality of the individual to allow any simple reconciliation of individual with social ends. The Toynbee Hall view never died altogether, but it had not a very wide appeal among ardent reformers. It was undermined even at Oxford by Green's own disciple and successor, Bernard Bosanquet.

Although Bosanquet condemned the materialism of his contemporaries, he sympathized wholeheartedly with 'the distinctive and modern spirit of what is known as Sociology'. The notion of a 'continuity between human relations and the laws of the cosmic order',[1] he explained, was entirely in the spirit of Plato, whose 'true passion was for the unity of things, and as guides to its nature, for science and goodness. . .'.[2] The sociological view had rightly made men sensitive to the fact that the crowning achievements of the human race, their states, their religion, their fine art, and their science all had their beginnings far back in the primitive organic world. It reflected a scientific enthusiasm that could be the parent of great things. But it misunderstood the true nature of the social organism.

Any view based on science or materialism made a false distinction between society and the self which set individual against social needs. This antagonism, however, was an illusion born of denying the continuity of nature and separating the ethical and cosmic process from 'lower' nature. Ultimate reality did not lie in the apparently independent existence of the physical individual, and it was only this that made government appear to be an encroachment on the self. The true reality, Bosanquet argued, was the 'social person'. He thereby identified the moral essence of the individual with society, and solved the problem that Stephen could but acknowledge.

Most men, Bosanquet explained, did not understand their real wants and knew only their superficial, private, selfish interests. But, in fact, it was not 'in the nooks and recesses of the sensitive self, when the man is most withdrawn from things and persons and wrapped up in the intimacies of his feeling, that he enjoys and asserts his individual self to the full. This idea is a caricature of the genuine experience of individuality'.[3] The correct view was that every man possessed individuality only as a part of a whole, and only to the degree that he identified himself with the social whole. The state was

[1] Bernard Bosanquet, *The Philosophical Theory of the State* (London, 1930), pp. 16, 19.
[2] Bernard Bosanquet, *Contemporary British Philosophers*, p. 55, in J. H. Muirhead, *Bernard Bosanquet and His Friends* (London, 1935), pp. 21 f.
[3] Bosanquet, *The Philosophical Theory of the State*, p. 117.

one with the 'real will' of the individual, that is, with his will to fulfil his highest capacities as a rational being. It was not something external to the individual, but his higher self.

In practice, Bosanquet advocated moulding the individual mind to the public purpose, rather than giving the state more power. He called himself a moral socialist and an economic individualist. Socialism correctly understood, he said, 'makes society the moral essence of the individual'. False, economic socialism neglected the profounder meaning of society and opposed to individualism nothing more than a theory that identified all social activity with that narrower 'legal and political form of cooperation which we call the State'.[1] Like every other attempt to compel men by force, economic socialism rested on moral individualism. Economic individualism, however, recognized the reality of the social organism.

For the rest, Bosanquet used the language of his scientific-minded contemporaries. He described society as a tissue of organizations, in which the capacity of every person is determined by the general nature and principle of the group considered as a whole. The social good, he said, was not 'composite, derivative, instrumental . . . the way in which millions of welfares could be best subserved',[2] but the good of a whole in which individuals, those illusions kept only by unreflective minds, are 'indivisible sides of the same thing'. He even likened society to an army, in which every unit is directed 'not by the movements and impulses of his immediate neighbours, but by the scheme or idea of the whole'. The army, he explained 'is a machine or an organisation, which is bound together by operative ideas embodied on the one hand in the officers, and on the other hand in the habit of obedience and the trained capacity which make every unit willing, and able to be determined not by the impulse of his neighbours, but by the orders of his officers'. What the public thought it wanted did not matter; the purpose of government is to satisfy real needs. Public discussion in parliament may be useful for educational purposes, but elected representatives need not necessarily decide public issues. True self-government is to be found in whatever system truly apprehends the needs of the whole and 'forces us to be free'.[3]

Bosanquet's theory was more clear-cut than Green's. It escaped both the conflicts implicit in any individualist view of politics, and the inhumanity of the views based on materialism. But it was not an easy theory—it impressed only those who could move easily among abstractions. And it did not pay sufficient homage to science.

It was left to another Oxford idealist to combine successfully the attrac-

[1] *Ibid.* p. xxxiii.
[2] Bernard Bosanquet, *Some Suggestions in Ethics* (London, 1918), pp. 42 f.
[3] Bosanquet, *The Philosophical Theory of the State*, pp. 156, 150, 310.

tions of both idealism and science. In *Darwinism and Politics*, published in February, 1889, six months before the first Fabian essays appeared, David G. Ritchie contrived a synthesis of Hegel and Darwin that made the image of the social organism irresistible and won him a footnote by Sidney Webb. Ritchie saw in Darwin's theory of evolution a scientific confirmation of Hegel's theory of history, and in Hegel's philosophy, a guide for drawing the political and ethical lessons from Darwin's discoveries. Both Darwin and Hegel, Ritchie claimed, described the same process: a continuous development from the simple to the complex that proceeded through struggle and the elimination of the unfit. They even used the same categories—Darwin's heredity and variation were but particular forms of Hegel's identity and difference.

The proper political and ethical lessons could be drawn from biological evolution, Ritchie warned, only by following Hegel's method. Hegel taught men to look for the meaning of a process in its end, and to discover this end by distinguishing the surviving, real elements in a process from those that were decaying, seeming, and transitory. This meant that one looked for the meaning of evolution in the 'later' stages, and regarded what characterized the earlier stages as primitive, low, undesirable.

In fact, Ritchie's conclusions were no different from those of Huxley, who did not appeal to Hegel. Unconscious and indirect adaptation, Ritchie argued, very much as Huxley had in *Evolution and Ethics*, was characteristic of the lower stages of evolution; conscious, deliberate adaptation appeared in the later stages and was a 'higher' form of adaptation. The ethical progress of society depended on combatting the cosmic process—the natural struggle for existence. When men first came to live in society, and the object of evolution changed from the adaptation of individuals to the adaptation of societies or social organisms, men were at first unaware of their real end. They continued the war of each against all, and the struggle between tribes selected those with the greatest internal discipline. But gradually, as reason developed, men came to realize that the real end of their lives was the preservation of the tribe, that is, the success of the social organism of which they were only parts. As men came to see that they were not independent beings, but parts of an organic whole, they accepted greater social discipline. Thus evolution taught that 'happiness is not the end of right action. My happiness is of no use to the community except insofar as it makes me a more efficient citizen; that is to say, it is rightly desired as a means and not as an end'.[1]

To pursue the good of the social organism consciously meant to Ritchie accepting political centralization. For if society were an organism with a

---

[1] D. G. Ritchie, *Darwinism and Politics* (London, 1901), p. 106; also D. G. Ritchie, *Darwin and Hegel* (London, 1893), p. 62.

unitary end, it could no more leave the individual to decide on what he required, than an animal could send out its cells to forage for themselves, or an army could leave its soldiers to determine when and where they would fight. Higher animals had more developed, more centralized nervous systems than lower organisms, and a society where the government did little was more like an amoeba than a noble animal. 'Apparently the social organism in Mr Spencer's ideal state'. Ritchie taunted, 'ought to resemble an animal drunk or asleep with its brain doing as little as possible'.[1] As an idealist, Ritchie was especially cautious about pressing the biological analogy too far, but that only meant, he argued, that in its highest development society was even more organic than a biological whole.

Finally, Ritchie could draw on the idealist denial of any opposition between government and individual. 'The state has as its end, the realisation of the best life by the individual'. All that was elevated and human in man—his rights, his culture, his morality—was created by the state: 'the state is not a mere means to individual welfare as an end; in a way, the state is an end in itself'.[2] Ritchie accordingly censured John Stuart Mill for thinking of liberty as opposed to the power of government. His own view eliminated the possibility of any such conflict.

Ritchie's theory effectively summed up and integrated the most attractive elements of the new views of science and politics that became current among later Victorians. It came to be popular, however, not in its own right, but as part of a more eclectic theory with more precise and certain prescriptions for politics. How the new influences were combined and grafted on to old views to transform the picture of political activity is most sharply illustrated in the life of Beatrice Webb.

[1] D. G. Ritchie, *Principles of State Interference* (London, 1896), p. 21.
[2] *Ibid.* p. 102.

341

CHAPTER XXVIII

THE MAKING OF A SOCIALIST

THE POTTER FAMILY

BEATRICE WEBB was born Beatrice Potter, on January 2, 1858, into a prosperous business family. The Potters had risen in the usual way. Richard, Beatrice's grandfather, came from a farm in the North, where his family also kept a draper's shop. His elder brother William, convinced that young men could rise most easily in trade, urged Richard to apprentice himself to a merchant, and against his inclination, Richard did. Afterwards he moved to Birmingham, and in 1792, to Manchester, where he and his brothers set up a cotton warehouse. William, for all his generosity with moral and prudential precepts, was too fond of drink, but his brothers followed his advice and quickly became rich. What time they could spare from business, Richard and Thomas devoted to politics, and Potter's Plotting Parlour became a favourite resort of Manchester Radicals. Thomas was elected the first Mayor of Manchester, and Richard, the first member for Wigan in the reformed parliament.

Richard, Junior, the father of Beatrice, was brought up as a gentleman. He was sent to school at Clifton; then, because he was a Unitarian, to University College, London; as he had no desire to enter the family business, he was permitted to go to the Bar. But shortly after his marriage in 1844 to the daughter of a Liverpool merchant, his father's death enabled him to give up his profession and enter upon the life of a country gentleman with an interest in politics. When, however, the crash of 1847 wiped out most of his fortune, he accepted his father-in-law's offer of a directorship in the Great Western Railway, and a few years later, thanks to a schoolmate, he became a partner in a timber works at Gloucester. The Crimean War, and especially the decision of the British and French armies to house soldiers in wooden huts, enabled him to restore his fortune. Before long, he was chairman of the Great Western Railway, president of the Grand Trunk Railway of Canada, promoter and director of a number of firms ranging from the Hudson Bay Company to a small concern manufacturing railway wagons. He left a fortune of nearly a hundred and fifty thousand pounds.[1]

Business, as Richard Potter, Jr, knew it, was very different from what it had been for his father and uncle, who had refused to support a joint-stock bank in Manchester because 'A man is successful in business only when he

[1] January, 1892. Somerset House, 188.

342

can watch with his own eyes everything that is going on'.[1] The great age of railways was almost over; the conquests had been made; rate wars had been abandoned as wasteful and the railways had learned to settle conflicts by agreements as broad as ten-year treaties or outright amalgamation. What remained was to extend and consolidate. Richard Potter's work was accordingly mainly financial and administrative; he was a promoter and speculator rather than founder, somewhat like Trollope's Mr Melmotte, though without any of his vices. His was an industry where competition was neither practised by businessmen nor encouraged by the state, where nationalization was the topic of the day, and the manager was applauded more for tact and orderliness than for aggressiveness.

In politics, Richard Potter began as a Liberal, turned Peelite, and finally joined the Conservatives after they gave up protection. He stood for parliament, as a Conservative for Gloucester, and lost by twenty-eight votes. Nevertheless, he distrusted Disraeli scarcely less than Gladstone, and dismissed Cobden and Bright as fanatics who deceived themselves as well as others by 'wire drawn logic and moral platitudes'.[2] Religion gave him no trouble. Though brought up as a Unitarian, he attended Anglican services, and without becoming a member, took the sacrament and enjoyed reading the lesson. Morning and night, he repeated the prayer his mother had taught him: 'Gentle Jesus, meek and mild, look upon a little child . . .'[3] and was all that a Christian gentleman should have been.

In every other way, too, he was practical and easy-going, with wide uncommitted tastes. He heard and read everything with good humour, and good-humouredly disbelieved most of it. His reading included Carlyle, Burke, and Newman, along with Dante, Shakespeare and Plato. Although he saw a great deal of Herbert Spencer and enjoyed talking with him, he was not in the least tempted by his theories. 'Words, my dear, mere words', he told his daughter: 'Experience tells me that some businesses grow diverse and complicated, others get simpler and more uniform, others again go into the bankruptcy court. In the long run and over the whole field there is no more reason for expecting one process rather than the other. . . .' 'Poor Spencer, he lacks instinct, my dear, he lacks instinct—you will discover that instinct is as important as intellect'. Ideas and tastes so difficult to classify made his daughter think that her father's preferences were 'inspired by emotional thought rather than pure reason'.[4]

Mindful of his duties as a father of nine daughters, and obliged besides to

[1] C. H. Grindon, *Manchester Banks and Bankers* (1877), p. 241, quoted in J. H. Clapham, *An Economic History of Modern Britain* (Cambridge, 1926), vol. I, p. 278.

[2] Beatrice Webb, *My Apprenticeship* (London, 1926), pp. 9–10.

[3] *Ibid.* p. 8.

[4] *Ibid.* p. 10.

entertain business associates, Potter kept open house for a varied company, including as many eminent men as he could muster. To Beatrice it seemed a very brilliant and mixed society: business men ranging from American railway presidents to Scandinavian timber merchants, British Imperial Company promoters and managers of local works, representatives of London society, and intellectuals of all varieties. She met some scientific celebrities like Tyndall and Huxley, who were probably introduced by Spencer, the Potters' closest family friend; she also met religious leaders—Cardinal Manning, Dr Ellicott, the Dean of Gloucester and Bristol, as well as Frederick Harrison. But the family seems never to have entertained or interested themselves in the writers, artists, or journalists of the day. Swinburne, Morris, and Rossetti, Matthew Arnold, Leslie Stephen, or Morley were outside their range. Nor does their large, white, ungainly house in the Cotswolds, later converted into a county hospital, suggest that they might have been among the admirers of Morris wallpapers, blue vases, and Liberty prints.

In society, their position was on the fringe. Beatrice Potter did all the things appropriate to a young lady entering society, without ever establishing her place in it. She rode in Rotten Row, paid calls, dined and danced, went to Hurlingham and Ascot, but all within her family circle and their restricted set. If she ever encountered the literary lions, she was not much impressed, or else she did not get on with them. Years later she confessed an unfounded prejudice against William James, 'as the brother of Henry James whom I had known in London Society and heartily disliked, a dislike which was reciprocated'.[1] In sum, she found London boring and her acquaintances tedious. Later, as Mrs Webb, she met some of that brilliant and unconventional circle of aristocrats known as the Souls, and became very fond of the Balfours, but as Miss Potter she had not been noticed. Lady Amberley, who once met the Potter girls, described them merely as 'great friends of Herbert Spencer's', and saw no more of them. The Potters were a self-contained middle class family, absorbed in the business of living.

Even so, Beatrice found the company she did meet almost too much for her. What it lacked in breadth, it made up for by rapid change, leaving her vague memories of people coming and going, along with a succession of servants, governesses, and tutors. Her mind was exposed to a similarly quick procession of ideas. For amusement on Sundays in London, father and daughters went to Hyde Park, in search of the most exciting speaker on religion or metaphysics—'we would listen with equal zest to Monsignor Capel or Canon Liddon, Spurgeon or Boysey, James Martineau or Frederick Harrison; dis-

---

[1] Beatrice Webb, unpublished diaries, entry for July 16, 1921. The dates given in the footnotes that follow refer to entries in the unpublished diaries of Beatrice Webb, at the London School of Economics. For entries that have been published, the reference is given to the published work.

cussing on the walk back across the London parks the religious rhetoric or dialectical subtleties of preacher or lecturer'.[1] Beatrice was stimulated but confused, and could not sort out what she heard.

Despite all the visitors, she was a lonely child, drifting idly about the house, finding companionship chiefly among the servants. She imagined death-bed scenes in which she forgave everyone their neglect; dreamt of lovers—many, brilliant, and ardent; suffered from an assortment of minor ailments; and kept a bottle of chloroform against the time when life might become too difficult (but the chloroform evaporated). She read at random whatever fell into her hands, and at fourteen began her diary, in which she meant to enter abstracts and criticisms of her reading. Soon afterwards, she added a periodic stock-taking in the Puritan or Evangelical manner, and at sixteen she wrote: 'I think that the great benefit one receives from keeping a diary is that it often leads one to examine oneself and that it is a vent for one's feelings, for those feelings in particular that one cannot communicate to other people'.[2]

In the first few years, the diary mixed the reflections of a romantic girl, who felt herself to be in an 'indecent way of thinking of men, and love',[3] with resolutions to be 'a good and useful woman in this world, and a companion of our Lord in the next'.[4] But she was willing to be amused by new sights and sounds. When her father took her to America in 1873, she was delighted with New York, 'the cleanliness and elegance about the town', and with Central Park, which 'beats all our town parks to pieces'; she carefully noticed as well whether the people she met would count as gentry in England. In Yosemite valley, she was for a short spell moved to become a painter. In San Francisco, she fled from a Chinese theatre after five or six minutes, because 'being in such close quarters with John Chinaman was not exactly pleasant'.[5] Once back at home, with no new adventures to divert her, she became more and more absorbed in what she regarded as 'the problem of her life'. She wanted to see clearly the final shape of her life: How would she live? What would she do between breakfast and tea-time, tea-time and bedtime? How should her time be divided between reading and social life? She searched for some measure for a 'good day', a purpose that her hours might serve.

In this she was probably inspired partly by her mother, who was sterner and more ambitious than Richard Potter. Mrs Potter had been an impressive girl and was no less so as the mistress of the Potter household. A visitor from France, a friend of Taine's, sent back a eulogy of a woman who not only

[1] *Apprenticeship*, p. 55.
[2] December 11, 1874.
[3] March 6, 1874.
[4] December 23, 1872.
[5] October 24, 1873.

345

knew much more Greek than himself, but was also 'a woman of the world, and even stylish. Moreover, she has nine daughters, two nurses, two governesses, servants in proportion, a large well-appointed house, frequent visitors; throughout all this, perfect order; never noise or fuss; the machine appears to move at its own accord'.[1] But at the same time, and even though she attended the Anglican Church with her husband, she was severe in her piety; she spent hours studying the Greek testament and the Fathers of the Church, and practised religious rites with unfailing regularity. She read the *Imitation of Christ* morning and night, and according to her daughter, 'longed for the mystical consolations and moral discipline of religious orthodoxy'.[2] Towards the end of her life, she collected grammars, and hoped to know twelve languages before she died. She had been disappointed in her hopes for intellectual comradeship with her husband, and for a life of more intellectual distinction, such as she supposed might have been the lot of a country gentleman's wife. Her children, too, failed her—she had lost her only son, generally disliked women, and found her daughters far from the intellectual sort of women she could admire. Beatrice described her as 'cursed with a divided personality', not at peace with herself.

To her daughter, she was a 'remote personage', mysteriously hostile, who rarely, but arbitrarily, interfered in her life. Mrs Potter, for her part, recorded in her diary that Beatrice was the only one of her children below the average in intelligence. After her mother's death, Beatrice began to feel that although she had known her father better, and her mother hardly at all, she had learned the most important things from her mother, whose pressure had been wholesome and in the right direction. Some years later, when she had begun doing social research, Beatrice suddenly felt a new closeness to her mother, who now seemed to belong more to her than to the rest of the family. When she became prominent, she congratulated herself on achieving what her mother had always wanted.

The other Potter girls were content to await their destiny as wives of well-established, possibly prominent men. (They succeeded in marrying a merchant, a lord, a millionaire millowner, a banker, an eminent surgeon, a barrister later raised to the peerage, and a member of a great Liberal family). But Beatrice was less confident, as well as more restless. She was handsome enough and had two or three partners for every dance at her first ball—'How I did enjoy that'.[3] Yet she felt she was somehow not lovable, and the fear that no one cared about her was a constant torment. When her mother's death gave her the job of running the household, she worried that her family, though dependent on her, felt little affection: 'I was not made to be loved,

[1] Michael Chevalier to Taine, in *Apprenticeship*, p. 15 n.
[2] *Ibid.* p. 14.
[3] *Ibid.* p. 75.

there must be something repulsive in my character'.[1] Later, and indeed throughout her life, she worried in the same way about all her friends. With new acquaintances, she was inclined to exaggerate in her own mind the significance of any attention paid to her, only to find that she had meant less to the other person than she had supposed. As she could never bear to discover that an old friendship had weakened or broken, she yearned for a 'recognised ethic of friendship', for rules to govern the making and breaking of friendships and end the 'anarchy', the 'lack of permanency' in human relations.[2]

The excitement, the exhilaration, and disappointments of being with other people, especially as a young lady in the market for a husband, were too painful for her: 'How well I recollect those first days of my early London seasons: the pleasurable but somewhat feverish anticipation of endless distraction . . . as one form of entertainment was piled on another, the pace became fast and furious; a mania for reckless talking, for the experimental display of one's own personality, ousted all else from consciousness'. The social round was followed by depression, indigestion, insomnia, and a host of disquieting doubts about herself and others.[3] Late at night, after a party, she would sit up writing in her diary that her suffering was all due to vanity, worthless and sinful, that she could avoid such pain by dedicating herself to a better life. Unlike her father, she did not enjoy the game of meeting and conquering the world, nor was she in the least inclined to find her predicaments amusing. Even as Mrs Webb, she felt the same and shunned direct participation in political life: 'I do not, and have never liked political life—there is too big an element of intrigue—too continuous a conflict of personality—too little essential comradeship'.[4] Yet she also wanted to make a name for herself. Far from accepting the conventional duty of late Victorian ladies 'to be as quiet and retiring and unobtrusive as possible . . .',[5] she wanted her energy and talents recognized somehow.

Whatever the conventions, by the latter decades of the nineteenth century a number of women had been recognized for their work. Lady novelists had become quite common and successful—Jane Austen, Charlotte Bronte, Mrs Gaskell, and, of course, George Eliot, who was at the height of her popularity when Beatrice Potter was searching for a vocation. Journalism and polemics for some worthy cause offered other openings: Hannah More and Harriet Martineau might have served as models. Or a lady might devote herself to improving some institution, like Florence Nightingale in the hospitals,

---

[1] February 1, 1883.
[2] May 10, 1915.
[3] *Apprenticeship*, pp. 48–9.
[4] December 5, 1925.
[5] *The Amberley Papers*, ed. by B. and P. Russell (London, 1937), vol. I, p. 142.

or Elizabeth Fry in prisons. The settlement houses, of course, made it easy to work among the poor. And finally, and most traditional, though more difficult to insure, a woman might become important by marrying an important man, and influence leading public figures, perhaps even campaign directly in public meetings, as both Lady Churchill and Lady Amberley did. Between 1872 and 1888, Beatrice Potter toyed with each of these possibilities.

THE STRUGGLE BETWEEN REASON AND PASSION: RELIGION, ART AND SCIENCE

But her first attempt to find her way to a 'meaningful and peaceful' life was through religion. She filled her diary with analyses of religious difficulties, in the manner of the famous Victorian doubters, and described herself, then and later, as having suffered over her loss of faith. Yet her spiritual upbringing was distinguished mainly by its difference from that of the classic nineteenth century doubters. Whereas Beatrice strolled in Hyde Park to be amused by the latest attacks on Christianity, Hale White had sat every Sunday in a crowded, foul smelling chapel through three services. At the age when George Eliot was writing, 'When I hear of the marrying and giving in marriage that is constantly being transacted, I can only sigh for those who are multiplying earthly ties',[1] Beatrice Potter was considering making the sacrifice of not coming out, and failed to keep her resolution. In fact, her first religious confession was neither of faith nor of doubt, but of search for a faith: 'I must make a faith for myself, I must work, work, until I have'.[2] Later on, she thought of herself as having been a religious young woman. But by the time she was twenty-two, the day when she could still 'pray in all sincerity of spirit to my Father in Heaven'[3] was well behind her.

It is difficult to say what inspired her desire for religious faith. Perhaps she tried to attract her mother's attention by a display of religious zeal. But it would not have been easy to live up to her mother's strict Puritanism, or to hide any shortcomings from her unsympathetic insight. Having failed as a believer, Beatrice may have tried to make herself interesting as a doubter. Whatever moved her at the beginning, it was the formlessness of her life, her lack of clear-cut convictions that soon came to trouble her most. The elegant pastime that agnosticism had become for some, like her father, was not for her.

From time to time, she took the Holy Sacrament and congratulated herself on being a good Christian, but her elation never lasted. It was the doctrine of atonement, she told herself, that was so difficult to accept. Like other good

---

[1] Joan Bennett, *George Eliot, her Mind and her Art* (Cambridge, 1948), p. 6.
[2] April 14, 1874.
[3] November 14, 1880.

rationalists, she saw in it only the substitution of Jesus for the true sinners, without feeling either thankfulness or awe for a god who went so far to save men. To her matter-of-fact mind, the sacrifice of Jesus seemed a pointless act, unjust, because an innocent man died, and to no good purpose, because wicked men ought not to be saved.[1] Besides, as her one firm belief, no doubt part of her family's way of life, was in the evil of wasting time and effort, she preferred to believe that Jesus could and did save the world not by dying, but by the less wasteful means of preaching.

Though for a while she declared herself devoted in some sort of way to Jesus, her sentiments were not those of someone clinging to the remains of faith. To many of the doubters, the 'dissolution of Jesus into mythologic vapour' was nothing less than the death of their dearest friend. To others, however difficult it became for them to accept the doctrine of atonement, the story of Jesus' sacrifice remained meaningful and touching, the great example of a noble life. George Eliot, even while devotedly translating Strauss's destructive *Leben Jesu*, could hardly bear his dissection of 'the beautiful story of the crucifixion'. Yet Beatrice, who thought of herself as struggling painfully toward religion, wrote quite calmly: 'I hope I may have an opportunity of studying Christianity some day, then perhaps I may find . . . reasons of the acceptance of Christianity by the greatest nation of the world . . .'.[2]

Nevertheless some of the beliefs and emotions associated with Christianity came easily to her. She found no difficulty in accepting the distinction between man's higher and lower nature, between reason and the passions. The beliefs she held to firmly for the rest of her life were the very ones that many of the doubters shed when they gave up Christianity. George Eliot, to whom Beatrice likened herself, had felt liberated by Spinoza's arguments on the difficulties of distinguishing good from evil, on the innocence of many worldly pleasures that 'one man may enjoy without hurting another'. When she turned against her religion, she rejected above all the rigid censoriousness it had taught her. But Beatrice, in her new spiritual state, disapproved of Spinoza. And when she read *Jane Eyre*, instead of feeling as George Eliot had, that the self-sacrifice had been somewhat unnecessary, she pronounced it an 'impure' book, where the 'author's conception of love is a feverish, almost lustful passion. Her hero is frankly speaking a bad and immoral man whom she endeavours to render attractive by giving him a certain force of character and much physical and intellectual power'.[3] Even though Charlotte Bronte believed as Beatrice did that the right path demanded the greatest sacrifice of self-interest, her descriptions of passion made her a sinful writer.

[1] March 27, 1875.
[2] Sept. 13, 1877.
[3] Sept. 6, 1875.

Beatrice disapproved of mixing duty with passion. Duty meant to her precisely what doubters like George Eliot had rejected—judicious self-abnegation, sustained wholly by intellect and utterly free of emotion, which belonged to the world of sin. She divided the world into two ethical parties: one that defended the senses, and the other that demanded self-sacrifice and repression. The renunciation of Job or the fortitude of Bunyan was the only kind of heroism she could understand. The Old Testament characters generally pleased her best because they were so actively engaged in struggling against the passions,[1] and Romans taught her that the Jews were favoured because they were readier to obey conscience than to follow their passions. She was inclined to assimilate passion of any kind to the crudest physical lust, and to condemn it as impure and immoral. But it was also associated in her mind with any emphasis on personality, or on the emotions. While she insisted that she would not renounce all emotional experiences, she wanted religion to provide a refuge from them, certainly from any concern with personality. The ideal religion, she felt, must be utterly impersonal. The kind of feeling that animated Christians like Robert Elsmere, the 'passionate memory' of great men who have spoken 'most audibly of God and of eternal hope', was repulsive to her. To remember Christ's personality was to be reminded of her own and thus be plunged further into turmoil. Peace and salvation lay not in anything connected with passion, emotion, or personality, but in the supremacy of reason, conscience, and self-abnegation. But it was not until later that she came to understand the source of her difficulty with Christianity: 'My real trouble is that I do not admire, still less reverence, human personality. All my religious feeling streams away from it to something higher'.[2] As she grew older, she could confess boldly:

To me, human personality as I know it—myself and others—is a tragedy. If it be the end of nature's processes, the experiment is a failure and had better be wound up.... I long to rid myself of my personality—and, having by all my strivings after knowledge and kindliness transformed some more of the ether into pure intellect and impersonal love, cease to exist—breathe out my life in Prayer.[3]

From an easy-going, prosperous, mid-Victorian, business family upbringing, Beatrice Potter made her way back to the sterner discipline of her forbears. The desire to discipline and rationalize her life, her idealization of labour as the only source of health and holiness, her opposition to all leisure and luxury, her worship of an iron will and cool intelligence—all could have been drawn directly from Puritan copy-books. She stood ready to do Baxter's bidding: 'Be wholly taken up in diligent business of your lawful

---

[1] July 11, 1875.

[2] October 29, 1925.

[3] February 28, 1930.

callings, when you are not exercised in the more immediate service of God'. But unfortunately she could neither discover the calling nor believe in God.

When she finally abandoned the attempt to be a Christian, she explained it as the result of a conflict between emotion and reason. Not that it was her only explanation. Christianity, she also told herself, was essentially selfish: 'the idea of doing good and believing blindly in order to arrive at eternal bliss is through its selfishness an immoral doctrine; I believe also that as soon as our religion becomes truly unselfish, enormous interest in the speculation as to the future existence of the individual will die out'.[1] But most persistently, Beatrice described herself as torn between emotions that demanded something 'worthy of absolute devotion and devout worship', and remained unsatisfied even by anything like 'Plato's Idea of the Beautiful or Perfect', and reason that condemned 'the great Father and Creator, the perfect object for devotion'.[2] She wanted both to believe wholeheartedly and to base her convictions only on demonstrable truth.

For a moment, Catholicism promised a solution, even though to her Protestant eyes St Peter's could never look like a proper church: 'There is a solemnity in its gorgeousness, but surely it is not Christian'.[3] The ritual was moving, and there was perhaps a chance that Catholicism, by substituting authority for intellect, 'on a point where individual reason has been proved inadequate', could reconcile reason and emotion. Perhaps, by surrendering one's judgement in some matters, one could comfortably accept the supremacy of reason in all others. But though her intellect almost accepted this compromise, the Church's lapses from 'pure morality' broke the spell. Later, when she visited Cologne and felt a certain 'superstitious awe' in the cathedral, she was relieved to hear Spencer explain that awe arises only because one senses that powerful men, 'Princes of the Church who were military chieftains and as bloodthirsty as their secular neighbours', had built the cathedrals.[4] In the end, she reduced Catholicism to a useful sort of mental hygiene, and as such, she praised it to the end of her life. A brief entry in her diary of February 1882 suggested what was to come of her meditations on Christianity:

Surely there are two ways of viewing the sacrifice of the Mass: one as an atonement to an exacting Deity, the other as a grand symbolical expression of the greatest of human characteristics, the power of self-sacrifice in the individual for the good of the community. . . . What a curious psychological fact is that great and mysterious joy in the prostration of soul and body before the symbol of infinite goodness uniting all individuals in one aspiration.[5]

[1] March 31, 1878, *Apprenticeship*, p. 97.
[2] November 14, 1880, *Apprenticeship*, p. 99.
[3] November 8, 1880.
[4] July 2, 1882.
[5] *Apprenticeship*, p. 101.

From time to time, other more 'rational' religions had captured her fancy. Buddhism was, for a moment, an appealing candidate. It seemed safe because Buddha's personality seemed nowhere near as important as Christ's: 'The majestic impersonality of Sakyamuni; his aloofness from the joys and sorrows of mortal man; his very lack of what is called humanity attracted me . . . the mysterious Nirvana, and the attainment of this unconditional blessedness of ridding yourself of your own personality, fascinated my imagination'.[1] But Buddhism offered nothing definite to worship. Its obligations were not concrete enough for someone interested in activity rather than contemplation and it provided no external discipline. For in one respect Beatrice was very different from the Puritan who believed that he had to stand alone face to face with God, and that no one and nothing could help him. She did not count such thorough-going self-sufficiency as a virtue, but was inclined rather to consider it a delusion. She did not expect herself to rely solely on her own strength.

The Religion of Humanity, as Harriet Martineau described it, was no more satisfactory. It seemed a selfless faith, but it had too little mysticism. It was 'bleak and dreary, in sorrow and ill-health'.[2] For the same reason, Beatrice rejected Lewes's positive philosophy, which was free of both metaphysics and theology, but gave her nothing to work for. All that remained of her exposure to positive philosophy was summarized by a quotation from Comte: ' . . . to live for others is the only means of developing the whole existence of man. Towards humanity, who is the only true great Being, we, the conscious elements of whom She is the compound, shall henceforth direct every aspect of our life, individual and collective . . .'[3] Neither God, Jesus, Buddha, nor Humanity could give Beatrice Potter the moral support and guidance she was seeking.

As religion failed her, she began turning over other possibilities. Partly she just read at random, hoping for a stray inspiration. Spencer's *First Principles* reassured her by 'its fearless conviction that no advance of science can take away the beautiful and elevating consciousness of something greater than humanity'.[4] She also read history and criticism—Froude's *English in Ireland*, Ruskin's *Modern Painters*, Buckle—always taking great pains to summarize what she had learned and to decide whether the writer should be praised or censored. Some of her comments foreshadowed her later opinions: against Grote on Greece, she argued, as Mill had in *Representative Government*, 'that if a perfectly democratic government is in the abstract the only perfectly right one', it may be destructive for a civilization in the early stages, even if,

[1] *Apprenticeship*, p. 88.
[2] March 8, 1878, *Apprenticeship*, p. 96.
[3] (1884) *Apprenticeship*, p. 149.
[4] December 15, 1877.

as in Athens, it produces 'a precarious development'. After reading Thucydides, she pronounced Pericles a man of 'high moral nature' and noted that he 'supported his comparatively just and humane policy by arguments of expediency, not as is often now the case, supporting an expedient policy by arguments of justice and humanity'.[1] Whatever her conclusions, she was always positive of them and very rarely changed her mind.

But some of her reading had a more consistent pattern. She was thinking of becoming a novelist, and filled her diary with notes and essays on novels as well as sketches of people she met and things she saw. Again, however, she took an odd view of her vocation. George Eliot's novels seemed good to her because they made her feel 'happier, more contented', because the author was never cynical and always earnest. Even so, when she read *Daniel Deronda*, it was not the picture of rootlessness or Daniel's discovery of a duty to his people that impressed her, but the author's preference for 'emotive over purely rational thought . . .', her almost 'naive belief in human nature, which most English readers would call morbid idealism. . .'.[2] Nor did Beatrice Potter share the enthusiasm of her contemporaries for George Sand. She saw nothing of what George Eliot described as her 'truthfulness', 'nicety of discrimination', 'tragic power', and 'loving, gentle humour'.

For portraits of how people felt and behaved were of little interest to Beatrice Potter; if a book did not make for spiritual or moral improvement, it bored and often repelled her. A novelist, she believed, had to teach a moral lesson. *Les Miserables* was a good novel because it was 'a glorious drama' and 'the description of the Bishop and the criminal is simply splendid', but mostly because Victor Hugo was 'such a pure writer': 'There is no hidden sensuality. He describes vice not as a cool and somewhat enjoying observer like George Sand, but as a great pitying moralist'.[3] Of Balzac, she strongly disapproved: he did not believe in the 'progress of human nature', and his characters were all corrupt except for the peasant who does not think or analyse. Balzac's only saving grace was his admiration of characters capable of self-devotion, but unfortunately, it was self-devotion of an 'inconsiderate, thoughtless' kind. His books seemed to her 'profoundly melancholy and enervating' because the wicked always prospered, and the woman's only nobility lay in 'self-immolation to her lover and child . . . it is the purely instinctive and not the spiritual love that he describes—The wife is the mistress of her husband, if it is between husband and wife that the love exists, which is rare. . .'.[4]

---

[1] Nov. 8, 1879 (Notes made Oct. 30, 1879 to Feb. 4, 1880).
[2] January 22, 1881.
[3] June 15, 1877.
[4] March 20, 1881.

The moralist's attitude to life was deep-rooted in Beatrice Potter, and she judged living people in the same way as she judged characters in a novel. When she visited Germany in 1878, she found the music delightful, but difficult to enjoy in 'the company of half washed and unshaved foreigners and Germans'. They were, she felt, 'such dirty slovenly looking creatures, so underbred and rowdy looking'.[1] The Viennese were gayer—'if happiness be the aim of existence, they understand the latter better than we do', but she was far from convinced that they had the right aim.[2] When she visited galleries, she wanted the paintings, like novels, to uplift her: Raphael's *Madonna and Child* in Dresden pleased her immensely because it was such an excellent 'representation of a perfect soul',[3] and Perugino's frescoes of the *Transformation and Nativity* captivated her for the same reason. But Titian's *Divine and Human Love*, although 'simply divine in its colouring', showed her 'nothing beautiful in the spirit or much in its motive'.[4]

After about two years of dabbling in novel-writing, Beatrice decided that it was not after all her vocation. She spoke of putting aside 'art' and devoting herself instead to 'science'. Her ambition to be a novelist and the time spent on reading novels now appeared to her as laziness and vanity, although Balzac's observations might prove useful for a 'future science of the mental life of the community'. She had wanted to be a novelist, she thought, because the novelist avoids 'the drudgery of mastering a difficult and tedious groundwork'.[5] He does not correct his theories by research, for he finds his verification very easily in nothing more than the reader's knowledge of himself. Writing literature was harmless, perhaps, but certainly frivolous, or, as she put it in a more poetic moment: 'the amateur', meaning the novelist, 'may wander over moorland and bogland with the delightful sensations of elasticity underfoot and variety around him, and in the happy consciousness that his path differs somewhat from that of any fellow wanderer'.[6] Science was quite another matter.

Science replaced instinct with principles; it assured the triumph of reason over passion. The scientific mind was 'the most purely rational' because the only test science allowed was the demonstrable accordance of idea with fact. It developed self-controlled effort and generated 'intellectual conscience'. It produced 'the same transformation in the realm of thought as we have watched in the development of morality, whereby principles have been accepted in lieu of instinct as the guide of the individual in his conduct toward

---

[1] June, 1878.
[2] October 5, 1878.
[3] October 13, 1878.
[4] November 9, 1880.
[5] January 2, 1883.
[6] January 2, 1883.

the community. . .'.[1] When occasionally Beatrice felt herself thinking about writing novels, she scolded herself for a moral lapse. The temptation returned, even at the age of thirty, but was staunchly resisted:

I have been haunted (lately) . . . by the vulgar wish to write a novel. There is intense attractiveness in the comparative ease of descriptive writing. Compare it with work in which movements of commodities, percentages, depreciations, averages, and all the ugly horrors of commercial facts are in the dominant place, and must remain so if the work is to be worthful . . . (but) what have the whole lot of [novels] accomplished . . . in the advancement of society on the one [and] only basis that can bring with it virtue and happiness—scientific method?[2]

In keeping with her decision, Beatrice began to concentrate on scientific reading. She worked in the laboratory, preparing biological specimens with her surgeon brother-in-law, Willie Cripps. She plodded through texts of physiology. She read the works of Herbert Spencer, and discussed the nature of science with him at length. And she began to develop the pattern for living to which she kept for the rest of her life—an unshakable routine and detailed schedules of research. This, she thought, was the scientific life. It was the life of reason and of virtue. Opposed to it was the life of passion, emotion, or instinct, a life with no discipline, no clearly laid out plan or stated purpose and rules.

As she prepared biological specimens, she found that she could breathe more freely—'one leaves behind all personalities and strives hard to ascertain the constitution of things, a constitution which to us is eternal and dependent on no one manifestation of it'. One must think, she now realised, not of men and women, but of 'persons, past, and present', as groups of qualities 'bound up for a time in one form'.[3] Ordinary social life could teach one very little because it was too marked with individual personalities to let one see the great wave of humanity. When she walked down Tottenham Court Road, and jostled up 'against the men and women of the "people", with their various expressions of determined struggle, weak self-indulgence and discontented effort', she could not resist the conviction that 'the fate of each individual is governed by conditions born of the distant past'. She did not, she now felt sure, want to know this or that man, but a 'bird's eye view of mankind'.[4]

At one point, she considered doing Settlement House work. Her sister, Kate, had introduced her to it. In fact, Kate became so attached to East London that when she married Leonard Courtney, she held her wedding there, and invited her fashionable friends from the West End to join the

---

[1] January 2, 1883.
[2] September 30, 1889.
[3] June 3, 1883.
[4] June 3, 1883.

parishioners of St Jude's in the East End. But Beatrice never did Settlement House work. Instead, she went to work for the Charity Organization Society, described by Canon Barnett, who was the guiding spirit of Settlement House work, as an attempt to substitute 'a relief giving machine for a helping hand'.[1] Barnett disliked their impersonality, their tendency to treat human beings as cases, and he left the Society, he explained, mainly because he felt that the only way to improve society without leaving worse evils behind was through personal work, through friendship. This was almost the exact contrary of what Beatrice Potter believed. And it is nicely illustrated in her misunderstanding of why the Barnetts left the Charity Organization Society—she thought it was because they had become socialists, and the Society was not socialist enough. Their true objection was incomprehensible to her.

Her own feelings were all against a concern with personality or individuals as the basis of reforming society. This was made clear in her reactions to her experience of working among the poor. When her sister married, Beatrice took over her job as a rent collector in a working class housing project, which had been set up in the East End to improve housing for the workers. Whereas Kate Potter had seen her work there as a chance to live among the poor, Beatrice described it as an opportunity to observe the people without intruding on them too much. For all her conscientious and efficient effort, it was more than she could bear. The job required getting to know the tenants and their habits well enough either to discipline them or exclude them. Speaking with the tenants left her at the end of the day drained of all energy, and longing to escape and devote herself exclusively to observation. She could spend hours considering dreary statistics about the buildings, their facilities and floor space, but the personal contacts were another matter. After one such day, she wrote in her diary: 'this East End life, with its dirt, drunkenness and immorality, absence of co-operation or common interests, saddens me and weighs down my spirit. I could not live down here; I should lose heart and become worthless as a worker. And practical work does not satisfy me; it seems like walking on shifting sand. . .'.[2]

She never ceased to be grateful to Herbert Spencer for what he had taught her about 'scientific method'. In 1901, while summing up her life thus far, she wrote that after her mother's death in 1881 'came the spring of my nature into health and vigour and a rich seed time of intellectual life. My life became inspired with the spirit of modern science. . . . This phase of my life was connected with my relations to Herbert Spencer; unmeasured admiration for his intellect, on my side, and affection for my personality, on his part'.[3] Although,

[1] H. Barnett, *Canon Barnett, His Life, Work and Friends* (Boston, 1919), vol. II, p. 263.
[2] November 8, 1886, *Apprenticeship*, p. 276.
[3] New Year's Day, 1901 (Vol. 20, Conclusion).

like everyone else, she came to think of Spencer as a 'mummy', too devoid of ordinary emotions, and although she became critical of his political dogma, neither her friendship nor her admiration for him ever weakened. He had shown her the true, impersonal way of seeing the world, and he had taught her that it was the social whole, the human race, that mattered most.

At the same time, he allowed her to think of herself as not having altogether lost her religious instincts. Beatrice Potter was probably one of the last to find solace in the Great Unknowable, and when she spoke or wrote of it later in her life, her friends were inclined either to laugh or suspect her sincerity. But it genuinely made her feel easier about having moved from what she regarded as grave religious probings to science. It set her free to worship the scientific method without asking herself uncomfortable questions. She could feel that she had kept her sense of mystery without letting it interfere with daily life, as orthodox religion inevitably did. Later the Great Unknowable helped to fortify her insistence that the economic and political policies she advocated affected only the means and not the ends of human life, and need therefore be judged only by their efficiency for achieving scientific objectives. While she always had to supplement the formless worship of the Unknown, and although after a time it ceased to satisfy her, for several decades it helped to reassure her that she had not become an unfeeling reasoning machine.

In another way too, Beatrice insisted that she was not a convert to arid intellectualism. She never, she would point out, denied the importance of emotion, only it had to be 'pure' emotion. Throughout her life, she continued to praise that 'state of mind, which for lack of a better word, we call Love—some call it Heavenly Love, to distinguish it from Animal Love'.[1]

JOSEPH CHAMBERLAIN

The final shape of Beatrice's life work was decided by an intense personal attachment between 1883 and 1888. Before then, though she read many books and thought about a great variety of subjects, though she later believed that she had always been interested in politics and politicians, her diary totally ignored the exciting political events of the 'seventies and 'eighties. She speculated about democracy in general, but not about the Franchise Act. She never did become interested in political issues and men as such, but only as connected with some broad social change. But even politics in this sense did not seriously absorb her until she came to connect it with her scientific interests. The new science had in fact already become associated with Radical Liberalism through the *Fortnightly*. But the association was casual, and Morley never claimed to support a systematic policy, though he lamented the lack of one. Beatrice had to make the connection for herself.

[1] November 14, 1915.

At a dinner in June, 1883, she met Joseph Chamberlain. His tall, spare, impeccable figure, with his monocle and an orchid in his lapel, was one of the best known in England. He was President of the Board of Trade, and heir apparent to the leadership of the Liberal Party. For the moment, he was the *enfant terrible* of the Gladstone Cabinet, at loggerheads with most of his colleagues and especially with Gladstone. But by creating the National Liberal Federation that reorganised the Liberal Party in the constituencies, he contributed so much to Gladstone's victory in 1880 that he could not be kept out of the Cabinet. He was the established leader of the agitation for social reform and local government; earlier, he had founded the National Education League advocating universal, free, compulsory, and unsectarian primary education; he had sparked the movement for municipal reform, publicly made violent remarks against the House of Lords and the Church of England, and generally declared himself an advocate of moderate socialism. In foreign affairs, he held what Sir Charles Dilke called 'strongly patriotic and national opinions' that foreshadowed his later role as defender of the empire. He opposed Home Rule for Ireland, had favoured sending aid to General Gordon when Gladstone hesitated, and on other occasions supported policies that led some to consider him the foremost jingoist in the Cabinet. Although he never became a socialist in the Webbs' sense, the policies he advocated during the years when Beatrice knew him were very similar to those she and Sidney later tried to implement.

At the dinner where they met, Chamberlain 'talked passionately', she recorded in her diary, of getting hold of other people's property for the masses. He impressed her as a man of action, a leader of radical politics, altogether a lively contrast to Herbert Spencer, the only other 'great man' she knew at all well. She soon found herself thinking of him steadily, and became convinced that he meant to propose marriage to her. At the end of the year, she invited him to a house-party and discussed with her family the possibility of marrying him. Precisely what happened then is difficult to tell. A week later she reported in her diary that they had talked in the abstract about the relation between men and women, and that she had opposed his belief in egalitarianism in politics. She interpreted the conversation as a sparring about their own relationship in which her unwillingness to grant any man intellectual mastery over herself was tantamount to a refusal of marriage. From later entries, it seems clear that in any case he did not plainly offer to marry her. But this was just the beginning of a long, painful episode.

They met again from time to time, and in her own mind Beatrice played constantly with the 'problem' of marrying Chamberlain. But often, too, she felt there was no chance of her ever knowing personal joy and tried instead to find her way towards 'doing something for others'. Her diary recorded the moral: 'We have learnt that we can neither see, think, nor feel alone—much less live without the help of others; therefore we must live for others. . .'. Slowly, what she called her personal and objective interests were coming to meet in a concern with the why and wherefore of misery in this world.[1]

Politics, or rather, the nature of the relation between society and government began to interest her more. Chamberlain argued that the government should give the people what they want; she wondered whether it might not be wrong for the governing class to 'gratify the sensations of the great social organism', whether it should not rather impose the right remedies 'irrespective of the longings of the patient. If the government is an outside force to be directed by the ablest minds . . . then it is a question of correct diagnosis and of a most deeply thought out treatment. . .'.[2] At times when she grew sceptical about her dream of a bird's eye view of the past that would provide a glimpse into the future, she would review her 'little hoard of facts' in the hope that they would lead her 'to untie the knots of human destiny'. For the first time, she discussed the political parties in England: 'The liberal party are still bound together . . . by that metaphysical doctrine that each responsible individual has an equal right to a say in the government of his country'.[3] She knew that she opposed the democratic view that had transformed 'the doctrine of the equal rights of individuals into that of the absolute right of the majority—tacitly asserting the infallibility of the judgement of the great working masses on social questions. Practically this means that social laws are not discoverable by the scientific method—that the only guide to political action is the will of the people'.[4] This sort of democracy did nothing but crown the self-interest of the working class, which was no better than the self-interest of the upper class. Beatrice preferred that social science, 'a comprehensive knowledge of social facts, past and present',[5] should come to rule.

In the midst of these political reflections, she continued to hope that the role of wife and mother was not closed to her, while reminding herself in black moments that 'altruism is after all the creed of those who are suffering personal misery and yet do not intend to sink into abject wretchedness—it used to be devotion to God, under one form or another—now this God is dead it must be devotion to other human beings'.[6] Most of the time she was unhappy and morbid, and finally in a moment of despair she wrote to Chamberlain a frank declaration of her feelings.[7] His reply was polite, but discouraging. She was told besides by a friend who knew Chamberlain well

[1] October 15, 1884.
[2] September 26, 1883.
[3] November 6, 1884.
[4] November 6, 1884.
[5] November 6, 1884.
[6] November 19, 1884.
[7] January 29, 1885.

that he did not think of marrying her.[1] The following week, she took the Sacrament and declared,

This morning took the Sacrament—the great symbol of sacrifice—of the sacrifice of individual life and happiness . . . I have passed through months and months of hardness and vain endeavour after foolish things . . . the last two years I have been striving after the fulfilment of my lower nature. . . . *Now*, surely I am humbled ? . . . Shall I resist the querulous grief at missing the greatest happiness of a woman's life. Now I must more than ever, decide my life's way. . . . Is it vanity, this intense desire to devote my life to clearing up of social questions. . . . If I believed I had in my intellect and character the fit instrument for scientific inquiry and that I should strike truth—I could pass years in uneventful learning—living to work, sleeping to rest from work in order to work again.[2]

Still her attachment to Chamberlain lived on, and it was not until November, 1888, when he was actually married to the daughter of an American governor that she became resigned to her fate. As she continued to follow his career closely, she found consolation in the reflection that had she been his wife he would have been a far nobler politician.

Her dream of marrying Chamberlain was Beatrice's last attempt to find a personal object for devotion. The pain she suffered went a long way towards convincing her that she must find the meaning of her life in some more remote, impersonal object. Marriage was not altogether out of the question, but it would not be the sole or highest light in her life.

A CONVERT TO SOCIALISM

By the time the Chamberlain episode was over, Beatrice was almost completely converted to socialism. Hints of her conversion had been appearing for some time. She had begun to use some of the catchwords that marked her later work. In August, 1885, after saying that she was inclined to look more favourably again on Spencer's view that the state's duty was 'the free and right administration of justice between individuals', she began considering whether the wrongs of 'great classes of men' could perhaps be corrected by 'taking from a whole class that which has been stolen. . .'.[3] Not long afterwards, she criticized Spencer for 'trying to palm off illustrations as data by transcribing biological laws into terms of social facts and then reasoning by them as social laws'. She soon became certain that his view of the state was wrong, and her reading during these years was directed towards studying the two functions of state interference: 'enforcing respect in the individual for the health of others . . . and secondly, that more doubtful natural function—its

[1] March 6, 1886.
[2] March 15, 1886.
[3] August 7, 1885.

attempt to supplement by direct constructive activity the work of voluntary enterprise and of individual effort'.[1]

She had been coming to see a way of linking social investigation with political action. The direction appeared first in an article on 'Social Diagnosis' (May 6, 1886) where she tried to show how much men were influenced by descriptions of social facts, and especially how personal observation was liable to err unless checked by the statistical method. Studying political economy led her to conclude that both Adam Smith and Karl Marx had seen only the economic aspect of human nature, and that the political economy of Adam Smith, having originated as a 'crusade of the eighteenth century against class tyranny', had become the 'Employer's Gospel' of the nineteenth.[2] By the autumn of 1886 she had determined to study German socialism and English history with a view to writing a history of industrialism. In general, she was dwelling more and more on the unimportance of the individual. A visit to Leonard Courtney's constituency inspired the following comments on a talk with a non-conformist farmer:

our conversation another instance of the entire novelty of the scientific view of society—of the hopeless misunderstanding of the motto (my motto) to know in order to act. According to these excellent persons it is individual suffering that must be relieved, not the common good considered. And I maintain that I am the true Socialist through my willingness to sacrifice the individual to the community. But this man had not thought of the social question, except from the religious and political point of view—charity and love of freedom were the qualities seeking expression in his earnest single-minded opinion.[3]

By March, 1889, Beatrice was able to write: 'These last months I have been trying to set my nature to the higher note of self-forgetting effort for the Public Good. It has been a spiritual struggle—against bitterness and resentfulness on the one hand—one long prayer against the evil passions of body and mind'.[4] The diary was now divided into two journals, one in which she recorded her social observations, and the other where she wrote of personal things. When her friend, Auberon Herbert, teased her about being 'a woman without a soul, looking on struggling society like a young surgeon looks on a case',[5] she was flattered. Peace of mind had at last come to her—'I have found the life that suits me. . . . My work now absolutely absorbs me'.[6]

Her painstaking study of details was leading her towards a knowledge of the whole, of the 'forces which are swaying to and fro, raising or depressing

[1] September 15, 1885.
[2] July 30, 1886.
[3] March 15, 1887.
[4] March 10, 1889.
[5] February 8, 1888.
[6] March 28, 1888.

this vast herd of human beings . . .'.[1] At the same time, she had been gaining recognition as a social investigator. In the spring of 1887, she began assisting her cousin, Charles Booth, in his inquiry into the *Life and Labour of the People of London*. Her first assignment was to study dock labour. In September, 1887, an article on 'Dock Life in the East End of London' appeared in the *Nineteenth Century*, followed by others on the tailoring trade of East London. As a social investigator, she could even 'enjoy the life of the People—the reality of their effort and aims; the simplicity of their sorrows and joys'.[2] She was very good at interviews, sympathetic and careful, but she regarded interviewing as 'social investigation', not at all like the personal work she disliked. And she succeeded in giving a vivid account. Characteristically, what appalled her most in the conditions of work was the importance of the 'personal element'. There was no longer any question in her mind that individual efforts to improve society were useless—'An enlightened selfishness in men and women cannot bring about the Peace of an unselfconscious, self-devotion of all individuals to the Public Good'.[3]

Her personal outlook had also become firmly defined and did not change for the rest of her life. Its character is easiest to see in her opinions about literature. She condemned the French Realist School 'as pandering to fruitless curiosity, as rousing latent passion to a degrading and artificial satisfaction through the imagination, weakening alike to the physical and the moral fibre of the great majority of readers'.[4] In later writers like Aldous Huxley and D. H. Lawrence, she lamented the 'utter absence of any kind of ethical code, and of any fixed scale of values. Judging by the types of character they choose to portray there is a preference for men and women who combine a clever intellect with unrestrained animal impulse'.[5] Lawrence was especially wicked. His attitude to the relation between men and women was contemptible:

Like so much else in modern art and literature, Lawrence's ideal is deliberately subhuman: a device to revert to the pre-human animal. I prefer the hard hygienic view of sex, and the conscious subordination of sexuality to the task of 'building up Socialism' characteristic of Soviet Russia; it may lack a sense of humour, as well as a sense of beauty, but it is more likely to lead to a healthy mind in a healthy body than Lawrence's morbid obsession about the 'phallic consciousness' as the be all and end all of human life.

His views on economics and politics were as bad—'the dominant note is insistent anarchism, a dislike to anything that is fixed. . .'.[6] Virginia Woolf

[1] May 5, 1888.
[2] May 5, 1888.
[3] March 10, 1889.
[4] August 4, 1889.
[5] December 5, 1925.
[6] October 30, 1932.

was less offensive and personally very attractive, but her novels were dull and trivial: 'Her men and women do not interest me—they don't seem worth describing in such detail . . . no predominant aims, no powerful reactions from their mental environment. . . . To the aged Victorian this soullessness is depressing—doubtless our insistence on a Purpose, whether for the individual or the Universe, appears to them a delusion and a pernicious delusion'.[1] There were few commendable novels like Paul Gourget's *Clime d'Amour*, where he described so vividly the 'separation of, and antagonism possible between deep passion on the one side, and of conscience and the affection which springs from judgement on the other'.[2]

Novelists were not generally very worthy people, and the personal conduct of George Eliot was perhaps no worse than one might have expected. She had light-heartedly 'left the beaten track of morality' and 'taken to herself all the good things of the world without seeking out the less gifted and fortunate'.[3] Beatrice, however, had been saved from such dangers by her scientific work. She had been thoroughly cleansed of ambition and vanity, and made aware of her responsibility for the welfare of others; she had become conscious of a special mission, 'a duty to society at large rather than to individuals',[4] which made even drudgery far more satisfying than the 'restless craving for personal recognition which haunted me years ago'.[5] All her interests were now united: 'Search after Truth—the careful measurement of facts—is the Enthusiasm of my life: and of late it has been combined with a realisation of the common aims of the great army of Truth-seekers—the ennobling of Human life'.[6]

Her general views of society and politics had, however, still to be translated into policies. She had long felt certain that nothing good in politics could come of emphasizing rights. 'Renunciation, that is a great fact we all—individuals and classes, have to learn—in trying to avoid it we bring misery to ourselves and others'.[7] Socialism meant politics based on renunciation, a readiness to sacrifice the individual along with class to the common good. But whether this required the abolition of profit-making industry, she decided somewhat later. Toward the end of 1889, she was wondering

whether a system of standard salaries and standard wages such as is being gradually evolved in Joint Stock and Cooperative enterprise is not a higher form of industrial organisation? Should not the use of a man's faculties after he has received sufficient to keep them in full working order be dedicated to Society? And are we not through the force of Public Opinion and the natural evolution of industry tending that way?[8]

[1] February 5, 1927.   [2] September 1, 1889.
[3] January 29, 1885.   [4] August 28, 1888.
[5] August 20, 1889.   [6] August 17, 1889.
[7] January 29, 1885.   [8] October 30, 1889.

In the course of preparing her book on the cooperatives, which she began early in 1889, she saw a movement towards an 'unconscious realisation of the socialist ideal of officially managed business on the basis of voluntary association', enlivened by the 'religious element of work for humanity'. By 1890, she could declare, 'At last I am a Socialist',[1] meaning that she now accepted not only the spirit, but also the policies of state socialism.

Against friends who believed that socialism meant equal pay, or giving to each according to his needs, she argued firmly that it meant rewarding services according to 'their competitive worth to the community'.[2] Her conversion to socialism had come, she explained, 'not because I believe it would ameliorate the conditions of the masses (though I think it would do so), but because I believe that only under communal ownership of the means of production can you arrive at the most perfect form of individual development—at the greatest stimulus to individual effort'.[3] In *My Apprenticeship*, however, she preferred to emphasize the importance of her growing awareness of poverty and her rejection of an upper class bias in making her a socialist.

She began to work subtly for her objective. When asked to participate in a report, she tried to suggest measures, however insignificant in themselves, that would increase the government's control over industry. The role she was to play in public investigations was perfectly clear to her: 'Though I am suspected of socialism, my anti-sensationalism gives me a footing among the sternest school of laissez-faire economists—and this position I must guard jealously if I am to be of even little use as a reforming agency'.[4] She no longer felt lonely or unhappy. She had friends and fellow workers, as well as a vision that took her out of herself: 'My whole thought and feeling has drifted far out into the Future—present persons seem to me so many shadows; it is for future generations, for their noble happiness that I live and pray'.[5] Science had taught her that only the future and only the human race as a whole mattered.

[1] January 30, 1890, *Apprenticeship*, p. 408.
[2] February 15, 1890.
[3] February 15, 1890.
[4] February 9, 1890.
[5] April 26, 1890.

CHAPTER XXIX

THE APOTHEOSIS OF POLITICS

How science could dispense with politics in the traditional sense Beatrice
Potter discovered after becoming Mrs Sidney Webb.[1] From early on one of
Sidney Webb's favourite arguments for socialism had been that nations
should be thought of as social organisms engaged in a struggle for survival.
In his contribution to the *Fabian Essays*, 'The Historic Basis of Socialism',
he warned Englishmen that, 'The cultivated Athenians, Saracens, and
Provençals went down in the struggle for existence before their respective
competitors, who, individually inferior, were in possession of a, at that time,
more valuable social organisation'. The Germans had defeated the French,
he explained, 'not because the average German was an inch and a half taller
than the average Frenchman, or because he had read five more books, but
because the German social organism was, for the purposes of the time,

---

[1] She met Sidney in 1890 and married him in 1892, after her father's death. She hesitated at
first but in the end could not resist Sidney's 'resolute, patient affection, his honest care for my
welfare. . .'. There was consolation, too, in the thought: 'But if I marry—though I shall be
drawn to it by affection and gratitude—it will be an act of renunciation of self, and not an
indulgence of self as it would have been in the other case'. (May 22, 1891) The differences
between Sidney and Beatrice Webb are aptly summed up in her comment on their tastes in
conversation with their friends: 'The relation of man's mind to the Universe is constantly
present as a background in my own thought and with some of our more intimate acquaintances—with Harvey, Masterman, Haldane, Russell—I have long talks. But the subject
bores Sidney as leading nowhere and as not capable of what he considers valid discussion—
exactly as he dislikes discussing what train you will go by, before he has got hold of the
Bradshaw. He prefers reading a statistical abstract of LCC agenda'.
    She had dedicated herself in this marriage to an exclusively 'brainworking' life but
continued to think of 'motherhood' as a woman's true vocation: 'First and foremost I
should wish a woman I loved to be a mother. . . . From the first I would impress on her the
holiness of motherhood. . . . But for the sake of that very motherhood I would teach her
that she must be an intellectual being—that without a strong deliberate mind she is only
capable of the animal office of bearing children, not of rearing them. It pains me to see a
fine intelligent girl, directly she marries, putting aside intellectual things as no longer
pertinent to her daily life. . .'. (July 25, 1894) 'And yet, the other alternative,—so often
nowadays chosen by intellectual women—of deliberately foregoing motherhood seems to
me to thwart all the purposes of their nature. I myself—or rather we—chose this course on
our marriage—but then I had passed the age when it is easy and natural for a woman to
become a child bearer. . . . If I were again a young woman and had the choice between a
brainworking profession and motherhood, I would not hesitate which life to choose (as it
is I sometimes wonder whether I had better not have risked it and taken my chance).'
(July 28, 1894).

365

superior in efficiency to the French'. If Englishmen wished to hand down their influence, and not merely leave the memory of their excellence, they had better remember that it was even more important 'to improve the social organism of which we form part, than to perfect our individual developments'. They had to realize that the interests of the individual unit often clashed with those of the whole and that the latter must take precedence. And Webb offered the same consolation that Ritchie had—in yielding to the whole, the individual realized his highest capacities, for 'the perfect and fitting development of each individual' consisted in filling 'in the best possible way, of his humble function in the great social machine'.[1]

The Webbs never deduced rules of social organization from the social organism, and in general preferred to deny the propriety of biological analogies. Nevertheless, the 'social organism' was more than an image pressed into service for polemical purposes. It summed up for them the nature of society and made possible clear-cut, scientific answers to political problems that otherwise seemed difficult. Questions such as whether the empire was to be preferred over the rights of national self-determination were easily settled.

The answer was derived from the requirements of progress in the social organism. The direction of progress, the Webbs argued, was towards larger, more complex, and more highly integrated organisms. The course of evolution made it inevitable that the world would ultimately be united into one grand social organism, which would be identical with Humanity, and divided into smaller units only for administrative purposes. It followed that, 'The abstract right to unfettered freedom in self-government, which we all see that we must deny to the individual, cannot be accorded to the family, the tribe, the race, the parish, the city, the county, the province, or the state. . .'. Nothing but a retrogressive, atomic conception of society, the Webbs argued, lay behind 'much of the feeling of nineteenth century Liberalism with regard to foreign and colonial policy'. Progressive twentieth-century politics had to be based not on the rights of 'nationalities', but on 'the concrete administrative necessities of definitely organized commonwealths; not on racial autonomy whatever the geography—an obsolete tribal notion which would give us an empire of the Jews—but on territorial democracy, whatever the mixture of races'.[2]

The British Empire not only testified to England's superiority in its struggle with other nations, but was clearly a step on the way to the all-embracing social organism of the future. Of course, it was not to be run for the profit of England and it had to be organized so as to 'promote the maximum individual

---

[1] Sidney Webb, 'The Historic Basis of Socialism', in *Fabian Essays* (London, 1948), p. 54.
[2] Sidney Webb, 'Twentieth Century Politics', *Fabian Tract* 108, p. 5.

development of each geographical unit within its bounds'. But as in all other matters, this 'maximum of individual development' could not be secured by 'allowing each unit to pursue its own ends without reference to the welfare of the whole'.[1] Therefore the Webbs did not hesitate to declare themselves thoroughly against Irish Home Rule: 'We at any rate, are precluded from assuming or admitting that any distinct "nationality", just because it imagines itself to have ends which differ from, and, perhaps conflict with, the common interests of the Empire as a whole, has, therefore, an abstract right to organize an independent government and pursue those ends at whatever costs to its colleagues or neighbours'.[2] The agitation for Irish Home Rule was hardly short of ridiculous, for a small nation that had no real claim to being a grand social organism should not be encouraged in idle day-dreams. The Webbs' position on the Boer War was similar—better management might perhaps have avoided the war, but once it broke out, they were determined to 'face the fact that henceforth the Transvaal and the Orange Free State must be within the British Empire'.[3] It was only when England seemed utterly unable to hold a colony, as by 1930 had become clear in the case of India, that the Webbs were ready to support independence.[4]

The image of society as an organism made it reasonable also to derive an argument for socialism from the experience of England during the first World War. This was the moral of the *Decay of Capitalism*, written in 1920. The Webbs felt certain that the war had made England ripe for a fundamental change: 'The state of things brought about by the war is, in fact, the greatest of opportunities for a big step forward that the world has ever seen—indeed a radical revolution is the only alternative to ruin. We are at the end of one civilization: the question is are we at the beginning of another'.[5] But even more, the war had pointed out what the next step had to be. England had succeeded in the war because she had recognized consciously that she was engaged in a struggle for survival with other social organisms, and had accordingly subordinated all other interests to winning that struggle. It remained only to recognize that a state of war is but a more intense phase of the perpetual struggle for existence, that national survival had always to come before individual interests, however noble: 'The lesson of evolution seems to be that inter-racial competition is really more momentous in its consequences than the struggle between individuals. It is of comparatively little importance in the long run that individuals should develop to the utmost, if the life of the

---

[1] *Ibid.* p. 6.
[2] *Ibid.* p. 5.
[3] Beatrice Webb, *Our Partnership* (London, 1948), p. 189.
[4] May 4, 1930.
[5] December 11, 1917.

community in which they live is not thereby served'.[1] It followed that the extensive government controls that England had found effective in winning the war would serve her equally well in so-called peace, where the objectives were no different.

At the same time, even though that was not the primary aim, the lives of many individuals would be radically improved. Poverty would have to be eliminated because poverty weakened national efficiency and drained away 'the vitality of the race'. A national minimum in wages was imperative, Sidney Webb declared, 'not merely, or even mainly, for the comfort of the workers, but absolutely for the success of our industry in competition with the world'. Only a programme of national efficiency could 'breed an even moderately Imperial race'. Education, too, had to be improved because 'It is in the classrooms . . . that the future battles of the Empire for commercial prosperity are being already lost'.[2] Incidentally individuals as such would benefit from society's recognition of a true order of values.

But the Webbs also argued more directly from the analogy of the social organism to the need for socialism. The 'new scientific conception of the Social Organism', Sidney Webb affirmed, 'has put completely out of countenance the cherished principle of the Political Economist and the Philosophical Radical. We left them sailing gaily into Anarchy on the stream of Laissez-Faire'. The Webbs agreed with Spencer's and Kidd's critics that since competing individuals acted only for their self-interest, a competitive society resembled an organism where each cell was left to forage for itself. Competition was to them nothing but a free struggle of warring atoms which some strange optimists hoped would unconsciously result in the best social state. It was the opposite of a 'conscious, deliberate organization of society', and science had shown that 'conscious "direct adaptation" steadily supplants the unconscious and wasteful "indirect adaptation" of the earlier struggle for existence . . .'.[3] In the Webbs' vocabulary, individualism and competition were synonymous with anarchy. Nations with centralized governments and a high degree of social discipline were superior social organisms. And a practical demonstration of this truth was furnished by Japan's success in the war with Russia. Mrs Webb predicted that the Japanese triumph would 'alter not merely the balance of power, but the balance of ideas—it will tell against Christianity as the one religion, against materialistic individualism, against autocracy, against luxury, in favour of organization, collective regulation, scientific education, physical and mental training—but on the whole

[1] Sidney Webb, 'Difficulties of Individualism', *Problems of Modern Industry* (London, 1920), p. 250.

[2] Webb, 'Twentieth Century Politics', pp. 8, 9, 14.

[3] Webb, 'The Historic Basis of Socialism', p. 54.

not in favour of democracy'.[1] She concluded that it did not matter which creed or training a nation adopted so long as it produced discipline and self-lessness. Because these qualities were lacking in Russia, her disintegration was inevitable. Russia's fate taught 'the terrible object lesson of the failure even in the struggle for existence of the race which has lacked conduct, abstinence from physical pleasures, and trained intelligence in the bulk of its people. . .' .[2] The only consolation for the Russians was that the Chinese were even more hopeless—'a race of ants or bees of gregarious habits but incapable of the organization of the ant-hill or the hive. They show us, indeed, what homo sapiens can be if he does not evolve into the social organism'.[3]

The most interesting consequences of thinking in terms of the social organism appeared in the Webbs' proposals for running a society entirely by science. Although their *Constitution for a Socialist Commonwealth* was not very much noticed and is of all their books one of the least remembered, to the Webbs it became a crucial work: 'The publication of the Socialist Constitution was an event in our lives: the summing up of our observation and reasoning about political and industrial organization'.[4] It was not primarily a plan for a society in which the state owned all the resources; it was above all a plan for replacing politics with science, politicians with scientific experts. It designed a government in which the uninformed public, and its haphazardly trained representatives, were made to recognize and submit to the knowledge of social scientists. It explained why the Webbs had pledged themselves 'to establish on a firm basis a Science of Society',[5] the purpose that animated their research and their efforts for the London School of Economics. Nationalization of the means of production and distribution interested them only secondarily, as a way of insuring the application of scientific method to social problems.

The key to the *Constitution* appeared as early as the Webbs' second book, *Industrial Democracy*: 'Whether in political or in industrial democracy, though it is the Citizen who, as Elector or Consumer, ultimately gives the order, it is the Professional Expert who advises what the order shall be'. The older notion of democracy that 'meant an "equal and identical" sharing of the duties of government' was declared obsolete; for now men could rely on a 'specially selected and specially trained class of professional experts'.

---

[1] *Our Partnership*, p. 299. [2] February 20, 1905.

[3] Sidney and Beatrice Webb, 'China in Revolution', *Crusade against Destitution*, III (March, 1912), p. 55. Edgar Snow's *The Red Star Over China* convinced Mrs Webb that China no longer displayed the hopeless anarchy of the past—'What interests me most is . . . the new philosophy of life and code of conduct that has transformed the Chinese from passive to active agents of human progress. . . . Mao and his comrades are not interested in their own personality, nor even in their own prowess and success: they are impersonal in their outlook, absorbed in the welfare of the Chinese race, and humanity as a whole'. (October 18, 1937).

[4] January 1, 1921. [5] May 22, 1900.

The Webbs pointed out that on the basis of the steadily increasing information discovered by doctors and physiologists, a 'Select Committee' could easily determine what was 'the maximum working day, consistent in any particular industry with the health, existence, home life, and citizenship of the average workman'.[1] In the course of preparing *Industrial Democracy*, the Webbs came to see how the scientist could decide even more, and their picture of new sorts of political institutions took definite shape: 'Out of our study of Trade Unionism we are developing a new view of Democracy and I think quite an original set of Economic and Political Hypotheses'.[2]

In the ideal commonwealth, the governing apparatus was arranged so as to allow the scientist to decide. To this end the Webbs distinguished, in a manner reminiscent of Mill's *Representative Government*, between the functions of 'deciding' and 'controlling'. The latter was left to parliament, which was divided into two parts: a political parliament would attend to the traditional tasks of government, and a social parliament would look after all the new economic and social activities. In these parliaments, young gentlemen could continue their undergraduate debates. They would discuss and suggest, criticize and question, but not actually conduct the affairs of the country. The real work would be done by experts appointed to advise standing committees of parliament. These experts, whose status would be like that of civil servants, would conduct their own investigations, gather comparative statistics, make audits and inspections. They would oversee the administration of industry, decide in general what was needed, and advise the Standing Committees accordingly. The detailed administration of each industry would be in the hands of a National Board, which could decide particular questions and occasionally reverse certain higher decisions. But the National Board's budget, its contemplated expenditures, and its general policy had to be approved by the appropriate Standing Committee in accordance with the verdict reached by the experts.

The same principles governed the Webbs' proposals for the relations between the National Boards of industry and the workers. Any concession to guild socialism was firmly opposed. The issue between syndicalism or guild socialism and state socialism, Mrs Webb felt, was simply whether emotion or reason should govern. The opponents of state socialism relied on 'impulse', and showed contempt for intellect. They consisted of artists, anarchists, and aristocrats, who, under the inspiration of an idealized image of manual workers, had become enamoured of the cruder forms of democracy espoused by guild socialism. That the worker should decide the conditions of his work

[1] Sidney and Beatrice Webb, *Industrial Democracy* (London, 1913), pp. 845, 843, 592.
[2] September 16, 1896.

was unthinkable. Workers should not expect to capture through trade unions the power to interfere with the efficient administration of industry. As the Webbs had shown in *Industrial Democracy*, union officials 'are of course, ignorant, if not incapable, of understanding the complications and subtleties of the law. Their suggestions are one-sided and often impracticable and their opinion can never be accepted as decisive'.[1] How much truer this would be under scientific socialism. Then everything, whether factory, mine, railway station or steamship, would be run scientifically and would have to 'conform to the rules, and to obey the orders emanating, not from the particular workers concerned, but from a distant superior, transmitted through a hierarchy of managers and foremen'. This would probably seem to the workers, the Webbs admitted, very like the 'government from above' that prevailed under capitalism. But in time the workers would learn that in a scientific society it was no longer meaningful to make distinctions between decisions 'from above' or 'from below'. Nor would they be concerned with just how their superiors were appointed. For the decision or appointment would be the scientifically correct one.

No decision, the Webbs emphasized, would be political in the old sense. No one would really 'decide', because governing bodies would not have to depend on 'the spontaneous promptings of their members' minds' or even on mere information, but could count on 'a stream of reports from independent and disinterested experts, retained expressly for this professional service'. These reports would 'reveal the results, material and moral, of each establishment or of each industry, in comparison alike with its own past, with the corresponding results of analogous cases elsewhere, and with the possibilities opened out by new discoveries great and small'.[2] And the comparison would make the right policy obvious. Since science meant, as the Webbs explained over and over again, 'measurement; it means the objective testing of persons and policies', the expert would simply be giving technical advice.

There was, therefore, no need to fear his power. The spirit of the civil service, the Webbs predicted, would come to animate all employees of the Socialist state. The expert would seek nothing but the truth: 'His personality will find expression, and his freedom will be exercised without limitation, in the process of discovery and measurement, and in the fearless representation

[1] Webb, *Industrial Democracy*, p. 830. Later, Mrs Webb expressed even stronger antipathy to Trade Union leaders: 'The Trade Union movement has become like the hereditary peerage, an avenue to political power through which stupid, untrained persons may pass up to the highest office if only they have secured the suffrages of the members of a large union. One wonders when able rascals will discover this open door to remunerative power'. (June 7, 1917).

[2] Sidney and Beatrice Webb, *A Constitution for the Socialist Commonwealth of Great Britain* (London, 1920), p. 197.

371

of whatever he finds, without regard either to the *amour-propre* of the management or the rebellious instincts of any grade of employees'.[1] Society would be run by selfless intellects, who asked for nothing more than freedom to conduct and publish their research. In this, of course, the expert would not differ from the rest of the community, all of whom would realize themselves in a life of duty and service to the social organism.

With the disappearance of old-fashioned political decisions, democracy would acquire a new meaning. The Webbs explained that it was reactionary to think, as the framers of the American constitution did, that the best way to safeguard liberty was to prevent any great concentration of power: 'Now no one fears tyranny; what a modern democracy requires is the conduct of affairs with efficiency, integrity, and with due regard to the wishes of the whole community. This combination of efficiency with popular control is exactly what cannot be brought about by the theory of checks and balances'.[2] In the new democracy, the 'citizen-elector' would have no power to reverse the government's decision, for that would be sheer folly; it would mean substituting the ignorant voice of 'the average sensual man' for the knowledge of the scientist. Democracy would mean rather the power to discuss, and the Webbs therefore always stressed the importance of 'publicity'.

This would become the main function of the member of parliament. He would have to read a great number of documents, compare reports, and sift evidence, so that he could raise questions of his own. But above all he would serve as intermediary between the experts and the public. By transmitting the reactions of his constituents, he would inform the expert of the state of public feeling, thus serving the expert as 'foolometer' and his constituents as publicity agent.[3] But even more important, he would also act as a propagandist for the government, by 'educating' the public to understand and appreciate the experts' proposals. The government would not confine itself to Hansards and Bluebooks; it would use every method available by which knowledge of its activities could be brought home to the average citizen. Only in this way could 'consciousness of consent' be assured. This 'consciousness of consent' was the essence of the new democracy. And it depended on widespread and intensive education as well as on continuous public discussion, especially of the meaning of science. 'A government is said to be an autocracy, or a dictatorship', the Webbs wrote in their study of Soviet Russia, 'if the chief authority enacts laws or issues decrees without submitting them beforehand to public discussion and criticism by the people themselves or their authorised representatives, in order to be guided by their decision'.[1] As long as

---

[1] *A Constitution for the Socialist Commonwealth*, p. 198.
[2] June 11, 1898.
[3] *Our Partnership*, p. 231.

there was widespread discussion, the fact that the people did not decide was irrelevant. The USSR, the Webbs found, encouraged discussion of government decisions before they were pronounced final and so it was a democracy.

Eventually the need for political parties in the old sense would disappear: 'With the increase in an educated community both of public spirit and of interest in public affairs, this diversion of voluntary effort from political parties to propagandist bodies may be expected to be progressive'.[2] Although a need for final decision of the old sort might remain for a time, the Webbs felt confident that

A steadily increasing sphere will, except in matters of emergency, be found for consultation among grades and sections concerned, out of which will emerge judgements and decisions arrived at, very largely by common consent. This common consent will be reached by the cogency of accurately ascertained and authoritatively reported facts, driven home by the silent persuasiveness of the public opinion of those concerned.[3]

For once society is regarded as an organism, it is understood to have a unitary good and all the old political controversies become obsolete. The problem of reconciling conflicting desires of individuals, or of compromising between conflicting views of national ends, disappears. There remains only one end, the health of the social organism, and what every man should have can easily be determined by his function in the social machine. Since, moreover, social health is measured by the society's ability to survive in the struggle among nations, there is a clear, concrete end towards which social scientists can orient their research and prescriptions. The test for public support of an institution becomes not whether all individuals subscribe to or support it, but whether it makes for national success. Discussion of policies, whether in education or industry, would dwell on the contributions of the alternatives to England's power among nations. That this is the only relevant consideration everyone would agree. They would see that social health is not an ethical, but an empirical category, and that its requirements are independent of any man's preferences.

The opportunity to put this view into practice in England never came because the revolution that the Webbs had thought imminent continued to dawdle on the way. But they came to believe that their ideal commonwealth had been realized in Soviet Russia. Their attitude to Soviet Russia underwent a number of changes, but throughout they remained certain that Soviet

---

[1] Sidney and Beatrice Webb, *Soviet Communism* (London, 1947), pp. 344 f.
[2] *A Constitution for the Socialist Commonwealth*, p. 145 n.
[3] *Ibid.* p. 196.

Communism was a creed dedicated to science, and Soviet society accordingly superior to any other in efficiency and morality.[1] Their book on *Soviet Com-*

[1]The Webbs' early opposition to the Russian Revolution came of their believing it to be an outbreak of anarchism: 'The account of the Russian Revolution brought back by Sanders and West from Petrograd is tragic disorder drifting into anarchy. We all comfort ourselves with the story of the French Revolution, though I see little real comfort in it since Napoleonic Imperialism was the outcome. But the Sanders-West account does not tally with that analogy—it looks more like a drift toward a Chinese individualist pacifism—based on indifference to the Commonwealth'. (Aug. 5, 1917). At another time Mrs Webb declared, 'The Bolshevik creed was the latest edition of the philosophy represented in Western Europe by Syndicalism and Guild Socialism—a philosophy which had its foundation in a contempt for intellect and an almost equal contempt for "conduct". It relied on impulse, more especially the impulse to violence'. (Feb. 19, 1918).

Gradually, the Webbs gave up this interpretation of the Bolshevik Revolution. Their interest in the later developments was probably in part a reaction to their disappointment in the progress of socialism in England, especially in their hopes for immediate success after the war. The success of Soviet Russia over the counter-revolutionary armies impressed them and they saw in Lenin's and Trotsky's military, administrative, and diplomatic successes and in 'the humiliation of the capitalist governments' signs of a movement to the 'Left'. It was hopeful that the Bolshevik government was being transformed, Mrs Webb noted, into a bureaucratic administration exercising far-reaching coercive power over the life and liberty of the individual citizen. (Feb. 25, 1920). The first sign of the later enthusiasm came (Sept. 4, 1920) after hearing Kamenev and Krassin speak of the Soviet emphasis on 'working to a plan, elaborated by scientific experts'. Krassin said, Mrs Webb wrote in her diary, 'that two sources of Soviet power were the fervour of the Faithful organised in the Communist Party; and the scientific knowledge of the experts specially trained to serve that Party in all departments of social and industrial life. . . . Payment in kind, with a small balance of money for "supplementary needs" was to supersede the ordinary wage system so that the consumption of commodities by individuals might lead to the maximum mental and physical development of the race'.

The Soviet reliance on force remained for some years an impediment to the Webbs' enthusiasm, and as late as 1930, they condemned Communist fanaticism, although they were already enthusiastic about the progress 'from the lowest type of magic to idolization of science', (June 22, 1930), and beginning to think of Communism as the religion of the future. By the end of 1930, Mrs Webb described Soviet Russia as 'struggling with fanatic fervour to bring about, for the first time in the history of the world, an equalitarian state, based on an uncompromising scientific materialism'. (Oct. 30, 1930). In the end, the economic crisis of the 'thirties swung the Webbs entirely over to Communism as the only vital force in the world. The design to visit Russia became explicit at the end of 1931. They wished to see: 'What is the value of this strange combination of Science without free thought, and Fanaticism without religion, which is possessing the Russian race?' (Christmas Day, 1931). When in 1932 Tawney returned from a brief visit to Moscow, the Webbs found him 'converted to the equalitarian state in practice as well as in theory, but frightened at the absence of personal freedom—and not an admirer of communist mentality'. Mrs Webb commented: 'All the same, he and we find ourselves in agreement on world affairs'. (Feb. 1, 1932). A month later, she wrote: 'What we have to prove is the connection between the economic system of Communism with its moral superiority—the *higher standard* of the *collective man*' (Feb. 28, 1932).

Mrs Webb began reading Lenin and Russian writers: 'What strikes me in the various novels which have been translated (the most striking are *Sot* and *Free Love*) is the emergence of the new ethic—of the collectivist State—the subordination of the life of the individual to the service of the community, "socialist emulation" replacing pecuniary self-interest'. (March 1, 1932). By May of 1932, just before leaving for Russia, she had sketched hypothetical conclusions about Russia. Immediately upon returning, Mrs Webb wrote that she was impressed above all with the moral elevation achieved by Communism, though she found the puritanism, priggishness, and humourlessness too much even for her tastes. Economically, she felt, Russia still had far to go—and she deplored the lack of freedom. 'Hence, I doubt' she concluded, 'whether Soviet Russia will be for the next twenty years a sufficiently attractive exemplar to be deliberately chosen as a model. . .'. (July 28, 1932). For the rest of the year, she deliberated on the question of freedom and slowly convinced herself that the Russians had not perhaps erred so severely, arguing along the lines indicated in her summary of the Communist attitude to death: 'There is no conception of the Rights of Man in Soviet Philosophy; there is only the welfare of the Community, present and future. If the death of one man will raise the standard of life, mental or physical, of the masses, then the one man must die—a painless death. And why trouble about it? No man can avoid death, the only question is the time and the manner of it. Time is of no account; when the allotted spell is over; and the manner of dying without illness is merciful and to be desired'. (August 31, 1932).

Very shortly thereafter, her enthusiasm for Soviet Communism was complete: (Nov. 9, 1932)—'Shall we ever rid ourselves of the *thought* of Soviet Communism? today we are obsessed by it . . . as things are, present day Soviet Communism presents itself as the only alternative social order to that of decaying Capitalism. All who are concerned with public affairs must take their stand on one or the other social order. . . .'

Dec. 1, 1932—'Oh! Where oh! Where is the sower of the new seed? This advancing spiritual desert, this deadness of any aim in human life is woeful for the young people and deepens the darkening shadow of all age. In the U.S.A. the reaction is crime; in Great Britain it is just apathy. Herein lies the attraction of the USSR with its fanatical faith and its boundless optimism'.

The trials and purges that began in 1936 came as a shock, but were soon being explained sympathetically, although never entirely excused. Mrs Webb replied to critics of the USSR by saying that 'an elementary teacher could not preach communism, atheism, and republicanism in the U.K.' (Aug. 27, 1937), or by describing the terror as 'clearings up of counter-revolutionary activities' (August 30, 1937). Yet, while accepting the necessity of the purges, when they continued, she more and more deplored the lack of freedom in the USSR: 'I am still inclined to back the USSR but I wish they would get rid of their disease of orthodoxy, of the human parrot and the human herd'. (Letter to G. B. Shaw, 11/19/39). The Russian attack on Finland—'Another shock to the friends of the Soviet Union!' (Dec. 1, 1939)—even more the verbal attacks on Finland, outraged the Webbs. The immediate response was—'We are not responsible for the foreign policy of the "New Civilisation",' observes Sidney, 'don't worry about it'. (Nov. 24, 1939). By the end of the year, the new shock, too, was absorbed: 'Our sympathies are still with the "New Civilisation" in spite of Stalin's bad behaviour about Finland. I am worried about the morale of the Red Army and the chance of a sensational defeat of the Red Army and the rise of a new anti-Communist front in which Great Britain and France would be included'. (Dec. 15, 1939).

The reports of the suppression of free opinion in Soviet Russia continued to disturb Mrs Webb, but whatever the shortcomings, she invariably concluded, it was after all The New Civilisation: 'The USSR, in spite of the acceptance of a vocation of leadership based

munism, as its organization and headings make plain, illustrates in detail the society outlined in the *Constitution for a Socialist Commonwealth*.

What the Webbs found especially attractive in Soviet Russia, Beatrice perhaps more than Sidney Webb, was its devotion to 'the higher freedom of corporate life'. With all its excesses, Communism was at least headed in the right direction—it was inspired by a far nobler conception of individual happiness than that prevailing in capitalist countries. Soviet Communism demonstrated that a socialist society would develop citizens distinguished not only for their devotion to the social good, but also for their self-control, selflessness, indifference to material goods, and freedom from physical desires. The superiority of such a character was not, Mrs Webb liked to point out, a truth discovered by science. But it was the ideal that governed all her preferences. As she grew older Mrs Webb was more than ever convinced, and she practised what she believed, that the good life meant a simple life, and above all 'abstemiousness from all harmful if not unnecessary, physical indulgence and vain display'.[1] Her old puritanical sentiments took the form of a conviction

that man will only evolve upwards by the subordination of his physical desires and appetites to the intellectual and spiritual side of his nature. Unless this evolution be the purpose of the race, I despair,—and wish only for the extinction of human consciousness. . . . It is this purpose, and this purpose only, that gives a meaning to the constantly recurring battles of good and evil within one's own nature—and to one's persistent endeavour to find the ways and means of combatting the evil habits of the mass of men.[2]

The ideal man of the future, she prophesied, would be

an Impersonality . . . perpetually disentangling the material circumstances of the universe by intellectual processes, and by his emotional will, casting out all other feelings, all sensations other than that of an all embracing beneficence. Physical appetites are to me The Devil: they are signs of the disease that ends in death, the root of the hatred, malice, and greed that make the life of man a futility.[3]

Socialism would help the individual to achieve this higher ideal partly by emphasizing the superiority of public activity over private pursuits. The relationship of 'mutual obligation' between the individual and the community that she envisioned was, Mrs Webb said, 'taken straight out of the

on a particular creed, and of the disease of orthodoxy, is superior as a civilisation [to one] based on the discordant triplet of the Christian religion, capitalist profit-making, and political democracy'. Russia's success against Hitler brought final confirmation: 'and after all it is pleasant, as I observe to Sidney, to have been proved to be right about Soviet Communism: A New Civilisation, the only civilisation which will survive the war. . .'. (April 10, 1943).

[1] *Our Partnership*, p. 340.
[2] *Ibid.* p. 366.
[3] November 14, 1915.

nobler aspects of the medieval manor . . . really a very old idea that has been thrust out of sight in order to attain some measure of equality in political rights'.[1] Anything like the handicraft society ideals of William Morris, she regarded as not only utopian but base, a way of encouraging preoccupation with unworthy trivialities. Mrs Webb agreed with John Mill and Leslie Stephen that the highest happiness lay in action, in performing one's social duty, not in retirement from society, certainly not in mere enjoyment or contemplation. Besides, this was the only sort of happiness suitable to 'modern society in densely crowded communities with highly developed industrial enterprises of magnitude, and a closely integrated economic life . . .'.[2] Under socialism, Mrs Webb hoped, Englishmen would learn to prefer earnest public discussion to pottering in the garden.

In addition, the socialist state would actively exert itself to improve the inner life of the individual, as much as his external circumstances. 'I do not believe that the ordinary man is capable of prescribing for the diseases of the soul any more than he is for the diseases of the body. We need the expert here as elsewhere'.[3] This implied for Mrs Webb that 'the national life should have its consciously religious side. . . . I should desire the Church to become the home of national communal aspirations as well as of the endeavour of the individual towards a better personal life'.[4] She had always argued against friends like Bernard Shaw that only religion, that is, some form of 'communion of the soul with some righteousness felt to be outside and above itself . . . a faith, a hope, a devotion to a wholly disinterested purpose' could save society from becoming a rabbit warren.[5] Religion was also a most useful form of 'mental hygiene', and the High Church doctrine was probably more suitable for the purpose than the Evangelical.[6] But one need not rely solely on church rituals. There were many new ways of scientifically guiding the individual's spiritual life. Radio broadcasting, for instance, made it possible to direct people by suggestion. All sorts of purposes might be served by

perpetually reiterated suggestion instead of by legislative enactment. Also you might do the job not by public administration, but merely by public control—or merely by publicly organised experiment . . . it leaves open for research and experiment how exactly the deliberate purpose shall be attained, and, indeed, what the deliberately pursued ideal should be! All that is postulated is a conscious creation of social environment as distinguished from allowing it to arise haphazard according to the interests, instincts, and impulses of a congeries of men.[7]

[1] July 19, 1907.
[2] *A Constitution for the Socialist Commonwealth*, p. 101.
[3] *Our Partnership*, pp. 209–10.
[4] *Ibid.* pp. 210, 206.
[5] March 13, 1910.
[6] *Our Partnership*, p. 206.
[7] July 24, 1928.

In short, politics would comprehend everything. Anyone who attempted to exclude government from some activities, or in any way to separate politics from the rest of life, would be advocating a return to anarchy and preventing human beings from realizing their highest potentialities. No worries about the dangers of authority interfered with these ideals. For under scientific socialism, personalities and personal judgments, with all their uncertainty, were dispensed with. The rule of science eliminated matters of opinion. Everything could be reduced to a question of social health, and settled rationally, efficiently, and impersonally.

INDEX

Under certain abstract entries, individual views are indicated by the placing of initials (in brackets) after the sub-headings as follows:

B	Jeremy Bentham	M	John Stuart Mill
EB	Edmund Burke	JM	James Mill
C	S. T. Coleridge	CP	The Cambridge Platonists
SC	Samuel Clarke	JFS	Fitzjames Stephen
TC	Thomas Carlyle	LS	Leslie Stephen
H	David Hume	W	Beatrice Webb
FH	Francis Hutcheson	WW	William Wollaston
L	John Locke		

Adam Bede, 294
Adams, Henry, 327
Addison, Joseph, 24
Africa, 163
Agnosticism, 195, 327, 348
Albert, Prince, 289, 291
Alembert, J. Le R. d', 16
Algiers, 112
Amberley, Lady, 344, 348
Amberley, Lord, 315
America (USA), 13, 113, 114, 117, 122, 153, 163, 176, 178, 180, 251, 286, 301, 305, 331, 345, 372, 374*n*
Annan, Noel, 334*n*
Annandale, Marquis of, 13
Annual Register, 193
Anschutz, R. P., 280*n*
Apostles, the, 224
Apothecaries, Society of, 212
Argyll, Duke of, 16
Aristotle, 158, 203, 276–7
Arnold, Matthew, 219, 322–3, 325, 331, 344
Arnold, Thomas, 292
Art, attitude to, and political divisions, 3; Kirk's view of, 21, 22, 24; role of, in religion (H), 26; imagination and senses (CP), 32; Shaftesbury on morals and art, 34; in absolute and free governments (H), 89, 99; civilized taste and political judgment (H), 111; fanatics' indifference to (H), 110, 116; Bentham's view of, 129–30, 139, 158–9, 216; James Mill's view of, 195–6, 201; in John Mill's education, 203; threatened by industrial society (Carlyle), 214–15; *Westminster Reviewers* on, 218–20; Coleridgeans on English attitudes to, 225–7; and antipathy to utilitarianism, 227, 251–2; Mill's view of, 235–9, 295, 305, 316; opposed to philosophy, 238; role in Mill's friendship with Harriet Taylor, 240; Mid-Victorian, 294–

295; Victorians on function of in civilization, 322–5; equated with moral laxity, 324–5; in Potter family, 344; Beatrice Webb's views on, 352, 353, 354, 362   See also Education, Luxury, Science
Atheism, 56
Athenaeum, The, 220
Athens (ancient), 88, 96, 106, 117, 152, 353, 365
Austen, Jane, 347
Austin, Charles, 207, 217
Austin, John, 233, 294
Austin, Sarah, 229
Australia, 180
Authority, balanced with Liberty (H), 80–1; must be stable (H), 102
Avignon, 314–15

Bacon, Francis (1561–1626), 24, 139, 152, 166, 185–6
Bagehot, Walter, 252, 280, 290, 291, 293, 296, 333–4
Bailey, Samuel, 206
Bain, Alexander, 194, 315
Balzac, H. de, 353, 354
Bank of England, 178, 221
Barebones, P. G., 110
Barnett, Canon, 328, 329, 356
Barrington, D., 131
Bavaria, 176
Bayle, Pierre (1647–1706), 14, 24, 36
Beccaria-Bonesana, Marchese de (1735–94), 131, 139, 171–2, 174
Bell, Andrew, 213
Bennett, Joan, 348*n*
Bentham, Jeremiah, 130, 131–2
Bentham, Jeremy (1748–1832), 4, 9, 12, 82, 120, 123, 191, 192, 194, 198, 202, 206, 212, 215–18, 220, 223, 233, 235, 239, 241, 262, 264–6, 271, 276, 299, 300, 301, 307,

Bentham, Jeremy–*continued*
309, 335; his political philosophy in outline, 7–9; utility as a basis for law, 127–9;
sketch of his life and character, 129–36;
view of science, 130, 131, 184–7; on
pleasures and pains, 137, 144–5; dangers
of benevolence, 138, 143–5; utility in
morals, 139–40; utility in politics, 140–46;
self-preference, 141, 159; natural law,
141–3; denies natural harmony, 146–7
and *n*; place of government in economics,
146–8; and in other fields, 148–50; 'the
greatest happiness paramount,' 150–1;
arguments for democracy, 151–4; style of
writing, 155–9; view of clarity and truth,
158–9, 188; criticisms of English law,
163–4; and of Roman law, 164–5; on the
requirements of an ideal code, 165–6;
interpretation and modification of law
unnecessary, 166–8; on evidence, 169;
and juries, 170; disagreement with J. F.
Stephen, 170–71; and with Beccaria, 172;
agreement with Blackstone, 172; influence
on penal law, 171–3; and the police, 174–
175; his evasion of practical opportunities, 134, 176–7; his influence on
details of law, 177; some reactions to
events, 178–80; panopticon, 180–82; his
place in history, 183–8
Bentham, Samuel, 132, 133, 134, 204
Berkeley, Bishop G. (1685–1753), 48, 85,
328
Berlin, 134
Bernoulli, J., 47
Birmingham, 178, 342
Blackheath, 315
Blacklock, T., 114*n*
Blackstone, Sir William (1723–80), 127–9,
131, 133, 156, 163, 171–2
Blackwell, Professor T., 20
Boccaccio, G., 219
Bolingbroke, Lord (Henry St John), 78–9,
83, 84, 85, 87–8
Booth, Charles, 362
Bosanquet, Bernard, on the social person,
338–9
Boston, Thomas, 20, 21, 23
Boswell, James, 16, 23, 120
Boufflers, Madame de, 16
Bowood, 133, 178
Bradlaugh, Charles, 314
Bray, Charles, 329–30, 336
Briggs, Asa, 292*n*
Bright, John, 343
Brissot, J. P., 142
British, the (coffee-house), 73
British Association, 321 322, 326
Brodie, George, 207–8, 209

Brontë, Charlotte, 347, 349
Brougham, Lord, 136, 213
Buckingham, Duke of, 94, 104
Buckle, H. T., 352
Buddhism, 352
Burke, Edmund (1729–1797), 16, 82, 98, 113,
114*n*, 156, 252, 343; agreement with
Hume, 120; extravagance, 120–21; belief
in Divine Reason, 121–2; on empire and
war, 122–3
Bute, Earl of, 115
Byron, Lord, 219, 294

Caird, Edward, 232–3
Calvinism, 18, 29, 32, 33, 114*n*, 191, 226, 307
Cambridge, 224, 228, 272, 273; Union, 217,
221
Cambridge Platonists, the, reason as the
'candle of the Lord', 29–30, 44; the spirit-
ual world alone real, 32
Camden, Lord, 129, 133
Cameronians, the, 23
Campbell, Dr, 17
Canada, 206, 260–1, 342
Capitalism, 3, 12, 337, 371, 374*n*
Capital Punishment, 173, 214
Carlton House, 194
Carlyle, Thomas (1795–1881), 194, 214–15,
224, 233, 234, 236, 238, 255, 271, 280,
294, 305, 343; on inadequacy of British
philosophy, 225; his search for a new
faith, 226; reaction to German thought,
228–9; re-interpretation of duty, 231–2;
his Gospel of Work, 232; his friendship
and breach with Mill, 242
Carswell, John, 106*n*
Catherine the Great, 134
Catholicism, Roman, 12, 18, 19, 36, 94, 104,
208–9, 221, 292, 304, 351
Causation, in Locke, 43; as seen by Hume,
45–7, 49–51; and by others, 47–8; practical belief defended (H), 87; in Mill's
philosophy, 268
Chadwick, Edwin, 313; proposal for standing committee on legislation, 288–9
Chamberlain, Joseph, 358–60
Chancery, Court of, 160, 164
Charity Organization Society, 356
Charles I, 78, 94, 101, 103, 108, 109, 114*n*,
208–9
Charles II, 78, 101, 103, 105
Chartism, 257, 261, 262, 291
Chatham, Earl of (William Pitt), 16, 112,
113, 119–20, 122; as seen by Hume,
115–16; his nature, policy and methods,
116–18
Cheyne, Dr, 39, 74
China, 369

Chirnside, 13, 22–3

Chrestomathia, 215, 217–18

Christianity, its view of man, 5; its austerity, contrasted to pagan religion (H), 25; seeks union of mind with God (H), 33; its values (FH), 36; its assessment of pride and humility (H), 63; its values a vicious dogma (B), 140; importance for James Mill, 192–3, 195-8; acceptance without real belief (by Sterling), 227; Carlyle's interpretation, 232–3; Arnold's ideal, 292; reduced to respectability, 292, 294; its negative features (M), 295; value of the Gospels (M), 249, 317–18; affected by theory of evolution, 321–2; doctrine of self-denial, 325; reconciliation with science, 329–30; becomes Homage to Unknowable, 329; in the Potter family, 343, 346; interest to Beatrice Potter, 348–351, 357; importance under socialism, 377

Cicero, 54, 74, 129, 203

Civil War, the, 81, 94–6, 100, 106, 171, 193, 194–5, 207–10

Clarke, Samuel (1675–1729), 24, 47, 85; religion and morality with mathematical proof, 30–1; on the fury of human passions, 32; influenced by Locke, 42, 44; on space and time, 47*n*; echoed by Fielding, 68

Cleriheugh's (tavern), 14

Clerk-Maxwell, James, 326

Clifton, 342

Cobban, Alfred, 123*n*

Cobden, Richard, 343

Coleridge, Samuel T. (1772–1834), 228, 234, 238, 262, 266, 294, 305; attacks recent philosophy, 224–5; his terror of duty, 226; on understanding and reason, 230; in poetry and morals, 230–1

Collectivism, see Socialism

Cologne, 351

Colonies, see Empire

Commerce, changes in methods, 212

Committees, Standing, 288–90

Commonwealth, the (1649–60), 102, 108, 209, 295

Communism, 374–6

Competition, see Economics

Comte, Auguste (1798–1857), 280, 285, 327, 328, 352; on Humanity, 244–5; on social progress, 246; his influence on Mill, 252, 264, 268; ignored induction, 265

Conservatism, 262, 343

Conway, General, 16, 114*n*

Copernicus, 57

Corn Laws, 291, 294

Corruption, Political, Hume's views, 81–3

Corsica, 105

Courtney, Leonard, 355, 361

Covenanters, 18–19, 23, 24, 25, 33, 233

Cripps, W., 355

Cromwell, Oliver, 18, 94, 95, 104, 108, 109, 114*n*, 171, 210, 219

Cromwell, Richard, 108

Crystal Palace, 291

Custom, in Hume's philosophy, 48–51; its significance in history (H), 100–1, 103; and political integrity, 102–4; its importance to Burke, 120; censured, (B) 152, 184, (JM) 201, (M) 208; imposes public opinion (M), 297; valid only for ordinary people (M), 298; needed by majority (JFS), 299; an impediment to progress (M), 300

Darwin, Charles (1809–1882), 11, 294, 322, 323, 327, 332, 334, 340

Declaration of Rights, the, 179

Decline and Fall of the Roman Empire, 127

Deffand, Madame du, 16

Deism, 33, 42, 107

Delphi, 26

Democracy, preferred by Bentham, 151–3; a mechanism to muzzle power (B), 153–4, 188; in America (B), 180; not a panacea (B), 188; advocated by James Mill, 199–200; in setting of 1820's, 222; opposed to popular government, (M) 250–1, (W) 359, 372; Mill's disenchantment with, 261; conflict between democracy and efficiency (M), 288; the rule of mediocrity (M), 301; representative, effects on moral progress, (JM) 199–200, (M) 308–10; unsuitable at some stages, (M) 310–11, (W) 352–3; in industry, retrogressive (W), 369–72; founded on science (W), 369–70; discussion and consent (W), 372 See also Representation, Science

Democritus, 54

Denmark, 163

Descartes, R. (1596–1650), 13, 30, 54, 224, 271, 276

Devonshire House, 194

Dickens, Charles, 294

Diderot, D., 16

Dilke, Sir Charles, 358

Discretion, see Politics

Disraeli, Benjamin, 313, 324, 330, 331, 343

Dresden, 354

Dryden, John, 24

Dumont, P. E. L., 134, 158, 169

Dunning, John (Lord Ashburton), 129, 133

Durham, Lord, 260–1

Duty, 226, 232, 350, 377

East India Company, 221–2, 311

Economics, character of (H), 90–92; the nature of competition, (B) 146–7, (Adam Smith) 146*n*, (Elie Halévy) 146–7*n*; *Westminster Reviewers* laud study of, 218; distortion of, by *Westminster Reviewers*, 220–1; Mill's training in, 282; laws of distribution modified (M), 283; scope widened (M), 284–5; in relation to justice and morality (M), 287; the function of competition, (Spencer) 333, (Kidd) 335–336; inefficiency of competition, (LS) 335, (Huxley) 340, (Ritchie) 340–1, (W) 367–8

Edinburgh, 13, 14, 15, 16, 36, 327; University, 13, 23–4, 226

Edinburgh Review, 170, 199, 228, 262

Education, the source of moral distinctions (Mandeville), 60; not the province of government, (H) 97–8, (B) 143–4, 157; views of Locke and James Mill compared, 197; promoted indirectly by good government, (JM) 199, (M) 285, 287, 308, (W) 374*n*, 376–7; development of vocational training, 212–13, 215, 217–18; new efficiency in (Lancaster and Bell), 213; usefulness of *Chrestomathia*, 215; liberal, defended, (Peacock and F. D. Maurice) 215, (M) 316, (Arnold) 322–3; scientific and technical praised (*Westminster Reviewers*), 217–18; national, 262, 337, 358; dependence on science of ethology (M), 270; in the Public Schools, 292; state monopoly of, opposed (M), 298; dependence on coercion (JFS), 299; changes in the universities, 321; controversies about science and art in, 321–4; imperial importance (W), 368

Edward II, 101

D'Eichtal, Gustave, 262

Eldon, Lord, 164

Eliot, George, 294, 321, 347, 348–50, 353, 363

Elizabeth I, 104

Ellicott, Dr C. J., 344

Elliot, Gilbert, 16, 115

Elm Court, 129

Elsmere, Robert, 337, 350

Emmanuel College, Cambridge, 29

Empire, disadvantages of, (H) 113–14, (B) 149–50; glory of (EB), 122; and as seen by Chatham, 122; England's duty to (M), 311; difficulties with, 331; Joseph Chamberlain on, 358; a superior organism (W), 366–8

Empiricism, 41, 185, 245, 279

Encyclopedia Britannica, 199, 316

Enthusiasm, Philosophical, 74; Religious, pretentious nature of, 24, 27; harmful effects, 95–6; Hume versus Burke, 123

Epicurus, 54, 195

Episcopalianism, 18–19, 23

Equality, (H) 96, (B) 150–1, 153, (W) 359, 364, 374*n*

Erskine, Rev. H., 23

Evangelicism, 11, 19, 23, 292, 377

Examiner, The, 256

Exhibition, Great (1851), 291

Fabian Society, 4

Faraday, Michael, 326

Fawcett, Henry, 315

Fichte, J. G., 228, 229

Fielding, Henry (1707–54), moral attitude in his novels, 68–9

Filmer, Sir Robert, 170

Finland, 374*n*

Flèche, La (Jesuits' college), 13, 74

Flower, Eliza, 240

Fontenelle, B. le B. de, 36

Ford, Abbey, 134, 203–4

Fortune, 98

Fourier, J. B. J., 303

Fox, C. J., 116, 132, 191, 193

Fox, W. J., 220, 240

Fragment on Government, 127, 132, 133

France, 13, 16, 73, 97, 103–4, 112, 117, 118, 123, 174, 176, 193, 204, 206, 225, 250, 287, 331, 345, 365, 374*n*

Franklin, Benjamin, 113*n*, 133, 135

Free Trade, 149, 222, 291

Free Will, see Liberty, of Will

Freemason's Tavern, 207

French Revolution (1789), 123, 132, 175, 176, 178, 179–80, 295; (1848), 294

Froude, J. A., 321, 352

Fry, Elizabeth 348

Galileo, G., 279

Garrick, David, 16

Gaskell, Mrs, 347

Gay, John, 130

George II, 114*n*

George III, 114*n*

Germany, 12, 13, 228, 233, 286, 331, 354, 365; thought and literature, 228–30, 231, 233, 235–6, 238, 272, 304

Gib, Adam, 21

Gibbon, Edward, 16, 110, 114*n*, 127, 192

Gladstone, W. E., 292–3, 331, 343, 358

Glasgow, 15

Glory, 94; dangers of (H), 96–7, 102 See also Empire

Gloucester, 342, 343

Goethe, J. W. von, 228–9, 237–8, 239, 303–4

Goldsmith, Oliver, 132
Gordon, General, 331, 358
Gordon Riots, 178
Gourget, Paul, 363
Government, controversies about, 3; its limited scope, (H) 6–7, 97–9, (B) 144; requiring technical skill (B), 7–8; whether a means to human perfection, (M) 10, (H) 97–9, (EB) 122, (B) 143–4, 157, (JM) 199, (M) 285, 287, 308, (W) 374n, 376–7; as a system of life (W), 11–12; origins of and theory of original contract, (H) 79, (B) 157; innovation in, (H) 80, 97, 98, 99–100, (M) 316; mixed, least vulnerable (H), 84–90; differences of form not clear-cut (H), 89; over-active and capricious under Chatham (H), 118; responsibility to governed, (B) 140, (M) 200; utility principle opposed to paternalism (B), 143; drawbacks inherent in (B), 145–6, 183; provision against indigence (B), 147; and for security and information (B), 148; syllogisms about (JM), 199; growth of technical efficiency in, 213–14; not a mechanism (M), 247–8; new activities of, in Mid-Victorian England, 295–6; by discussion (Bagehot), 334; in social organism, 332–41; liberal versus scientific view of, 359 See also Democracy, Economics, Politics, Progress, Representation
Grafton, Duke of, 105
Greece (ancient), 163; (modern), 176, 219
Green, T. H., 339; opposes scientific vogue, 336–7; provides social gospel, 337–8 See also Morality
Gregory, Dr J., 140
Grenville, George, 16
Grey, Lord, 260
Grote, George, 136, 206, 255, 256, 294, 315, 352
Grote, John, 272
Grotius, Hugo, 142

Halévy, Elie, 146–7n
Hamburger, Joseph, 248n
Hamilton, Sir William, 267, 271, 272
Hampden, John, 209
Happiness, its three ingredients (H), 67; always qualified (H), 76–7; 'the greatest happiness of the greatest number', (B) 127, 140–1, 150–1, (M) 210, 335; as fulfilment of desires (B), 139; and activity, (M) 302–5, (W) 377; ruled out for individual (LS), 335–6; and marriage (W), 358–60, 365n; under communism (W), 376; under socialism (W), 376–7 See also Morality, Virtue
Hare, Julius, 224, 227, 228

Harrington, James, 89
Harrison, Frederick, 12, 324, 344
Hartley, David, 131, 196–8, 206, 267
Hastings, Warren, 122
Hayek, F. A., 245n
Haymarket Theatre, 100
Hazlitt, William, 155
Hegel, G. W. F. (1770–1831), 340
Helvetius, C. A. (1715–71), 131, 133, 139, 201
Hendon, 134
Herbert, Auberon, 361
Herbert, Lord, 42
Herder, Johann, 229
Herschel, Sir J. F. W. (1792–1871), 249; influence on Mill, 272–3; on scientific laws, 275
Hertford, Earl of, 16, 114n
Himmelfarb, G., 332n, 334n
History, nature of, (H) 92, 94–5, (EB) 144, (JM) 193, (M) 207–10, 246, 263–4
Hobbes, Thomas (1588–1679), 9, 30, 32, 81, 85, 92, 200, 206, 328, 332–3, 337; empiricism and reasoning, 41–2; his amorality, 43; emphasizes the will, 69; denies right to revolution, 107
Holland, 103, 105
Holland House, 194
Holland, Lord, 178
Home, George, 23
Home, Henry (Lord Kames), 14, 15
Honour (H), 68, 103–4, 105, 106, 109 and n, 110
Howard, John, 139
Hugo, Victor, 295, 353
Human Understanding, Essay on, 42
Humanity, 244–5; the religion of, 246, 318, 352; as world-wide social organism (W), 366
Humboldt, Alexander von, 325
Hume, David, 4, 12, 127, 128–9, 131, 139, 140, 155–6, 171, 184, 187, 192–3, 207–10, 239, 271, 276, 307, 328; his philosophy in outline, 5–7; on motives and character, 8; on the limits of human powers, 9; on man as a balanced whole, 11; his life and character summarized, 13–17; reactions to influence of Kirk, 22–5, 27–8; paganism contrasted with Christianity and abstract theism, 25–7; influence of Hutcheson, 33; and of Montaigne, 36–9; motive of his philosophy, 39; his illness, 39–40; his reaction to Hobbes and Locke, 41–5; 'impressions', 'ideas' and 'association', 45; on space, time and causation, 45–51; on limitations of human knowledge, 51–2; reason linked to nature, 52–3; on mind and matter, 54–6; a world of flux and change, 57–8; on passions and

Hume, David—*continued*
the unity of man, 59–60; on the nature of virtue, 61–2; on suicide, 62; on pride, 62–3; the uses and limits of general rules, 63–6; on the ingredients of happiness, 67; on honour, 68, 103–4, 105, 106, 109 and *n*, 110; virtue and right instinct, 68–9; his philosophy a liberation, not a system, 69–71; philosophical doubts and compensations, 72–3; a phase of philosophical enthusiasm, 74; the man of moderation takes over, 75; the merits of diffidence, 76–7; views on current issues, 78–80, 112–15, 115–18; liberty versus authority, 80–1; degree even in corruption, 81–3; a moderation of disagreement, 84; political and social maxims, 85–8; the value of carefully framed laws, 88; fact more important than theory in government, 89–90; some observations on economics, 90–2; caution needed in political science, 93; political disposition preferred to doctrine, 94; the force of circumstance in history, 95, the dangers of zeal and heroism, 95–7; function of government not to change men, 97; but to mediate, reconcile, encourage and protect, 98–9; true public spirit a devotion to rule of law, 100; custom and integrity in politics, 101–6; a place for discretion, 106–8; the acceptability of failure, 109; politics as an art, 110–11; his standards unsuited to new era of Chatham, 118–19; contrasted with Burke, 120–23.
Hume, Joseph, 216*n*
Huskisson, William, 214
Hutcheson, Francis (1694–1746), opponent of Covenanters, 33; bases morality on moral sense, 34; reverses place of reason and passion, 35, stresses ascetic virtues, 36
Hutton, R. H., 321
Huxley, Aldous, 362
Huxley, T. H. (1825–95), 12, 322, 328, 340, 344; views on art and science, 323–4; on a science of social life, 331–2
Huygens, C., 47

Imagination, in relation to space and time (H), 49; as a receptive power (H), 69; leading from experience to belief (H), 72; as ingredient of political order (H), 121; excluded from politics (B), 184; as a source of illusions (Roebuck), 223; importance in poetry (C), 230; in relation to happiness (M), 317
India, 167, 192, 200, 311, 367; India House, 206, 210, 254, 312

Indies, East, 113
Induction, required in social science, 265; Mill and Whewell opposed, 273–9; success of Mill's views, 280 See also Science
Industry, growth of impersonal organization, 212
Integrity, importance in government (H), 102–3; its expediency and dependence on discretion (H), 106–8; based on decency and moderation (H), 108–9; a summary of Montaigne's, 109*n*; Mill's views on, 255–6, 258–9, 260, 312–13; Radicals', 256
Ireland, 174, 178, 259, 331, 337, 358
Italy, 103, 205

Jamaica, 313
James, Henry, 344
James I, 104, 209
James II, 78, 101, 104
James's Court, 16
Japan, 368
Jevons, Stanley, 321
Jews, the, 350, 366
Johnson, Samuel, 17, 94, 114*n*, 116, 120, 129, 132, 226
Justice (H), 63–6 See also Bentham, Law

Kamenev, 374*n*
Kames, Lord (Henry Home), 14, 15
Kant, Immanuel (1724–1804), 228, 229, 271, 277; divorces reason from nature, 53–4; man's pursuit of rational goals, 69
Kelvin, Lord, 326
Kemble, J. M., 221
Kemp Smith, Norman, 35*n*
Kepler, J., 264, 274–5
Kidd, Benjamin, 335–6, 368
Kirk, the, 18, 29, 32, 74, 75, 191, 192, 193, 195–6, 198, 201, 252 See Chapter II
Krassin, 374*n*

Laissez-faire, 3, 146*n*, 368
Lancaster, Joseph, 213
Land, William, 21
Lansdowne House, 134
Laplace, Marquis de, 213, 264
la Rochefoucauld, F. de, 36
Laud, William (Archbishop of Canterbury), 26, 111, 208
Law, importance to Hume, 7; Bentham's conception, 8; necessary but not fully just (H), 65–6; must fit changing circumstances (H), 80; importance of careful framing (H), 88; as basis of liberty (H), 99, 102; as a part of moral perfection (EB), 121; Blackstone criticized, 127–8; tested by utility, reduced to statute and universally applicable (B), 128, 166–8;

legal fictions (B), 128, 162–4; concentric with morality (B), 143; inevitable limitations (B), 145; inadequacies of common law (B), 159–60; its two particular defects (B), 160–2; arguments in its defence (B), 162–3; its inferiority to statute law (B), 163–4; character of, 164; criticisms of equity, 160, (B) 164; and of Roman law (B), 164–5; legal procedure (B), 168–71; suggestions on penal law (B), 171–5; extent of Bentham's influence, 177; his reputed aims, 183; reform welcomed by Mill, 209; legislation as a profession (M), 250; as work of a commission (M), 287

Law, Natural, (H) 64, (EB) 121, (B) 141–3, 146–7n, (JM) 200

Law, Rule of, equated with liberty (H), 99; essence of government (H), 99–100; endangered by revolution (H), 100; importance of (EB), 120; requires exact definitions (B), 153; endangered by Bentham's law reforms, 168–72, 174–5; in Mid-Victorian England, 293–4; meaning of, under scientific socialism, 369, 371–2, 378

Lawrence, D. H., 362

Leibnitz, G. W. (1646–1716), on time and space, 47–8

Lenin, 374n

Lessing, G. E., 228, 229

Leucippus, 54

Lewes, G. H., 328, 334

Liberalism, 249, 261, 293, 308, 312, 337, 343, 358, 359, 366

Liberty, balanced by authority (H), 80–81; dependent on law (H), 99, 102; endangered by enthusiasm for (H), 100; and by dissimulating politicians (H), 104; dependent on integrity (H), 109; excesses in name of (H), 112, 115; whether safeguarded by constitutional provisions (B), 142; interfered with by law (B), 145; threatened by philanthropy (M), 295–7; and by collective opinion (M), 297; and by custom (M), 298; a means to progress (M), 300; compatible with restrictions by government, 338–41, (W) 365–6, 376–7; for national self-government, retrogressive (W), 366–7; for workers' self-government, retrogressive (W), 370–2.

Liberty, of the Press, (H) 107–8, (B) 143, 154

Liberty, of Taste, (H) 147, (M) 301–2

Liberty, of Will, and regularity in human behaviour (H), 87; and causality (H), 87n; unimportance of (B), 140; significance for Coleridgeans, 227; relation to sociology (M), 266–7

Liberty, On, 297, 299–301, 305–8

Lilburne, T. W., 110

Lincoln's Inn, 131, 160

Lind, John, 131, 132, 133

Literary Journal, The, 192, 194

Literature, attitude of Westminster Review, 218–19; views of (W), 353–4, 362–3 See also Art

Liverpool, Lord, 179, 214

Locke, John (1632–1704), 9, 12, 24, 30, 41, 131, 200, 224, 229, 328; human knowledge limited to experience and observation, 42; but reason able to discern moral law, 43; on cause and effect, 43; distinguishes creative and passive powers of mind, 44–5; seeks a unifying vision of life, 69; a difference from Hume, 70n; quoted by rival parties, 78; supports right of political resistance, 81; differences from Bentham, 185; and from James Mill, 196–8

Logic (Mill), 270, 272, 287

London, 14, 16, 73, 82, 113, 115, 180, 191, 192, 222, 337, 344

London Debating Society, 207, 224, 244

London Review, The, 201, 254–5

London School of Economics, 369

Lucian, 17, 129

Luxury, (H) 66, 68, (W) 368, 369, 376

Lyell, Sir Charles, 321, 322

Macaulay, Lord, 141, 199–200, 201, 207, 246, 264, 265

Machiavelli, N., 103

Mackintosh, Sir James, 179, 200, 201

Magnanimity, 110

Malebranche, N., 36, 55

Manchester, 342

Mandeville, B., 60

Manning, Cardinal, 344

Mansel, H. L., 267, 271

Mansfield, Lord, 129–132

Mao Tse-tung, 369n

Maria Theresa, 13

Marmontel, J. F., 211

Martineau, Harriet, 347, 352

Marx, Karl, 361

Maurice, Frederick D., 215, 221, 231, 234; influenced by German thought, 231

Mechanics Institute, the, 213

Melbourne, Lord, 212, 255, 260

Mill, James (1773–1836), 12, 134, 136, 203, 206, 209, 210–11, 212, 216, 220, 221, 223, 226, 227, 235, 239, 241, 245, 247, 252, 264–6, 269, 282, 287, 297, 303; disciple of Bentham, 4; puritan concept of government, 10; his early life and outlook, 191–4; changes of view, 194–5; a new creed and its sources, 196–8; politics in axioms and syllogisms 199–201; Bentham's gadgets evolved into a creed, 202

Mill, John Stuart (1806–1873), 4, 12, 171, 192, 195, 321–7 *passim*, 336, 341, 351, 370, 377; his political philosophy in outline, 9–10; his puritan background, 10; science as a technique, 11; his education in England, 203–4; and in France, 204–6; his debating clubs, 206–7; his assessment of Hume, 207–10; his first mental crisis, 211; spiritual malaise, 223; his new friends, 224; their search for a new faith, 224–8; his horizon of thought enlarged, 233–4; a reverence for poetry and art, 235–6; many-sidedness, 237; beauty as handmaid to truth, 238–9; insistence on clear categories, 239–40; influence and support of Harriet Taylor, 240–2; breach with Carlyle, 242; contact with Positivism and 'Humanity', 244–5; a creed of social progress, 246–7; leadership by experts, 248–51, 288; agrees with Tocqueville, 251; new conclusions to inherited principles, 252; political activity through journalism, 253–5, 257–9; he advocates an independent Radical party, 260–1; retires from politics, 262; his enlargement of sociology, 263–6; on the relation of social science to free will, 266–7; on psychology and ethology, 267–70; he remains faithful to logic and observation, 270–1; the impact of his *System of Logic*, 272; his idea of Induction, 274; disagreement with Whewell, 274–8; popular appeal of theory of science, 279–80; forerunner of new politics, 280–1; turns to political economy, 282–3; modifies classical economics, 284–5; his successive visions of socialism, 285–7; on the economist's function, 287; on commissions for law-drafting, 288–90; his reaction to mid-century events, 294–5; and to paternalism, 295–7; on individualism, liberty and progress, 297–302; on state education, 298–9; on the ideal individual, 302–4; and the active character, 304–5; on the leadership of the superior few, 306–7; the reconciliation of liberty and progress, 307–8; on representative government, 309–10; and stages towards it, 310–11; his three years in parliament, 312–14; Avignon and Blackheath, 314–15; last thoughts on education and socialism, 316–17; on imagination and religion, 317–18

Milman, 292

Milnes, R. M., 207

Milton, John, 24, 135

Missions, 337, 355–6

Mitford, Mary, 292

Molesworth, Sir William, 254–5, 261

Molière, 129

Monk, General, 108

Monotheism, 26

Montaigne, M. de (1533–1592), 95, 98, 102; prefers catholicism to protestantism, 12; on the loveliness and diversity of virtue, 36—7; spirit and matter not in conflict, 38; human fallibility, 41; adapted by Hume, 52–3; on the element of chance, 98; on decency and public interest, 106*n*; on integrity and discretion, 109*n*

Montesquieu, C. L. de S., 90, 129, 152, 166–7, 171–2

Moore, Thomas, 218

Morality, secondary to faith (Presbyterians), 20–1; objective and eternal (CP), 29; as an exact science (SC and WW), 30–2; based on 'the moral sense' (FH), 34; discernible by reason (L), 43–4; certain but not absolute (H), 61; compared with a watershed (H), 65; requires no hierarchy of pleasures (H), 67–8; relation between principles and judgment (H), 69–70; and impersonality (H), 70; and personal identity (H), 70; must derive from reality of human nature (H), 85–6; not in conflict with expediency (H), 105, in relation to politics, 106; as seen by Burke, 121; as scientifically based happiness (B), 127, 137; as cloak for despotism (B), 138; insufficiency of Christian tradition (JM), 195; founded on reason (C), 230–1; need for one standard (M), 263; as concern of economists (M), 287; dependence on coercion (JFS), 299; must distinguish between higher and lower (M), 305–6; revealed by the superior few (M), 305–7; united to physical truth (Spencer), 329; as performance of social function (LS), 334–5; through self-imposition of duty (Green), 337; instinct replaced by principles (W), 354 See also Passion, Reason, Virtue.

More, Hannah, 347

More, Sir Thomas, 89

Morellet, Abbé, 176–7

de Morgan, A., 276

Morley, John, 107, 295, 300, 315, 344, 357

Morris, William, 324, 344, 377

Napoleon, 117

Nationalization, 343, 369

Nationalism, see Empire

Natural Harmony, existence of not assumed by Bentham or Adam Smith, 146–7 and *n*; nor by Spencer, 333; the ultimate end, (Spencer) 328, (LS) 334–5

Nature, creation of (H), 54–6; opposed to reason (H), 63; and rules of justice (H), 63; Hume's defence of and natural judgments, 64 and *n*; in Fielding, 69; and solution of human problems (H), 81; ultimate mystery of (H), 86–7; and free will (H), 87; and uniformity in history (H), 97–8; described, (JM) 196, 200, (M) 303, (Kidd) 335–6, (Ritchie) 340, (W) 354, 367, 368, 369; ultimate mystery of, acknowledged by science, 329–30 See also Law, Natural

Nesbitt, G. A., 220*n*.

Newcastle, Duke of, 81, 116

Newman, Francis, 321

Newton, Sir Isaac (1642–1727), 12, 24, 30, 35*n*, 86, 131, 152, 185, 213, 264, 275, 276; his method adopted by Hume, 45; experiments and concepts, 47–8

Niebuhr, B. G., 228, 229

Nightingale, Florence, 347

Ninewells, 13

North, Lord, 113

Novalis (Friedrich von Hardenberg), 228

Oakeshott, Michael, 41*n*, 111*n*, 121*n*

O'Brien, B., 261

Origin of Species, The, 294, 321

Owenities, the, 206

Oxford, 129, 131, 228, 272, 321, 336, 338, 339

Oxford Movement, the 291

Packe, Michael St John, 206*n*

Paganism, 6, 19, 25, 41

Paine, Tom, 179

Palmerston, Lord, 293–4

Panopticon, the, 134, 180–2, 241

Papinian, 165

Paris, 16, 95, 136, 179, 204, 224

Parkin, Charles, 121*n*

Parliament, Long, 209

Pascal, B., 36

Passions, set against reason, 5, 32, 68, 196, 198, 231, 232, 302, 349; tolerated by Mill, 9; as seen by Clarke and Wollaston, 32–3; as source of good (FH), 35; French views, 36, 303; not opposed by reason (H), 37; a form of sensation (H), 59; in conflict with each other (H), 106; as a key to moral law (EB), 121; affected by analytic habits (M), 223; condemned by Beatrice Webb, 349, 350, 353, 354, 357, 361, 362

Passmore, J. A., 85*n*

Pater, Walter, 324–5

Paternalism, 143, 145, 297, 337

Patriots, the, 78–9

Pattison, Mark, 321

Paulus, 165

Peacock, T. L., 215, 220

Peel, Sir Robert, 214, 259, 292, 294

Pericles, 96, 106, 353

Petty, Sir William, 184

Philanthropy, 295–6

Philosophy, and Christianity, 5; nature of (H), 75–6, 77; British, criticized, 224–5, 229–31; British, character of, 227–8; German, attractions of, 229–30, 233; opposed to art, 238; metaphysical, contrasted to positivism, 245; of history, 246; continuous with natural science, 249–50, 327–30, 338, 340; medieval, on social organism, 332

Pitt, William, see Chatham, Earl of

Pitt, William (the younger), 123, 133, 179, 289

Place, Francis, 136, 203–4, 216*n*, 257, 259, 261

Plato, 5, 32, 34, 77, 89, 121, 158, 196, 200, 201, 203, 247, 323, 333, 338, 343, 351

Pleasure, with pain as governing mankind (B), 137; in fourteen varieties (B), 137; related to individual needs (B), 138; circumstances of its value (B), 144; general importance in politics (B), 150; in relation to logic (B), 159; in relation to penal law, 172–3; as test of right and wrong (JM), 195; affected by analytic habits (M), 223; graded by Mill, 305–6 See also Morality

Poetry, philistine attitude of *Westminster Review*, 218–19; importance of imagination (C), 230; to balance science (M), 235; Mill's homage, 236–8 See also Art

Police, 174–5, 214

Political Economy (Mill), 287, 291, 298, 300, 309

Politics, differences in approach, 3–4; destroyed and sanctified (W), 11; claims Hume's attention, 78; as a matter of degree (H), 81; importance of parties, (H) 83–4, (EB) 120; must be based on reality (H), 85; as a science, (H) 87–8, (M) 263; needing caution (H), 93; the necessary disposition (H), 94; in relation to morals (H), 106; discretion essential in (H), 106–9; as a part of social life (H), 110; an art, not a science (H), 111; a new style epitomized by Chatham, 115–17; suited to new conditions, 118; in relation to public opinion, 119; Burke's views, 120–3; utility and tolerance (B), 140; no good is unalloyed (B), 146, 183; seen as a technique (B), 150, 187; but not as all-embracing (B), 188; spiritual basis needed (M), 247–8; as an experimental science (Herschel), 250; as sociology (M), 266; as business of ex-

Politics-*continued*
 perts, 287; the mid-Victorian view, 292-3;
 sway of public opinion (M), 301; scope
 for service (M), 308-9; general reduction
 to science, 333; regeneration through
 citizenship (Green), 337; science to take
 over (W), 369; all-comprehending (W),
 378 See also Government, Integrity
Poor Laws, 182, 214
Pope, Alexander, 24, 31
Popper, Karl, 280*n*
Portugal, 176
Positivism, asserts subjective unity of man-
 kind, 244; Humanity and social progress,
 245-7
Potemkin, Prince, 134
Potter, Beatrice, see Webb, Beatrice
Potter, Kate, 337, 355-6
Potter, Richard (senior), 342
Potter, Richard (junior), 342-4, 345; Mrs,
 345-6
Poverty, provision for (B), 147-8; Victorian
 concern with, 330-1; and science, 331-2;
 usefulness (Kidd), 335-6; elimination of,
 not first aim of socialism (W), 364
Presbyterianism, 12, 18, 22, 23, 74, 198, 226
Pride (H), 96-7
Priestley, Joseph (1733-1804), 178, 179
Principia, Newton's, 47
Progress, moral, not the function of govern-
 ment (H), 97, 98, 99; Bentham's belief in,
 127; and Bentham's optimism about de-
 mocracy, 152; proper concern of historian,
 (JM) 193, (M) 210; Mill's interest in, 245-
 9, 285, 300, 306-7; in social organism,
 (Spencer) 328, (LS) 334-5, (W) 366-8,
 373; opposed to reason, 336; ethical, op-
 posed to cosmic process, 340; proper concern of the arts (W), 353, 354; ideal to
 be achieved by (W), 376-7
Protestants, 25, 29, 36
Proudhon, P. J., 303
Prussia, 163, 331
Prynne, W., 110
Public Schools, the, 292, 321
Pufendorf, S., 142
Puritanism, rejected by Hume, 6, 25, 209;
 revived in new form by Mill, 9-10;
 adopted by Beatrice Webb, 10; back-
 ground to Hume's childhood, 13; in
 Scotland, 18-19; in Cambridge, 29; atti-
 tude to beauty, 34; and dogmatic theology,
 42; repellent to Bentham, 140; important
 in James Mill, 193, 195; in Coleridge,
 Carlyle and Sterling, 226-7; idealized by
 Carlyle, 233; modified by Mill, 298; in
 Beatrice Webb, 350-1, 352, 376
Pym, John, 94, 95, 116, 209

Queen Square Place, 134-5, 183
Queen's College, Oxford, 129

Radicals, Philosophical, 235, 262, 293; suc-
 cess in 1832 elections, 253; to be re-shaped
 through journalism, 254-5; manipulation
 of popular sentiment, 256; urged to
 action by Mill, 257-9; and to inde-
 pendence, 260; reasons for failure (M),
 263 See Chapter XXII
Radio, 377
Rainbow (coffee-house), 73
Ramsay, Allan, 14, 15, 24
Ramsay, Michael, 24
Rankenian Club, 24
Raynal, Abbé, 117
Reason, attacked by Hume, 5-6; as curb on
 emotion (M), 9, 252; equated with science
 (W), 10-11, 354-5; as key to moral law
 (CP), 29; source of eternal rules, (SC), 31,
 (WW) 31; as servant of passions (FH), 35;
 French views, 36; Hume and Montaigne
 on rational rules, 37; as revelation of God
 (L), 44; creative and passive reason, 44-5;
 and the causal inference, 47; a combination of imagination and sense-impression
 (H), 51; in animals (H), 52-3, 59; creative
 reason saved by Kant, 53-4; its inexplica-
 bility (H), 55; its limits (H), 59*n*; controlled
 by passions (H), 60; as judge of utility (H),
 61; as source of essential rules (H), 63;
 links politics to moral law (EB), 120-1;
 opposed by 'irascible appetite' (B), 140;
 in Plato, 196; as an austere overlord
 (JM), 198, 224; weakened by embellishment (JM), 201; contrasted with understanding (C), 230; the basis of morality
 (C), 231; with emotion as balance (M),
 235; in the ideal individual (M), 302-3;
 as outwork to imagination (M), 317;
 opposed to art, 324-5; enables discussion
 (Bagehot), 333-4; opposed to science
 (Kidd), 336 See also Passion
Reform Bill (1832), 250, 254, 259, 288;
 (1867), 313
Reformation, the, 18, 192, 295
Religion, see Christianity
Representation, the proper character of, (H)
 82, (B) 152, (M) 250-2, 288-90, (W) 372-
 373 See also Democracy
Representative Government (Mill), 251, 288,
 290, 308-10, 371
Restoration, the, 18, 108, 109
Revolution, rarely achieves its aims (H), 97;
 the natural revolution of human affairs
 (H), 98; endangers rule of law (H), 99-100;
 cannot be ruled out (H), 100; American,

(H) 113, (B) 142, 180; imminent in England, (H) 112–15, 118, (M) 221–2, 256–61, 314, (W) 367, 375–6n; salutary effects of (M), 295; gradual reform preferable (M), 316 See also Civil War, French Revolution

Ricardo, D., 136, 206, 216n, 282
Richelieu, Cardinal, 94, 116
Richter, J. P. F., 228, 229
Rights of Man, the, 119
Ritchie, D. G., 340–1
Robertson, William, 15, 193
Roebuck, J. A., 206, 223, 240, 261, 294, 313; lacks faith in aristocracy of intellect, 251; attitude to Radicals, 255–9
Rome (ancient), 88, 96, 100; (modern), 297
Romilly, Anne, 203
Romilly, John, 207
Romilly, Samuel, 134, 136, 175
Rossetti, D. G., 324
Rousseau, J.-J. (1712–1778), 16, 114n, 123, 303
Royal Society, The, 184
Rugby (school), 292
Rules, general, of good breeding and of justice (H), 63; distinguished from natural judgments, 64, 93; imperfect but indispensable (H), 65–6
Ruskin, John, 294, 352
Russell, Lord John, 255, 259
Russia, 134, 176, 331, 362, 368–9, 373–6, 374n

St Andrew's (university), 316, 321
St Clair, General, 13–14, 75
St James Chronicle, 192, 194
St Paul's Churchyard Club, 132
Saint-Pierre, Abbé de, 36
San Francisco, 345
Sand, George, 353
Sandwich, Earl of, 106
Savigny, F. K. von, 166
Scepticism, 75; emollient of intellectual pride (H), 76–7; in politics, 121–2
Schelling, F. W. J. von, 228, 229
Schiller, J. C. F. von, 228, 229
Schlegel, K. W. F. von, 228, 229
Scholasticism, 41, 42, 43, 186, 200
Science, equated with reason (W), 10–11, 354; as basis for politics, 10, 123–4, 188, 200, 332–6, 340–1, 359, 361–2, 365–78; controversy about Newton's theory, 47–8; Hume and Newton, 57, 85–6; and final causes (H), 57; whether descriptive or explanatory (H), 86; scientific distinguished from experimental method (H), 86; and political wisdom (H), 87–93; Bentham's

early interest in, 129; only source of truth (B), 130, 131; opposed to mystery (B), 144; views of Bacon, Newton, Bentham compared, 184–6; Royal Society, 184–5; opposed to history (M), 263–4; deduction and induction (M), 265, 272–81; and free will (M), 266–7; and intuition (M), 270–271; nature of progress in (M), 278–80; and religion, 321, 327, 329–30, 357; comparison between English and Continental, 325; relation to philosophy, 325–6, 327–330, 338; new theories in 19th century, 326; cure for poverty, 331–2; the true basis for morality, 354–5, 356, 363, 374–5n, 376; offers escape from personality (W), 356, 362, 376; associated with Radical Liberalism, 357; emphasizes future of race (W), 364

Scotland, 18–19, 21, 25, 174, 191, 259
Scott, Sir Walter, 219, 228
Self-preference principle, (B) 141, 154, (JM) 199
Seneca, 74, 75
Seven Years War, 116
Shaftesbury, Earl of (first), 104–5
Shaftesbury, Earl of (third) (1671–1713), the importance of beauty, 34; reason as man's dignity, 35
Shaw, G. Bernard, 377
Shelburne, Earl of, 16, 123, 133, 152, 184
Sidgwick, Henry, 325
Sidney, Algernon, 109
Smith, Adam (1723–90), 15, 90, 91, 114n, 127, 146n, 149, 282, 287, 361
Social Organism, The, 11, 332–3, 335–6, 338, 340–1, 359, 366, 368–9, 372, 373
Socialism, 3, 234, 266, 333, 336, 367–9, 374n, 377; communal ownership of means of production, 285, 364; Mill's qualified approval, 286; in contrast with competitive economy, 316–17; society as moral essence of individual (Bosanquet), 339; acceptance by Beatrice Webb, 360–1, 364; as politics based on renunciation (W), 363; opposed to Syndicalism, 370–1, 374n; and moral progress, 374–5n, 376–8
Sociology, 10, 11, 12, 85, 338; its objects and methods (M), 264–6; compatibility with free-will (M), 266–7; impeded by old Benthamites (M), 268; to be founded on psychology and ethology (M), 269; dichotomy in Mill's approach, 280; in politics (M), 287; as conceived by Huxley, 331–2; defines social welfare (LS), 335; and idealism (Bosanquet), 338; as key to government (W), 359, 369–78 See Chapter XXIII
Socrates, 129, 201

South Sea Bubble, 108

Space and Time, 225; as seen by Hume, 45–6, 48–9; and by others, 47–8

Spain, 113, 117, 119, 176, 205, 222

Spencer, Herbert (1820–1903), 11, 12, 315, 323, 330, 341, 343, 344, 351, 352, 355, 356–7, 360, 368; his theory of equilibrium, 327–9; on the social organism, 332–3

Spinoza, B. (1632–77), 30, 60, 70, 271, 328, 337, 349

Spirit of the Age, The (Mill), 242, 248, 249, 297, 321

Stalin, 374n

Stall, Marion Rush, 280n

Stamp Act, 116

Star Chamber, 168

Steele, Sir Richard, 24, 33

Stephen, J. Fitzjames, 170–1, 299–300

Stephen, Leslie, 344, 377; on morality and social function, 334–5

Sterling, John (1806–44), 224, 234, 241, 254, 266, 305; on superficiality of English philosophers, 225–6; his troubles of conscience, 226–7; reaction to German thought, 228; and interpretation of 'earnestness', 229–30; on Carlyle, 231

Sterne, Laurence, 35

Strabo, 62

Strafford, Earl of, 102

Strato, 54

Suffrage, Universal, 152, 188, 235, 248n, 253, 265, 312; Women's, 216, 314

Sulla, 109

Swift, Jonathan, 24

Swinburne, A. C., 294, 324, 344

Switzerland, 163

Taxes, 91–2

Taylor, Harriet, 240–2, 285–6, 296, 297, 306, 307, 312

Taylor, Helen, 312, 314–15

Taylor, Henry, 207

Temple, Richard (Grenville-Temple), 16

Temple, Sir William, 105

Tennyson, Lord, 321, 323

Thirlwall, Connop, 228

Thornton, W. T., 315

Thucydides, 203, 353

Tiecke, J. L., 228, 229

Tocqueville, Comte de, 251, 257, 261, 288

Toland, J. (1670–1722), on time and space, 48

Tolstoy, Leo, 95

Torrijos, General, 222, 224

Toryism, 79, 83, 165, 206, 219, 254, 260

Totnes, 82

Townshend, Charles, 16, 116

Toynbee, Arnold, 337

Toynbee Hall, 330–1, 337–8

Trade Unions, 370–1, 371n

Treatise on Human Nature (Hume), 13, 14, 35n, 39, 45, 48–9, 73, 74–5, 78, 79, 86, 87, 97, 114n

Trollope, Anthony, 291, 293, 296, 343

Trotsky, 374n

Truth, nature of, (H) 74–7, (B) 155–9, 188, (JM) 201–2, (M) 235–6, 296, 300, (W) 363

Tuell, A. K., 22n

Tunis, 112

Turgot, A. R. J., 115

Turin, 13

Tyndall, Professor J., 322, 326–7, 329, 344

Ukraine, the, 134

Ulpian, 165

University College, London, 321, 342

Utilitarian Society, the, 206

Utilitarianism, 282, 288, 294; its tradition and nature, 4–5; contrasted in Bentham and James Mill, 198; in J. S. Mill, 209, 211, 223, 239, 247; incomplete as a philosophy, 215–16; it becomes a dogma, 216–17, 227; and a way of life, 220; outmoded, 222; its neglect of the arts (M), 235; its conception of government, 248; adapted by L. Stephen, 335; and by Kidd, 335–6 See Chapters XII and XVIII

Utility, 62, 119, 128, 137, 139, 142, 151, 166, 198; applications of the principle to government (B), 143–5

Vane, Henry, 96

Venice, 88

Victoria, Queen, 291

Vienna, 13, 354

Villiers, H. and C., 207

Virtue, based on harmony (H), 6; rid of dismal dress (H), 28; invariable (rational moralists), 33; in a 'fair and pleasant plain' (Montaigne), 37; dependent on judgment (Mont.), 38; one with God (L), 44; in a natural shape (H), 59; as a perception (H), 61; as 'what is useful to men' (H), 62; continuous with vice (H), 64; as a balance of passions, 68; instinctive, of the benevolent man (Fielding), 68–69; and pleasure (B), 137–8; not to be enforced by state (B), 144; as described by James Mill, 195, 196, 198; requires activity, not contemplation, (M) 302–5, (LS) 335, (W) 377; in relation to social organism (LS), 335 See Morality.

Voltaire, F. M. A. de (1694–1778), 16, 129, 134, 192–3, 205

Wales, 224
Wallace, Thomas, 214
Walpole, Horace, 16, 106, 109, 112, 118
Walpole, Sir Robert, 78–9, 85, 87, 100, 108, 115, 116–17
War, views of Hume and Burke, 96, 123
War, Boer, 367; First World, 367
Warsaw, 134
Watkins, F., 85n
Wealth of Nations, 17, 127, 146n
Webb (Potter), Beatrice (1858–1943), 4, 12, 341; her political philosophy in outline, 10–12; her background and early life, 342–5; in relation to her mother, 346; her disappointments and ambitions, 346–8; her spiritual searchings in religion, 348–52, 359–60; and in wide reading and travel, 352–4; she turns to science, 354–5; and to disciplined impersonality, 355–7; her relationship with Joseph Chamberlain, 358–60; she finds her niche in Socialism, 360–4; her marriage to Sidney Webb, 365n; on social organisms and imperial responsibility, 366–7; on social discipline, 368–9; on a scientific democracy, 369–73; interest in Soviet Russia, 373–6; on the subordination of physical appetites, 349–50, 353, 355, 360, 361, 362–3, 376; on all-comprehensive government, 377–8
Webb, Sidney (1859–1947), 4, 10, 340, 358, 365n; on the social organism, 365; on a minimum wage and on education, 368; on a scientific democracy, 369–73; interest in Soviet Russia, 373–6

Westminster Hall, 160
Westminster Review, 12, 207, 217, 235, 254–5, 257, 295
Westminster School, 129
Whately, Richard, 206
Whewell, William (1794–1866), 228, 280n; on the history and methods of science, 272–4; on observation and conception, 274–5; disagreement with Mill, 275–8, 279–80; the human element in science, 278
Whiggery, 13, 78–9, 83, 105, 117, 127, 165, 206, 254, 258–60, 262
White, Hale, 321, 348
White, R. J., 238n
Wilberforce, William, 179
Wilkes, John, 112–13, 114
Willey, Basil, 224n, 232n, 235n
William of Orange, 18, 78
Wilson, George, 133, 140
Wollaston, William (1660–1724), uniformity of moral law, 31; on the corruption of human nature, 32
Woolf, Virginia, 362
Wordsworth, William, 235, 238, 294, 323
Work, Gospel of (Carlyle), 232
Working Men's Association, 257; International, 314
Working Men's College, 294

Young, Arthur, 184
Young, G. M., 120n, 228n, 292n